CHAPTERS
from the
American Experience

CHAPTERS

from the

Volume One

American Experience

edited by

Frank M. Fahey

and

Marie L. Fahey

Prentice-Hall, Inc., Englewood Cliffs, New Jersey

CHAPTERS
from the
American Experience

edited by
Frank M. Fahey
and
Marie L. Fahey

© 1971
by PRENTICE-HALL, INC.
Englewood Cliffs, New Jersey

C   13–128116–x
P   13–128108–9
Library of Congress Catalog Card No.: 75–103138
Printed in the United States of America
Current printing (last digit):

10 9 8 7 6 5 4 3 2 1

PRENTICE-HALL INTERNATIONAL, INC., London
PRENTICE-HALL OF AUSTRALIA, PTY. LTD., Sydney
PRENTICE-HALL OF CANADA, LTD., Toronto
PRENTICE-HALL OF INDIA PRIVATE LIMITED., New Delhi
PRENTICE-HALL OF JAPAN, INC., Tokyo

For

Sherry, Cindy, and Jim

An Invitation

No drama contrived by man can match the impact of his own story. Unfolding over the centuries, the plot has proved at once intricate and cohesive. Tragic flaws and inspirational hopes reach out across the klieg lights, at a high pitch sustaining suspense as to the ultimate end of the great protagonist, man.

One of the most exciting parts of this monumental work is the American story, which tells of the men who challenged a primeval continent, of the changes that unspoiled world wrought in them, and of the civilization which, together, they created. A lifetime is too short a span to explore all the ramifications of this adventure. Only a preview of it is attempted here. With these chapters from the annals of our civilization, we issue the reader an invitation to attend the wonderful realm of history, and there to view and participate in the evolving drama of American life.

Given a modicum of encouragement, man is a restless, questing creature, ever in search of physical and spiritual change. Coming from Renaissance Europe, where these forces had recently been reawakened, and finding in the New World opportunities to match his ambition, the American created a society where the two drives for change existed side by side.

Volume I of these Chapters traces the spirit of physical aggrandizement in the exploits of the first conquerors and settlers, in the repudiation of the tie with England, in the thrust of empire to the West, and in civil conflict.

At the same time, out of the moving frontier and out of an intermingling of many backgrounds and faiths, arises a common idealism—a dream of individual worth and individual rights. This yeasting, too, Volume I attempts to indicate.

Sometimes the two forces tear at or reject one another, as in the slave trade or the communal experiment at Brook Farm. Again, they reinforce each other, as in the Revolutionary and Civil Wars.

While Volume I deals primarily with these matters—with conquest and revolution, the clash of civilizations over the issue of slavery, and the rise of the American dream—there are also suggestions of new things to come. A Puritan turns Yankee, an election initiates the processes of mass persuasion, the first stirrings of Industrialism wreak their changes, and the braying of intolerance foreshadow racial confrontation.

Through all these themes runs a common thread—the human equation, man attempting to manipulate his varying environment with the same set of tools: the same noble strengths, the same ignoble frailties. The more things change, the more they are the same, says a French proverb. As the great literary tragedies of antiquity are made meaningful to us by this thread of continuity that is human nature, so too is the story of man. And this is the drama we have sought to capture here.

We would like to acknowledge the generous cooperation of the Stanford University library staff, the editorial department of Prentice-Hall, particularly Mr. Robert Fenyo, and reviewers James Newbill and William Mounkes, whose comments were invaluable.

In a more personal vein, we wish to express, however inadequately, our indebtedness to our mothers, Mrs. Lilian Fahey and Mrs. Ruth MacFadden Johnson, as well as to numerous mentors and friends, especially Mrs. Ruth G. Collier, Mr. Joseph E. Hall and Drs. Dorothy O. Johansen, Edgar E. Robinson, George E. Knowles, and Julio Bortolazzo.

Contents

CHAPTERS
from the
American Experience

Courtesy the Bancroft Library, University of California, Berkeley.

1

Iliad of the New World

Lord and King of ours, . . . forgive my daring. . . .
I walked to the seashore and I saw a kind of mountain
. . . moving about in the midst of the sea.[1]

The clash of civilizations that marked the coming of Europeans to the New World is an epic theme. Nowhere is this truer than in the confrontation between the Spanish conquistadores and the Mexican Aztecs. And, of all the colorful and conflicting accounts of this great conquest, none has a more epic flavor than that of the nineteenth-century American historian William Prescott. His work, from which most of the following reading is derived, betrays the prejudices of his time and place but is vibrant with the days and the men it portrays. It has the flaws and the virtues of the expansive, highly descriptive, and courageously interpretative style of the Romantic period.

When Hernando Cortez invaded the world of the Aztecs, in the spring of 1519, they ruled a far-flung empire, and their wealth and power were legendary. Their capital city, high on a mountain tableland and surrounded by the waters of a great lake, was rich with the tribute of subject peoples. Their emperor, the Lord Montezuma, ruled with a sway so absolute that none dared look on him, and carpets were spread before him as he walked so that his feet might never touch earth.

Against this empire Cortez thrust his 11 small sailing vessels and his

553 Spanish soldiers. For "Glory, God; and Gold," they came. Their enterprise would be "famous in times to come," he had promised them. 4 The "lust for glory extends beyond this mortal life . . . taking a whole world will hardly satisfy it." Furthermore, he had urged, it would be a "just and good war," waged in the name of Almighty God. The venture would be "wrapped about with great hardships," but there would be riches for all.[2] So, on Good Friday, April 21, these earthbound warriors of the faith came ashore on the silent sands of the Aztec Empire.

Receiving word that the men who had arrived "at the shore of the great sea" were white and wore long beards, Montezuma was "downcast and spoke not a word," for he knew that the hour of the prophecy had come.[3] The signs of disaster had long been heavy on the land. Flaming balls had streaked across the night skies, the waters of the lake had moved preternaturally without wind, and a fire in the temple had spread to the water they cast upon it. Now, in a 1-Reeds year, had come the white bearded ones.* Quetzalcoatl, bearded, white god of the wind, had in the days of antiquity come to the land, lived among them, and taught "by word and deed" the way of virtue, "saving them from vice and sin, giving them laws and good doctrine."[4]

But, seeing how little fruit his doctrine brought forth, he had gone away by the same road he had come, which was to the East, . . . and as he parted from them, he had said to them that at a future time, on a . . . [1-Reeds] year, he would return, and then his doctrine would be received, and his sons would be lords and owners of the lands, while they [the Mexicans] and their descendants would undergo many calamities and persecutions.[5]

Eager to propitiate the god, Montezuma ordered the governor of the province in which the Spanish had landed to greet them cordially, and soon an embassy of Aztec nobles bearing princely gifts appeared before Cortez.

Delicately wrought mats were unrolled, and on them the slaves displayed the articles they had brought—shields, helmets, cuirasses, embossed with pure gold; collars, bracelets, sandals, fans, and crests of the same metal, sprinkled with pearls and precious stones; imitations of birds and animals in wrought and cast gold and silver, of exquisite workmanship; coverlets and robes of cotton, fine as silk, interwoven with feather-

---

*The 1-Reeds year came only every fifty-two years in the Aztec calendar and was the predicted year of Quetzalcoatl's return.

work that rivalled the delicacy of painting. But the things which excited the most admiration were two circular plates of gold and silver "as large as carriage wheels." One, representing the sun, was richly carved with plants and animals.[6]

Even as he sent these tributes to the returning god, Montezuma must have entertained hopes that the invaders were really men and that they might still be encouraged to go away. He sent word that he regretted not being able to have a personal interview with his guests but that the "distance to his capital was too great," the journey "beset with difficulties, and with too many dangers from formidable enemies." It was best, he suggested, that the strangers accept his gifts as evidence of a "friendly disposition" and "return to their own land." Cortez sent a courteous response. The Emperor's munificence had "made him only the more desirous" of a personal interview, he said.[7]

In the months that followed, the conflict in Montezuma's mind deterred him from any vigorous action against the little force of Spanish soldiers that moved ever closer to his mountain citadel. Cortez soon discovered that the empire was torn by dissension, with many of its nations restive under the harsh Aztec control. As he moved across the coastal plain and up the mountain barrier, his skill in the art of persuasion and his military prowess won over large numbers of these subject peoples, even the Tlascalans, a sturdy mountain nation that had stubbornly maintained its independence from the Aztecs.[8]

By continued diplomatic maneuvers, by ambush, by every means short of open hostility, Montezuma tried to halt the invaders. But Cortez and his men continued up the mountains, and after an ascent of over 7,000 feet, they found themselves on the rim of the magnificent Valley of Mexico, or Tenochtitlan. Before them lay a panorama of cultivated plain—orchards, fruitful fields, and "shining cities."[9] On November 8 they marched over the long causeway across the lake and into Montezuma's stronghold.

Down the spacious central thoroughfare they moved, over bridges suspended above the canals that veined the city, amazed at what they saw—a metropolis of several hundred thousand people, homes of brick and stone with gracious inner courts, gardens in fragrant bloom, arcades, fountains, great markets, massive central buildings, turreted temples, and an alabaster incrusted palace. At least as great, says Prescott, was the amazement of the Aztecs

. . . as they heard, now for the first time, the well cemented pavement ring under the iron tramp of the horses, the strange animals which fear had clothed in such supernatural terrors; as they gazed on the children of the East, revealing their celestial origin in their fair complexions; saw the bright falchions and bonnets of steel, a metal to them unknown, glancing like meteors in the sun, while sounds of unearthly music—at least, such as their rude instruments had never wakened—floated in the air![10]

In a robe studded with pearls and emeralds, Montezuma came out to greet them. The "wonderful deeds" of the Spaniards and their fair complexions showed that they were the descendants of the "great Being" of Aztec tradition, he said. He honored them; he would see that everything they could want was provided, that their wishes were obeyed as his own.[11]

He feted the Spanish with exotically prepared foods and housed them in a giant palace near the center of the city and adjacent to one of the great temples. On a broad stone wall that encircled their quarters, Cortez stationed sentries and cannon.

Exploring the area, the commander found that, in the nearby temple, the walls and priests' robes were stained with blood and a golden platter on the altar contained still-bleeding hearts. Meanwhile the soldiers discovered within their quarters a wall in which the outlines of a door could be plainly seen beneath fresh plaster. Tearing it open, they came upon a room filled with the private treasure of Montezuma. "It seemed to me," recalled Bernal Diaz years later, "as if all the riches of the world were in that room."[12]

As the days went by and the Spaniards' status as honored guests remained unchanged, Cortez concluded that the conquest was moving too slowly. Seizing as an excuse the treachery of an Aztec governor against Spanish troops in a coastal garrison, the General insisted that the governor be killed, and, forcing Montezuma to come with him to the Spanish quarters, he held the emperor prisoner there. Montezuma adjusted resignedly to his role as Cortez's hostage, gave audience to his subjects in the apartment delegated to him, attended the temple in the company of a Spanish guard, and joined in the Spanish hunts.

But some of the Aztec leaders, resenting their sovereign lord's captivity, began secretly to organize a resistance. Hearing of the conspiracy, Cortez ordered Montezuma to call the offending nobles to him, and when they came, he imprisoned them.

He now felt sufficiently strong to demand that Montezuma formally recognize the sovereignty of the Spanish Emperor. The principal nobles of the kingdom were called together, and with tears in his eyes, Montezuma told them that the god Quetzalcoatl had sent the Spanish to reclaim the allegiance of the Mexican people.

"You have been faithful vassals of mine during the many years that I have sat on the throne of my fathers. I now expect that you will show me this last act of obedience by acknowledging the great king beyond the waters to be your lord also, and that you will pay him tribute in the same manner as you have hitherto done to me."[13]

Spanish soldiers accompanied the Aztec collectors on their rounds, and the booty they gathered, together with the personal contributions of Montezuma, made up a treasure such, said Cortez, "as no monarch in Europe could boast in his dominions."[14]

Cortez seemed now to have accomplished the great objects of the expedition. The Indian monarch had declared himself the vassal of the Spanish. His authority, his revenues, were at the disposal of the general. The conquest of Mexico seemed to be achieved, and that without a blow. But it was far from being achieved. One important step yet remained to be taken, towards which the Spaniards had hitherto made little progress—the conversion of the natives. Neither Montezuma nor his subjects showed any disposition to abjure the faith of their fathers. The bloody exercises of their religion, on the contrary, were celebrated with all the usual circumstance and pomp of sacrifice before the eyes of the Spaniards.

Unable further to endure these abominations, Cortez told the emperor that the Christians could no longer consent to have the services of their religion shut up within the narrow walls of the garrison. They wished to spread its light far abroad and to open to the people a full participation in the blessings of Christianity. For this purpose they requested that the great temple should be delivered up as a fit place where their worship might be conducted in the presence of the whole city.[15]

Montezuma heard this dictum with consternation. "Why," he asked, "will you urge matters to an extremity that must surely bring down the vengeance of our gods and stir up an insurrection among my people, who will never endure this profanation of their temples?" Cortez replied that if at least one of the sanctuaries in the temple were not given over to them, they would take it by force. "We fear not for our lives," he said, "for though our numbers are few, the arms of the true God are over us."[16] Montezuma and his priests concluded that the sanctuary should be given over to the Spanish. When it was cleansed and fur-

Iliad of the New World

nished with a crucifix and a figure of the Virgin, the conquistadores mounted the steps of the pyramid temple in solemn procession, and the

8 chant of the Te Deum drifted down to the people of Montezuma.

The plundering of their treasure and even the degradation of their emperor had not stirred such resentment as now swept through the city. Montezuma became cold and remote. Sensing the growing danger, the Spanish doubled their guard, slept in their armor, and kept their weapons constantly at hand and their horses ready to mount.

At this critical moment the news reached them that a ship bearing Spaniards hostile to Cortez had landed in Mexico, and the general, taking a small force with him, left the city and went down the mountain to meet them.* In the battle that ensued, he defeated his challengers and burned their ships. As he prepared to celebrate his triumph, messengers arrived with the news that the capital city had risen in rebellion against the conquistadores. The Aztecs had attacked and laid siege to the Spanish quarters. They had also destroyed the brigantines Cortez had built earlier as an emergency means of escape across the lake.

Leaving his sick and wounded, Cortez hastily gathered together an army—made up of his own small band, his coastal garrison, the Spanish forces he had defeated, and his Indian allies. They marched to the capital and along the now quiet streets through the palace gates into the Spanish quarters.

The uprising, he learned, had been precipitated when his men, under deputy commander Alvarado, had stalked a group of six hundred young Aztec noblemen celebrating an annual festival to their war god and had slaughtered them as they danced. Telling Alvarado he was a "madman," Cortez took inventory of his situation.

He now had under his command about 1,250 Spaniards and 8,000 native warriors. The forces he had brought had only increased the problem of subsistence for the besieged. Bitter engagements and unsuccessful forays made it clear to the commander that he would not be able to hold out long against the infuriated Aztecs. Word came that the drawbridges across the causeways had been removed, isolating the city. The great avenues leading to the Spanish quarters and the terraces and rooftops of the area were thronged with Aztecs.

Cortez now asked Montezuma to intercede in their behalf, and, after being assured that the Spanish would willingly leave the city, the Em-

---

*Governor Velasquez of Cuba, doubtful of Cortez's personal fidelity, had sought to revoke his commission shortly before he set sail for Mexico, but Cortez had slipped out of port and gone on with his venture in defiance of the Governor's wishes. Velasquez now sent a force to supersede him.

Chapters from the American Experience

peror consented. Attired in his imperial robes, he ascended the turret and emerged upon the battlements. The fierce tumult died down, and Montezuma addressed his people for the last time:

"Why do I see my people here in arms against the palace of my fathers? Is it that you think your sovereign a prisoner, and wish to release him? You are mistaken. I am no prisoner. The strangers are my guests. Have you come to drive them from the city? They will depart of their own accord, if you will open a way for them. Lay down your arms. The white men shall go back to their own land; and all shall be well again within the walls of Tenochtitlan."

As Montezuma announced himself the friend of the detested strangers, a murmur ran through the multitude. The swollen tide of their passions swept away all the barriers of ancient reverence, and, taking a new direction, descended on the head of the unfortunate monarch. "Base Aztec," they exclaimed, "coward, the white men have made you a woman." A chief, it is said, of high rank, bent a bow or brandished a javelin with an air of defiance, and, in an instant, a cloud of stones and arrows descended on the spot where the royal train was gathered. The Spaniards appointed to protect the emperor's person hastily interposed their bucklers. But it was too late. Montezuma was wounded by three of the missiles, one of which, a stone, fell with such violence on his head, near the temple, as brought him senseless to the ground. The Mexicans, shocked at their own sacrilegious act, experienced a sudden revulsion of feeling, and, setting up a dismal cry, dispersed panic-struck, in different directions. Not one of the multitudinous array remained in the great square before the palace.[17]

They did not long remain subdued. The battle continued for some days, the hordes of Aztecs increasing, and the Spanish diminishing, in strength. In the Spanish quarters, Montezuma lay dying.

Perceiving his end approach, some of the cavaliers present were anxious to save the soul of the dying prince from the sad doom of those who perish in the darkness of unbelief. They accordingly waited on him and in the most earnest manner implored him to open his eyes to the error of his creed, and consent to be baptized. But, when the Father, kneeling at his side, with the uplifted crucifix, affectionately besought him to embrace the sign of man's redemption, he coldly repulsed the priest, exclaiming, "I have but a few moments to live and will not at this hour desert the faith of my fathers."[18]

With the death of Montezuma, the protection his person had afforded the Spanish was gone. They made hasty plans to evacuate the city that night. They would, they decided, go by the shortest causeway across the lake. This Causeway of Tlacopan was broken by three large canals, and since the bridges over these openings had been removed, Cortez set his men to work building a portable wooden span that they could use at each canal in turn. Cortez assigned the strongest horses to the task of bearing the Spanish Emperor's fifth of the Mexican treasure and also Cortez's own share. The order of march was determined, and at midnight the soldiers, many of them burdened with gold, stood under arms awaiting orders.

Mass was performed, the gates were thrown open, and, early on the first of July, 1520, the Spaniards sallied forth from the walls of the ancient fortress.

The night was cloudy, and a drizzling rain, which fell without intermission, added to the obscurity. The great square before the palace was deserted. Steadily, and as noiselessly as possible, the Spaniards held their way. At length, a lighter space beyond the dusky line of buildings showed the van of the army that it was emerging on the open causeway.

But as the Spaniards were preparing to lay the portable bridge across the first uncovered breach, several Indian sentinels set up an alarm. The priests, keeping their night watch on the summit of the temples, instantly caught the tidings and sounded their shells, while the huge drum in the desolate temple of the war god sent forth those solemn tones which, heard only in times of calamity, vibrated through every corner of the capital. Before the Spaniards had time to defile across the narrow bridge, a plashing noise, as of many oars on the dark waters of the lake, was heard. Then came a few stones and arrows striking at random among the hurrying troops. They fell every moment faster and more furious, till they thickened into a terrible tempest, while the very heavens were rent with the yells and war-cries of myriads of combatants.

The Spaniards pushed steadily on through this arrowy sleet, though the barbarians, dashing their canoes against the sides of the causeway, clambered up and broke in upon their ranks. But the advance of several thousand men, marching, probably, on a front of not more than fifteen or twenty abreast, necessarily required much time, and the leading files had already reached the second breach in the causeway before those in the rear had entirely traversed the first. Here they halted, as they had no means of getting across, smarting all the while under ceaseless volleys from the enemy, who were clustered thick on the waters around this second opening. Sorely distressed, the vanguard sent repeated messages to the rear to demand the portable bridge. At length the last of the army had crossed and they endeavored to raise the ponderous framework. But it stuck fast in the sides of the dike. In vain they strained every nerve. The weight of so many men and horses and the heavy artillery had wedged the timbers so firmly in the stones and earth that it was beyond their power to dislodge them.

The tidings soon spread from man to man. All means of retreat were cut off. Each thought only of his own life. Pressing forward, he trampled down the weak and the wounded, heedless whether it were friend or foe. The leading files, urged on by the rear, were crowded on the brink of the gulf. Some succeeded in swimming their horses across. Others failed. The infantry followed pellmell, heaped promiscuously on one another. At last, the opening in the causeway was filled up with the wreck of matter which had been forced into it—ammunition-wagons, heavy guns, bales of rich stuffs scattered over the waters, chests of solid ingots, and bodies of men and horses till over this dismal ruin a passage was gradually formed. With the water up to his saddle-girths, Cortez endeavored to check the confusion. But his voice was lost in the wild uproar, and finally, hurrying on with the tide, he pressed forward with a few trusty cavaliers to the van. Here he found his advance guard halting before the third and last breach. It was wide and deep, though the passage was not so closely beset by the enemy as the preceding ones. The cavaliers again set the example by plunging into the water. Horse and foot followed as they could, some swimming, others with dying grasp clinging to the manes and tails of the struggling animals. Many were the unfortunate wretches who, weighed down by the fatal gold which they loved so well, were buried with it in the salt floods of the lake.

The first gray of the morning was now coming over the waters. It showed the hideous confusion of the scene—the masses of combatants stretching along the dike, struggling for mastery. The lake was darkened by canoes crowded with warriors, whose spears and bludgeons gleamed in the morning light.

To the front, the troops, in a loose disorderly manner, were marching off the causeway. The attention of the Aztecs was diverted by the rich spoil that strewed the battleground; little molested, therefore, the Spaniards were allowed to defile through the adjacent village.

There the Spanish commander dismounted from his jaded steed, and sitting down on the steps of an Indian temple, gazed mournfully on the broken files as they passed before him. The loss sustained by the Spaniards on this fatal night, with that suffered in the previous week, may have reduced them to something more than a third of the original force with

Iliad of the New World

which they entered the capital. Not a musket even remained, the men having thrown them away, eager to disencumber themselves of all that might retard their escape on that disastrous night. Nothing of their military apparatus was left but their swords, their crippled cavalry, and a few damaged crossbows.

Such were the disastrous results of this terrible passage of the causeway—so disastrous that the night on which it happened was branded with the name *noche triste,* or "sad or melancholy night."[19]

Nor were the trials of the Spaniards at an end. As they retreated toward the land of the Tlascalans, starving and ill, they found their way blocked by a vast and hostile army.

On the seventh morning, the army had reached the mountain rampart which overlooks the plains of Otompan. During all the preceding day they had seen parties of the enemy hovering like dark clouds above the highlands, brandishing their weapons.

As the army was climbing the mountain steeps which shut in the Valley of Otompan, they were warned that a powerful body was encamped on the other side. Turning the crest of the sierra, they saw spread out below a mighty host, filling up the whole depth of the valley and giving to it the appearance, from the white cotton mail of the warriors, of being covered with snow. Every chief of note had taken the field with his whole array gathered under his standard, proudly displaying all the pomp and rude splendor of his military equipment. As far as the eye could reach were shields and waving banners, fantastic helmets, forests of shining spears, the bright feather-mail of the chief, and the coarse cotton panoply of his followers, all mingled together in wild confusion, and tossing to and fro like the billows of a troubled ocean. It was a sight to fill the stoutest heart among the Christians with dismay. Even Cortez, as he contrasted the tremendous array before him with his own diminished squadrons, wasted by disease and enfeebled by hunger and fatigue, could not escape the conviction that his last hour had arrived.

But he gathered strength from the very extremity of his situation, for there was no alternative left to him. Escape was impossible. He could not retreat. He must advance—cut through the enemy—or perish. He hastily made his disposition for the fight. He gave his force as broad a front as possible, protecting it on each flank by his little body of horse, now reduced to twenty. Fortunately, he had not allowed the invalids, for the last two days, to mount behind the riders to spare the horses, so these were now in tolerable condition.

Chapters from the American Experience

It was a solemn moment—that in which the devoted little band descended on the plain, to be swallowed up in the vast ocean of their enemies. The latter rushed on with impetuosity to meet them, making the mountains ring to their discordant battle-cries, and sending forth volleys of stones and arrows which for a moment shut out the light of day. But, when the leading files of the two armies closed, the natives fell back before the charges of cavalry. The Spanish opened a wide lane in the ranks of the enemy. But, rallying, the Aztecs poured over and engulfed the little army deeper and deeper in their masses. The contest had now lasted several hours. The sun rode high in the heavens and shed an intolerable heat over the plain. The Spaniards began to relax in their desperate exertions. Their enemies, constantly supported by fresh relays from the rear, were still in good heart. With the tide of battle setting rapidly against them, Cortez' restless eye roved round the field and discerned at a distance, in the midst of the throng, the chief who, from his dress and military cortege, he knew must be the commander of the barbarian forces. He was covered with a rich surcoat of feather-work, and a panache of beautiful plumes, gorgeously set in gold and precious stones, floated above his head. Rising above this, and attached to his back, between the shoulders, was a short staff bearing a golden net for a banner—the singular but customary symbol of authority for an Aztec commander. He was borne on a litter, and a body of young warriors, whose gay and ornamented dresses showed them to be the flower of the Indian nobles, stood round as a guard of his person and the sacred emblem.

Turning quickly around to the cavaliers at his side, Cortez pointed out the chief, exclaiming, "There is our mark!" Then, crying his war cry and striking his iron heel into his weary steed, he plunged headlong into the thickest of the press. His enemies fell back, taken by surprise and daunted by the ferocity of the attack. The cavaliers followed close in the rear. On they swept, with the fury of a thunderbolt, cleaving the solid ranks asunder. In a few minutes they were in the presence of the Indian commander, and Cortez, overturning his supporters, sprang forward with the strength of a lion and, striking him through with his lance, hurled him to the ground. A young cavalier who had kept close by his general's side quickly dismounted and dispatched the fallen chief. Then tearing away his banner, he presented it to Cortez. It was all the work of a moment. The guard, overpowered by the suddenness of the onset, made little resistance, but, flying, communicated their own panic to their comrades. The Indians, filled with consternation, now thought only of escape. In their blind terror, they trampled one another as they fled.

The Spaniards and Tlascalans were not slow to avail themselves of their

Iliad of the New World

change in fortune. Their fatigue, their wounds, hunger, thirst, all were forgotten in the eagerness for vengeance; and they followed up the flying foe, dealing death at every stroke. Long did they pursue, till, the enemy having abandoned the field, they returned sated with slaughter to glean the booty which they had left. It was great, for the ground was covered with the bodies of chiefs at whom the Spaniards had particularly aimed, and their dress displayed all the barbaric pomp of ornament in which the Indian warrior delighted. Such was the famous battle of Otompan, which was fought on the 8th of July, 1520—undoubtedly one of the most remarkable victories ever achieved in the New World.[20]

The conquistadores returned to the land of the Tlascalans to recuperate and gradually build up their war machine for a final assault on the Aztec capital. This time the approach to the city was bitterly contested, but the Spaniards and their allies prevailed. They penetrated the outer bastions, encircled the heart of the city, and lay siege to it. Months went by. The citadel that had once flourished on the tribute of the surrounding country was completely severed from its supplies; its inhabitants were reduced to drinking the brackish water of pools saturated with salt from the lake. Still the Aztecs hung on, forcing the invaders to conquer their capital street by street and canal by canal.

As the Spaniards penetrated deeper into the city, they found the ground turned up in quest of roots and weeds, the trees stripped of their stems, foliage, and bark. Dead bodies lay unburied in the streets and courtyards and choked the canals. It was a sure sign of the extremity of the Aztecs, for they held the burial of the dead to be an imperative duty. "A man could not set his foot down," says Cortez, "unless on the corpse of an Indian!" A poisonous steam arose from the mass of putrefaction, under the action of alternate rain and heat, so tainting the atmosphere that it had bred a pestilence that swept off even greater numbers than the famine.[21]

Only with the capture of their valiant new emperor did the Aztecs finally capitulate. Cortez allowed the survivors to leave the capital, and for three days they moved across the causeways out of their city, their "wasted forms and famine-stricken faces" telling the story of their courageous resistance.[22]

Cortez distributed gifts among his Indian allies and dismissed them. The conquest of Mexico was achieved.

The Spanish conqueror, with his armor and his horse, his fortuitously white skin, his crusader's zeal, and his tremendous thirst for glory and

gold, had put down his boot on the New World. The proud and splen-
didly barbaric civilization of the Aztecs had given way to the sword and
the cross of the conquistadores.

Champlain's Battle with the Iroquois and Fort Ticonderoga, Huddle, July 1, 1609.

Primitive oil, R. Dowling. Courtesy Fort Ticonderoga.

2

The Challenge

I should be very happy to see the clause
in Adam's will which excluded me from my share
when the world should come to be divided.
—King Francis I[1]

In the century that followed Cortez's conquest of Mexico, the rising powers, France and England, gradually mounted a challenge to Spain's monopoly of the North American continent. For the first half of that period defiance emanated primarily from France, whose King Francis I sent out early pathfinders to the St. Lawrence and encouraged privateers to harass Spanish shipping in the Caribbean. In the late 1560s British privateers joined in the attacks on Spain's treasure ships and ports, and through the remainder of the century, as the two nations gathered strength, the challenge became more and more menacing to Spain. It remained, however, substantially a sea assault. A few unsuccessful attempts were made at colonizing during those decades, but not until after the beginning of the seventeenth century did the first permanent settlements of both the French and the English substantiate their claims to the New World. The following reading describes first the sea challenge as personified in the great English Sea Dog, Sir Francis Drake, and then the land challenge as embodied in the leading French empire builder, Samuel de Champlain.

By the winter of 1578–79 Sir Francis Drake had become a scourge to the Spanish, as he waylaid their ships and ravaged their Caribbean towns. His most daring and destructive raid against Spanish America,

17

however, came from a new direction when, early that winter, he descended upon the unsuspecting ports of the Pacific and struck at Spanish shipping there. Until his coming, the Spaniards in the "South Sea" had felt impervious to attack, having found the Straits of Magellan so treacherous that supplies reached them by land across the neck of Panama. There on the Pacific they built vessels for coastal shipping in what they considered their private sea.

Drake set out from England with a fleet of five ships, ran into near-mutiny and foul weather, and arrived in the Pacific with only his flagship, the *Golden Hind*. He slipped up the coast of Chile and sailed brazenly into the port of Valparaiso. The surprise was complete. One ship lay at anchor, and the Spanish crew, seeing the English vessel sail in, broke out a botija of wine and played a tune of welcome on their drums. Not until Drake's boarding party was on their ship shouting "Below dogs" did they realize their mistake.[2] Taking the vessel and the town, the English reprovisioned their ship and sailed off with 25,000 pesos in gold and a large emerald and gold cross.

The corsairs now found a secluded harbor in which they cleaned their ship, mounted her guns, and constructed a pinnace to serve as a tender. In mid-January, 1579, they again sailed north (toward Callao, the port of Lima), making small land raids and seizing ships as they went. A Spanish officer they captured left an interesting account of life on board the British galleon.

Drake is a man of about thirty-five years, short, with a ruddy beard, one of the greatest mariners and commanders on the sea. He treats his men with affection and they him with respect. He carries with him nine or ten gentlemen, cadets of high families in England. These are members of his council and are admitted to his table. He is served with much plate with gilt borders and tops and engraved with his arms and has all possible delicacies and scents, many of which he says the Queen gave him. None of the gentlemen sit down or cover their heads in his presence, without first being ordered once and even several times. They dine and sup to the music of violins. I understand that all the men he carries are paid, because when they plundered our ship, nobody dared take anything without his orders. He keeps very strict discipline and punishes the slightest fault. He has painters, too, who sketch all the coast in colors so true to nature that whosoever follows him can by no means lose his way.[3]

News of Drake's depradations began to spread, and he drove hurriedly up the coast to reach Callao before the Spanish there were forewarned. He approached that port at twilight.

The harbor was full of shipping; some twelve or fifteen of the finest ships in the South Sea trade were riding at one mooring with no watch kept. As night fell Drake stood in and anchored quietly in the midst of them. While the English searched the deserted ships, a vessel from Panama came in and anchored close to the *Golden Hind.* At the same time a boat from shore came alongside the English ship to inquire what she was. A man from the boat began climbing up the side, but suddenly finding himself confronted by the mouth of a great gun hurriedly jumped back, and the boat dashed away. In vain with a noiseless shower of arrows the Englishmen tried to stop her escape. The Panama ship took alarm and, cutting her cable, stood out again to sea. Drake at once gave the word to weigh anchor, and, quietly cutting the cables of every ship in the harbor and leaving them to the mercy of the wind, he gave chase. One shot through the Spanish ship brought her flag down. She was laden with goods, but more importantly bore the news that two weeks before, the *Nuestra Senora de la Concepcion,* the great glory of the South Sea, had left Lima for Panama, laden with bullion on its way to the King of Spain's treasury.

It was a long headstart, but, learning that she would stop en route, the English hoped they might overtake her. As ill luck would have it, before Drake was out of sight of Callao, it fell dead calm, and he drifted with his prize on a glassy sea. The Viceroy of Peru hurriedly manned two vessels and sent them in pursuit of the corsairs. Seeing the two large ships bearing down on him with the coming breeze, he cast off the Spanish vessel and, spreading every stitch of canvas, escaped his pursuers.

Meanwhile the breeze having increased to a gale, Drake flew northward after his prey. As they neared the Equator, the wind failed again, but in spite of the heat they took to their oars and rowed. On the second day they met and captured a frigate whose pilot told them that the chase was only three days ahead of them. Two days more brought them to another prize from which they learned they had gained another day. To insure against missing the great ship, (which was nicknamed the *Cacafuego,* or decently translated the *Spitfire*), the two English vessels now sailed in extended line, the pinnace close in-shore and the ship a league and a half to sea. Pressing on under every rag that could be carried, they crossed the Equator, and still there was not a glimpse of the *Cacafuego.* Another prize was stopped, and one of the prisoners revealed that the chase must be almost in sight. And then, a few hours later, the *Cacafuego* was sighted to the

The Challenge

seaward of them, quietly proceeding on her course. It was only midday, and Drake did not wish to attack before dark. To take in sail would have aroused the Spaniards' suspicions. He therefore hit on the ingenious device of trailing at his stern some empty wine jars, whereby his speed was reduced and the chase deceived as to his sail power.

By eight o'clock, it became obvious to all on board the *Cacafuego* that the strange vessel was making for them, and San Juan de Anton, her owner and captain, thinking that the Viceroy must be sending some message, went about and made toward the *Golden Hind.* Drake at once cut away his drags, and running under the Spaniard's stern came alongside. As the English approached, Anton hailed them, but there was no answer. He demanded what they were, and the answer came, "a ship of Chile." Anton continued to close the distance between them, only to discover his mistake as the strange ship laid hold of his. "English!" shouted the corsairs, "Strike sail!"

"Strike!" cried the indignant Anton. "What kind of a cruet-stand do you think this is to strike! Come aboard and do it yourselves!" Instantly there was a whistle, followed by a trumpet call and a volley of shot and arrows. In vain Anton tried to bear away. A chain shot from a big gun set his mizen overboard, and a rain of shot frustrated every attempt to repair the damage. His men fled below, and in another minute he found himself laid aboard to port by the pinnace, which he now saw for the first time. Some forty Englishmen were clambering over his sides. Resistance was hopeless. Almost without a blow Drake found himself in possession of the richest vessel in all the South Sea.

All that night, and the next day and night, the three ships sailed out direct from land, till Drake felt himself well out of the trade routes and secure from disturbance while he gutted his prize. One source says there were found in her thirteen chests of pieces-of-eight, eighty pounds of gold, and twenty-six tons of silver, besides jewels and plate. Furthermore, they were able to reprovision from the prize in the most luxurious way and supply themselves with all the sails, cordage, and ship's stores they required.

The prisoners were surprised at the treatment they received, for they were entertained, given gifts, and allowed to return to the Spanish settlements in the gutted *Cacafuego.*[4]

Droves of Spanish ships now emerged from Lima and Panama in a futile effort to track down the marauder. With his gigantic plunder serving as ballast, Drake slipped up the coast in search of the fabled Northwest Passage. Discouraged by the intense cold from continuing this quest, he returned to the coast of present-day California, where he added to his provisions by killing seals and seagulls. Then he sailed out across the Pacific on a course that would bring him, after another eventful year and a quarter, around the world and home to England.

In less than a decade Drake and other great leaders of the Elizabethan pirate fleet met and defeated the fabulous Spanish Armada. This British victory did not put an end to Spanish power in the New World, but it weakened it and heralded the rise of another and mightier sea power.

While French and English corsairs were harassing the Spanish Americas and England was building up her navy to defy Spanish sea power, a new type of challenge was emerging. In the 1560s France sent out, to the shores of present-day Florida, a colony that was to establish a French settlement in the New World. The story of this colony on the St. John River, of its struggle with the Spanish, and of its abandonment reads like a novel. And so does that of the lost colony of Roanoke, which was planted in Virginia by the British in 1587 and which also ended in failure.

Not until after the turn of the century did the new national powers succeed in establishing permanent settlements in America. Then in rapid succession came the founding by the French of Acadia and Quebec and the English colonization of Jamestown.

While the British were struggling in Virginia and events were underway that would soon lead to the Plymouth Plantation, one of the greatest of the builders of New France Samuel de Champlain was sent out by his nation to strengthen the claim he and Jacques Cartier had laid to North America by earlier explorations. These were the first of a long succession of Frenchmen who would carry the challenge to Spain across the Great Lakes, down the Mississippi River, and into her back yard. They represented a different breed of conqueror from the Spanish, and the Indians they found belonged to another age than the more advanced Aztecs whom the conquistadores had subdued in Mexico.

The handful of colonists that Champlain settled at Quebec owed their survival, in part at least, to the friendship of the neighboring Indians. These natives belonged to an alliance of tribes that had long been at war with the formidable Five Nations of the Iroquois. Leaders among these enemies of the Iroquois were the Hurons, a relatively advanced nation of farmers and traders, whose home lay on the upper shores of the Great Lake that bears their name. The cooperation of the Hurons could mean much to Champlain if he were to pursue his dream of finding a Northwest Passage to the Orient, and their trading contacts with the nomadic hunters of the northland could bring valuable furs to the French posts.

22   So in 1609 Champlain became involved with the Hurons and their allies in a military expedition into the heart of Iroquois country (in what is now New York state). From Champlain's journal comes an account of the strange confrontation between the Stone Age Iroquois and three Europeans clad in medieval armor. The journal picks up the story at the point where Champlain and his two French soldiers, with their allies, had worked their way south by the Richelieu River and the Lake of the Iroquois (Lake Champlain) to within a two- or three-day journey of the enemy's stronghold.

Now we did not advance any more except at night; by day we rested. Our Indians continued to practice their customary superstitions to find out whether the undertaking would succeed. As in all their camps, they had a *pilotois,* a soothsayer, who built a shelter surrounded by sticks and covered with his robe. He ensconced himself inside in such a way that he could not be seen. Then he took hold of one of the posts and shook it, muttering some words between his teeth, by which he said he invoked the devil, who appeared to him in the form of a stone and told him whether they would find their enemies and kill many of them. This pilotois lay flat on the ground motionless. Then suddenly he rose to his feet, talking and writhing in such a way that, although naked, he was all in a perspiration. All the people were squatted around the shelter. They told me that the shaking I saw was caused by the devil. I admonished them that I had seen otherwise and that this was sheer folly. The rogue disguised his voice and made it sound big and clear and spoke in a language that was unfamiliar to the other savages; and when he made it sound broken, they believed that it was the devil who spoke.

After they had learned from their soothsayer what was to happen to them, they took as many sticks, a foot long, as they themselves numbered, and represented their chiefs by others a little longer. Then they cleared a place five or six feet square, where the chief, as field sergeant, arranged all the sticks in the order that seemed good to him; then he showed them the rank and order that they were to keep when they fought their enemies. All the savages watched this attentively, studying the figure which their chief had made with these sticks. Then they mingled with one another, and then returned to the formation, repeating this two or three times until they were familiar with it.

On the evening of the 29th of July, we embarked in our canoes, and, as we were going along very quietly and without making any noise, at the end of a cape that projects into the lake on the west side [Ticonderoga], we met the Iroquois, and they were coming to battle. We both began to make loud cries, each getting his arms ready. We pulled out into the lake, and the Iroquois went ashore, where they arranged their canoes in a line along the shore and began to cut down trees with which they barricaded themselves very well.

Our men passed the whole night with their canoes drawn up close together, fastened to poles, so that they might not scatter. We were within arrow range of their barricades. When preparations had been made, our allies sent two canoes to learn from their enemies whether they wanted to fight. The Iroquois replied that they desired nothing more, but that, at the moment, there was too little light and that they should wait until daylight when they could recognize one another. It was determined that battle should open at sunrise.

While we waited, the whole night was passed in dances and songs, on both sides, with endless insults hurled across the water. After plenty of singing, dancing, and parleying, daylight came. My two companions and I remained concealed, as we did not want the enemy to see us yet. After arming ourselves in light armor, each took an arquebuse and went ashore in separate canoes.

I saw the enemy come out of their barricade, nearly 200 men, strong and robust, coming slowly toward us with a dignity and assurance that impressed me greatly. At their head were three chiefs. Our men also went forth in the same order. They told me that those who wore much larger plumes were the chiefs and that I should do all I could to kill the three of them. Our men began to run toward their enemy, who were standing firm. Now they opened their ranks so that I could advance to the front, and the enemy saw me for the first time.

They looked at me and I at them. Seeing that they were preparing to shoot at us, I rested my arquebuse against my cheek and aimed directly at one of the three chiefs. With that single shot two of the chiefs fell dead to the ground, and one of their companions was mortally wounded. I had put four balls into my arquebuse. When our men saw this shot so favorable for them, they began to shout so loud that thunder could not have been heard. Meanwhile the arrows flew from both sides. The Iroquois were much astonished that two men had been so quickly killed, despite their woven wood armor, which was proof against arrows. As I was reloading, one of my companions fired a shot from the woods. This completed their demoralization, and, abandoning the field and their fort, they fled into the depths of the forest. Pursuing them thither, we killed several and took ten or twelve prisoners. The rest escaped.

The Challenge

After we had gained this victory, the allies amused themselves by taking a great quantity of Indian corn and meal from their enemies, and also their arms, which they had left behind in order to run better. They celebrated, dancing and singing, and in three hours we set out on the return voyage.

Toward evening the Indians took one of the prisoners and, telling him that they were about to inflict on him the same cruelties his people had inflicted on them, they commanded him to sing. This he did, but it was a song very sad to hear. Meanwhile our men lighted a fire, and when it was blazing well, each took a brand and burned the poor wretch little by little, to make him suffer the more. Sometimes they stopped and threw water on his back. Then they tore out his nails and put the fire on the ends of his fingers. Afterward they flayed the top of his head and dripped on top of it a kind of gum all hot; then they pierced his arms near the wrists, and with sticks pulled the sinews, and tore them out by force. This poor wretch uttered strange cries, and I turned away from them, distressed. When they saw that I was not pleased, they called me and told me to fire a musket shot into him; which I did without his seeing it at all.

When we arrived at the river's rapids, the Hurons returned to their country. They were well pleased. So we separated with great protestations of friendship, and they asked me if I did not wish to come to their country. I promised to do so.[5]

It was 1615 before Champlain was able to carry out his promise to visit his allies in Huronia. In the intervening years the Hurons and French had built up a trading empire. From the tribes above distant Lake Superior and beyond, the Hurons procured the thick prime beaver skins to be found only in lands of intense cold. In return for these and other prize furs, they exchanged their vegetables and the French hatchets and trinkets that they received at the annual trading fairs on the St. Lawrence. It was a trade that brought rich profits to both the Hurons and the French.

By 1615 the Iroquois had become a serious threat to commerce and travel on the St. Lawrence; so Champlain was forced to take the circuitous route up the Ottawa River far to the north before descending to Lake Huron and the land of his allies. A week or so before him had gone Recollect Father Joseph le Caron, first missionary to the area, and twelve French soldiers with whom Champlain intended to join his Indian confederates in a full-scale war against the Iroquois. In the Huron village of Carhagouha he met the Recollect Father. A modern historian has recreated that meeting.

There were effusive greetings. "And what sort of a trip did you have, Father?"

Father Joseph shuddered. He said: " . . . I can hardly tell you the fatigue I suffered. I had to keep my paddle in hand all day long, and row with all my strength with the Indians. More than a hundred times I walked in the rivers over the sharp rocks, which cut my feet, in the mud, in the woods, where I carried the canoe and my small baggage, in order to avoid the rapids and the frightful waterfalls. And the hunger! We had only a little sagamité [a cornmeal mush that the natives often flavored with flies], which was dealt out to us morning and evening. Yet I must avow that amid my pains I felt much consolation. For alas! when we see such a great number of infidels . . . one feels an ardor which I cannot express to labor for their conversion and to sacrifice for it one's repose and life."

He had suffered not only because of his European softness. His Franciscan garb, gray undyed wool, bound with a knotted cord, his flat-soled, open-topped sandals, were ill adapted to forest and stream. His gown soaked up water like a sponge, and when he stepped into a canoe, it sprinkled water and sand, to the Indians' fury. His bare feet, puffed with mosquito bites* and thorn scratches, were tortured by the sandal thongs, wet or dried stiff. He had all the burden of the Mass vessels, crucifixes, communion wine, breviary. He had no time for his daily religious duties. And he must endure the strange agony of uncomprehending silence, for, alone with the sweating paddlers, he had no words to express his simplest needs or desires.

"And now?" said Champlain. "You are picking up a little of the language?"

Father Joseph sighed . . . a dreadful language, all vowels and grunts. Point to a tree, and one person will tell you one word, another, another. You begin to recognize words, but every time you hear them they have different endings. You can never know when an Indian is making a joke, telling you with a straight face some horrible obscenity when you ask the word for, say, the sacred chalice.

"How are my men behaving?"

"Badly. Very badly. The Huron girls are utterly shameless, and some of our French are more shameless than they. A few of the men are making surprising progress in the language, but I fear by unholy means. They have accommodated themselves quickly to the filth and sloth of the Indians, and spend their days hunting, fishing, and idling about the village."

---

*Such bites often swelled to the size of lemons before the whites developed partial immunity.

The Challenge

"Ah well, let them have their little vacation. We'll be on the march again soon."[6]

Due largely to the erratic and undisciplined behavior of his Indian allies, the campaign Champlain now launched resulted in total failure. But he did not hold it against the Hurons, writing tolerantly in his journal, "They must be excused, for they are not soldiers."[7] The Indians, chagrined and disillusioned as to the omnipotence of the white man, refused to let Champlain have the use of a canoe, and so he was obliged to spend the winter in Huronia. This he did in good spirits, improving his relations with them, learning a great deal about their language and their ways, and returning to Quebec the following spring in the company of one of the chieftains, who was deeply impressed by his glimpse of French civilization.

A few years later, the Jesuit order published a little handbook of instruction for the men sent out to New France. It reflected the experiences and the insights of Champlain and of Father Joseph as it cautioned its prospective missionaries:

You must have sincere affection for the savages. . . . To conciliate the savages, you must be careful never to make them wait for you in embarking. You must provide yourself with a tinder box or with a burning mirror, or both, to furnish them fire in the daytime to light their pipes, and in the evening when you have to encamp. These little services win their hearts. You should try to eat their sagamité or salmagundi in the way they prepare it, although it may be dirty, half cooked, and very tasteless. . . . You must . . . tuck up your gowns so that they will not get wet, and so that you will not carry either water or sand into the canoe. . . . It is not well to ask many questions, nor should you yield to your desire to learn the language and to make observations on the way. . . . Each one should be provided with half a gross of awls, two or three dozen little knives, a hundred fish-hooks, with some beads of plain and colored glass, with which to buy fish or other articles when the tribes meet each other. . . . Be careful not to annoy anyone in the canoe with your hat; it would be better to take your nightcap. . . . Do not undertake anything unless you desire to continue it; for example, do not begin to paddle unless you are inclined to continue paddling. . . . When you meet savages on the way . . . show them a cheerful face, and thus prove that you endure gayly the fatigues of the voyage.[8]

It was, then, in a spirit of accommodation that the builders of New France came to this continent and went among the Indians, adjusting to their customs, sharing in their wars, and creating with them a great trade network. And, while they labored in their way at the task of conquest, the English to the south were tenaciously clinging to the hostile continent. Privateers and pathfinders, the French and the British were challenging the might of Spain, encroaching upon a world she had considered hers alone.

Courtesy Jamestown Foundation.

3

The Starving Time

All was fish that came to net
to satisfy crewell hunger.

"Virginia grew up to be a great beauty, the mother of many distinguished men," writes historian George Willison, "but she was born an ugly duckling and had a childhood so terrible that at times it seems scarcely real."[1] From the day the colonists landed at Jamestown in May, 1607, they were beset by tribulations. The Indians, who had wiped out a Jesuit mission in the area thirty-six years before, were cautiously hostile. They traded with the English when the terms were satisfactory, and some tribes proved genuinely friendly. But the colonists soon realized that the natives were constantly assessing their strength. One direct assault was made on the fort during the first summer, and only the heavy guns of the ships drove off the attackers. Ambush presented an unceasing threat to any white who strayed from the company of his fellows.

Every day the Indians came, but no one ever saw them until it was too late. They lurked in the woods, or crept up to hide in the tall grass under the bulwarks, and the colonists, "by their disorderly straggling, were often hurt." One of the Gentlemen, while the palisade was going up, found nothing better to do than go for a stroll in the woods, unarmed. He soon came running into the fort, having six arrows through him, from which he died a few days later. Another, going out to answer a call of nature, was shot "in the somwhat, dangerously." When they could find no other targets, the Indians lofted arrows into the fort, scoring an occasional hit or amused themselves by shooting the English dogs.[2]

The site of Jamestown appealed to the colonists for two practical reasons. It was readily defensible, being almost completely surrounded by water, and a deep channel ran close to it, allowing them to bring their ships directly to the shore and moor them to the trees along the riverbank. But the choice proved disastrous. Dense woods had to be cleared to make way for their fort and fields. The lack of fresh-water springs in the area forced the settlers to drink "the murky waters of the river, which were salt at high tide and filled with muck at low." And the unwholesome air from the marshlands around the spot brought "summer sickness" and death.[3]

Into this fetid climate came a group of English "gentlemen" in heavy Elizabethan clothing and armor, many of whom were as unsuited temperamentally as they were sartorially to face the challenges of the land. Drinking the purest of water would have been a sacrifice to many of them, for they had been accustomed to use water only for bathing—their standard beverages, even for breakfast, had been wine and beer. The rigid English social system had poorly prepared them for grubbing manual labor. "After two months, no houses, not even dogholes, had been finished," and "little seed had been planted—they were not the kind to till the soil."[4]

The men who settled Virginia were bickering when they arrived from England, and they continued to squabble until most of them were dead. Their leadership was often inept and unstable. But their frailties can be overstressed; there were times when individual skill or fortitude or courage tipped the delicate balance of the colony in favor of survival. And there were errors on the part of others too, notably the Company at home in England, that often contributed to their trials. Along with these human elements, a capricious Chance dabbled often in their affairs—sometimes happily, sometimes with disastrous results.

In 1609 the Third Supply fleet left England with provisions for the Virginia settlers. But, under the blazing heat of a tropical midsummer, disease swept the ships; plague, fever, and scurvy killed a fifth of the crew. One ship foundered; one turned back. The flagship *Sea Venture* was swept away in a hurricane, bearing with it Sir Thomas Gates, whom the Company had appointed the first Governor of Virginia, together with his second and third in command. The provisions on the surviving ships were spoiled by high seas, so that when they came limping into Jamestown, their hungry passengers, instead of replenishing the colonists' supplies, further depleted them. By October, when the fleet returned to England, Jamestown's president (George Percy) and the council, taking inventory, found that the food supply was dangerously low. Ahead lay the winter that, with good reason, came to be known as the Starving Time.

There was less than two months' supply in the store, and it was at least ten months before they could reap a harvest, if any. No relief from home could be expected till late in the spring at least. No trade could be had with the Indians, who had been alienated by innumerable outrages. The Cape Merchant [Manager of Provisions] stretched the supplies as far as he could, giving everyone a starvation ration of a half pint of corn a day.

Winter came, as bitterly cold as the first one at Jamestown. Many of the weak and ailing, having pawned their clothes and their blankets for a capful of corn, froze to death in their beds. With the storehouse exhausted, all began to waste away. After they had eaten hogs, sheep, goats, and horses, devouring even their hides, they were "gladd to make shift with vermin, as doggs, catts, ratts, and myce." They ate boots, shoes, "or any other leather," said Percy, for "all was fish that came to net to satisfy crewell hunger."

When they had consumed everything eatable in the fort, men went into the woods "to feede upon Serpents and Snakes, and to digg for wylde and unknown Rootes." While they were foraging, many were cut down by the Indians. None could fish because all the nets had been allowed "to rot and spoile."

A ray of hope flashed in the darkening gloom when an offer of trade came from Powhatan [the Great Chief of all the tribes in the area]. The chief sent word that if a ship were sent with some copper, he would freight her home with corn, which was a godsend beyond the dreams of any.

Quickly dispatched with fifty men, Captain Ratcliffe came ashore at Orapaks, eager to trade, having most of his men with him. They were welcomed and feasted, but the next day there was trouble.

According to the more probable account, a quarrel developed when trading began, with each side complaining that it was being cheated. Someone struck a blow and the exasperated braves fell upon the English, slaughtering them almost to a man—about thirty in all—only two escaping.

The Indians also attacked the pinnace, which caused great concern, for this was something which they had never dared before in fear of its cannon. But the vessel, though nearly captured, finally got away and returned to Jamestown with its small crew "neare starved," bringing none of the corn so prayerfully expected, nothing but news of the slaughter.

Another blow immediately followed. Captain Francis West [a member of the council] was sent in the *Swallow* to see what trade could be found in more distant waters, for men were now dying by the scores. The remaining pinnaces, the *Discovery* and the *Virginia,* were sent down to Point Comfort [at the mouth of the river] to fish. With a crew of almost forty, recruited largely among those brought over in the Third Supply, West sailed up the Potomac, where the Indians proved to be friendly and ready to trade. But they valued their corn at more than the few trinkets they were offered. Enraged, West turned his ruffians loose on the Indians, killing many, wounding more, plundering and burning their villages, making "implacable enemies" of the friendly Potomac.

On her way back, well loaded with corn and other loot, the *Swallow* stopped at Point Comfort, where a small fort had recently been built. The commander there informed West and his men of Jamestown's desperate need, urging them, said Percy, "to make with all the speed they could to releave us." Instead, the ruffians ran up sail and put to sea, abandoning the poor wretches at Jamestown to a horrible fate, leaving them without a large vessel and therefore with no means of trade or escape. Eager for more and better loot, dreaming of "mountaines of gold and happie robberies," the runaways became "professed pirates." Nothing was heard of them until six months later when the *Swallow* crept into a small English port, having lost many of her crew from hunger, for she had not prospered under the Jolly Roger.

The flight of the *Swallow* reduced Jamestown to the ultimate horrors of the Starving Time. Nothing was "spared to maintaine Life and to doe those things which seem incredible," as Percy recalled almost twenty years later, still haunted by memories of those days when hunger drove men "to digge up dead corpses out of their graves and to eate them boyled and stewed with roots and herbes." Others "licked upp the bloode which had fallen from their weak fellowes." As one exclaimed, "It were too vile and scarce to be believed what we endured."

His mind unhinged, one man killed his wife, "powdered [salted] her, and had eaten of her before it was known," for which he was executed. "Now whether she was better roasted, boyled, or carbonado'd, I know not," remarked Captain Smith [in England], "but such a dish as powdered wife I never heard of."

Two out of three of those alive six months before were now in their graves. Quite hopeless, unable to escape, having only a small rowboat and an Indian canoe, the trapped survivors at Jamestown would have killed and eaten one another, according to Percy, but for the extraordinary pains and energy of the Cape Merchant, Captain Daniel Tucker. Almost unaided, the latter succeeded in building a large shallop, which offered some slight hope of trade and of escape if aid did not come soon.

Putting the new shallop to immediate use, Percy went down to Point Comfort to learn the fate of the small garrison there, as nothing had been heard of it for weeks. Though a few had died, most of the men there were hale and hearty, enjoying the fresh breezes that blew in from the sea and the abundance of shellfish to be found along the shore. The crabs these men fed their hogs "would have been a great relefe unto us and saved many of our Lyfes," Percy indignantly noted. But [the men at Point Comfort had] "concealed their plentie" from those at Jamestown because they planned to keep alive "some of the better sorte" and embark for home on the two pinnaces lazily riding at anchor in the roads, the *Virginia* and the *Discovery,* sent down to fish the Bay, which they had not done.

Half of the starving at Jamestown were going to be brought to the Point for relief, Percy announced. When these had recovered some strength, the other half would be brought down. If this did not suffice, he would bring down everybody and abandon Jamestown.

It would have been well if Jamestown had now been abandoned, as it ultimately had to be. But as happened so often in Virginia, Chance intervened. While Percy was at the Point, all were startled when two strange vessels appeared in the Bay late one afternoon. Fearing that these were hostile craft, perhaps Spanish, they kept close watch all night, only to discover in the morning that they were friendly vessels and carrying Sir Thomas Gates and almost all of the company of the long-lost *Sea Venture,* which had vanished in the "hurycano" almost a year before.

The ship had almost gone down in the hurricane. After working with pumps and buckets for four days and nights in an effort to clear the hold of the ship, which was ten feet deep in water, all had given up in despair, breaking out bottles of brandy and "other good and comfortable waters" to drink to their reunion in another world. In the midst of that "hell of darkness" something suddenly loomed up in the murk, the "dreadful coast" of the Bermudas, "said and supposed to be inchanted and inhabited with witches and devills and so wunderous daungerous of Rockes" that none could approach it without "unspeakable hazard of shippe wrack."

Rather than founder at sea they decided to take a desperate chance and try to run ashore anywhere at all. While still a half-mile out, the ship crashed into a rock, then into another. Though badly shaken, she did not go down, for she was so tightly wedged between the rocks that she was held upright, almost as if standing in the stocks. Favored by low tide, all of the bruised and battered company were soon safe on shore.

Far from being bewitched, the haunts of fiends and demons, a bedeviled land of "monstruous Thunderstorms and Tempests," Bermuda proved to be a delightful place—altogether, a fairyland.* All of their supplies had been lost in the shipwreck, but here they found fish, fowl, fruits and berries, and the woods were full of wild black hogs, fat and sweet, the descendants of swine off some Spanish shipwreck.

Gates ordered that some vessels be built to carry the company on to Virginia, which aroused great resentment. Many were quite content to stay where they were. In spite of murmuring and mutiny the company finally

*The marvels of the islands, the wreck of the *Sea Venture,* and the "hurycano," as described by one of the shipwrecked company, inspired Shakespeare to a great play, *The Tempest.*

The Starving Time

succeeded in accomplishing the seemingly impossible task of fashioning out of the wreckage of the *Sea Venture* and whatever was at hand not only one vessel, but two—a large pinnace and a smaller one.

Early in May, 1610, after nine pleasant months on the islands, with all in good health, Gates ordered the company on board. For the most part, it was reluctant to go and a few braver spirits, determined to remain, ran away and hid in the woods. Though they could easily have been well loaded, the ships were carrying only sufficient supplies for their voyage, for Gates assumed that he would find plenty of everything at Jamestown. Meeting Percy at Point Comfort, he was quickly disillusioned.

With no breeze stirring, the ships "plyed it sadly" up the river and finally reached Jamestown, which seemed rather the "ruins of some auncient fortification than that any people living might now inhabit it." It presented a grim and ghastly sight with the "pallisadoes downe, the ports open, the gates from the hinges, the church ruined." The houses of the dead had been torn down and used as firewood, for none dared to go into the woods for fear of the "watching, subtile, and offended Indian."

Of the three hundred people in the colony nine months before there were only sixty "most miserable and poore creatures," all so emaciated that they "looked like anatomies." As the ships tied up, they ran naked out of their beds and fell upon the newcomers, crying and moaning: "We are starved! We are starved!"

Having lost his mind, as had others, one came into the market place in a "furious, distracted mood," cursing and shouting that there was no God, for God would never have allowed his creatures to endure such agonies. In a frenzy he dashed out of the fort later that day and the Indians quickly put an end to his miseries.

Finding all things so contrary to his expectations, "so full of miserie and misgovernment," Gates first assembled the company to hear a "zealous and sorrowfull prayer." Then calling in some of the leaders, he asked their advice on what should be done, for he could see nothing to do to repair the calamitous situation.

The supplies brought from Bermuda would last only two weeks, and there were none to be had in the country. As the situation was obviously hopeless, all of the leaders except one agreed that there was only one thing to do "to preserve and save all from starvation." That was to abandon the colony and sail for home by way of Newfoundland, in the hope of meeting there with some English fishing vessels from which they might obtain supplies, for theirs would not see them across the Atlantic.

When Gates announced this, it was greeted "with general acclamation and a shoute of joy" by the still tottering survivors of the Starving Time. Many dreadful uncertainties remained—their small vessels might go down at sea, or they might perish from hunger along the way. But at least there was a ray of hope.

Personal belongings and the few precious stores were carried on board. As there was no space to carry them, the cannon were buried within the gates. Word was dispatched to inform the men at Point Comfort and order them to stand by until the ships came down from Jamestown in a day or two.

Hating Jamestown and all that it represented in their tortured lives, many wished to destroy the fort, threatening to burn it. But Gates objected, knowing that there was going to be trouble enough in satisfying the adventurers [of the Company] on his reasons for abandoning the country, which meant the wreck of all their hopes and the certain loss of their entire investment.

"My Masters," said Gates, "let the town stand. We know not but that as honest men as ourselves may come and inhabit here."

On June 7, 1610, two weeks after his arrival, three years after the first landing, Gates "commanded every man, at the beating of a Drum, to repair aboard"—and here was one command that was obeyed with alacrity and without any grumbling. Gates remained on shore to the last to prevent any attempt at arson and finally, at noon, the pinnaces moved out from the bank and started down the river, "giving a farewell with a peal of small shot." The wilderness had routed another proud presumptuous intruder. Virginia had fallen.

If they had been favored with a good breeze, the pinnaces could have cleared from Point Comfort and been well out to sea before nightfall. As it was, having no breeze at all, they drifted slowly with the tide and anchored that night off Hog Island only a few miles downstream. With any luck they would be well away to sea by noon the next day.[5]

But the luck proved to be of another sort—an incredible coincidence was about to reshape the history of Virginia. The next day, before they could make their escape out to the sea and away to the north, they met a small boat coming upstream. It bore word that the three ships of Lord de La Warr, newly appointed Governor of all the Virginias, stood at the mouth of the river and that the colonists were to bring their vessels about and sail back to Jamestown.

La Warr's fleet brought only scanty provisions, and over half of its complement of men consisted of "Gentlemen of fashion" and "a military guard of honor [for the Governor, together with] . . . a large number of retainers and personal servants, all in scarlet liveries."[6] But, dubious though the prospect seemed, a new start would be made. Virginia had not fallen.

Governor John Winthrop

4

The Genesis
of a Patriarch,
Puritan Style

Thus stands the case between God and us.
We are entered into a Covenant with Him for this work.
—John Winthrop[1]

When John Winthrop was a young man, he presided over his father's manorial court at Groton, judging the charges the tenants levied against one another. He attended Trinity College at Cambridge, studied the law briefly, married well, and became the local justice of the peace, a position held only by important men in Suffolk County. In his late thirties he was appointed common attorney in His Majesty's Court of Wards, a prestigious court, with nationwide jurisdiction. All this was in the best tradition of the English country squire.

But Winthrop was not destined to live out his life in the manner traditional to his class. He would, instead, sell his patrimony, cross the Atlantic, and devote his fortune and the last two decades of his life to the establishment in America of a New Canaan. For Winthrop was a Puritan. He drank his cup in the same round as Shakespeare, and yet the fresh breath of the Renaissance, the Great Bard's lust for life, his exaltation of Reason and the individual man did not touch Winthrop—

save as a temptation to be withstood. In family background and in personal inclination, Winthrop was, rather, a product of the Reformation.

The "fever of Puritanism,"[2] which had seized many middle-class businessmen in the towns and many of the lesser gentry in the country, was a compelling force for change. England, as it emerged into the modern era, suffered all the dislocations associated with the transition from Feudalism. The Puritans saw about them massive poverty and degradation at one end of the social scale and venality and corruption at the other. Yet the reforms they proposed were not concerned directly with social improvements or political change. For they believed that the ills they observed were only symptoms of a great underlying malaise—the degeneration of religious life. The Church of England, already too closely bound to the formalism of Rome, was moving closer. They would redirect it into the simpler paths of worship laid out in the Bible.

In private life also the Puritans demanded a return to the pure doctrine of the Scriptures. Man's earthly existence was a drop in the sea of time, a pilgrimage that should be devoted to the task of seeking out and submitting to the Will of God. To the early seventeenth-century Puritan, religion was not a Sunday exercise but, as Samuel Eliot Morison has phrased it, a complete "way of life based on the belief that the Bible was the word of God, and the whole word of God."[3] The ethical code the Puritan drew from his study of the Scriptures was rigidly exacting and laid its injunctions on his every action and thought. Deviation from it caused him great mortification. He was horrified to see how many of his countrymen squandered their precious time roistering at the theater, dallying at the pubs, and even defiling the Sabbath with pleasure-seeking. He would not fall into the lure of the earth's vanities. Life had been given him to erase, if he could, the stigma of original sin—it should only be regarded as a preparation for eternity.

The Puritan peopled his world with contending forces of good and evil constantly vying for his soul. He viewed himself as struggling, with the help of God and his fellow Puritans, to climb out of the pit of sin, despite the machinations of Satan and his human agents. Only when he had learned to submerge himself in the Will of God, could the regenerate man find his true identity and peace. This moment of conversion was the focal point of the Puritan's quest and an experience essential to his admission into the communion of the Saints. The letters and religious diary of John Winthrop constitute a priceless record of how this fever burned in one English squire, eventually driving him to lead into the New World wilderness a crusading army of Saints who would brand deep into the American mind the mark of Puritanism. The process of spiritual disciplining began early.

About ten years of age, I had some notions of God; for, in some frighting or danger, I have prayed unto God and found manifest answer. After I was twelve years old, I began to have some more savor of religion. I would occasionally write letters of mere vanity; and, occasionally I would write savory and godly counsel. About fourteen years of age, being in Cambridge, I fell into a lingering fever, which took away the comforts of my life, and I betook myself to God, who, I did believe, would welcome any that would come to Him, especially such a young soul and so well qualified as I took myself to be.[4]

His religion was still egocentric and superficial. Not until he had attained the age of eighteen and the status of a married man did "the ministry of the word" first come home to him "with power." Now he could "no longer dally with religion," but developed an "insatiable thirst after the word of God" so that he could not miss a good sermon, even though he had to go miles to hear it. But the pull of the flesh was still great, and there were innumerable backslidings. Worldly cares continued to invade his thoughts, and "a secret desire after pleasure and itching after liberty and unlawful delights."[5]

For almost another decade he vacillated agonizingly between the natural man and the Puritan conscience. Now the sins with which he wrestled were of the flesh, now of the mind.

After I had much displeased God by following idle and vain pastimes, such as sitting late up and omitting my family religious exercise, I was much unsettled. Yet God drew me to repentance and showed me sweet mercy.

Finding that the variety of meats draws me on to eat more than is good for my health, I have resolved not to eat more than two dishes at any one meal, whether at home or abroad.[6]

The sin that troubled him might be nothing more tangible than a vagrant thought. "On Sunday, being at sermon at Groton," he wrote, "I let in but a thought of my journey into Essex, but straight it delighted me, and being not very careful of my heart, I was suddenly, I know not how, so possessed with the world I could hardly recover myself till, praying, I found mercy."[7] More seriously, his ego kept interjecting itself into his communion with God.

The Genesis of a Patriarch, Puritan Style

Sometimes, in the midst of holy prayer or meditation, I let my affections cast an eye toward myself—thinking of myself as somebody in the performance of such a duty in such a manner, etc.—and the thought would destroy my peace, as cold water cast upon a flame, whereby I might see that God would teach me to go wholly outside of myself, and learn to depend upon Him alone.[8]

Occasionally he rationalized, as in the matter of hunting. Concluding that he could not indulge "with a good conscience" in shooting, he listed all the reasons why he should give up the sport—it was illegal, it wounds more than it kills, it wastes time, it is tiring and dangerous, etc. Finally, in the ninth and final item, he admits, "Lastly for mine own part I have ever been crossed in using it, for when I have gone about it (not without some wounds of conscience) I have gotten sometimes a very little but most commonly nothing at all to repay my cost and labor."[9]

Still, in matters of importance, Winthrop was starkly honest with himself, as all those passages which recount his efforts to tame his wayward mind make clear. "I found that the pride of my heart—these great thoughts of mine own gifts, credit, greatness, goodness, etc.—were like a canker eating out the comfort of all duties," he wrote in a characteristically candid moment.[10]

When tempted to waste his hours in pleasure, Winthrop would seek refuge in work. But it must be the Lord's work, not work for earthly rewards, riches, or renown.

The flesh is eagerly inclined to pride and wantonness, by which it plays the tyrant over the poor soul, making it a veritable slave. The works of our callings being diligently followed are a special means to tame it, and so is temperance in diet. For Idleness (under which term falls all such works as are done to fulfill the will of the flesh rather than that of the spirit) and gluttony are the two main pillars of the kingdom of the flesh.[11]

The training for salvation was a process of contracting his interests and energies into the narrowing funnel of religious absorption.

I saw my great folly in that I placed so much felicity in present outward things and in the hope of earthly things to come, whereas I am sure that I shall have them but for a short time, if at all. The danger and hurt of these earthly joys I find to be greater in that they diminish the joy of my salvation. Wherefore I have resolved, by the grace of God, to hold my affections in a narrower compass and not to suffer my heart to delight more in anything than in the comfort of my salvation.[12]

As the years went by, Winthrop became known for his piety; neighbors and friends sought him out for advice on spiritual matters, so that he began to consider leaving the law and taking up the ministry. But this too evoked the demon pride, and so he gave it up.

I grew to be of some note for religion (which puffed me up not a little), and divers would come to me for advice in cases of conscience; and, if I heard of any that were in trouble of mind, I usually went to comfort them. So that, upon the bent of my spirit this way and the success of my endeavors, I gave myself to the study of divinity, and intended to enter into the ministry. But as I grew into employments and credit thereby, so I grew also in pride of my gifts, which made me examine myself more narrowly.[13]

In June, 1615, when Winthrop was 27, his wife of ten years died. Six months later he married again, only to have this wife die on the day of their first anniversary, and, with her, her infant child. This succession of disasters set him to contemplating the vanity of the temporal world and the futility of man's efforts in it—a meditation that brought him at last the conversion and peace of mind he had so long sought.

I was now about thirty years of age. And now was the time come when the Lord would reveal Christ unto me, whom I had long desired. First, therefore, He laid a sore affliction upon me, wherein He laid me lower in mine own eyes than at any time before, and showed me the emptiness of all my gifts and parts. He left me neither power nor will, so as I became a child. I could now no more look at what I had been and what I had done, nor be discontented for want of strength or assurance. Mine eyes were only upon His free mercy in Jesus Christ. I knew I was worthy of nothing; for I knew I could do nothing for Him or for myself. I could only mourn and weep to think of free mercy to such a vile wretch as I was. Then the good Spirit of the Lord breathed upon my soul and said I should live. Now could my soul close with Christ and rest there with sweet content, so ravished with his love as to desire nothing, fear nothing. I was filled with joy unspeakable and glorious, and with a spirit of adoption.[14]

Also in his thirtieth year Winthrop married Margaret Tyndal, the daughter of a peer and an earnest Puritan who believed as firmly as did

The Genesis of a Patriarch, Puritan Style

her husband that God's purpose was "to exercise us with one affliction after another in love, lest we should forget ourselves and love this world too much."[15] Consistently Winthrop's letters to this "companion" of his "pilgrimage" alluded to the secondary nature of their love when compared with their love for Christ.[16]

We see how frail and vain all earthly good things are. There is no means to avoid the loss of them in death, nor the bitterness which accompanies them in the cares and troubles of this life. Only the fruition of Jesus Christ and the hope of heaven can give us true comfort and rest. The Lord teach us to lay up our treasure there, where our abiding must be forever.[17]

For Christ he reserved his most unrestrained passion.

Now Thou the hope of Israel, draw us with the sweetness of thine odors, that we may run after thee, that thou mayest possess us as thine own, in the love of marriage. Carry us into thy garden, that we may eat and be filled with those pleasures which the world knows not. Let us hear that sweet voice of thine, my love, my dove, my undefiled. Spread thy skirt over us, and cover our deformity. Make us sick with thy love. Let us sleep in thine arms and wake in thy kingdom.[18]

The love of John and Margaret Winthrop for each other, if less ecstatic than their love of God, was still a rich and enduring relationship. Four times a year he was called to the sessions of the Court of Wards in London—long wearisome sessions, fraught with the temptations of the flesh. His letters home to Groton were warm and loving; he "kissed his sweet wife" and longed for her; he prized her "above all things in the world."[19] She, in turn, sent him turkeys and fresh linen, her "best affections" and "a love increasing."[20] He had burned his hand, he wrote her, and back came the response: "I will not look for any long letters this term because I pity your poor hand. If I had it here I would make more of it than ever I did, and bind it up very softly for fear of hurting it."[21]

As Winthrop moved in the worldly circles to which his profession took him, he grew increasingly aware of the corruption around him. He struggled to keep his own standards above reproach and to raise those of the court. And, gradually, the realization sharpened in his mind that his responsibilities extended beyond himself, his family, his neighbors, and his profession—to England and the English people.

Like most Puritans, Winthrop believed that both Church and State

Chapters from the American Experience

were, ideally, grounded in covenants with God. Politically, this meant that God had made an agreement with rulers and subjects alike whereby He would care for them, and they would obey His laws—as interpreted by the learned clergy and magistrates. If the government performed these obligations satisfactorily, the people owed it complete obedience. If it did not, they had a responsibility to reform or replace it.[22]

For some time now, the Puritans in England had been asking themselves whether the time for rebellion had not come. With the accession of Charles I to the throne in 1625, the picture darkened perceptibly. The tendency of his father to tax his English subjects without their consent was put to shade by a host of new arbitrary exactions, and nonconformists of all kinds found themselves in constant danger of capricious arrest and punishment. But it was in the field of religion that Charles I and his ecclesiastical advisors galled the Puritans most deeply. Not only had the sovereign married a Catholic princess, but he began at once to give positions of prominence to opponents of the Puritan view, and the persecution of religious dissenters stepped up sharply. The Puritan-oriented House of Commons rose to the occasion by demanding reform in the Church. Charles responded by dissolving the Parliament and indicating that he intended to rule without it.

Here was a clear deviation from the path of righteousness. Winthrop realized that action of some kind could no longer be deferred. In a letter to Margaret, he poured out his sense of impending judgment. The times were "evil and declining," and the growing sinfulness of his countrymen gave Winthrop "great cause to look for some heavy scourge and judgment" to be coming upon the English people. "The Lord hath admonished, threatened, corrected, and astonished us, yet we grow worse and worse," he wrote. "His Spirit will not always strive with us; He must needs give way to His fury at last. My dear wife, I am verily persuaded God will bring some heavy affliction upon this land, and that speedily."[23]

Three courses of action seemed open to Winthrop. He might consider armed uprising, but open rebellion against his King was difficult for Winthrop to contemplate. Nor could he bring himself to the middle course of repudiating the Church of England as had the Puritan Separatists of Plymouth almost a decade before.

By a strange combination of circumstances a third possibility presented itself. In the spring of 1629, just a week before he dissolved the Parliament, Charles granted to a group of Puritan merchants a royal charter enabling them, under the name "Governor and Company of the

The Genesis of a Patriarch, Puritan Style

Massachusetts Bay in New England," to establish a settlement in the American colonies. Men involved in the Company urged Winthrop to join them. Here was an opportunity to cleave to his church and his country and yet to escape their sins—and even their control. For, because of the peculiar nature of the Company's charter, this would be an especially independent colony. Like the earlier London and Plymouth Companies, this corporation carried with it power to govern the area colonized. What was unique about the Bay Company was that its charter contained no clause specifying that its government be seated in any particular city. Taking advantage of this fact, the Company decided that—in order to induce "persons of worth and quality to transplant themselves and their families" to the New World—it would transfer the government of the colony to the colony itself.[24] This then would be no ordinary settlement, but a virtually independent land, where the laws of the Lord could be enforced without hindrance and where a model church and way of life could be established in the hope that the mother Church of England would see and be moved to reform herself.

Winthrop began to consider the project seriously. "If the Lord seeth it will be good for us, He will provide a shelter and a hiding place for us and others," he wrote Margaret in May, 1629.[25] He considered, step by step, the arguments in favor of such a move. It would carry the Gospel to the New World and "raise a bulwark against the kingdom of Antichrist which the Jesuits labor to rear up there." It would be a refuge for those the Lord meant "to save out of the general calamity." In England it was "almost impossible for a good and upright man to live comfortably in any of the arts and trades," and countryfolk struggled to "keep an acre or two." In the New World "a whole continent, just as fruitful" awaited them. In England the "fountains of Learning and Religion" were corrupted; across the seas their children could be properly educated. To the objection that the exodus of so many good people from England laid that country more open to judgment, he answered that their going might frighten others to "turn from their evil ways," that those who went could probably do more good in New England, and that the Church was universal and taught that the gospel should be spread to all corners of the world.[26]

On August 21, 1630, Winthrop's eldest son, John, whom he regarded very highly, returned from a trip to the Near East and, learning that Winthrop was considering the step, encouraged him to go. "It cannot but be a prosperous action which is undertaken by so religious and wise worthies of Israel," he told his father.[27] Within a week Winthrop had committed himself to the undertaking. He would go, the following spring, with the Massachusetts Bay Company. Together in that "hiding place" they would build a new kingdom for God.

In October the members of the Company met and elected Winthrop their governor. The responsibility for the entire expedition now fell upon him. "It hath pleased the Lord to call me to a further trust in this business of the Plantation than I either expected or find myself fit for," he wrote Margaret. "The only thing in this that gives me comfort is that I am now sure that my charge is from the Lord and that He hath called me to this work."[28]

In the months that followed, Winthrop wrote countless letters encouraging "persons of worth" to join the Company, soliciting funds, arranging the thousand details of the passage and the settlement. Margaret, who had become pregnant, would not go on this first voyage, and his letters home to her from London are filled with a tender effort to prepare her for the separation.

I must now begin to prepare thee for our long parting, which grows very near. I know not how to deal with thee by arguments; for if thou wert as wise and patient as ever woman was, yet it must needs be a great trial to thee, and the greater, because I am so dear to thee. That which I must chiefly look at in thee, for a ground of contentment, is thy godliness. If now Christ be thy Husband, thou must show what sure and sweet intercourse is between Him and thy soul, when it shall be no hard thing for thee to part with an earthly, mortal, infirm husband for His sake.[29]

When the expedition had been manned, equipped, and financed, when the colonists had gathered together to hear the farewell sermon of the brilliant young Lincolnshire minister, John Cotton, and had gone aboard their ships, there was a long delay because of bad weather. From the ship during the days while they waited, Winthrop wrote to his "Best Beloved," his "Joy," his "Sweet Wife" stirring notes of love for her to cherish.

And now, my sweet soul, I must once again take my last farewell of thee in Old England. It goeth very near to my heart to leave thee. But I know to whom I have committed thee, even to Him who loves thee much better than any husband can. Oh, how it refresheth my heart to think that I shall yet again see thy sweet face in the land of the living—that lovely countenance that I have so much delighted in.[30]

On April 8, 1630, the *Arbella* and three sister ships set sail for

The Genesis of a Patriarch, Puritan Style

America. The passage was cold and wearing, but not tragic, as many were in that day. Winthrop had provisioned them well, and he now routed them out daily to exercise and take fresh air, regardless of the weather or their inclinations. And he breathed into them his will to survive and to fulfill his covenant with God.

We have taken out a commission. The Lord hath given us leave to draw our own articles. Now if the Lord shall please to hear us, and bring us in peace to the place we desire, then hath He ratified this Covenant and sealed our Commission. As Moses said in his last farewell to Israel: "We are commanded this day to love the Lord our God, and to love one another, to walk in His ways and to keep His Commandments, and His Ordinance, and the articles of our Covenant with Him, that the Lord our God may bless us in the land whither we go to possess it."[31]

In June the four ships of the first migration, bearing 400 men, women and children, sailed into Salem harbor, where the company "went on shore and gathered store of fine strawberries."[32] Despite the fact that they were already too late to make proper provisions against the winter ahead, the Puritans set to work with enthusiasm. On the fertile land to the South of Salem, around the Bay of Boston, Winthrop and those of his men who survived the first harsh winter labored so eagerly and prospered so well that, by the fall of 1631, when Margaret joined him, Winthrop's friends brought welcoming gifts of "fat hogs, kids, venison, poultry, geese, partridges, etc., so as the like joy and manifestation of love had never been seen in New England."[33]

And, above all, they at once set about building a state that would enforce the Laws of God. Such a church-state, Winthrop believed, would make clear to the world the distinction between an individual's "natural liberty" (which was unguided license) and his "civil liberty" (which was his liberty to obey the voice of God, as enunciated by His magistrates). Only by "cheerfully submitting to authority," he warned his followers, could their "liberties be preserved."[34] It was a frankly aristocratic dogma. Democracy, said Winthrop, was "the meanest and worst of all forms of government." There was no precedent for it in the Scriptures, "no such Government in Israel." If man was to be raised from his fallen state, leadership must rest in the hands of the "called."[35]

Winthrop was acutely aware that this community would serve as a beacon to other men faltering in the dark. They would find that the God of Israel was among them—in the years to come men would make them "a praise and a glory" and would pray that succeeding plantations be like that of New England. "For we must consider that we shall be as a City upon a hill," he told them:

The eyes of all people are upon us. So that if we shall deal falsely with our God in this work we have undertaken, we shall be made a story and a by-word throughout the world. We shall open the mouths of enemies and shame the faces of many of God's worthy servants.[36]

And they did indeed "possess" the land, and future generations of Americans, migrating to the Ohio, the Oregon Country, Hawaii, would indeed strive to be "like New England" and would succeed. Standing on the threshold of this great, germinal plantation, the once self-doubting Squire of Groton had emerged as the foremost of the Puritan Patriarchs—determined, with the other magistrates and ministers, to create a New Canaan, a nation of Saints treasured of the Lord, a flaming proof that, under the stewardship of the chosen, man might fulfill his Covenant with God.

Herman A. MacNeil, The Hall of Fame for Great Americans,
New York University.

Roger Williams

5

The Rise of a Rebel,
Puritan Style

Liberty of searching out Truth . . . [is] hardly got, and as hardly kept.
—Roger Williams[1]

From the start there were those who questioned the right of the Massachusetts Bay magistrates to rule with such absolute sway, however well-meaning their intent. The Puritans' English legacy consisted of something more than authoritarianism. There was also a healthy strain of English Independency in their veins—a long tradition of challenging authority. Greatest of the Massachusetts rebels was Roger Williams, born in England around 1603. The son of a local guild merchant, Williams would normally have had little opportunity to move out of the lesser mercantile class had he not won the favor of the great jurist, Sir Edward Coke, under whose patronage he studied for five years at Cambridge, in preparation for the ministry.

Disgusted with Laud's England, Williams refused more than one good post in the Anglican Church (to keep his "soul undefiled") and spent a year or two, instead, as chaplain in the household of a prominent Puritan member of Parliament.[2] By 1630 he had become completely alienated from the Church of England and had subscribed to the doctrine of Separatism. Late that year, he and his bride sailed for the New World, arriving in February, 1631, at Massachusetts Bay. The ship had brought them "a godly minister," Governor Winthrop recorded in his *Journal.*[3]

Almost at once it became evident that this man, whom Cotton

Mather would call the "first rebel against the divine church-order established in the wilderness," was not as "godly" by Winthrop's lights as he should have been.[4] He was offered the position of "teacher" to the Boston congregation but refused it. "I durst not officiate to an unseparated people," he explained. Furthermore, he added, the magistrates had no right to punish violations of the first four Commandments (against idolatry, blasphemy and heresy). These Commandments, known as "the first table," dealt with matters of faith, and in such matters civil authorities had no right to enforce conformity.[5]

And so, before he had been in New England two months, Williams had defied the authorities by flatly opposing the fundamental tenet of theocracy—the concept of church and state as inextricably bound together. Williams' stand would, the magistrates and ministers believed, "open the door unto a thousand profanities" and "utterly take away from the authority all capacity to prevent the land from becoming such a 'sink of abominations' as would be the reproach and ruin of Christianity."[6]

Williams quickly found that the Bay Colony was in many ways less liberal than England had been. Only church members could be freemen (voters); and not all members of a congregation qualified as church members—only the inner circle known as the "Visible Saints." Biographer Samuel Brockunier discusses the power structure of the Bay Colony:

This limitation on the suffrage was decisive and insured domination by the close alliance of ministers and magistrates. . . . Puritan clergy . . . took care to admit only men zealous in orthodoxy and well affected to the dominant order; and before long, English Puritans were startled to hear that in the new Zion over the seas three-fourths of the people had been shut out from membership in the church. . . .

With a suffrage linked to sanctification, and clerical influence over the people employed as a stout crutch, . . . oligarchy served well the dual purpose of keeping democracy out and orthodoxy in. . . . [When] charter or English precedent would have tied their hands, . . . [the ruling group] sanctioned their conduct by Higher Law. . . . Only the husks of political rights had been conceded to the rank and file. . . . [The] vast body of yeoman farmers and common folk remained unenfranchised.[7]

It was inevitable that Roger Williams would challenge this system, the antithesis of his deepest convictions. For the philosophy that he had worked out was democratic in the fullest sense of the word, being rooted in the belief that all men are equal in the light of God's love for them. On this leveling principle he developed a concept of government as an instrument of the common good, subject to the common will. The state existed because the people, realizing that man's natural condition is anarchy, had agreed to establish such a community. It followed, 51 therefore, that a government which derived its power from the governed was responsible to them and was constantly subject to the people's judgment as to whether it was satisfactory—whether, in fact, it should survive. The "foundation of civill power lies in the People," Williams would write, and the people "may erect and establish what form of Government seemes to them most meete." The government they erect, he added, has "no more power, nor for any longer time" than the people entrust to it.[8]

In such a Christian commonwealth, built by men who love God and have confidence in their fellow men, government should do no more than maintain justice, and all men should be allowed to worship according to their consciences. Such religious freedom was one of the basic individual liberties.

It is the will and command of God that . . . permission . . . be granted to all men . . . [to follow] the most Paganish, Jewish, Turkish, or Antichristian [worship]. They are only to be fought . . . with . . . the Sword of God's Spirit, the Word of God. An inforced uniformity of Religion throughout a Nation or civill state . . . denies the principles of Christianity. . . . [Such] inforced uniformity (sooner or later) is the greatest occasion of civill Warre, ravishing of conscience, persecution of Christ Jesus in his servants, and of hypocrisie and destruction of millions of souls.[9]

Here was an irreconcilable confrontation of principles. The theory that the right to govern is derived from a compact among all the governed had been raised in defiance of the belief that the chosen few rule by virtue of their covenant with God. The democratic right of consent had been flung at an oligarchy that considered democracy the "meanest" form of government, the unlikeliest way to achieve the good of the people.[10] Williams' days in the Bay Colony were numbered.

Hoping to find a more congenial climate, he now moved from Boston to Salem. Shortly, Governor Winthrop received word that "they of Salem had called Mr. Williams to the office of a teacher."[11] A conference took place in Boston, and a letter went forth to John Endecott, Salem assistant (i.e., representative of the oligarchy there), pointing out that Williams had taken a hard-nosed Separatist stand in Boston, and further, that he had "declared his opinion that the magistrate might not punish the breach of the Sabbath" or any other offense against the first table. They "marvelled" therefore that Salem should "choose him without advising with the council." The leaders of Salem would "forbear to proceed" until they had had an opportunity to "confer" with Boston about it.[12] Williams was not given the position.

He went to Plymouth Colony, which was outside the jurisdiction of Massachusetts Bay and which offered him a post as minister. But the Pilgrims had relaxed a little on their Separatist stand, and Williams continued to press his unorthodox views. "He this year [1633]," wrote Governor Bradford of Plymouth, "began to fall into some strange opinions, and from opinion to practice."[13] "His turbulent and singular opinions," Cotton Mather later recorded, not finding the acceptance he had expected at Plymouth, he asked for "a dismission back to Salem," and the Pilgrims, perceiving how his "giddy courses" might "endanger" them, "wisely humour'd" him.[14]

In Salem again Williams was appointed assistant to the ailing pastor Samuel Skelton this time without any formal objection from Boston. Almost immediately he became involved in a dispute over the independence of the individual congregations. He found threatening the fact that ministers had begun to meet regularly to discuss questions "of moment." This seemingly innocuous practice would, he feared, grow into a "superintendency" that would "prejudice" the liberties of the individual churches.[15]

By December, 1633, Williams had turned to the question of land ownership. Winthrop, horrified, noted in his *Journal* that Williams was challenging the right of the King of England to make grants of land in the New World except by agreement with the Indians. He was disputing the colonists' "right to the lands they possessed."[16] Williams had spent much time with the Indians, had become "great friends" with their sachems, was intent on saving "native souls." He would not be silent while they were cheated of their rights.[17] Even if one conceded that the whites had any right to Indian land, which he did not, he said bluntly, King James had been guilty of "a solemn public lie" in claiming to be the "first Christian prince" to discover America.[18] Dismayed as they were at these impolitic aspersions on the father of the king, the magistrates did not formally censure Williams. Winthrop made it clear, however, that his stand on the land question was in error. Citing biblical precedent, he announced that Indians only had "natural" or squatters' rights. "Soe if we leave them sufficient for their use," he said, "we may lawfully take the rest."[19]

Williams' criticisms continued on all fronts, and in November, 1634, the general court brought charges against him for "preaching that the churches of England were false churches" and for arguing "publickly against the king's patent."[20] He was summoned to appear at the next court. This time, however, John Cotton, minister of the Boston church, interceded in his behalf. He felt, he said, that Williams' "violent course" did not stem from "seditious" intent but rather from errors of conscience.[21] John Cotton's account of his intervention, says Brockunier, "throws a shaft of light on the dual authority of church and state."

"I presented (with the consent of my fellow-Elders and Brethren) a serious Request to the Magistrates, that they would be pleased to forbeare all civill prosecution against him, till our selves (with our Churches) had dealt with him in a Church way, to convince him of sinne." . . .
. . . [This device for] dealing with offenders . . . already had proved a formidable weapon of social pressure. A battery of confident and capable Puritan priests was generally an irresistible answer to a doubting Thomas; nor were such advice and admonition unavailing with Williams. Although there is no evidence that he yielded his Separatist position as to the churches of England, the brethren won him to silence on the score of the patent.[22]

It was the last time the ministers would shield Williams from the wrath of the magistrates. Cotton and his fellow clergymen soon despaired of the unregenerate rebel. Further, they had no inclination to tangle with their co-rulers in the Bay oligarchy.

In April, 1634, the magistrates ruled that henceforth everyone not a freeman should take a "resident's oath" swearing to submit to the laws and "authority of the governor and magistrates" and to "give speedy notice" of any sedition "plotted or intended against the . . . government."[23] Such an oath was anathema to Williams, who, wrote Cotton, "vehemently withstood it, and dissuaded sundry from it."[24] In the face of this serious threat the magistrates summoned Williams before the court in the spring of 1635. There he was heard, says Winthrop, "before all the ministers and very clearly confuted." There is some question, however, as to how clear his confutation was to the population as a whole. Opposition to the oath became so general that, Cotton recorded, "the Court was forced to desist from that proceeding."[25]

In July, Williams was again in court, facing the charge of having agitated against the magistrates' right to enforce the first table.

When he faced his accusers on July 8, . . . [Williams] discovered that leading ministers were there by special request. Their faces were hostile. . . . [When] in the course of the lengthy proceeding, the magistrates called for advice, the clergy replied that . . . such a man should "be removed."[26]

In the midst of the trial the Salem congregation invited Williams to become their minister, a post left vacant by the death of Skelton. Incensed at this insubordination, the oligarchy issued a statement again condemning Williams' views and chastising Salem for its "great contempt of authority."[27] The magistrates also exerted a little economic pressure on the rebellious congregation. Salem had petitioned for a section of land in Marblehead Neck to which it had a claim. The request would not be considered, the court announced frankly, "because they had chosen Mr. Williams."[28]

The Salem congregation, roused to the point of rashness, held an "indignation meeting" and wrote the other congregations of the colony asking them to "admonish the magistrates" for their "heinous sin."[29] This heresy was effectually scotched, however, for the elders of the other churches cooperatively suppressed the letters and neglected to read them in their congregations. A heated note of protest now went from Salem to the Bay. It was not up to the elders to determine what letters should or should not be delivered to their congregations, it affirmed. Salem did not accept the theory that "the people are weak . . . giddy and rash, and therefore should not enjoy such liberties."[30]

The oligarchy struck and struck hard. The general court unseated the deputies of the town and sent them home; the freemen, or Visible Saints, of Salem were to have no representation until they disclaimed the church letters, nor would the court hear their claim to land in the Neck until the church repented of its choice of Williams. . . . Dismayed, yet furious, John Endecott appeared defiantly before the authorities and attempted to justify the Salem letters. . . . Peremptorily refusing him a hearing, the court ordered Endecott imprisoned for contempt. There had been no more vigorous and independent figure in the ruling class of the Bay than John Endecott, but it was now shown him that he would reap little if he opposed his fellow-dignitaries. . . . In a little while his head cooled, and "he came and acknowledged his fault, and was discharged."

The tide had begun to turn. Salem had moved surprisingly far, and a part of the congregation were ready to follow their pastor into absolute separation, even if it meant exile; but if the majority had to make choice between Roger Williams and the Puritan oligarchy, the choice was not to be Williams.[31]

Having driven a wedge between Williams and his constituents, the oligarchy met in general court on October 8, 1635, and issued against him a decree of banishment. "Whereas Mr. Roger Williams hath broached and divulged divers newe and dangerous opinions against the authoritie of magistrates . . . and yet maintaineth the same without retraction," read the decree, "it is therefore ordered that the said Mr. Williams shall depart out of this jurisdiction."[32]

Because Williams was recovering from an illness and his wife was pregnant, the time of exile was deferred until the following spring, on the condition that Williams refrain from going "about to draw others to his opinions." But this was expecting too much. Hearing that Williams "did use to entertain company in his house, and to preach to them, even of such points as he had been censured for," the magistrates, early in January, determined to send Williams to England at once.[33]

Williams, however, had no intention of returning to England, and while the magistrates sent a ship especially for him, he slipped away into the forest. Years later he would remember bitterly the difficulties of that "sorrowful winter's flight."[34] With the help of the Indians, he survived, and in late spring four men joined him at the upper tip of Narragansett Bay, where they bought land from the natives, planted a crop, and began building homes.

Then came a letter from the Governor of Plymouth, "professing his own and others love and respect to me," wrote Williams later, "yet lovingly advising me, since I was fallen into the edge of their bounds, and they were loath to displease the Bay, to remove but to the other side of the water."[35]

Once more heading westward, Williams and his followers crossed the . . . river to the peninsula jutting down into the upper reaches of Narragansett bay. . . . [There] they picked a site bulwarked at the back by a towering hill. Again Williams purchased the land, this time from the Narragansett sachems. Believing that at last he had found a safe refuge, Williams called the place Providence—"in the sense of God's merciful providence unto me in my distress."[36]

Here others joined him, and together they built a commonwealth that would be known to history as a pilot experiment in democracy. Its constitution was a testament to man's right to political and religious freedom and embodied such democratic ideals as frequent popular elections and maximum home rule for local governments.

The Bay rulers exerted pressure on Parliament to give them a mandate over the rebels, but supported by English Independents, Williams continued his experiment. Despite the antagonism of the Massachusetts theocracy toward him, Williams was able, almost immediately after his banishment, to do the Bay Colony a great service when his negotiations helped prevent a war between Massachusetts and the Narragansett Indians. In the summer of 1636 an English trader was killed by four Narragansett chiefs. Canonicus, the head sachem and a friend of Williams' from Plymouth days, asked Williams to explain that he and the Narragansett people did not sanction the deed. At the same time Governor Winthrop sent word to Williams asking him to use his linguistic gifts

The Rise of a Rebel, Puritan Style

and his friendship with the Indians in behalf of the Bay Colony. Despite the efforts of another tribe to effect an antiwhite pact with the Narragansetts, Canonicus signed a treaty with Massachusetts. Over the years many occasions arose for Williams to use his talents in this area. "The Indeans sent for Mr. Williams & made a greeveous complainte," Governor Bradford once recorded, but "Mr. Williams pacified them."[37]

These services arose not only from Williams' ability to turn the other cheek to the men who had ousted him, but also from his enduring friendship toward the Indians. He understood their "treacheries" and their "fierce pride," and his heart went out to them in their tribulations.[38]

His house was a council chamber, a hospital, an inn, whatever was needed at the moment. "5 or 6 Indians at my house," [he wrote, and on another occasion, someone] "took sick" on the way, and would stay until he was well. If they needed a canoe, shelter in "foul weather," food, . . . "Mr. Williams, his house" was the answer. To read the casual allusions to such services in his letters makes one wonder whether there was ever a time when his household . . . did not include several . . . who had "turned in" for some service or other. . . . "I have fixed mine eye on this little one with the red about his neck," he wrote . . . [of an Indian youngster captured] in war. He would bring the child up in his own home.[39]

Years later he would explain his reasoning in a letter to the Massachusetts General Court. He had, he said, allowed himself to be "used" in all their "great transactions" with the natives because it was his deep desire that "the whole land, English and natives, might sleep in peace securely."[40]

Even Cotton Mather, while still protesting that Williams had "less light than fire in him," was forced to admit that the "first rebel" had "in many things acquitted himself so laudably that many judicious persons judged him to have had the 'root of the matter' in him." There was a "constant correspondence" between him and "many worthy and pious people" in Massachusetts, wrote Mather, but, because he "still continued so many of his dangerous principles," the Bay was "unable to take off the sentence of his banishment."[41]

The great English historian, James Bryce, has assessed the contributions of Williams and Rhode Island in this way:

Roger Williams was the founder of Rhode Island in a clearer and ampler sense than any other single man—scarcely excepting William Penn—was the founder of any other American colony; for he gave it a set of principles which, so far as the New World was concerned, were peculiarly his own,

Chapters from the American Experience

and these principles long continued to affect its collective life. The men of Virginia were ordinary Englishmen of the class then dominant in England. The men of Massachusetts and Connecticut were Puritans of the normal seventeenth-century type, earnest and God-fearing, but almost as ready to persecute heretical opinions as they had found the church of Archbishop Laud in England ready to persecute them. Roger Williams had a new doctrine. He was the first apostle in New England of the theory of absolute freedom for the individual in matters of religion, with the consequent denial of the right of the civil magistrate to intermeddle in any wise with such matters.

Upon this foundation, and upon the [allied] principle of the fullest recognition of the rights of the individual in the civil sphere also, the commonwealth of Rhode Island was built. A no less honorable and scarcely less important part of Williams' doctrines was his recognition of the right of the native Indians to their lands. His respect for their rights, his wish to deal fairly and live peaceably with the aborigines are among the most attractive features of his character. Roger Williams was in a sense before his time; and he may not in some respects have fully appreciated the results of his own principles. But the principles spread, and the work told.[42]

Courtesy Library of Congress.

Hon. Samuel Sewell, Esq.

6

The Emergence of a
Yankee, Puritan Style

I name my little daughter Judith, and may she follow Christ,
being not slothfull in Business, fervent in Spirit, serving the Lord.
—Samuel Sewall[1]

Twenty-five years after Roger Williams left Boston, there arrived in the Bay Colony a boy of nine who was to become one of the colony's staunchest supports—Judge Samuel Sewall, chief justice of the Massachusetts Supreme Court, pillar of the South Church, a man of means and distinction. If Sam Sewall had not kept a diary, this is about all we would have remembered of him—this and the fact that he was involved in the witchcraft trials. And our impressions of life in Boston during the second and third generations after the founding would have been much less graphic. For, the introspections, judgments, and village news that Sewall jotted down over half a century make up one of the most revealing journals of colonial America. The image the diary casts is that of gradual transition. A frontier community founded in a rigid theocratic mold is growing and developing its own pattern. And a man, still earnestly orthodox in doctrine, is at the same time unwittingly turning to new and disruptive values.

Most of Sewall's neighbors would have testified that he lived by the traditional Puritan virtues. He accepted with a deep sense of responsibility his "calling" to share in the administration of the government and believed, as firmly as had John Winthrop, that the power of the church-state should not be questioned. It was "intolerable," he said, "for private persons to print Reflections and Censures on the highest Acts of Government."[2]

Equally orthodox were his views on religion. Although he put a little less emphasis on man's sin than did some of the ministers who were bewailing the "diseases of New England" and her "sucking of false principles," he was as firmly convinced as they of the need for inner regeneration.[3] Being of a positive disposition, he translated the quest for salvation into a healthy effort to live with his fellow men in accordance with the highest Christian precepts. "The Lord help me not to do, or neglect anything that should prevent the dwelling of brethren together in unity," he wrote, and his life was a testament to how seriously he meant this prayer.[4] With all the opportunities which fifty years of private diary writing offered him, he proved remarkably free from malice. There are many indications that he looked on his fellow wayfarers' frailties with a realistic eye but none that he took pleasure in gossiping about them. Life on the shelf of an alien continent was fraught with danger. Sewall attended innumerable death watches, held the "flaming" hands of many friends, and helped give them a "lift heavenward."[5] And his friends did the same for his family. To Sewall this was natural and right, for the commitment to work with and for his neighbors was deep in him. They were his brothers. In their redemption lay his own. Only in the light of this conviction of sacred duty does Sewall come into true focus—as a warmly human, gentle and constructive man, in the finest sense his brother's keeper. It was in such a spirit of stewardship for the Puritan conscience that he reacted to the situations described in the following entries:

August 12, 1676. Just as prayer ended Tim Dwight sank down in a Swoun, and afterwards, kicked and sprawled, knocking his hands and feet upon the floor like a distracted man. The Sabbath following I asked him, being alone with him, whether his troubles were from some outward cause or spiritual. He answered, spiritual. I asked him why then he could not tell it his master, since it is the honour of any man to see sin and be sorry for it. He gave no answer, as I remember. Asked him if he would goe to meeting. He said, 'twas in vain for him; his day was out. I asked, what day. He answered, of Grace. I told him 'twas sin for any one to conclude themselves Reprobate. He said he would speak more, but could not, &c. Notwithstanding all this semblance (and much more than is written) of compunction for Sin, 'tis to be feared that his trouble arose from a maid whom he passionately loved; for that when Mr. Dwight and his master had agreed to let him goe to her, he eftsoons grew well.

November 12, 1685. The ministers of this town come to the court and complain against a dancing master who seeks to set up here and hath mixed dances, and his time of meeting is lecture day [a second Sabbath among the Puritans]; and 'tis reported he has said that by one play he could teach more divinity than Mr. Willard or the Old Testament. Mr. Moodey said 'twas not a time for New England to dance. Mr. Mather struck at the root, speaking against mixed dances.

February 1, 1696. Sam Haugh came to speak about Frank's burial. I spoke to Sam about his Mistress' maid being with child, and that she laid it to him, and told him if she were with child by him, it concerned him seriously to consider what were best to be done; and that a father was obliged to look after mother and child. I could not discern that any impression was made on him.

September 10, 1696. Letter to Mrs. Martha Oakes: "Not finding opportunity to speak with you at your house, nor at my own, I write to persuade you that your striking your daughter-in-law in my house is not justifiable. Though 'twas but a small blow, 'twas not a small fault. As for New England, it is a cleaner country than ever you were in before, and, therefore, with disdain to term it *filthy,* is a sort of Blasphemie. I write this not to upbraid, but to admonish you, with whom I sympathize under your extraordinary provocations and pressures."

June 10, 1701. Having last night heard that Josiah Willard had cut off his hair (a very full head of hair) and put on a Wigg, I went to him this morning. Told his Mother what I came about, and she call'd him. I enquired of him what Extremity had forced him to cut off his own hair and put on a Wigg? He answered none, but that his hair was straight, and that it parted behinde. I said God seems to have ordain'd our Hair as a Test, to see whether we can bring our minds to be content, or whether we would be our own Carvers and come no more to Him. Pray'd him to read the Tenth Chapter of the Third book of Calvin's Institutions. He seem'd to say would leave off his Wigg when his hair was grown. I spake to his Father of it a day or two after. He thank'd me for having discoursed his Son and told me that when his hair was grown to cover his ears, he promis'd to leave off his Wigg.[6]

If Sewall used his weight in the community against such advanced ideas as mixed dancing and wigs, he indoctrinated his own children with the same stern and orthodox precepts.

September 15, 1688. Corrected Sam for breach of the 9th Commandment, saying he had been at the Writing School, when he had not.

November 6, 1692. Joseph threw a knob of brass and hit his sister, Betty, on the forehead so as to make it bleed and swell; upon which, and for his playing at prayer-time, and eating when Return Thanks, I whipped him pretty smartly.

The Emergence of a Yankee, Puritan Style

January 13, 1696. When I came in, past 7 at night, my wife met me in the Entry, saying that a little after dinner Betty burst out into an amazing cry, which caus'd all the family to cry too; Her Mother ask'd the reason; she said she was afraid she should goe to Hell, her Sins were not pardon'd. She was first wounded by my reading a Sermon of Mr. Norton's on the text: "Ye shall seek me and shall not find me," and the words "Ye shall seek me and shall die in your sins," ran in her mind and terrified her greatly. And staying at home Jan. 12 she read out of Mr. Cotton Mather: "Why hath Satan filled thy heart," which increas'd her fear. Mr. Willard came and prayed excellently. The Lord bring Light and Comfort out of this dark and dreadful Cloud, and Grant that Christ's being formed in my dear child, may be the issue of these painfull pangs.

February 22, 1696. Betty comes into me almost as soon as I was up and tells me the disquiet she had when waked; told me was afraid should go to Hell, was not Elected. Ask'd her what I should pray for, she said, that God would pardon her Sin and give her a new Heart. I answer'd her Fears as well as I could, and pray'd with many Tears on either part; hope God heard us. I gave her solemnly to God.[7]

All things lay, he believed, in the "good Hand of God."[8] When Sam Junior's cousin died of smallpox, the judge improved the occasion by pointing out his son's need to prepare for his own "dying hour." The lesson of submission to the will of God came hard for young Sam, who had already suffered the traumatic experience of seeing three of his little brothers buried within as many years and of peering into the family tomb at the coffins piled up in its dark depths.[9]

Richard Dummer, a flourishing youth of 9 years old, dies of the Small Pocks. I tell Sam of it and what need he had to prepare for Death, and therefore to endeavour really to pray when he said over the Lord's Prayer: He seem'd not much to mind, eating an Apple; but when he came to say, Our father, he burst out into a bitter Cry, and when I askt what was the matter and he could speak, he burst out that he was afraid he should die. I pray'd with him, and read Scriptures comforting against death, as, O death where is thy sting, &c. All things yours. Life and Immortality brought to light by Christ, &c.[10]

This fortitude born of piety, which Sewall tried to share with his young son, was a net of survival to the Puritans in those pioneer days when death and disaster were always near. Fires swept through the villages. Smallpox struck in almost every house. Drums beating for volunteers told of Indians raiding and scalping in the outlying areas. And, between and in the midst of these cataclysms, runs an incessant flow of dying and burying, described in the diary with terse stoicism. Infant mortality was staggering. Small coffins with a single year (for birth and death) hammered on in nails accumulated in the Sewall tomb until, in 1693, the judge recorded a poignant list of eleven children born to him and his wife, Hannah, of whom four had died in earliest infancy and two others before the age of two. In all, the Sewalls had fourteen children, and only three survived them. "Lord teach me to profit," wrote the judge.[11]

Childbearing also represented a hazard of daily life. In Sewall's family and among his friends, fever and death followed on confinement with a regularity that suggests that ignorant midwifery was a greater killer than smallpox. Frequent notations to the effect that a dying baby made "a kind of snoaring as it breathed" or that a friend died "drowned in flegm" point to another common killer—inadequate protection against the harsh New England winters.[12] "Very thin Assemblies this Sabbath and last, great Coughing," noted Sewall[13] and again: "Bread was frozen at the Lord's Table; though 'twas so cold, yet John Tuckerman was baptized. At six o'clock my ink freezes so that I can hardly write by a good fire in my wife's chamber."[14]

In all these ways, Sam Sewall was typical of the better Puritan leaders. The political and religious orthodoxy, the sense of a calling to public duty and of stewardship for his fellows, the stern parental discipline, the fortitude in the face of disaster—all help make up the conventional aspect of the diary's image. Sewall also shared most of the prejudices of his time. He hated the Quakers at least as ardently as did his brother Puritans. As a young man, he noted with disgust how a "female Quaker in a Canvas Frock, her hair disshevelled," had invaded their church and disrupted the sermon.[15] In middle age he wrote: "A petition for building a Quaker Meeting House passed the Selectmen and Justices of the Town; was offer'd to the Gov. and Council. I oppos'd it—said I would not have a hand in setting up their Devil Worship."[16]

Nor was he more enlightened than his contemporaries regarding the witchcraft trials, in which he served as one of the judges. But, after the reaction to the trials set in and many participants preferred to forget the roles they had played, Sewall showed more courage than most. Asking his minister to read his statement of guilt in church, he stood with bowed head while the congregation heard his penitent words:

Samuel Sewall, sensible of the reiterated strokes of God upon himself and family; and being sensible that he is, upon many accounts, more concerned than any that he knows of, Desires to take the Blame and shame of it, Asking pardon of men, And especially desiring prayers that God, who has an Unlimited Authority, would pardon that sin and all other his sins.[17]

In race relations, Sewall was in many ways a child of his era. (He once speculated on whether a Negro going to Heaven would be given a white skin.) But in an age thorny with prejudice he showed liberal tendencies. Amid entries noting that Indians had been branded in court and had their ears cut off for burglary, he recorded with pride that, in Council, he had "essayed to prevent Indians and Negroes being rated with horses and hogs," though he "could not prevail."[18] And his informal chats with apprentices and grave keepers suggest a bit more interplay between the classes, a shade less condescension and subservience than had prevailed in earlier days.[19]

In race relations, Sewall was in many ways a child of his era. (He once
    If these changes were intangible, Sewall departed noticeably from tradition in one basic matter. His attitude toward material well-being, like that of many of his contemporaries, represented a decided falling away from one of the cardinal beliefs of the earlier Puritans. John Winthrop had struggled to put the spiritual above all other values, had rejected the temptation to work for the goods of this world, had considered the possibility that work could become a "snare." But in Sewall there was a frank concern for the physical. Of all the failings that weighed on his conscience from time to time, his interest in money and the things it could buy seems to have been a relatively slight burden. Picnicking on plump turkeys, taking a ten-quart jug of Madeira to a barn-raising, observing with concern who attended the better dinner parties and weddings, who received gloves and rings at the funerals, Sewall appears more as a plump Dutch burgher than as an ascetic Puritan. (By 1721 he weighed 228 pounds, despite his shortness of stature.[20]) He noted with satisfaction that he had sent Increase Mather a "hanch of very good Venison," and that a visiting churchman whom he housed would find that his "library was convenient."[21] As the years went by, an increasing number of entries dealt with the pursuit of mammon—with the leasing of houses, the collecting of bills, the affairs of the Company. One night in July, 1709, his wife awakened him saying she smelled smoke. He jumped out of bed (put on his "cloathes except Stockings"), and while his wife checked on the welfare of the children, he found the source of the fire in his closet, extinguished it, and saved some business papers that lay nearby. "Thus with great Indulgence GOD saved our House and substance, and the Company Paper," he wrote. "This night, as I lay down in my Bed, I said to my Wife, that the Goodness of God appeared in that we had a Chamber, a Bed, and Company."[22]

    Nowhere does his acquisitiveness come into sharper focus than in his courting of the Lady Winthrop during his declining years. The fact that

Mme. Winthrop outdid him in bargaining suggests that the ministers were not far amiss in complaining of a general decay of interest in things spiritual.

When his wife of many years died in 1717, he mourned her deeply. "God is teaching me a new lesson," he said. "Lord help me to learn; and be a Sun and Shield to me, now so much of my comfort and defense are taken away."[23] By the next spring, his friends were busily suggesting various likely replacements. In the fall of 1719 he married, was widowed again the following May, and, shortly thereafter, began courting Madame Katherine Winthrop.

October 1, 1720. I spoke to Madam Winthrop saying, I had resolved that I would not make my court to any person without first consulting her. Had a pleasant discourse about 7 single persons sitting in the fore-seat [i.e., prominent ladies in the church]. She propounded one and another for me; but none would do.

October 3. Waited on Madam Winthrop again. I ushered in discourse about the names in the fore-seat; at last I prayed that Madam Winthrop might be the person for me. She instantly took it up in the way of denial, as if she had caught at an opportunity to say no. Said she could not leave her children. I prayed her consideration and asked when I should wait on her again. Gave her Mr. Willard's *Fountain.*

October 6. Madam seemed to harp on the same string. Must take care of her children; could not leave that house and neighborhood where she had dwelt so long. I told her she might do her children as much or more good by bestowing what she now laid out in housekeeping on them. Said her son would be of age the 7th of August. I said it might be inconvenient for her to dwell with her daughter-in-law, who must be mistress of the house. I gave her a piece of Mr. Belcher's cake and gingerbread wrapped up in a clean sheet of paper. My daughter Judith was gone from me, I said, and I was more lonesome.

October 12. At last I got my chair in place, had some converse, but very cold and indifferent to what 'twas before. Asked her to excuse my rudeness if I drew off her glove. Inquiring the reason, I told her 'twas great odds between handling a dead goat and a living lady. Got it off. I told her I had one petition to ask of her—that she would take off the negative she had laid on me. She readily answered she could not. She could not leave her house, children, neighbors, business. I told her she might do some good to help and comfort me. She thanked me for my book. When she insisted on the negative, I prayed there might be no more thunder and lightning, I should not sleep all night. I gave her Dr. Preston, *The Church's Marriage and the Church's Carriage,* which cost me 6 shillings at the sale. She sent Juno home with me with a good lantern.

October 19. Madam Winthrop took occasion to speak pretty earnestly

The Emergence of a Yankee, Puritan Style

about my keeping a coach. I said 'twould cost 100 pounds per annum; she said 'twould cost but 40.

October 20. Madam Winthrop took one of the candles and went into the best room, closed the shutters, sat down upon the couch. She told me the coach must be set on wheels, and not rusting. She spoke something of my needing a wig. I said, I am keeping you in the cold [of the unheated room], and asked if she would be at home tomorrow night. She could not say.

October 21. About 6 o'clock I go to Madam Winthrop's. Sarah told me her mistress was gone out, but did not tell me where. I read Dr. Sibb's *Bowels,* the first two sermons. Still nobody came. After a good while, she came in. I mentioned something of the lateness; she bantered me, and said I was later. She received me courteously. I asked when our [betrothal] proceedings should be made public. She said they were like to be no more public than they were already. Offered me no wine that I remember. I prayed her that Juno might light me home. She opened the shutter, and said 'twas pretty light abroad. Juno was weary and gone to bed. So I came home by starlight as well as I could.

October 24. I enquired whether she could find it in her heart to go and dwell with me at the South End. I think she said softly, Not yet.

I told her it did not lie in my lands to keep a coach. If I should, I should be in danger of being brought to the state of her neighbor (who was a little while before sent to prison for debt). Told her I would give a portion of my estate with myself, and I supposed she would do so. As to a periwig, my best and greatest Friend found me with hair before I was born, and had continued to do so ever since; I could not find it in my heart to put on another. She commended the book I gave her *The Church's Marriage,* quoting the author as saying 'twas inconvenient not following a fashion commonly used. She gave me a dram of Black-Cherry Brandy and a lump of sugar.

November 2. Gave her about 1/2 pound of sugar almonds, cost 3 shillings per pound. She seemed pleased with them, asked what they cost. Spoke of giving her 100 pounds per annum if I died before her. Asked her what sum she would give me, if she should die first. Said I would give her time to consider it. She said she heard that I had given everything to my children by deeds of gift. I told her 'twas a mistake, Point Judith was mine &c. That in England I owned property with an income of 20 pounds per annum; she thought 'twas 40. I think when I was reluctant to press this, she seemed to think 'twas best to speak of it; a long winter was coming on.

November 4. I asked Madam what fashion of necklace I should present her with. She said, None at all. I mentioned what I had offered to give her; asked her what she would give me. She said she could not change her condition, had said so from the beginning. She charged me with saying that she must put away Juno, if she came to me. I utterly denied it; it never came into my heart. Yet she insisted on it. About 10 I said I would not disturb the good order of her house and came away. November 7. Found Mad. Winthrop rocking little Katee in the cradle. I excused my coming so late. She set me an armed chair and cushion—and so the cradle was between her chair and mine. Gave her the remnant of my almonds. She did not eat of them as before, but laid them away. I said I came to inquire whether she had altered her mind since Friday, or remained of the same mind. She said, Thereabouts. I told her I loved her, and was so foolish as to think that she loved me. She said had a great respect for me. I told her I had made her an offer without advice. She had had so many to advise with that 'twas a hindrance. The fire dwindled to one short brand besides the block. At last it fell to pieces, and no recruit was made. I think I repeated again that I would go home and bewail my rashness in making more haste than good speed. I would endeavor to contain myself and not go on importuning her. As I came down the steps she bid me have a care. I did not ask her to draw off her glove as sometime I had done. Her dress was not so clean as sometime it had been. Jehovah jireh![24]

A touching self-revelation of a very human individual, who had the courage to record a story that made him look rather silly and to smile at himself in the process. And a testament to the acquisitive spirit.

So, while the journal of Sam Sewall is a document of Puritan orthodoxy, it also announces the coming of Yankee materialism. In Sewall and his friends there is clearly betrayed a blending of the religious and the secular. An autocratic and conventional view of the church-state mingles with a slight tendency toward social democracy and a strong upsurge of economic self-interest. It was only a subtle shift in emphasis. But a cleavage had been opened that Sam Sewall never willed. Taken together with the intellectual rebellion spearheaded by Roger Williams, that cleavage would spell disaster to the theocratic oligarchy.

Bartering for Slaves

National Maritime Museum

7

Blood on the Quarterdeck

Next to a pirate give me a slaver.[1]

A sordid but spectacular chapter in American colonial history was written at sea—on the slavers and pirate ships that plied their nefarious trades in the waters of the Atlantic. Two early-eighteenth-century documents recount these sagas of gore and thievery: a *Collection of Voyages,* telling of the barbaric triangular trade in African slaves, and a *General History* of the exploits of pirates off the Carolina coast.

The first slaves imported into the British American colonies were brought to Jamestown by a Dutch vessel in 1619. But the coming of this handful of Negroes marked no revolutionary change in the colonies' economy. It was not until the second half of the century—as great tobacco and rice plantations spread over the Southern tidelands—that the need developed for a supply of unskilled labor far greater than that furnished by white indentured servants. As this market opened up, British and American ships descended upon the Guinea coast to barter for human cargoes, which they transported to the West Indies (to be "seasoned" in the sugar fields before being resold to continental planters). Anyone inclined to be optimistic about the concept of Progress will take heart to read of the skulduggery which in that age went by the respectable name of the slave trade.

At the mouths of the rivers along the African coast, a corps of native middlemen set up shop. Shrewd merchant kings collected cargoes of slaves to barter for the white captains' goods. Their merchandise con-

sisted partly of criminals and of individuals who had bargained themselves away (or been bargained away by their families) in periods of
70 famine. But for the most part these human goods were acquired through kidnapping and warfare. Fleets of war canoes moved up the rivers on slave-hunting expeditions, and the various tribes of those upper regions also preyed on one another, selling their captives either to white traders or to the coastal middlemen. Sometimes the native kings along the coast dealt directly with the ship captains, and sometimes they sold their merchandise to white factors (resident agents) who held the victims in corrals near the harbors until their company ships arrived.[2]

The following accounts of two English voyages made in the late 1690s were written by the captain of one ship and an owner of the other. The horrors of the trade are therefore not made explicit, but they are evident to the twentieth-century reader.

When the *Albion Frigate* entered the mouth of the New Calabar River in Guinea around mid-June, 1699, she carried as supercargo one of the owners (Mr. James Barbot), who kept a detailed record of the voyage. The ship navigated the tricky channel and dropped anchor off a small village, where it fired a salute to the ruling King of Bandy. Going ashore to initiate trading, the captain and owner found that the king had raised his prices and was questioning the quality of their "basons, tankards, yellow beads," and other merchandise.[3] After a while the barterwise king and his officials were invited aboard the ship.

He had on an old-fashioned scarlet coat, laced with gold and silver, very rusty, with a fine hat on his head, but was bare-footed. His brother, Pepprell, came with him and was a sharp blade and a mighty talking black, always making sly objections against something or other. It were to be wished that such a one as he were out of the way, to facilitate trade.

We filled them with drams of brandy and bowls of punch, till night, at such a rate that they had such loud clamorous discourses among themselves, as were hardly to be endured. With much patience, however, all our matters were at last adjusted.

All the regulations having been agreed upon, supper was served, and it was comical, as well as shocking, to observe the behavior of the blacks, both King and subjects talking together and emptying the dishes as soon as set down; everyone filling his pockets with meat as well as his belly.

Two days afterwards the King sent aboard thirty slaves, men and women, out of which we picked nineteen and returned him the rest, and so from day to day, either by means of our armed sloop making voyages to New Calabar town and to Dony, or by our contract with the King, by degrees we had aboard 648 slaves of all sexes and ages all very fresh and sound, very few exceeding forty years of age.[4]

Captain Phillips, of the British ship *Hannibal,* which also arrived at the Gold Coast in the last decade of the seventeenth century, recorded how he, too, filled the hold of his ship. The black traders (*cappasheirs*) had sought to outfox him, he wrote:

> The cappasheirs each brought out his slaves according to his degree and quality, the greatest first &c., and our surgeon examined them well in all kinds, to see that they were sound of wind and limb, making them jump, stretch out their arms swiftly, looking in their mouths to judge their age; for the cappasheirs are so cunning, that they shave them all close before we see them, so that let them be never so old we can see no grey hairs in their heads or beards; and then having sleeked them with palm oil, 'tis no easy matter to know an old one from a middle-aged one, but by the teeth's decay. But our greatest care of all is to buy none that are pox'd, lest they should infect the rest aboard. And that distemper which they call the yaws is very common here, and discovers itself by almost the same symptoms as the clap does with us; therefore our surgeon is forc'd to examine the privities of both men and women with the nicest scrutiny. When we had selected from the rest such as we liked, we mark'd the slaves we had bought in the breast, or shoulder, with a hot iron, having the letter of the ship's name on it, the place being before anointed with a little palm oil, which caused but little pain, the mark being usually well in four or five days, appearing very plain and white after.[5]

Captain Phillips also complained about the unhealthy swamps, the "little malicious musketoes," and the long rainy season through which the natives could not be "prevail'd upon to stir out of their huts," the rain falling in hot "fountains."[6] But he praised the skill with which the natives thrust their great canoes through the pounding surf to the long-boat and the cooperativeness of the Negro "captain," who for a generous fee, guaranteed delivery of the slaves on board ship.

When our slaves were come to the sea-side, our canoos were ready to carry them off to the longboat, if the sea permitted, and he convey'd them aboard ship, where the men were all put in irons, two and two shackl'd together, to prevent their mutiny, or swimming ashore.

The negroes are so wilful and loth to leave their own country, that they have often leap'd out of the canoos, boat and ship, into the sea, and kept under water till they were drowned, to avoid being taken up and saved by our boats, which pursued them; they having a more dreadful apprehension of Barbadoes then we can have of hell, tho' in reality they live much better there than in their own country; but home is home, &c. We have likewise seen divers of them eaten by the sharks, of which a prodigious number kept about the ships in this place, and I have been told will follow her hence to Barbadoes, for the dead negroes that are thrown overboard in the passage. I am certain in our voyage there we did not want the sight of some every day, but that they were the same I can't affirm. We had about twelve negroes did wilfully drown themselves, and others starv'd themselves to death; for 'tis their belief that when they die they return home to their own country and friends again.[7]

The owner of the *Albion Frigate* recorded with pride how well the slaves were treated on their ships.

[We] lodged the two sexes apart, by means of a strong partition at the main-mast. We built a sort of half deck along the sides so the slaves lay in two rows, one above the other, and as close together as they could be crowded.

We were very nice in keeping the places where the slaves lay clean and neat, appointing some of the ship's crew to do that office constantly and several of the slaves themselves to be assistants to them, and thrice a week we perfumed betwixt decks with a quantity of good vinegar in pails, and red-hot iron bullets in them, to expel the bad air, after the place had been well washed and scrubbed.

[The slaves] took their meals twice a day, at ten in the morning and five at night, which [latter meal] being ended we made the men go down again between decks. As for the women, they were almost entirely at their own discretion to remain upon deck as long as they pleased. The first meal was of our large beans boiled, with a certain quantity of Muscovy lard. The other meal was of pease or of Indian wheat.

As for the sick and wounded, our surgeons, in their daily visits betwixt decks, finding any indisposed, caused them to be carried to the *lazaretto* under the fore-castle, a room reserved for a sort of hospital, where proper remedies could be applied. This could not leisurely be done between decks because of the great heat that is there continually, which is sometimes so excessive that the surgeons would faint away and the candles would not burn, and besides, in such a crowd of brutish people there are many so greedy that they will snatch from the sick the fresh meat or liquor that is given them.

One day, about one in the afternoon, after dinner, according to custom we caused them, one by one, to go down between decks, to have each his pint of water. Most of them were yet above the deck and many of them were provided with knives which we had indiscreetly given them two or three days before. It afterwards appeared that others had pieces of iron which they had torn off the forecastle door, having premeditated this revolt. They had also broken off the shackles from the legs of several of their companions, which also served them [as weapons]. Thus armed they suddenly fell upon our men and stabbed one of the stoutest, who received fourteen or fifteen wounds from their knives so that he expired shortly. Next they assaulted our boatswain and cut one of his legs so round the bone that he could not move, the nerves being cut through.

Others cut the cook's throat to the pipe and yet others wounded three of the sailors. From the quarterdeck [we] fired on the slaves, of whom we killed some and wounded many, which so terrified the rest that they gave way and dispersed themselves. Many of the most mutinous leaped overboard and drowned themselves with much resolution, shewing no manner of concern for life.[8]

Aside from the losses involved in this mutiny, the *Albion Frigate* made the voyage with fewer than the usual casualties. The *Hannibal*, on the other hand, was swept by a fatal epidemic, which cut severely into the profits and which Captain Phillips regarded as a gross injustice to himself and to the company that had commissioned him.

We often at sea, in the evenings, would let the slaves come up into the sun to air themselves, and make them jump and dance for an hour or two to our bag-pipes, harp, and fiddle, by which exercise to preserve them in health; but notwithstanding all our endeavour, 'twas my hard fortune to have great sickness and mortality among them.

We spent in our passage from St. Thomas to Barbadoes two months eleven days, in which time there happened such sickness and mortality among my poor men and negroes, that of the first we buried 14, and of the last 320, which was a great detriment to our voyage, the Royal African Company losing ten pounds by every slave that died, and the owners of the ship ten pounds ten shillings. The distemper which my men as well as the blacks mostly died of, was the white flux, which was so violent and inveterate, that no medicine would in the least check it; so that when any of our men were seized with it, we esteemed him a dead man.

The negroes are so [vulnerable] to the small-pox, that few ships that carry them escape without it, and sometimes it makes vast havock and destruction among them; but tho' we had 100 at a time sick of it, and that it went thro' the ship, yet we lost not above a dozen by it. All the assistance we gave the diseased was only as much water as they desir'd to drink, and some palm-oil to anoint their sores.

But what the small-pox spar'd, the flux swept off, to our great regret, after all our pains and care to give them their messes in due order and season, keeping their lodgings as clean and sweet as possible, and enduring so much misery and stench so long among a parcel of creatures nastier than swine; and after all our expectations to be defeated by their mortality.

Blood on the Quarterdeck

I deliver'd alive at Barbadoes to the company's factors 372, which being sold, came out at about nineteen pounds per head.

Having got aboard near 700 hogsheads of sugar some cotton and ginger we got all clear to sail to England.[9]

While Captain Phillips and the owner of the *Albion Frigate* were recording their adventures aboard the slavers, other sailing vessels were making history off the coast of America, and their exploits would soon be entered in Captain Charles Johnson's *General History of the Robberies and Murders of the Most Notorious Pirates.*[10] Captain Johnson's tales seemed so incredible that for many years their scholarship was suspect, but modern researchers have tended to substantiate his storybook findings.

During the early eighteenth century the seaboard of North Carolina swarmed with pirates, who used coves and inlets as bases from which to prey on coastal shipping. Most notorious of these outlaws was Edward Thatch, known throughout the colonies as Blackbeard—a rampaging, posturing barbarian, who devoted much energy to perpetuating his image as a devil incarnate.

His massive black beard (which came up to his eyes) he plaited into numerous separate tails, and each of these he tied with a ribbon. When preparing for action, he wore a sling over his shoulders with three brace of pistols hanging in holsters. He made matches of large, loosely twisted cord dipped in saltpeter and lime, which he stuck under his hat and ignited as he went crashing into battle. Burning along on either side of his black, beribboned bush of a face, they set his eyes to glowing, fierce and wild, and made him, all-in-all, such a figure that the imagination could not conjure up a Fury from Hell more frightful.

On one occasion, drinking in his cabin with his pilot and another crony, he drew a pair of small pistols without any provocation, blew out the candle, and, crossing his arms under the table, fired the pistols at random. The pilot was shot through the knee and lamed for life. Being asked the meaning of this behavior, he shouted theatrically: "Damn you, if I did not now and then kill one of you, you would forget who I am."

Once, when he and his men had seized an exceptionally valuable cargo, not wishing to share the booty with all of his men, he marooned the ones he liked least on a small sandy island where there was neither bird, beast, nor herb for their subsistence, and where they would surely have perished had not another pirate ship happened along two days later.

His fourteenth wife (or thereabouts) was a girl of sixteen to whom he was wed by the Governor of North Carolina, while about a dozen of his other spouses were still living. This young girl he habitually pandered to his brutal crew, five or six in a night.[11]

This tyrant was received in the homes of officials and plantation owners in North Carolina, and the fruits of his piracy found a ready market along the entire coast. After the conclusion of Queen Anne's War, many privateers who formerly had their sovereign's blessing in stalking the enemies of England now turned to outright piracy, striking at ships of all nations, including those of British registry. This greed forced the Crown to drive them from the Indies and to take stringent measures against them in South Carolina. By 1718 many of the outlaws transferred their bases to the hidden coves of North Carolina. There the government was weak and acquiescent, and the freebooters came and went, secure from official molestation.

Nor were they harassed by the colonists in general as they ranged up and down the seaboard, bartering their stolen goods. For there were substantial economic gains to be had from this illicit trade, which brought the buyer a dazzling array of goods from all parts of the world —goods forbidden him by the Navigation Acts and offered now at a fraction of their usual cost. Especially welcome were the pirate shipments of Spanish gold, which bolstered an economy suffering an unfavorable trade balance that constantly drew colonial currency to England.

So the pirates were allowed to go about their business, until finally they went too far. Events in both the Carolinas were brought to a head in 1718 by the mounting excesses of Blackbeard. He had been, on balance, a dashing, spectacular fellow, bringing into North Carolina considerable treasure and lavishly repaying the hospitality of her planters and traders with rum and delicacies. But when his supplies ran low between ventures, his largess slowed. His personal orgies (usually in the village of Bath, near his base in the Ocracoke Inlet) became increasingly offensive, and he began indiscreetly to seize more and more ships belonging to local traders. The number and animosity of his enemies grew.

Blackbeard's descent from power began at Charleston, South Carolina. Commanding over 400 men and a fleet of 3 sloops and a 40-gun ship, he defied the government of that colony.

He commenced operations by capturing the pilot boat which was stationed on the bar outside Charleston, and within the next few days took no less than eight vessels, as they emerged from the harbor. Among these captures was a ship bound for London, carrying a member of the Council of the province, Mr. Samuel Wragg. The pirates determined to make the best of their good fortune. The fleet was in need of certain medicines, and Thatch had his surgeon prepare a list of the desired articles and proceeded to demand them of the Governor. Arming a boat, he sent three of his men and one of the prisoners, a Mr. Marks, to the city to lay the situation before the Governor. They were to inform his Excellency that, if the necessary supplies were not immediately forthcoming and if the men did not return unharmed, the heads of Mr. Wragg and the other gentlemen would be separated from their owners and delivered to him.

Marks was given two days in which to accomplish his mission, and the prisoners, who had been told of the demands, waited in intense anxiety. Two days passed, and the envoys did not return. Thatch notified Wragg that his entire party should prepare for death. He was persuaded, however, to stay his bloody order for one day, and before that time had expired, a message arrived from Marks saying that their boat had been overturned by a squall and that they had now reached Charleston and were proceeding with their mission. Thatch gave the prisoners the freedom of the vessel until the third day, when, losing patience again, he swore that he would put Wragg and his fellows to an instant death. To save themselves, the prisoners then made a desperate and not too heroic offer. If the pirate messengers were actually being detained by the town's authorities, the prisoners, to earn a reprieve, would pilot the pirate fleet into the harbor and help Thatch batter down the defenseless town. Blackbeard granted a further stay.

Meantime, Charleston was in a state of desperation. Marks had laid the pirate demands before the Governor, who convened his Council and laid the situation before it. The members conceded that they must capitulate to the insolent demands. The colony was in no condition to repel a sea invasion at this time. The harbor was wholly unprotected, with not an armed vessel in hundreds of miles. Recent Indian wars had bankrupted the treasury, so it was impossible to arm any of the merchant vessels in the harbor.

The pirate emissaries were parading up and down the principal streets, and their impudent behavior aroused the indignation of the people. If the infuriated populace attacked the pirates, as it was clear they might at any moment, it would be the death warrant of Thatch's prisoners and would in all probability bring the guns of the pirates to bear on the city.

The medicines were hurriedly prepared, and in a few hours Marks and his guard were on their way back to the vessels. The pirate demands were now satisfied, and their holds full of spoils. Thatch set the prisoners ashore half-naked at some little distance from Charleston and sailed away to North Carolina.

[On returning to Ocracoke Inlet, he secured a pardon under a general amnesty offered to pirates, and went through the motions of disbanding

Chapters from the American Experience

his company in keeping with the terms of the amnesty.] He retained for himself and a few chosen companions one small sloop, and this he fitted out for an alleged trading expedition. In a few weeks, however, he returned to Bath with a large French vessel loaded with sugar and other costly merchandise, and, going brazenly up to Governor Eden, he made the incredible assertion that he had found this valuable ship drifting abandoned at sea. Whereupon, Tobias Knight, the Collector of the Port and Vice-Admiralty Judge, cooperatively condemned the French vessel as a legitimate prize and permitted Thatch to bring the cargo of the stolen ship ashore. The pirate then discharged the goods and, taking the ship along the coast, beached and burned her.

Thatch had for some time been living in terms of great intimacy with many of the principal inhabitants of the area and was a frequent visitor at Knight's residence. Being in favor with the officials, he enjoyed a perfect immunity from punishment for his various outrages. Complaints to the proper authorities were of no avail. But the license he was granted soon made him so arrogant that he aroused the bitter enmity of many of the inhabitants who might otherwise have continued to tolerate his residence there.

Seeing his intimacy with the North Carolina officials, Thatch's enemies realized they would have to look elsewhere than to their own government for help. Since Governor Spotswood of Virginia had helped the colony before, they applied to him for relief. The case of the French prize had become notorious in the province. Whatever Eden and Knight might pretend to think of it, everybody knew that it was a clear case of piracy and that, instead of trying to apprehend the pirates, the authorities had connived at their crimes and had, it was generally believed, been well paid for their connivance.

Information as to the situation was sent to Governor Spotswood, and the Virginia Assembly offered a reward of 100 pounds, for the arrest of Thatch. Not satisfied with this, however, Spotswood, feeling that his own coasts were in danger, determined to take steps toward the immediate capture of Thatch and his crew.[12]

The Governor ordered two small sloops built. Manned from a pair of British men-of-war and under the command of Lieutenant Robert Maynard, the little force set out in the greatest secrecy.

When the sloops reached the mouth of the Ocracoke Inlet, they stopped all entering vessels to keep news of their approach from reaching Blackbeard. The pirate, however, had already been informed of the plan by Mr. Knight, who wrote him a letter of warning. But Blackbeard had received several such reports in the past, all of which had proven unfounded, and

Blood on the Quarterdeck

so he gave little credence to this one. Nor was he convinced of danger until he saw the sloops at the mouth of the inlet. He thereupon put his vessel in a position for defense, but he had at most only twenty-five men on board. Having made such preparations as he could for battle, he sat down and spent the night in drinking.

Lieutenant Maynard came to anchor, for the place was shoal and the channel intricate so that it was impossible to get in that night. In the morning he weighed anchor and sent his boat ahead of the sloops to take soundings. When they came within gunshot, the pirate fired his cannon. Whereupon Maynard hoisted the King's colors and made directly toward him as fast as sails and oars could take him. Blackbeard cut his cable and tried to make a running fight, keeping up a continual fire with his guns. Not having any guns mounted, Maynard replied with small arms, while some of his men labored at their oars. Shortly, Thatch's sloop ran aground, and, since Mr. Maynard's vessel drew more water than that of the pirate, he ordered all his ballast to be thrown overboard and the watercasks to be staved in. Then he ran toward his antagonist. Upon which Blackbeard hailed him with: "Damn you for villains, who are you?" The lieutenant answered: "You can see by our colors we are no pirates." Invited to send a delegation to the pirate ship, the Englishman replied, "I cannot spare my boat, but I will come aboard of you as soon as I can—with my sloop."

After these preliminaries, Blackbeard, having in the meantime gotten his ship afloat, fired broadside at the two Virginia ships, killing and wounding many, and disabling one of the two sloops. Finding that his own sloop was making directly for Thatch, the lieutenant ordered all his men down for fear of another broadside. Mr. Maynard and the helmsman alone kept on deck. The men in the hold were ordered to get their pistols and swords ready for close-in fighting and to be prepared to come up the moment he commanded.

As the two ships came together, Blackbeard's men tossed into the attacking ship several hand-made grenades. These savage bottles, filled with powder and small shot, slugs, and pieces of lead or iron and lit by quick fuses, usually did great damage. But they were not effective in this case, since the men were in the hold. Seeing so few on board, Blackbeard called out, "They are all knocked on the head but three or four. Cut them to pieces!"

Under cover of the smoke from one of his bottle grenades, Blackbeard and fourteen of his men boarded Maynard's sloop, and simultaneously the English leader signalled his men. When they emerged in an instant and attacked the pirates, a melee ensued. Blackbeard and the lieutenant singled each other out, each firing his first pistol shot at the other. The pirate was wounded. Then they engaged one another with swords until the lieutenant's broke. He stepped back to cock a pistol, and Blackbeard was about to bring his cutlass down when one of Maynard's men slashed a terrible wound in Blackbeard's throat.

They were closely and heatedly engaged—the lieutenant and his twelve men against Blackbeard and his fourteen. The sea was tinctured with blood around the vessel. The shot that Blackbeard received from Lieutenant Maynard's pistol and the neck slash were not his only wounds. It is said that he received twenty-five in all, five of them from gunshot. At length, as he was cocking another pistol, he fell down dead. By this time eight more of the fourteen pirates who had boarded had been dropped, and the rest, badly wounded, called out for quarter. It was granted—but it only prolonged their lives for a few days. Maynard's other sloop now came up and attacked the men that remained in Blackbeard's sloop with equal bravery, until they too cried for quarter.

Before leaving his ship, Blackbeard had posted a faithful Negro follower in the powder room with the command to blow up the ship if the English were victorious and came aboard. Fortunately two prisoners of Blackbeard managed to dissuade the pirate from carrying out his captain's orders. Letters and papers were found in the pirate sloop, including correspondence between Blackbeard and Governor Eden.

When the lieutenant came ashore at Bath, he seized sixty hogsheads of sugar in the Governor's storehouse and twenty from honest Mr. Knight, which, it seems, was their dividend of the plunder taken in the French ship.

After the wounded men had been cared for, the lieutenant sailed back to the James River in Virginia. On board were fifteen prisoners, in the hold lay the captured booty, and dangling from the front of the bowsprit hung the great shaggy head of Blackbeard.[13]

COLONIAL DAYS IN NEW YORK.
CORNER LIBERTY AND WILLIAM STREETS.

Colonial Days in New York

8

Travelers to the Middle Colonies

What is the American?

Hector St. John de Crevecoeur, a Frenchman who lived in New York during the closing years of the colonial period, paid this sweeping tribute to the "new man" he saw emerging in America.

What is the American, this new man? He is either a European, or the descendant of one, hence that strange mixture of blood, which you will find in no other country. I could point out to you a family whose grandfather was an Englishman, whose wife was Dutch, whose son married a French woman, and whose present four sons have now four wives of different nations. *He* is an American, who leaving behind him all his ancient prejudices and manners, receives new ones from the new mode of life he has embraced, the new government he obeys, and the new rank he holds. In this broad land individuals of all nations are melted into a new race of men, whose labours will one day cause great changes in the world.[1]

America had been a melting pot (or a "salad bowl") for generations before Crevecoeur wrote his classic words of praise.[2] From the days of earliest settlement she had attracted men of different nationalities and conflicting persuasions. No section reflected this polyglot character as clearly as the Middle Colonies. During the first half of the eighteenth century, three diarists—a New England schoolmistress, a Maryland physician, and a young Swedish botanist—visited this section and recorded their impressions of it.

Sarah Kemble Knight was a proper Bostonian. In 1704 she set out on horseback on a long and daring journey to New York. She followed the old Pequot Path, traveling with the mail carriers, or "posts," for protection. Her journal describes the difficulties of such early travel (especially at a time when England and France were at war and massacre was in the air). It also reveals her timorous humor and her social and racial prejudices.

About two in the afternoon, arrived at the Post's second stage, where the western Post met him and exchanged letters. Here, having called for something to eat, the woman brought in a twisted thing like a cable, but something whiter; and laying it on the board, tugged for life to bring it into a capacity to spread. She served what I suppose was the remains of dinner in a dish of pork and cabbage. The sauce was of a deep purple, which I thought was boiled in her dye kettle; the bread was Indian, and everything on the table service equivalent to these. I, being hungry, got a little down, but what cabbage I swallowed served me for a cud the whole day after.

Went on with my third guide, who rode very hard. We came to a river which they generally ride through, but I dared not. So the Post got a lad and canoe to carry me to t'other side, and 'twas so small and shallow that I sat with my hands fast to each side, my eyes steady, not daring so much as to lodge my tongue a hair's breadth more on one side of my mouth than t'other, till we came ashore.

The only glimmering we now had was from the spangled skies. Each lifeless trunk, with its shattered limbs, appeared an armed enemy; and every little stump like a ravenous devourer. Nor could I so much as discern my guide, which added to my terror.[3]

After several days of such travel she was in Connecticut, where she observed that her hosts were "too indulgent to their slaves, suffering great familiarity from them, permitting them to sit at table and eat with them, so that into the dish goes the black hoof as freely as the white hand."[4]

Arrived at last in New York, Mrs. Knight described the town as a "pleasant, well compacted place, situated on a commodious river."[5]

The buildings, brick generally, very stately and high, are still not altogether like ours in Boston. The bricks in some of the houses are of divers colors and laid in checkers, being glazed very agreeably. The inside of them are neat to admiration; the woodwork, the supporting beams and joists are planed and kept very white scoured.

They are generally of the Church of England, and have a New England gentleman for their minister and a very fine church. There are also a Dutch and divers "conventicles" as they call them, i.e., Baptist, Quakers, etc. They are not strict in keeping the Sabbath as in Boston. They are sociable to one another and courteous and civil to strangers and eat well. The English go very fashionable in their dress. But the Dutch, especially the middling sort, differ from our women, wearing loose dresses and French muches (which are like a cap and a head band in one, leaving their ears bare). Their fingers are hooped with rings and old and young wear ear pendants.[6]

The appearance and manners of the Dutch attracted the comment of many visitors to New York. The aristocratic Dr. A. Hamilton, coming from Maryland a few decades later, also observed the Dutch women's "comical" dress; he expressed resentment at their "staring upon one like witches" and concluded that they were the "hardest favored" women he had ever seen.[7] However, in Albany, he found the Dutch generally a "civil and hospitable people," though "rustic and unpolished." They lived "very frugally and plain," commented the Southerner with a touch of hauteur. "The chief merit among them seems to be riches, which they spare no pains or trouble to acquire." That he was in the heart of the patroon country is clear from his remark that the inhabitants "talked of 30, 40, 50, and 100 thousand pounds as of nothing, but I soon found that their riches consisted more in large tracts of land than in cash."[8]

The feel of the frontier is in his description of the fortifications which the outpost village maintained:

The city of Albany . . . consists of three pretty compact streets, two of which run parallel to the river . . . and the third cuts the other two at right angles, running up towards the fort, which is a square stone building about 200 foot square with a bastion at each corner, each bastion mounting eight or ten great guns, most of them 32 pounders. . . . The greatest length of the streets is half a mile. In the fort is kept a garrison of 300 men under the King's pay. . . . This city is enclosed by a rampart or wall of wooden palisadoes about 10 foot high and a foot thick, being the trunks of pine trees rammed into the ground, pinned close together, and ending each in a point at top. Here they call them stockades. At each 200 foot distance round this wall is a block house, and from the north gate of the city runs

Travelers to the Middle Colonies

a thick stone wall down into the river. . . . [The] city militia keep guard every night, and the word "All's well" walks constantly round all night long from sentry to sentry and round the fort.[9]

The town of New York was a little more to his taste. The English ladies were "handsome," appeared in public more than they did in Philadelphia, and dressed much more gaily. "When the ladies walk the streets in the day time," he wrote, "they commonly use umbrellas, prettily adorned with feathers and painted."[10] He was especially interested in the club life of the city, into which he was readily accepted and toward which he took a rather supercilious view.

[The surgeon] . . . carried me to the tavern which is kept by one Todd, an old Scottsman, to sup with the Hungarian Club of which he is a member and which meets there every night. The company . . . saluted me very civily, and I . . . returned their compliments. . . . We went to supper, and our landlord Todd entertained us as he stood waiting with quaint saws and jack pudding speeches. . . .

After supper they set in for drinking. . . . They filled up bumpers at each round, and I would drink only three. . . . Two or three topers in the company seemed to be of opinion that a man could not have a more sociable quality or endowment than to be able to pour down seas of liquor and remain unconquered while others sank under the table. . . . I left the company at 10 at night pretty well flushed with my three bumpers and, ruminating on my folly, went to my lodging at Mrs. Hogg's in Broadstreet. . . .

To drink stoutly with the Hungarian Club, who are all bumper men, is the readiest way for a stranger to recommend himself, and a set among them are very fond of making a stranger drunk. To talk bawdy and to have a knack at punning passes among some there for good sterling wit. Governor Clinton himself is a jolly toper and gives good example and, for that one quality, is esteemed among these dons.[11]

Most informative of the three diaries is that of Peter Kalm, a young scientist from Sweden. His journal is a rambling account of conditions, mineral, plant, and animal, in colonial Pennsylvania and New York. There are carefully compiled classifications of flowers, trees, and wild life and lengthy discourses on blackberry wine, the hypnotic power of snakes over birds, and Iroquois remedies for toothache.[12] And, sandwiched among these, are illuminating commentaries on such aspects of human life as New York trade, the "privileges" of Jewish people, Pennsylvania city life and agriculture, and the conditions of (and prejudices against) the slave population of the Middle Colonies.

New York probably carries on a more extensive commerce than any town in the English North American provinces. They export grains, timber, skins, and the produce of the West Indies to London. In return every article of English growth or manufacture is imported from England, together with all sorts of foreign goods. England profits immensely by its trade with the American colonies, which import so many articles from her that all their specie must go to England to pay their accounts there, and still are insufficient.[13]

The freedom of the country enables many people of different language and religion to live peacefully together. Besides the different sects of Christians, many Jews have settled in New York. They possess great privileges, have a synagogue, own their own dwelling houses, own large country seats, and are allowed to keep shops in town. During my residence in New York, I was frequently in company with Jews and in their synagogue, where I sat in a special seat set apart for strangers or Christians.[14]

We arrived in Philadelphia about ten o'clock the morning of September 15, 1748. This town, next to Boston the largest in North America, was built around 1682 by the well-known Quaker William Penn. Charles II granted this whole province to him after Sweden gave up its claims to it. The area which is now Philadelphia belonged then to three Swedish brothers who had settled it. They resisted leaving the place, which was very advantageously situated. At last they were persuaded to it by Penn, who gave them twice as much land a few miles away.[15]

The town's streets are regular, fine, and generally 50 feet wide. There are many different churches, for God is served in various ways in this country. The Quaker meeting houses have in them, according to the customs of this people, neither altars, nor pulpits, nor any other ornaments usual in churches; but only seats and some sconces. They meet thrice every Sunday and at certain times each week.[16]

I took up my lodging with a grocer who was a Quaker, and I met with very good honest people in this house, such as most folk of this persuasion appeared to be. My companion and I had a room, candles, beds, attendance, and three meals a day for twenty shillings per week.[17]

Mr. Benjamin Franklin, to whom Pennsylvania is indebted for its welfare, and the learned world for many new discoveries in electricity, was the first who took notice of me and introduced me to many of his friends. He showed me kindness on many occasions.[18]

The Delaware is exceedingly convenient for trade, for the greatest ships

Travelers to the Middle Colonies

can sail right up to Philadelphia and anchor beside the bridge. On the south side of the town near the river, a fort was erected to prevent French and Spanish privateers from landing. But this was done after very strong debate. For the Quakers opposed all fortifications, as contrary to the tenets of their religion, which allow not Christians to make war, either offensive or defensive, but direct them to place their trust in the Almighty alone. Several papers were distributed for and against the project. But the enemy's privateers having taken several vessels belonging to the town in the river, many of the Quakers, if not all of them, found it reasonable to support the building of the fortification, at least by supplying money.[19]

The Quakers from almost all parts of North America have their great assembly here once a year. The town has also two great fairs annually, one in May and the other in November, to which the country people bring victuals and other produce, which is a great advantage to the town.[20]

I have not been able to find the exact number of inhabitants of Philadelphia. In the year 1746 they were reckoned above 10 thousand, and have since increased incredibly. The Quakers, who are the most numerous in this town, never baptize their children, so there are no such records among them.[21]

Everyone is of the opinion that the American savages were good-natured if not attacked. Nobody is so strict in keeping his word as a savage. If any one of their allies comes to visit them, they show him more kindness than he could have expected from his own countrymen. When they send their ambassadors to the English colonies, in order to settle things of consequence with the governor, they sit down on the ground, as soon as they come to his presence, and hear his demands with great attention. His demands are sometimes many, yet they have only a stick in their hand, on which they make marks with a knife. When they return the next day to give their answers, they respond to all the governor's articles in the same order in which he delivered them, without leaving one out or changing the order, as accurately as if they had had a full written account.[22]

Again and again as we traveled through the forests of Pennsylvania we saw little fields which had been cleared in the woods. These farms were commonly very pretty, and a walk of trees frequently led from them to the road. Every countryman, even a common peasant, has an orchard with many fruits and a house of brick or stone. The valleys were frequently graced with little crystal-clear streams.[23]

Europeans coming to America found a rich, fine soil lying loose between the trees. They had only to cut the wood and clear the dead leaves away. This easy method of getting a rich crop has spoiled the settlers and induced them to adopt the same method of agriculture as the Indians, that is, to sow uncultivated ground as long as it will produce a crop without manuring and to turn it to pasture as soon as it can bear no more and take on a new spot, covered since time immemorial with woods.[24]

The servants used in the English-American colonies are either free persons or slaves, and the former are of two different sorts. The free servants are either those who work by the year or those who, coming from Europe without money enough for their passage, agree to be sold for a few years on their arrival.

The Negroes make up the third kind of servants, the slaves, who belong to their purchasers as long as they live. However, it is not permitted a master to kill his Negro for a fault, but he must leave it to the magistrates to proceed according to the laws. A man who kills his Negro is, legally, punishable by death, but there is no instance here of a white man's ever being executed for this crime. A few years ago it happened that a master killed his slave. His friends and even the magistrates secretly advised him to make his escape. This leniency was employed toward him that the Negroes might not have the satisfaction of seeing a master executed for killing his slave, for this would lead them to all sorts of dangerous designs against their masters.

In regard to the marriage of slaves, they proceed as follows: if you have both male and female slaves, they must intermarry, and then the children are all your slaves. If you possess a male only and he has an inclination to marry a female belonging to a different master, you do not hinder your Negro in so delicate a point, but it is of no advantage to you, for the children belong to the master of the female. It is therefore advantageous to have Negro women.

Many people cannot conquer the idea that it is contrary to the laws of Christianity to keep slaves. Not only the Quakers but also several Christians of other denominations sometimes set their Negroes at liberty. When a gentleman has a faithful Negro who has done him great services, he sometimes declares him independent at his own death. This is, however, very expensive; for the masters are obliged to make a provision for the Negro thus set at liberty, to afford him subsistence when he is grown old, that he may not be driven by necessity to wicked actions or become a charge to anybody. But the children which the free Negro has begot during his servitude are all slaves, though their father be free.

To prevent any disagreeable mixtures of the white people and Negroes, and to hinder the latter from forming too great opinions of themselves, to the disadvantage of their masters, I am told there was a law passed prohibiting the whites of both sexes to marry Negroes, under pain of death, with the clergyman marrying them being deprived of rights.

It is greatly to be pitied that the masters of these Negroes in most of the English colonies take little care of their spiritual welfare, letting them live on in pagan darkness. There are even some who would, by any means, hinder their Negroes from being instructed in the doctrines of Christianity. To this they are led partly by the conceit of its being shameful to have a spiritual brother or sister among so despicable a people; partly by thinking that they would not be able to keep their Negroes so meanly afterwards; and partly through fear of the Negroes' growing too proud on seeing themselves upon a level with their masters in religious matters.[25]

Finally, Kalm cast a prophetic shadow of Revolution across his pages.

Each English colony in North America is independent of the other, each has its own laws and coinage and may be looked upon in several lights as a state by itself. Hence it happens that in time of war things go on very slowly and irregularly here. Not only is the opinion of one province sometimes directly opposite to that of another [as in the case of the Dutch at Albany and the English, who hate each other], but frequently the views of the governor and those of the assembly of the same province are quite different. It is easy to see, therefore, that while the people are quarreling about the best and cheapest manner of carrying on the war, an enemy has it in his power to take one place after another.

The English colonies in this part of the world have increased so much in their numbers and their riches, that they almost vie with Old England. Now, in order to keep up the authority and trade of their mother country and to answer several other purposes, they are forbidden to establish new manufactures which would turn to the disadvantage of British commerce. They are not allowed to dig for any gold or silver, unless they send it to England immediately. These and other restrictions cause the inhabitants of the English colonies to grow less tender for their mother country, and this coldness is kept up by the foreigners, Germans, Dutch, and French, who have no particular attachment to Old England.

As the whole country which lies along this seashore is unguarded, and on the land side is harassed by the French in times of war, these dangerous neighbors are sufficient to prevent the connection of the colonies with their mother country from being quite broken off. But I have been told by Englishmen, and not only by such as were born in America but

Chapters from the American Experience

even those who came from Europe, that the English colonies in North America, in the space of thirty to fifty years, would be able to form a state by themselves, entirely independent of Old England.[26]

It was a ten-league canvas these three diarists were splashing on. Before the century was out, the men and women of the colonies would stand back and see that, out of all these origins and faiths, and despite the prejudices and the enduring differences, something unique had been created. The opportunities of the New World, the shared sense of danger from the enemy to the North, the common anger at the stifling repressions of the mother country would frame that canvas and hang it in the sky for all to see—the composite portrait of the American.

Home of Washington

Engraving by Thomas Oldham. Courtesy Library of Congress.

9

The Tidewater
Gentleman

A good estate on healthy soil
Not got by vice, nor yet by toil.

George Washington's great grandfather came to Virginia in 1650, which, as it turned out, was just the right time. This son of an Anglican minister had no great fortune to begin with, but he worked and acquired land and served in various public offices; and his son and grandson did the same. When Washington's father died, he left an estate of over 10,000 acres and about fifty slaves.

In all this the Washingtons were typical of the tidewater gentry who emerged during the decades around the middle of the seventeenth century. These were not the sons of the early Jamestown gentlemen, who played dice instead of planting crops and who fared badly under the harsh imperatives of the New World. They were sons of humbler Englishmen—indentured servants, laborers, and especially members of the British middle class.[1] They found Virginia a relatively open society where land was cheap, opportunities were abundant, and no property qualifications barred them from a voice in the making of the law. Men with only modest capital or none at all amassed fortunes, founded new dynasties, and assumed the responsibilities of government.

By the turn of the century the picture had changed. The best lands had been taken up, indentured servants were being replaced by black slaves, the less wealthy immigrants were moving across Virginia to more promising frontiers, and the vote had been restricted to men who owned either 25 acres with a house and plantation or 100 acres of uncultivated land. "The effect was unmistakable," says historian Daniel Boorstin. "Virginia had become an aristocracy."[2]

By the beginning of the 18th century not more than five per cent of the newcomers were becoming landowners. The "best" families tended to intermarry and by mid-century probably not more than a hundred families controlled the wealth and government of the colony.

Virginia had arrived at a society strangely resembling that of the English countryside, but the resemblance was less in content than in form. It was as if the landed families of Virginia had brought with them the text of a drama long played on the English stage which now would be played on the American. The English Country Gentleman was now played by The American Planter; The English Peasant, by The Negro Slave; The Steward, by The White Overseer. The Virginia (like the English) Country Gentleman rode in a coach, ate off silver inscribed with his family coat of arms which had been approved by the College of Heralds in London, sat on the bench as justice of the peace, served as vestryman of the local Anglican church, read the books of a gentleman, and even flavored his conversation or his letters with an occasional literary allusion in a classic language.[3]

When George Washington was a schoolboy, he entered in his copy-book the following poem:

These are the things which once possess'd
Will make a life that's truly bless'd:
A good estate on healthy soil
Not got by vice, nor yet by toil:
Round a warm fire, a pleasant joke,
With chimney ever free from smoke:
A strength entire, a sparkling bowl,
A quiet wife, a quiet soul,
A mind as well as body whole:
Prudent simplicity, constant friends,
A diet which no art commends:
A merry night without much drinking,
A happy thought without much thinking:
Each night by quiet sleep made short,
A will to be but what thou art:

Possess'd of these, all else defy,
And neither wish nor fear to die.[4]

In neat, classical couplets the verse expressed the life goals and the ethical code of the Virginia gentleman.

Washington was raised, as were most younger sons of the planters, without benefit of an education in England. By the laws of primogeniture most of the lands left by his father went to his older brother Lawrence. George received a modest holding and with it an education calculated to help him increase it—a solid grounding in arithmetic and geometry, in the practical details of plantation life, and in the arts of shooting and horsemanship. By the age of sixteen, having acquired a respectable knowledge of soils and boundaries, he went on his first surveying expedition to the frontier regions along the Shenandoah River. In the next two years he saved enough from other surveying jobs to purchase 1,450 acres for himself in that broad upland valley. When he was twenty, his brother Lawrence, who had greatly increased the family holdings by marrying into the powerful Fairfax family, died, leaving George a vast estate. After a rigorous and disillusioning stint as head of the Virginia militia during the French and Indian War, Washington resigned his commission, married a widow with great holdings of her own, and settled down to the management of their plantations.

The life the Washingtons led during the decade and a half before he was called away by the Revolution was one that he would always look back on with yearning. Much of his thought and energy went into the administration of his lands and the acquisition of new ones. He also fulfilled the usual duties of his class—was justice of the peace, judge of the county court, a member of the Virginia House of Burgesses, and a vestryman in the local branch of the Church of England.

After these duties were finished, however, there was still time for the ample pleasures of a Virginia gentleman. Many pleasant hours were given over to dancing, horse racing, drinking, fishing, and hunting. A little journal that he kept, entitled "Where and How My Time was Spent," indicates that in one year he participated in fox hunts on forty-nine days and went to church on fifteen.[5]

It was obviously with tongue in cheek that he wrote a friend that he was surprised to receive a letter written on Sunday, when his correspondent should have been in church. "Could you but behold with what religious zeal I hie me to church on every Lord's day," he wrote, "it would do your heart good."[6] Of a sermon that had been sent him from a more ardent section of the colonies, he said: "I presume it is good coming all the way from New Hampshire, but do not vouch for it, not having read a word of it."[7] Like most of his peers, Washington was a deist. He referred to his God most frequently as "Providence." How things would come out, he said, was known only to the "great ruler of events; and confiding in His wisdom and goodness, we may safely trust the issue to Him, without perplexing ourselves to seek for that which is beyond human ken, only taking care to perform the parts assigned to us in a way that reason and our own consciences approve of."[8] It was the code of the eighteenth-century Enlightenment: he would live each day as his reason told him he should and leave concern about first cause and final destiny to those whose tastes so inclined.

He expressed a healthy respect for learning, but his own reading remained spotty, and, in vetoing a suggestion that his stepson's education be discontinued, he hastened to make clear that his opposition was not due to any belief that "becoming a mere scholar is desirable education for a gentleman."[9]

In Williamsburg (where his wife had an elegant house with six chimneys) and especially at Mount Vernon, the Washingtons entertained with open hospitality, and they rode out frequently in their handsome coach to visit neighboring plantations.

But despite his enjoyment of the amenities of life, Washington was no dilettante aristocrat. And in this too he was typical of his class.

For several reasons a successful planter was likely to remain something of a merchant, constantly seeking new investments for his capital. First, there were the characteristics of Virginia's tobacco-agriculture. Since Virginians did not replenish the nitrogen and potash which growing tobacco sucked from the soil, it was only on virgin land that tobacco could flourish; the second crop was usually the best. After the fourth season land was customarily abandoned to corn and wheat, before finally being turned back to wild pine, sorrel, and sedge. Under this system a prudent planter dared not put more than a small portion—say, ten per cent—of his acreage in tobacco at any one time. Foresight required that he continually add to his landholdings since every year he was, in the Virginia phrase, "using it up." A prudent planter thus had to be a land speculator, alert to opportunity, ready to make new purchases.

The second factor which stimulated a mercantile and enterprising spirit among the planters was the lack of large towns. Tidewater Virginia was cut into fingers by several deep and navigable rivers. Each finger was in turn [veined by] smaller rivers, many of which were large enough to carry traffic toward the ocean. These were the circulatory channels of economic

Chapters from the American Experience

life. Up came ships carrying Negro slaves from Africa and the West Indies, clothing and household furnishings from London; down went ships laden with hogsheads of tobacco from the vast plantations. Each of the larger planters had his private dock. The tobacco grower could load his hogsheads directly from his own dockside onto the ship which went to his agent in London; his imports could be landed at his private port-of-entry. For this reason Virginia had no commercial capital, no Boston or Philadelphia, during the colonial period; her commerce dwelt in these scores of private depots scattered along the riversides.

Life on a large plantation was far from that in a simple agrarian economy. There were hundreds of slaves, white craftsmen, overseers, stewards, and traders who were producing tobacco as a money-crop, raising food, and manufacturing tools, farm instruments, and clothing for their own use and for sale. A Virginia plantation was an eighteenth-century version of a modern "company town" rather than a romantic rural village. The plantation-owner needed both business acumen and a large store of practical knowledge to run his little world of agriculture, trade, and manufacturing.[10]

Washington's Mount Vernon, sprawling along the Potomac, grew steadily as he purchased neighboring parcels over the years until it was one of the greatest plantations in Virginia. The soil, however, was of variable quality, and it was only by carefully studying farm methods, by being on horseback with the first morning light to visit his various farms and oversee his "overlookers," and by working on his books after dinner that he made the great holding pay.[11] The journal which he kept at first recorded many difficulties and disappointments. He was angry with a Mr. French, who raised the price of pork after making a firm commitment; his Negroes were ill; his crops were not adequate to cover necessities. But as the years went by, his efforts began to show results. The tone of the diary became contented. The seasons changed. Mares were bred, fields were plowed. The master himself planted trees at the head of the cherry walk, and the hound bitch brought forth pups, one of whom he named "Sweetlips." He tested the soil for fertility. He tinkered at night with a new plow design.[12] The fishery, with its own vat for curing fish seined from the river and its own cooper shop, began to show a profit. A new barn of revolutionary design went up; the number of slaves increased. The spinning house, the gristmill, the distillery made their contributions. And the great manor house grew, as wings were added, and sat proudly on the land with its neatly laid out classical gardens, its private wharf, its great stable and kitchen-house.[13] Out of the broad holdings and an enterprising spirit, Washington had created a manorial domain that took its place among Virginia's greatest.

In his restrained way Washington wrote now that he was "pleased" with farming and could "no where find so great satisfaction as in those innocent and useful pursuits," so much more delightful than the "vain glory" of a military career.[14] Ironically, the more Washington indulged his love for the land, the more he encouraged another force (which also had its appeals) to draw him away from it. For, as his land holdings became ever larger, his political involvements grew. Boorstin describes the relationship between the plantation gentry and the government of the colony.

Just as the owner of a large plantation had thrust on him tasks of management which he could not escape so he had political duties which he could not shirk. The successful planter developed perforce the habit of command. He came to manage the affairs of the colony with the same self-assurance he showed in managing his private estate. If the plantation was a little colony in itself, which had to be governed with tact, authority, and prudence, the colony of Virginia was in turn ruled like a large plantation. The major dignities and decisions rested on those who held the largest stake.

The upward political path from the seat of the vestryman or justice of the peace to the Governor's Council was guarded all along the way by the local gentry. Seeking a political career without their approval was hopeless. And the House of Burgesses was hardly more than the political workshop of a ruling aristocracy. Here were made the major decisions about the price and quality of tobacco, taxation, education, Indian relations, and religion.

The Virginia Burgesses were, of course, "elected." Their election, if less corrupt and more open to talent, much resembled the English "election" of members of Parliament in the same period. It was nothing like a free-for-all in which any ambitious young man could seek his political fortune; the election was a process in which freeholders made their choice from among the gentlemen. Technically the qualifications for a Burgess were no greater than those for a voter, but in practice the candidates for the House were members of the gentry.

Elections took place in an intimate atmosphere of protocol and conviviality. Convention forbade a candidate's soliciting votes, or even voting for himself, and there was no party organization. A candidate was, however, expected to use indirect (usually gastronomic) means of persuasion; no one could hope for election without "treating" the voters. Large quantities of rum punch, ginger cakes, and barbecued beef or pork persuaded prudent voters that their candidate possessed the liberality and the substance to represent them properly in the Assembly. Such entertainment was expensive. George Washington's expenditures when he stood for Burgess were never less than 25 pounds and on one occasion about 50 pounds. Such a sum was several times what it would have cost a man to buy the house and land required to qualify him as a voter.

Voting took place in the county courthouse or, in good weather, on the courthouse green. It differed from a modern American election mainly in the publicity given to every voter's choice and in the resulting opportunity for gratitude or resentment between the candidate and his constituents. By an almost unbroken custom, candidates were expected to be present at the voting-place. At a table sat the sheriff, the candidates, and the clerks. The voters came up one at a time to announce their choices, which were recorded publicly like a box-score. Since anyone present could always see the latest count, a candidate could at the last minute send supporters to bring in additional needed votes. As each voter declared his preference, shouts of approval would come from one side and hoots from another, while the betting-odds changed and new wagers were laid. The favored candidate would rise, bow, and express thanks to the voter: "Mr. Buchanan, I shall treasure that vote in my memory." This personal acknowledgment of the voter's confidence was so customary that in the rare case when the candidate could not be present he delegated a friend to make his obeisances for him. When George Washington's command of the Frederick militia kept him at Fort Cumberland during the 1758 election, his friend James Wood, the most influential man in the county, sat at the poll and thanked each voter individually for his compliment to the absent colonel.

The gentry chose the sheriff from among themselves, and the sheriff managed the elections. He decided whether any individual was qualified to vote; he set the date of the election; he fixed the hour for opening and closing the polls; there was no appeal from his decisions except to the House of Burgesses, which was always reluctant to override local officials.

"Gentlemen freeholders," the sheriff would finally proclaim from the courthouse door, "come into court and give your votes or the poll will be closed." Sometimes the election would be ended by two o'clock in the afternoon, but if the sheriff found that many voters had been kept away "by rain or rise of watercourses," he might prolong the election into another day. What modern candidate would not envy the Virginia gentleman his power to keep the polls open until the winning votes had been rounded up!

Virginia law permitted a gentleman freeholder to vote in every county where he possessed the property qualification. If he was qualified in three

The Tidewater Gentleman

counties he could vote for three sets of Burgesses. Since a man could represent in the House of Burgesses any district where he could vote, this further widened the political opportunities of the larger planters. They could choose to run where their chances seemed best. Many great Virginians, including George Washington, used their extensive and dispersed landholdings to advance their political fortunes.[15]

This "well-oiled machinery of aristocracy" did not, Virginians believed, "thwart" the people's will, but saved it from error. The large planters, who understood better than most the economic and political problems of Virginia, knew they belonged in the Burgesses, and they were confident that, year after year, their constituents would put them there. This confidence had its advantages, says Boorstin.

This security of social position bred a wholesome vigor of judgment which made the Virginia House of Burgesses a place for deliberation and discussion rarely found among modern legislatures. Burgesses came close to Edmund Burke's ideal of the representative who owed allegiance not to the whim of his constituency but only to his private judgment. The voters in colonial Virginia had just enough power to prevent the irresponsibility of their representatives, but not enough to secure their servility.

The seriousness, wisdom, honesty, and eloquence in the deliberations of the Burgesses during the crucial years of the Stamp Act was not due only to the greatness of the men and the issues. These men were not satisfied to be spokesmen of their voters' whims. Their speeches were serious and sometimes subtle arguments directed to fellow-legislators.

These men were talking to each other; none of them was much impressed by the flowery phrase. With the conspicuous exception of a few like Patrick Henry, Virginia's representatives talked in sober and conversational style.

As the ruling Virginians admired the ideal of the English gentleman, the genteel canon they most scrupulously followed was Moderation. Unlike some of their English gentlemen-contemporaries, they did not despise trade or labor, nor did they admire an idle aristocracy. Nor, unlike some leveling democrats, did they particularly idealize the horny-handed laborer.[16]

A "leveling democrat" of this sort, inspired perhaps by De Toqueville, might suggest that, desirable as may be the search for excellence which characterizes aristocratic government at best, such a government is, by natural tendency, grounded in class favoritism. He would point out that these rulers of Virginia made greedy use of their power over the disbursement of land, that Washington, for example, netted 24,100 acres for himself as a result of his crusade for land-awards to veterans of the French and Indian War.[17] But, after all the eulogizing and the criticism, it would have to be conceded that these were aristocrats with a difference.

The leadership of Virginia had, indeed, become a gentleman's club. But it was an eighteenth-century club in a New World, and the idea of progress and the dream of revolution that were stirring Europe worked their subtle leaven even more effectively on the shores of a virgin continent. Out of this aristocratic gentleman's club would come makers of a new nation, dedicated to the self-evident truth that all men are created equal, and a president who would choose not to be king, but the father of his country.

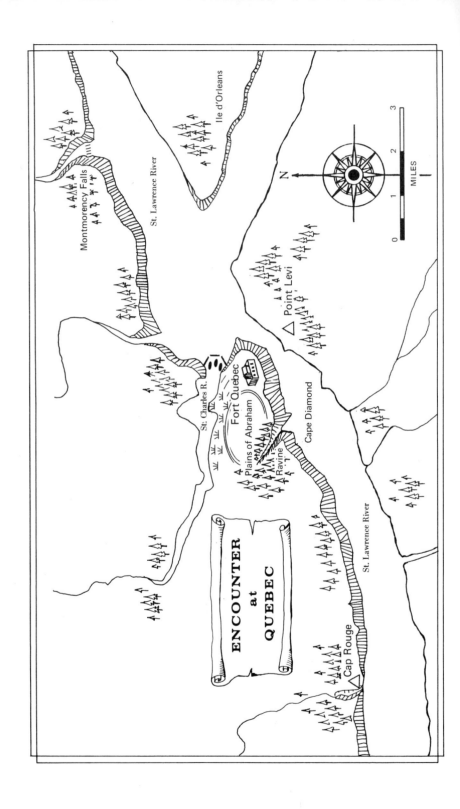

ENCOUNTER at QUEBEC

Montmorency Falls

St. Lawrence River

Ile d'Orleans

Point Levi

St. Charles R.

Fort Quebec

Plains of Abraham

Ravine

Cape Diamond

St. Lawrence River

Cap Rouge

N

MILES

0 1 2 3

10

Encounter at Quebec

The paths of glory lead but to the grave.
—Thomas Gray

While, along the Atlantic seaboard, the English colonies were evolving these various cultures—so diverse, yet all rising from and cherishing the British concept of representative government and the rule of law —New France was developing a quite different civilization. The French Canadian hierarchy ruled in authoritarian splendor over the little Versailles at Quebec, great feudal domains worked by peasants lined the St. Lawrence, an established Catholic Church dominated faith and morals, and the entire empire reflected the absolutist structure of pre-Revolutionary France. The men of the British colonies viewed this civilization as alien to their heritage and to the concepts of freedom they had developed—an anachronistic offspring of England's ancient enemy, a model of traditional colonial subservience, a spawning ground for the repressions of another age and another world.

Nor were the French satisfied to spread this civilization to Canada. By pushing up the St. Lawrence to the Great Lakes and down the Mississippi to New Orleans, they had laid claim to the broad heart of the continent—to everything north of Mexico and west of the Alleghenies as far as the Rocky Mountains.

Shortly after the middle of the eighteenth century, as the advance guard of the British pushed over the barrier of the Alleghenies into the Ohio country, the inevitable showdown between the two powers began. By the late 1750s the contest for empire between England and France had spread throughout the world, and the struggle in the forests and on the rivers of North America had become an adjunct to global conflict.

Almost a century after this conflict had wrought its epochal change in the course of empire and had been overshadowed by the Revolution, it was vividly recaptured by the artistry and sound scholarship of Francis Parkman. Parkman, a Bostonian of the Romantic school and one of America's most eminent historians, climaxed his epic of the rise and fall of New France with an account of the stirring struggle for the Canadian capital of Quebec in the summer of 1759. Although the British victory that ended that struggle was clear-cut, it was not decisive. The British hold on Quebec would for a while prove tenuous, and four more years of global strife and tortuous negotiations would ensue before the issue was resolved. But Quebec was a herald of things to come. It was a dramatic moment in the struggle for the continent. And its drama was recorded imperishably by a great historian and heightened by the heroic qualities of the contending leaders—Louis Joseph, Marquis de Montcalm, and the British general James Wolfe.

Montcalm was in his middle years at the time of the battle for Quebec. Born of an aristocratic family in southern France, he had brought with him to Canada his courtly ways and high standard of living. He wrote long nostalgic letters to his wife, children, and mother, assuring them of his tender love, inquiring about the affairs of his estate and chateau, and asking his wife to send him an array of delicacies including "anchovies, muscat wine, sausages, confections, cloth for liveries, and bottles of English lavendar."[1] But, although Montcalm had the mannerisms of a French courtier, he was a diligent, shrewd commander, engrossed in the task of molding a motley army into a strong defense for the Canadian empire.

As for British General Wolfe, says Parkman, never was the soul of a hero put in so unsuitable a frame. "The forehead and chin receded; the nose, slightly upturned, formed the point of an obtuse triangle; the mouth was by no means shaped to express resolution." His "narrow shoulders, slender body, and long thin limbs" testified to a life of poor health.[2] But his was a dauntless and militant spirit. He had been spurred from childhood by dreams of warriors' exploits, at sixteen he had entered the military service, and now, at thirty-three, he was entrusted with the command of the assault on Quebec. "All that I wish," he wrote prophetically, "is that I may at all times be ready and firm to meet that fate we cannot shun, and to die gracefully and properly when the hour comes."[3]

It was in the early summer of 1759 that the French at Quebec received word of a British fleet approaching the St. Lawrence. Quebec, secure on the cliffs above the river, was a natural bastion. The French hurriedly set about making it impregnable. Confident that the cannon of Quebec would bar penetration any farther up the waterway, Montcalm brought his entire force downriver from the city, strongly fortifying the eight miles of the river's north bank below him to the point where the wild cascade gorge of the Montmorenci River protected his left flank. Along the cliffs he set up earthenwork defenses from which a few men could repel an army. Near Quebec, on the mudflats of another great river, the St. Charles, which ran down to the St. Lawrence under the walls of the city, they set up redoubts, batteries, and entrenchment lines. Across the St. Charles River itself they chained a boom of logs, behind which lay a floating battery and an array of fire ships. To man these defenses, the French mustered more than 16,000 men—regulars, Canadian militia, and Indians. Against this formidable barrier Wolfe brought land forces totaling less than 9,000.

The British fleet arrived late in June, negotiated the treacherous Lower St. Lawrence, and sailed upriver to a point three or four miles below Quebec. There they disembarked their soldiers on the Island of Orleans, off the south shore. From the island Wolfe could see:

. . . the desperate nature of the task he had undertaken. Before him Quebec sat perched upon her rock, a congregation of stone houses, churches, palaces, convents, and hospitals; the green trees of the Seminary garden and the spires of the Cathedral. Beyond rose the loftier height of Cape Diamond, edged with palisades and capped with redoubt and parapet. Batteries frowned everywhere—on the rock above, and on the strand, where the dwellings and warehouses of the lower town clustered beneath the cliff.

Full in sight lay the far-extended camp of Montcalm, stretching from the St. Charles, beneath the city walls, to the chasm and cataract of the Montmorenci. Above the city, Cape Diamond hid the view; but could Wolfe have looked beyond it, he would have beheld a prospect still more disheartening. Here, mile after mile, the St. Lawrence was walled by a range of steeps, often inaccessible, and always so difficult that a few men at the top could hold an army in check; while at Cap-Rouge, about eight miles distant, the high plateau was cleft by the channel of a stream which formed a line of defence as strong as that of the Montmorenci. Quebec was a natural fortress.[4]

With little opposition, Wolfe seized Point Levi, on the heights across the St. Lawrence from Quebec, from which he bombarded the city. Its citizens fled to the country, but, aside from the effect on morale, the

Encounter at Quebec

attack accomplished little, for—as the French were quick to point out —the British could in that manner demolish Quebec, but they could not capture it. Next he took the eastern bluff of the Montmorenci River, but the broad torrent still separated him from Montcalm's headquarters, and, from the forest at his back, Indians attacked him, making his position all but untenable.

On July 18, the British carried off a maneuver that made possible their ultimate victory.

The French commanders had thought it impossible for any hostile ship to pass the batteries of Quebec; but about eleven o'clock at night, favored by the wind, and covered by a furious cannonade from Point Levi, the ship *Sutherland,* with a frigate and several small vessels, sailed safely by and reached the river above the town. Now, for the first time, it became necessary for Montcalm to weaken his army at Beauport [his headquarters between the Montmorenci and Quebec] by sending six hundred men to defend the accessible points in the line of precipices between Quebec and Cap-Rouge. Several hundred more were sent on the next day, when it became known that the English had dragged a fleet of boats over Point Levi, launched them above the town, and dispatched troops to embark in them. Thus a new feature was introduced into the siege operations, and danger had risen on a side where the French thought themselves safe.[5]

The British assaulted the French side of the Montmorenci but were repulsed with heavy losses. They attacked and burned outlying districts. Summer wore on, and still Wolfe was really no closer to his objective of a face-to-face trial of strength between his disciplined and loyal troops and the numerically superior but undependable French forces.

Montcalm let the parishes burn, and still lay fast intrenched in his lines. He would not imperil all Canada to save a few hundred farmhouses; and Wolfe was as far as ever from the battle that he coveted. Hitherto, his attacks had been made chiefly below the town; but, these having failed, he now changed his plan and renewed on a larger scale the movements begun above it in July. With every fair wind, ships and transports passed the batteries of Quebec [under cover of] hot fire from Point Levi, and generally succeeded, with more or less damage, in gaining the upper river. A fleet of flatboats was also sent thither, and twelve hundred troops marched overland to embark in them.

Yet the difficulties of the English still seemed insurmountable. Dysentery and fever broke out in their camps, the number of their effective men was greatly reduced, and the advanced season told them that their work must be done quickly or not done at all.[6]

The number of days that the British fleet could safely ply the St. Lawrence before freezing weather locked it in dwindled; the naval commanders became restive. Wolfe fell so dangerously ill that he and his army held little hope for his recovery, but he rallied and settled on a desperate plan for one final attack before withdrawing. The encampment at the Montmorenci was evacuated. Troops from the south bank of the St. Lawrence were reimbarked on the vessels above Quebec, and the heavy artillery was removed from the batteries at Point Levi. The French interpreted these movements as probable preliminaries to a British retreat. But the English had decided on a surprise attack up a small ravine cutting the cliffs near the Plains of Abraham just above Quebec. Parkman's story of the incredible feat of the small British force in bringing the city to its knees is the climax of his work.

For several successive days the squadron of Holmes [commander of the British fleet above Quebec] was allowed to drift up the river with the flood tide and down with the ebb, thus passing and repassing incessantly between the neighborhood of Quebec on one hand, and a point high above Cap-Rouge on the other; while Bougainville [French leader at Cap-Rouge], perplexed, and always expecting an attack, followed the ships to and fro along the shore, by day and by night, till his men were exhausted with ceaseless forced marches.

At last the time for action came. Wolfe, from the flagship *Sutherland,* issued his last general orders. "The enemy's force is now divided, great scarcity of provisions in their camp, and universal discontent among the Canadians. Our troops below are in readiness to join us; all the light artillery and tools are embarked at the Point of Levi; and the troops will land where the French seem least to expect it. The first body that gets on shore is to march directly to the enemy and drive them from any little post they may occupy; the officers must be careful that the succeeding bodies do not by any mistake fire on those who go before them. The battalions must form on the upper ground with expedition, and be ready to charge whatever presents itself. When the artillery and troops are landed, a corps will be left to secure the landing-place, while the rest march on and endeavor to bring the Canadians and French to a battle. The officers and men will remember what their country expects from them, and what a determined body of soldiers inured to war is capable of doing against five weak French battalions mingled with a disorderly peasantry."

The spirit of the army answered that of its chief. The troops loved and

Encounter at Quebec

admired their general, trusted their officers, and were ready for any attempt. Wolfe had thirty-six hundred men and officers with him on board the vessels of Holmes; and he now sent orders to Colonel Burton at Point Levi to bring to his aid all who could be spared from that place and the Point of Orleans. They were to march along the south bank, after nightfall, and wait further orders at a designated spot convenient for embarkation. Their number was about twelve hundred, so that the entire force destined for the enterprise was at the utmost forty-eight hundred. With these, Wolfe meant to climb the heights of Abraham in the teeth of an enemy who, though much reduced, were still twice as numerous as their assailants.

Admiral Saunders lay with the main fleet in the Basin of Quebec. This excellent officer, whatever may have been his views as to the necessity of a speedy departure, aided Wolfe to the last with unfailing energy and zeal. It was agreed between them that while the General made the real attack, the Admiral should engage Montcalm's attention by a pretended one. As night approached, the fleet ranged itself along the Beauport shore; the boats were lowered and filled with sailors, marines, and the few troops that had been left behind; while ship signalled to ship, cannon flashed and thundered, and shot ploughed the beach, as if to clear a way for assailants to land. In the gloom of the evening the effect was imposing. Montcalm, who thought that the movements of the English above the town were only a feint, that their main force was still below it, and that their real attack would be made there, was completely deceived, and massed his troops in front of Beauport to repel the expected landing. But while in the fleet of Saunders all was uproar and ostentatious menace, the danger was ten miles away, where the squadron of Holmes lay tranquil and silent at its anchorage off Cap-Rouge.

It was less tranquil than it seemed. All on board knew that a blow would be struck that night, though only a few high officers knew where. Colonel Howe, of the light infantry, called for volunteers to lead the unknown and desperate venture, promising, in the words of one of them, "that if any of us survived we might depend on being recommended to the General." As many as were wanted—twenty-four in all—soon came forward. Thirty large bateaux and some boats belonging to the squadron lay moored alongside the vessels; and late in the evening the troops were ordered into them, the twenty-four volunteers taking their place in the foremost. They held in all about seventeen hundred men. The rest remained on board.

Bougainville could discern the movement, and misjudged it, thinking that he himself was to be attacked. The tide was still flowing; and, the better to deceive him, the vessels and boats were allowed to drift upward with it for a little distance, as if to land above Cap-Rouge.

The day had been fortunate for Wolfe. Two deserters came from the camp of Bougainville with intelligence that, at ebb tide on the next night, he was to send down a convoy of provisions to Montcalm. The necessities of the camp at Beauport, and the difficulties of transportation by land, had before compelled the French to resort to this perilous means of conveying supplies; and their boats, drifting in darkness under the shadows of the northern shore, had commonly passed in safety. Wolfe saw at once that, if his own boats went down in advance of the convoy, he could turn the intelligence of the deserters to good account.

Towards two o'clock the tide began to ebb, and a fresh wind blew down the river. Two lanterns were raised into the main-top shrouds of the *Sutherland.* It was the appointed signal; the boats cast off and fell down with the current, those of the light infantry leading the way. The vessels with the rest of the troops had orders to follow a little later.

To look for a moment at the chances on which this bold adventure hung. First, the deserters told Wolfe that provision-boats were ordered to go down to Quebec that night; secondly, Bougainville countermanded them; thirdly, the sentries posted along the heights were told of the order, but not of the countermand; fourthly, [the French commander at the point of attack] had permitted most of his men to go home for a time and work at their harvesting, on condition, it is said, that they should afterwards work in a neighboring field of his own; fifthly, he kept careless watch, and went quietly to bed; sixthly, the battalion of Guienne, ordered to take post on the Plains of Abraham, had, for reasons unexplained, remained encamped by the St. Charles; and lastly, when Bougainville saw Holmes's vessels drift down the stream, he did not tax his wary troops to follow them, thinking that they would return as usual with the flood tide. But for these conspiring circumstances the fruitless heroism of Wolfe would have passed, with countless other heroisms, into oblivion.

For full two hours the procession of boats, borne on the current, steered silently down the St. Lawrence. The stars were visible, but the night was moonless and sufficiently dark. The General was in one of the foremost boats, and near him was a young midshipman, John Robison, afterwards professor of natural philosophy in the University of Edinburgh. He used to tell in his later life how Wolfe, with a low voice, repeated Gray's *Elegy in a Country Churchyard* to the officers about him. Probably it was to relieve the intense strain of his thoughts. Among the rest was the verse which his own fate was soon to illustrate—

"The paths of glory lead but to the grave."

As they neared their destination, the tide bore them in toward the shore, and the mighty wall of rock and forest towered in darkness on their left. The dead stillness was suddenly broken by the sharp *Qui vive!* of a French sentry, invisible in the thick gloom. *France!* answered a Highland officer

Encounter at Quebec

from one of the boats of the light infantry. He had served in Holland and spoke French fluently.

À quel régiment?

De la Reine, replied the Highlander. He knew that a part of that corps was with Bougainville. The sentry, expecting the convoy of provisions, was satisfied, and did not ask for the password.

Soon after, the foremost boats were passing the heights of Samos, when another sentry challenged them, and they could see him through the darkness running down to the edge of the water, within range of a pistol-shot. In answer to his questions, the same officer replied, in French: "Provision-boats. Don't make a noise; the English will hear us." In fact, the sloop-of-war *Hunter* was anchored in the stream not far off. This time, again, the sentry let them pass. In a few moments they rounded the headland above [their objective]. There was no sentry there. The strong current swept the boats of the light infantry a little below the intended landing-place. They disembarked on a narrow strand at the foot of heights as steep as a hill covered with trees can be. The twenty-four volunteers led the way, climbing with what silence they might, closely followed by a much larger body. When they reached the top they saw in the dim light a cluster of tents at a short distance, and immediately made a dash at them. [The French], taken by surprise, made little resistance. One or two were caught, the rest fled.

The main body of troops waited in their boats by the edge of the strand. The heights near by were cleft by a great ravine choked with forest trees; and in its depths ran a little brook, which, swollen by the late rains, fell plashing in the stillness over a rock. Other than this no sound could reach the strained ear of Wolfe but the gurgle of the tide and the cautious climbing of his advance-parties as they mounted the steeps at some little distance from where he sat listening. At length from the top came a sound of musket-shots, followed by loud huzzas, and he knew that his men were masters of the position. The word was given; the troops leaped from the boats and scaled the heights, some here, some there, clutching at trees and bushes, their muskets slung at their backs. The narrow slanting path on the face of the heights had been made impassable by trenches and abattis; but all obstructions were soon cleared away, and then the ascent was easy. In the gray of the morning the long file of red-coated soldiers moved quickly upward, and formed in order on the plateau above.

The day broke in clouds and threatening rain. No enemy was in sight. [Wolfe] had achieved the most critical part of his enterprise; yet the success that he coveted placed him in imminent danger. On one side was the garrison of Quebec and the army of Beauport, and Bougainville was on the other. Wolfe's alternative was victory or ruin; for if he should be overwhelmed by a combined attack, retreat would be hopeless.

Chapters from the American Experience

He went to reconnoitre the ground, and soon came to the Plains of Abraham. At the place that Wolfe chose for his battle-field the plateau was less than a mile wide. Thither the troops advanced, marched by files till they reached the ground, and then wheeled to form their line of battle, which stretched across the plateau and faced the city. The front line, when all the troops had arrived, numbered less than thirty-five hundred men.

Quebec was not a mile distant, but they could not see it; for a ridge of broken ground intervened about six hundred paces off. The first division of troops had scarcely come up when, about six o'clock, this ridge was suddenly thronged with white uniforms. It was the battalion of Guienne, arrived at the eleventh hour from its camp by the St. Charles.

Montcalm had passed a troubled night. Through all the evening the cannon bellowed from the ships of Saunders, and the boats of the fleet hovered in the dusk off the Beauport shore, threatening every moment to land. The General walked the field that adjoined his headquarters till one in the morning. At daybreak he heard the sound of cannon above the town and about six o'clock he mounted and rode thither. As they advanced, the country behind the town opened more and more upon their sight; till at length they saw across the St. Charles, some two miles away, the red ranks of British soldiers on the heights beyond. [Montcalm] set spurs to his horse, and rode over the bridge of the St. Charles to the scene of danger. He rode with a fixed look, uttering not a word.

The army followed in such order as it might, crossed the bridge in hot haste, passed under the northern rampart of Quebec, entered at the Palace Gate, and pressed on in headlong march along the quaint narrow streets of the warlike town: troops of Indians in scalplocks and war-paint; bands of Canadians whose all was at stake; the colony regulars; the battalions of Old France, a torrent of white uniforms and gleaming bayonets. So they swept on, poured out upon the plain, and hurried, breathless, to where the banners of Guienne still fluttered on the ridge.

Montcalm was amazed at what he saw. He had expected a detachment, and he found an army. Full in sight before him stretched the lines of Wolfe: the close ranks of the English infantry, a silent wall of red, and the wild array of the Highlanders, with their waving tartans, and bagpipes scream-ing defiance. Montcalm and his chief officers held a council of war. His men were full of ardor, and he resolved to attack before their ardor cooled.

The English waited the result with a composure which, if not quite real, was at least well feigned. Three field-pieces plied them with canister-shot, and fifteen hundred Canadians and Indians fusilladed them in front and flank. Over all the plain, from behind bushes and knolls and the edge of cornfields, puffs of smoke sprang incessantly from the guns of these hid-den marksmen. Skirmishers were thrown out before the lines to hold them

Encounter at Quebec

in check, and the soldiers were ordered to lie on the grass to avoid the shot. It was towards ten o'clock when, from the high ground on the right of the line, Wolfe saw that the crisis was near. The French on the ridge had formed themselves into three bodies, regulars in the centre, regulars and Canadians on right and left. Two field-pieces, which had been dragged up the heights [by the British] fired on them with grape-shot, and the troops, rising from the ground, prepared to receive them. In a few moments more they were in motion. They came on rapidly, uttering loud shouts, and firing as soon as they were within range. Their ranks, ill ordered at the best, were further confused by a number of Canadians who had been mixed among the regulars, and who, after hastily firing, threw themselves on the ground to reload. The British advanced a few rods; then halted and stood still. When the French were within forty paces the word of command rang out, and a crash of musketry answered all along the line. The volley was delivered with remarkable precision. In the battalions of the centre, which had suffered least from the enemy's bullets, the simultaneous explosion was afterwards said by French officers to have sounded like a cannon-shot. Another volley followed, and then a furious clattering fire that lasted but a minute or two. When the smoke rose, a miserable sight was revealed: the ground cumbered with dead and wounded, the advancing masses stopped short and turned into a frantic mob, shouting, cursing, gesticulating. The order was given to charge. Then over the field rose the British cheer, mixed with the fierce yell of the Highland slogan. Some of the corps pushed forward with the bayonet; some advanced firing. The clansmen drew their broadswords and dashed on, keen and swift as bloodhounds. At the English right, though the attacking column was broken to pieces, a fire was still kept up, chiefly, it seems, by sharpshooters from the bushes and cornfields, where they had lain for an hour or more. Here Wolfe himself led the charge, at the head of the Louisbourg grenadiers. A shot shattered his wrist. He wrapped his handkerchief about it and kept on. Another shot struck him, and he still advanced, when a third lodged in his breast. He staggered, and sat on the ground. Lieutenant Brown, of the grenadiers, one Henderson, a volunteer in the same company, and a private soldier, aided by an officer of artillery who ran to join them, carried him in their arms to the rear. He begged them to lay him down. They did so, and asked if he would have a surgeon. "There's no need," he answered; "it's all over with me." A moment after, one of them cried out: "They run; see how they run!" "Who run?" Wolfe demanded, like a man roused from sleep. "The enemy, sir. Egad, they give way everywhere!" "Go, one of you, to Colonel Burton," returned the dying man; "tell him to cut off their retreat from the bridge." Then, turning on his side, he murmured, "Now, God be praised, I will die in peace!" and in a few moments his gallant soul had fled.

Chapters from the American Experience

Montcalm, still on horseback, was borne with the tide of fugitives towards the town. As he approached the walls a shot passed through his body. He kept his seat; two soldiers supported him, one on each side, and led his horse through the St. Louis Gate. On the open space within, among the excited crowd, were several women, drawn, no doubt, by eagerness to know the result of the fight. One of them recognized him, saw the streaming blood, and shrieked, "Oh my God! My God! the Marquis is killed!" "It's nothing, it's nothing," replied the death-stricken man; "don't be troubled for me, my good friends."[7]

Montcalm died before dawn. The following afternoon the British marched without opposition through the gates of Quebec and raised their flag above the city. And thus, says Parkman, "the capital of New France passed into the hands of its hereditary foes."[8]

Benjamin Franklin

11

Benjamin Franklin: Universal American

Jack of all trades,
master of each and mastered by none—
the type and genius of his land.
—Herman Melville[1]

There was little about the youth of seventeen who came walking up Philadelphia's Market Street that Sunday morning in October, 1723, to suggest that he was to become one of America's giants. It had been a harrowing journey from Boston—thirty hours without food on a small boat caught in a storm, a siege of illness, an overland trek in soaking rain, and finally a night lost along the river above the town, warmed only by a fire of old fence rails. In his inimitable *Autobiography* Franklin recalled the amusing circumstances of his arrival in Philadelphia:

I was in my working dress, my best clothes being to come round by sea. I was dirty from my journey; my pockets were stuffed out with shirts and stockings; I knew no soul, nor where to look for lodging. I was fatigued with travelling, rowing and want of rest. I was very hungry, and my whole stock of cash consisted of a Dutch dollar and about a shilling in copper. The latter I gave the people of the boat for my passage, who at first refused it on account of my rowing; but I insisted on their taking it, a man being sometimes more generous when he has but a little money than when he has plenty, perhaps through fear of being thought to have but little. Then I walked up the street, gazing about, till near the Market House I met a boy with bread. I had made many a meal on bread, and inquiring where he got it, I went immediately to the baker's he directed me to in Second Street; and asked for biscuit, intending such as we had in Boston, but they it seems were not made in Philadelphia, then I asked for a three-penny loaf, and was told they had none such: so not considering or knowing the difference of money and the greater cheapness nor the names of his bread, I bade him give me threepenny worth of any sort. He gave me accordingly three great puffy rolls. I was surprised at the quantity, but took it, and having no room in my pockets, walked off, with a roll under each arm, and eating the other. Thus I went up Market Street as far as Fourth Street, passing by the door of Mr. Read, my future wife's father, when she standing at the door saw me, and thought I made as I certainly did a most awkward ridiculous appearance.[2]

But ridiculous as he may have appeared, Benjamin Franklin was awkward neither in mind nor in body. He was already a skilled printer and successful newspaper publisher and had read "abundantly" in such works as *Plutarch's Lives* and Locke's *Essay Concerning Human Understanding*. Moreover, he had been an active youth, adept in sports, particularly swimming, and a leader among his peers.

Living near the water, I was much in and about it, learned early to swim well, and to manage boats, and when in a boat or canoe with other boys I was commonly allowed to govern, especially in any case of difficulty; and upon other occasions I was generally a leader among the boys, and sometimes led them into scrapes, of which I will mention one instance, as it shows an early projecting public spirit, though not then justly conducted. There was a salt marsh that bounded part of the Mill Pond, on the edge of which at high water, we used to stand to fish for minnows. By much trampling, we had made it a mere quagmire. My proposal was to build a wharf there fit for us to stand upon, and I showed my comrades a large heap of stones which were intended for a new house near the marsh, and which would very well suit our purpose. Accordingly in the evening when the workmen were gone, I assembled a number of my playfellows, and working with them diligently like so many ants, sometimes two or three to a stone, we brought them all away and built our little wharf. The next morning the workmen were surprised at missing the stones, which were found in our wharf; enquiry was made after the removers; we were discovered and complained of; several of us were corrected by our fathers; and though I pleaded the usefulness of the work, mine convinced me that nothing was useful which was not honest.[3]

Apprenticed to his brother, James, at the age of twelve, Benjamin offered to feed himself if his brother would give him half of the money he would normally have spent on his food. Given this sum, he spent half of it for food (often only a slice of bread, a few raisins, and water). With the rest he bought books. He studied arithmetic, navigation, grammar, and logic and sharpened his wits in long erudite arguments with a studious friend. Coming upon a copy of Addison's *Spectator Papers*, he made use of the work of that great English essayist to develop a witty, concise style of his own.

I took some of the papers, and making short hints of the sentiment in each sentence, laid them by a few days, and then without looking at the book, tried to complete the papers again, by expressing each hinted sentiment at length and as fully as it had been expressed before, in any suitable words that should come to hand. . . . I took some of the tales and turned them into verse. And after a time, when I had pretty well forgotten the prose, turned them back again. I also sometimes jumbled my collections of hints into confusion, and after some weeks, endeavored to reduce them into the best order, before I began to form the full sentences, and complete the paper. This was to teach me method in the arrangement of thoughts. By comparing my work afterwards with the original, I discovered many faults and amended them; but I sometimes had the pleasure of fancying that in certain particulars of small import, I had been lucky enough to improve the method or the language.[4]

When James Franklin became embroiled with the magistrates and religious leaders of Boston and was jailed for "contempt," Benjamin temporarily took over the task of publishing his brother's newspaper. Circumspectly he succeeded in expressing his equally rebellious opinions without coming into direct conflict with the authorities. Writing under the guise of an anonymous contributor, he twitted the magistrates of Boston:

It has been for some time a question with me whether a commonwealth suffers more by hypocritical pretenders to religion or by the openly profane. But some late thoughts of this nature have inclined me to think that the hypocrite is the more dangerous person of the two, especially if he sustains a post in the government.[5]

Having tried his wings, the apprentice did not prove sufficiently pliable when his brother returned from jail. "Perhaps I was too saucy and provoking," he conceded.[6] At any rate, the tension between them was more than Benjamin chose to bear, and, selling some of his books for funds, he ran away.

In the seven years that followed his inauspicious arrival in Philadelphia, Franklin rose quickly from a journeyman printer to the master of his own shop. Examining the traits which his fellow citizens expected to see in a young tradesman, Franklin set about living up to their ideal:

In order to secure my credit and character . . . I took care not only to be in *reality* industrious and frugal but to avoid all *appearances* of the contrary. I dressed plainly; I was seen at no places of idle diversion. I never went out a-fishing or shooting; a book, indeed, sometimes debauched me from my work, but that was seldom, snug, and gave no scandal; and, to show that I was not above my business, I sometimes brought home the paper I purchased at the stores through the streets on a wheelbarrow.[7]

While he was thus playing the role of "the complete tradesman," Franklin devoted his free moments to analyzing his own character and devising a set of standards by which, in typical Enlightenment manner, he determined to perfect himself. He would order his life rationally— would establish a precise code of behavior and force the unruly elements of his nature to obey the dictates of Reason. He constructed a list of thirteen virtues which he resolved to pursue: *Temperance* ("Eat not to dullness; drink not to elevation"), *Silence* ("Speak not but what may benefit others or yourself"), *Order* ("Let all your things have their places; let each part of your business have its time"), *Resolution, Frugality, Industry, Sincerity, Justice, Moderation, Cleanliness, Tranquility* ("Be not disturbed at trifles, or at accidents common or unavoidable"), *Chastity,* and *Humility* ("Imitate Jesus and Socrates").[8]

I made a little book, in which I allotted a page for each of the virtues. . . . I determined to give a week's strict attention to each of the virtues successively. Thus, in the first week, my great guard was to avoid every the least offense against *Temperance,* leaving the other virtues to their ordinary chance, only marking every evening the faults of the day. . . . Proceeding thus to the last, I could go through a course complete in thirteen weeks, and four courses in a year. And like him who, having a garden to weed, does not attempt to eradicate all the bad herbs at once . . . so I should have (I hoped) the encouraging pleasure of seeing on my pages the progress I made in virtue . . . till in the end, by a number of courses, I should be happy in viewing a clean book."[9]

Franklin was surprised at the trouble some of the virtues (especially *Order*) gave him, but his progress toward *Humility* (or rather the semblance thereof) pleased him:

A Quaker friend having kindly informed me that I was generally thought proud; that my pride showed itself frequently in conversation; that I was not content with being in the right when discussing any point but was overbearing and rather insolent, of which he convinced me by mentioning several instances; I determined endeavoring to cure myself, if I could of this vice or folly among the rest. . . . I cannot boast of much success in acquiring the reality of this virtue, but I had a good deal with regard to the appearance of it. I made it a rule to forbear all direct contradiction of the sentiments of others and all positive assertion of my own. . . . I soon found the advantage of this change in my manners. The conversations I engaged in went on more pleasantly. The modest way in which I proposed my opinions procured them a readier reception and less contradiction; I had less mortification when I was found to be in the wrong, and I more easily prevailed with others to give up their mistakes and join with me when I happened to be in the right.[10]

During these years Franklin organized a self-improvement club, the Junto, which was to bring him numbers of helpful, life-long friendships and to broaden and deepen the intellectual interests of many future leaders of the city. In his superb biography of Franklin, Carl Van Doren, following the story of his subject's development from a brash youth to a great and gentle sage, pauses to analyze this period in Franklin's life:

No single thread of narrative can give a true account of Franklin's life during the years 1726–32, for he was leading three lives and—most of the time—something of a stealthy fourth, each distinct enough to call for a separate record and yet all of them closely involved in his total nature. There was his public life, beginning with his friendships in the club he organized in 1727, and continuing with larger and larger affairs as long as he lived. There was his inner life, which was at first much taken up with reflections on his own behaviour, and, after he had more or less settled that

Benjamin Franklin: Universal American

in his mind and habit, grew to an embracing curiosity about the whole moral and physical world. There was his life as workman and business man, which greatly occupied him and was to occupy him until, after twenty years in Philadelphia, he was able to retire from an activity he had never valued for itself. In time all three were to be fused in the spacious character of a sage in action, but in 1726–32 they were still distinct if not discrepant. Moving in the familiar, fallible world, he showed few signs of the inner life which ran incessantly through his studious days and nights, and from which his influence and charm rose to pour over Philadelphia.[11]

Before Franklin retired from active business, at the age of forty-two, he had expanded his influence to newspapers in other colonies, published *Poor Richard's Almanac*, become Postmaster of Philadelphia, and run a general store where he sold everything from ink powders, codfish, and scarlet cloth to lottery tickets and the unexpired time of indentured servants. He fathered an illegitimate son, whom he raised in his home and sponsored in a successful political career. He married the girl who had smiled as he came bedraggedly into Philadelphia. And he returned to New England to make amends with his dying brother by taking home James' ten-year-old son and training and equipping him as a printer.

Meanwhile, having come to terms with himself, Franklin directed his passion for improvement toward the needs of his fellow men. Science for its own sake was not his primary concern; abstract metaphysical speculation did not interest him. Focusing on the many difficulties of existence for most people of the eighteenth century and on the lack of social organization in the young colonies, Franklin turned his mature energies to the scientific investigations and the public services that would make life easier and fuller for all.

Because fire was a great hazard in those times, Franklin contrived the lightning rod and set up the first fire-protection and fire-insurance companies in the colonies. The drafty houses, so inadequately heated against the rigorous winters, turned his thoughts toward the invention of the Franklin stove, which made skillful use of physical principles to create and warm air currents. For defense against the marauding Indians and the French, Franklin organized a volunteer militia and personally supervised the establishment of a series of frontier fortresses. To Philadelphia he helped bring a hospital, a library, and a university, as well as paving, lights, and patrols for its streets. In the course of many years as an assemblyman, he made the interests of the people of Pennsylvania his own and represented them at the Albany Conference and in England.

Examining a portrait of the middle-aged Franklin of this period, when he was about to expand his sphere of interest to international diplomacy, Van Doren says:

Franklin had not yet grown to that look of benevolence, sometimes shy and always sage, which is familiar from his later likenesses. He was not in appearance unmistakably a philosopher. His eyes were open, full, and bold, the line of his mouth straight and even a little hard. His heavy chin was stubborn if not assertive. He still had the marks of the self-made man which he was, not yet refined to the ripe native genius which Europe took him for. He looked successful rather than superior.

In various respects he was the quintessence of provincial America. Born of the "middling people," he had emerged from his class without deserting it, and he never pretended or wanted to belong to the aristocracy. He had prospered along with many other men in Pennsylvania and in the other colonies. Though he talked about frugal living and was indifferent to hardships on his travels, he lived comfortably at home, liked rum punch and Madeira, and was on his way to gout. In his impulse toward intellectual pursuits he was not too much ahead of his society. There had been a dozen ambitious young tradesmen in his Junto, and enough men of learning in America to make up, however slowly, the American Philosophical Society.[12]

But the drive that set these organizations (and so many others) in motion was Franklin's. And this creative force continued to make Franklin a leader of the Enlightenment for more than three decades to come. As he went about the business of his nation in the courts of Europe, his mind was always questioning and exploring. He loved to concoct magic number squares; he created an instrument of musical glasses (which Marie Antoinette studied); he tangled with the problem of the common cold, experimented with the uses of oil on water, and studied ways in which English spelling might be improved so that each sound would have its own letter and each letter would represent only one sound. A hundred years before Europeans in general learned the advantages of wearing white in the tropics, Franklin made a simple but ingenious experiment.

"I took a number of little square pieces of broadcloth from a tailor's pattern card, of various colours. There were black, deep blue, lighter blue, green, purple, red, yellow, white, and other colours or shades of colours. I laid them all out upon the snow in a bright sunshiny morning. In a few

Benjamin Franklin: Universal American

hours the black, being warmed most by the sun, was sunk so low as to be below the stroke of the sun's rays; the dark blue almost as low, the lighter blue not quite so much as the dark, the other colours less as they were lighter; and the quite white remained on the surface of the snow, not having entered it at all."[13]

Perhaps the most compelling aspect of this versatile genius was his warm personal magnetism. Wherever he went (except among English Tories in the hour of revolution), he captivated and swayed men of every status. The letters that remain reflect the warm glow of his relationship with others. Van Doren cites these revealing letters generously. One, for instance, was to a young girl, whose parents' hospitality Franklin had enjoyed in England. He had given her a gray squirrel from Pennsylvania, and, when the pet died and the girl asked him to compose an epitaph for it, he wrote:

"I lament with you most sincerely the unfortunate end of poor Mungo [or Skugg, as they also called him]. Few squirrels were better accomplished; for he had had a good education, travelled far, and seen much of the world. As he had the honour of being, for his virtues, your favourite, he should not go, like common skuggs, without an elegy or an epitaph. Let us give him one in the monumental style and measure, which, being neither prose nor verse, is perhaps the properest for grief; since to use common language would look as if we were not affected, and to make rhymes would seem trifling in sorrow." He wrote her an epitaph which happily parodied the pompous style of many epitaphs in the grand style of contemporary graveyards. Then he reduced even that to a simile which has become proverbial. "You see, my dear Miss, how much more decent and proper this broken style is than if we were to say, by way of epitaph:

Here Skugg
Lies snug
As a bug
In a rug.

And yet there are people in the world of so little feeling as to think that this would be a good enough epitaph for poor Mungo."[14]

Thus warming the hearts of his many friends, probing the frontiers of knowledge, skillfully and patiently upholding the interests first of Pennsylvania and then of all the colonies in England, Franklin passed

Chapters from the American Experience

his middle years. And, once the Revolution had come, he turned all the force of his personality on the French court, adroitly seeking and securing vital financial, diplomatic, and military assistance.

Franklin's wit, his suave charm, his infinite tact, and genial tolerance enchanted the French and opened to him doors that remained closed to Americans less perceptive of the Gallic temperament. Now in his seventies, and sporting a fur cap and a new image as the homespun philosopher from the provinces, Franklin became overnight such a legend that his *bons mots* were on every tongue, and statuettes of him appeared in homes all over the country. Nevertheless, even Franklin had difficulty in charming funds from the nearly bankrupt French treasury. Van Doren describes the problems Franklin faced and the difference between his approach and that of his fellow diplomat, prickly John Adams. Listing the very substantial loans which Franklin had negotiated, the biographer says:

All these sums Franklin had to obtain from a ministry burdened with France's own war against England. He was not left to the exercise of his judgment as to when to apply for loans. Congress would authorize him to apply and then, without waiting to hear from him, would draw upon the funds which he had been told to apply for. "The drafts of the treasurer of the loans coming very fast upon me," Franklin wrote, "the anxiety I have suffered and the distress of mind lest I should not be able to pay them has for a long time been very great indeed. To apply again to this court for money for a particular purpose, which they have already over and over again provided for and furnished us, was extremely awkward." Congress, he thought, should dig more and beg less. France operated upon an annual budget, settled in advance, and the ministers disliked what Franklin called the "afterclap" demands made by Congress. [John Adam's blunt assertions that the French were acting solely from self interest were complicating negotiations] Franklin explained to the president of Congress. "Mr. Adams has given offence to the court here by some sentiments and expressions contained in several of his letters written to the Count de Vergennes [the French Foreign Minister]. He thinks, as he tells me himself, that America has been too free in expressions of gratitude to France; for that she is more obliged to us than we to her; and that we should show spirit in our applications. I apprehend that he mistakes his ground, and that this court is to be treated with decency and delicacy." Louis XVI, Franklin believed, took a pleasure in reflecting that he was benevolently aiding an oppressed people. "I think it right to increase this pleasure by our thankful acknowledgments, and that such an expression of gratitude is not only our duty but our interest.

Benjamin Franklin: Universal American

"M. Vergennes, who appears much offended, told me yesterday that he would enter into no further discussions with Mr. Adams, nor answer any more of his letters. It is my intention, while I stay here, to procure what advantages I can for our country, by endeavouring to please this court; and I wish I could prevent anything being said by our countrymen here that may have a contrary effect." Franklin knew well enough that France had her own interests and would look out for them. But so long as those interests were on the whole the same as America's, Franklin could see no reason why the allies should not conduct their diplomatic affairs with cosmopolitan good breeding.[15]

Franklin was a principal architect of the peace treaty that concluded the revolution on terms highly favorable to the United States, and he returned home to render his last great service as a delegate to the Constitutional Convention. Now, eighty-two years old and seriously ill, he attended the meetings regularly and brought the force of his tremendous prestige to bear in favor of federation and mutual accommodation.

Franklin's influence in the Convention was conciliatory, aimed rather at keeping the delegates in agreement than at leading them in a particular direction. His favourite legislative ideas—a single legislature, a plural executive, the non-payment of officers—were none of them adopted. His principal contribution was a compromise. Yet the most single-minded politicians could never long forget that there was a philosopher among them, incomparably able, when he chose, to speak with large wisdom, the pleasantest humour, and a happy grace. When he had more than a few words to say in the midst of debate he wrote out his speech in advance and, because standing was painful, had it read for him.

The final day of the Convention Franklin rose with a written speech which Wilson read. "I confess that there are several parts of this Constitution which I do not at present approve, but I am not sure I shall never approve them; for, having lived long, I have experienced many instances of being obliged by better information or fuller consideration to change opinions, even on important subjects, which I once thought right but found to be otherwise. It is therefore that the older I grow the more apt I am to doubt my own judgment and to pay attention to the judgment of others.

"I agree to this Constitution with all its faults, if they are such; because I think a general government necessary for us, and there is no form of government but what may be a blessing to the people if well administered; and believe farther that this is likely to be well administered for a course of years and can only end in despotism, as other forms have done before it, when the people shall become so corrupt as to need despotic government, being incapable of any other. Thus I consent, Sir, to this Constitution because I expect no better, and because I am not sure that it is not the best. The opinions I have had of its errors I sacrifice to the public good. On the whole, Sir, I cannot help expressing a wish that every member of the Convention who may still have objections to it would, with me, on this occasion doubt a little of his infallibility, and, to make manifest our unanimity, put his name to this instrument."[16]

On this fitting note, Franklin concluded his public service. For his last year he was confined quite closely to his bedroom. Still he maintained a lively interest in general affairs and in the welfare of a host of friends.

"The deafness you complain of," he wrote [to an old friend] on 17 February 1789, "gives me concern, as, if great, it must diminish considerably your pleasure in conversation. If moderate, you may remedy it easily and readily by putting your thumb and fingers behind your ear, pressing it outwards, and enlarging it, as it were, with the hollow of your hand. By an exact experiment I found that I could hear the tick of a watch at forty-five feet distance by this means, which was barely audible at twenty feet without it. The experiment was made at midnight when the house was still." But numerous friends came to see him, and he followed the course of the world in the newspapers with his old curiosity. "For my own personal ease," he wrote to Washington, "I should have died two years ago; but, though those years have been spent in excruciating pain, I am pleased that I have lived them, since they have brought me to see our present situation"—with the new government at last established and Washington at its head.

Pain seems to have had little effect on Franklin's memory or wit, and none on his cheerfulness. In his last summer, so emaciated from loss of appetite that, as he said, "little remains of me but a skeleton covered with a skin," Franklin wrote his sister Jane one of his most cheerful and charming letters to her. He was pleased to hear that she had not had a misunderstanding with a relative of theirs. "Indeed, if there had been any such, I should have concluded it was your fault; for I think our family were always subject to being a little miffy. By the way, is our relationship in Nantucket quite worn out? I have met with none from thence of late years who were disposed to be acquainted with me, except Captain Timothy Folger. They are wonderfully shy. But I admire their honest plainness of speech. About a year ago I invited two of them to dine with me. Their answer was that they would if they could not do better. I suppose they did better, for I never saw them afterwards, and so had no opportunity of showing my miff, if I had one."

Benjamin Franklin: Universal American

About the first of March [six weeks before his death] Franklin's pain ceased, and he wrote his famous letter to Ezra Stiles, president of Yale. "You desire to know something of my religion. It is the first time I have been questioned upon it. But I cannot take your curiosity amiss, and shall endeavour in a few words to gratify it. Here is my creed. I believe in one God, Creator of the universe. That He governs it by His providence. That He ought to be worshipped. That the most acceptable service we render Him is doing good to His other children. That the soul of man is immortal, and will be treated with justice in another life respecting its conduct in this. These I take to be the fundamental principles of all sound religion, and I regard them as you do in whatever sect I meet with them.

"As to Jesus of Nazareth, my opinion of whom you particularly desire, I think the system of morals and his religion, as he left them to us, the best the world ever saw or is likely to see; but I apprehend it has received various corrupt changes, and I have, with most of the present Dissenters in England, some doubts as to his divinity; though it is a question I do not dogmatize upon, having never studied it, and think it needless to busy myself with it now, when I expect soon an opportunity of knowing the truth with less trouble. I see no harm, however, in its being believed, if that belief has the good consequence, as probably it has, of making his doctrines more respected and better observed. I have ever let others enjoy their religious sentiments, without reflecting on them for those that appeared to me unsupportable and even absurd. All sects here, and we have a great variety, have experienced my good will in assisting them with subscriptions for building their new places of worship; and, as I never opposed any of their doctrines, I hope to go out of the world in peace with them all."[17]

Van Doren closes his biography of this many-sided, kindly genius with a fine tribute:

Franklin was not one of those men who owe their greatness merely to the opportunities of their times. In any age, in any place, Franklin would have been great. Mind and will, talent and art, strength and ease, wit and grace met in him as if nature had been lavish and happy when he was shaped. Nothing seems to have been left out except a passionate desire, as in most men of genius, to be all ruler, all soldier, all saint, all poet, all scholar, all some one gift or merit or success. Franklin's powers were from first to last in a flexible equilibrium. Even his genius could not specialize him. He moved through his world in a humorous mastery of it. He could not put so high a value as single-minded men put on the things they give their lives for. Possessions were not worth that much, nor achievements. Comfortable as Franklin's possessions and numerous as his achievements were, they were less than he was. Whoever learns about his deeds remembers longest the man who did them. And sometimes, with his marvellous range, in spite of his personal tang, he seems to have been more than any single man: a harmonious human multitude.[18]

125

Boston Tea Party, December 18, 1773

Engraving by D. Berger, 1784.
Courtesy Library of Congress.

12

John Adams,
Reluctant Revolutionary

Politics are an ordeal path among red hot ploughshares.
Who then would be a politician for the pleasure of running about
barefoot among them? Yet somebody must.
—John Adams[1]

The coach-and-four rolled southward over the road to Philadelphia. Behind its red silk curtains the occupants fell into a weary silence. It had been more than a fortnight since they left Boston (on August 10, 1774). They had been greeted and feted and sped on their way in triumphal splendor through the provinces of Massachusetts and Connecticut. It seemed to John Adams that the salutes of cannon, the ringing bells, the corteges of dignitaries, the solemnly cheering citizenry would all have been more fitting to a royal processional than to this journey of four Massachusetts delegates to the First Continental Congress.[2] Nevertheless, it had been most gratifying.

And yet, it had made the weight of responsibility almost unbearable. What, after all, did he and his three companions know of such broad affairs of state—of the techniques of communication at the inter-colonial level, of the differing and sometimes antagonistic trade interests that the various provinces would face in the event of a non-intercourse agreement against England? He had learned that Connecticut's concern lay with the West Indies trade, with whether a continental market could be found for the lumber and the "great quantities of provisions, cattle, and horses" she normally shipped to the Indies for rum, sugar, and molasses.[3] What specific dislocations to trade faced the other provinces, and how could adjustments be made to ease the problems of them all? Or would it prove impossible to agree on any effective measures? Would the Congress founder on the selfish interests and widely differing cultures of the colonies—go down in history as a miserable failure?

The men of Connecticut had assured him that "they would abide by whatever should be determined, even to a total stoppage of trade to Europe and the West Indies." Boston had "suffered persecution" and must be supported, they had said. But even here there had been those who maintained that a non-importation agreement would not be observed—that Congress did not have the "power to enforce obedience to their laws."[4]

In New York the atmosphere had, predictably, proved less enthusiastic. He had been taken to see the fort, had marveled at the streets ("vastly more regular and elegant than those in Boston") and the houses ("grand and neat," all painted, even the brick buildings), had climbed up into the new Dutch church steeple for the view, and had been entertained at "elegant" homes.[5] But his sensitive antennae had detected cause for alarm. There existed in New York ample prejudice against a stoppage of commerce with Britain. And there was obviously an old and solid wall of resentment against the religious and political views of New England. (Had not one been so indelicate as to mention Massachusetts' hanging of the Quakers—as if it had happened yesterday instead of a hundred years ago?) Furthermore, he had been authoritatively informed that a large group of New Yorkers feared that the "levelling spirit of the New England Colonies should propagate itself into New York" and that another powerful party had only been induced to agree to the Congress after assurances that no step beyond a "peaceful cessation of commerce" was contemplated.[6] Analyzing the various New York delegates to see which would wield the power, which would stand for united action, he had found one a "downright, straightforward man" but a blusterer, another "soft and sweet," and a third possessed of a "sly, surveying eye."[7] All in all, Adams concluded, he did not much care for New Yorkers:

> With all the opulence and splendor of this city, there is very little good breeding to be found. We have been treated with an assiduous respect, but I have not seen one real gentleman. At their entertainments there is no conversation that is agreeable. There is no modesty, no attention to one another. They talk very loud, very fast, and altogether. If they ask you a question, before you can utter three words of your answer, they will break out upon you again, and talk away.[8]

The Congress would be a ghastly failure—or at least he was "unequal to the business."[9] Why had he put himself in a position to be associated with the "levelling spirit of New England"? Why had he come off on such a futile errand, leaving Abigail to protect herself and the children as best she could from the Redcoats who swarmed over the Massachusetts countryside, and with the situation so tense that it was bound to explode at any moment? He had tried for so long to hold himself aloof from politics. As the red and yellow wheels of the coach rolled ever nearer the City of Brotherly Love, Adams calmed himself by going systematically over the course of events that had brought him there.

It had begun almost fourteen years ago, in early 1761—had begun with a small angry stirring as he listened to Otis' flaming speech against the Writs of Assistance. These search warrants, intended to help control smuggling, were couched in such general terms that any vengeful or ill-humored man might search his neighbor's or any other house at will, breaking locks and everything in his way. They were an invasion of man's castle, of his essential English liberties, and a violation of the constitution.[10] Listening to the arguments, the young lawyer had been deeply moved:

The views of the English government towards the colonies, and of the colonies towards the English government from the first of our history to that time appeared to me to have been directly in opposition to each other and were now, by the imprudence of administration, brought to a collision. A contest appeared to me to be opened, to which I could foresee no end, and which would render my life a burden, and property, industry, and everything insecure.[11]

But the mood had passed. Generally, his attitude at the time had been anything but revolutionary. At twenty-five he had completed a classically oriented education at Harvard, and he had since been supplementing his knowledge with voracious reading in the *belles lettres*, in political theory, and in the law. He had driven himself, had, on the whole, wasted little time, and had entertained ambitious hopes. If he rose late (eight o'clock) he chided himself: "Three and a half hours after sunrise is a sluggard's rising time. It is a stupid waste. Three and a half —one-seventh of the twenty-four—is thus spiritlessly dozed away. I shall never shine till some animating occasion calls forth all my powers."[12]

It had been his father's expectation that he go into the ministry, but he had come to dread the prospect of being confined to the traditional dogma, had chosen instead the less prestigious profession of the law. He had already begun to make a name for himself in his little practice in the village of Braintree. His thoughts were devoted to getting ahead

John Adams, Reluctant Revolutionary

and to raising his profession by outlawing "pettifoggers" and "dirty dabblers in the law" from practicing it.[13]

Further, he had developed a deep distrust of gullible and unthinking people and of demagogues who preyed on them. "An artful man," he recorded in his diary, "who has neither sense nor sentiment, may by gaining a little sway among the rabble of a town, multiply taverns and dram shops, and thereby secure the votes of taverner and of all. And the multiplication of taverns will make many who may be induced by flip and rum to vote for any man whatever."[14] Already he had no illusions about the perfectibility of man: "Vice and folly are so interwoven in all human affairs that they could not possibly be wholly separated from them without tearing and rending the whole system of human nature and state."[15]

By the spring of 1765, when news of the Stamp Act reached Boston, Adams was still reading deeply in the laws of ancient and medieval civilizations, had made "frequent additions" to his small farm in Braintree, was commuting to the court sessions in Boston, and had married the Reverend Mr. Smith's daughter, Abigail. He knew of the radical Caucus Club, which met in Tom Dawes' garret and controlled Boston politics—controlled it in a manner that confirmed Adams' cynicism about the political animal:

> There they smoke tobacco till you cannot see from one end of the garret to the other. There they drink flip, I suppose, and there they choose a moderator, who puts questions to the vote regularly; and selectmen, assessors, collectors, wardens, fire-wards, and representatives are regularly chosen before they are chosen in the town.[16]

Adams' own affiliation was not with the Caucus Club, but rather with the sedate Sodality, a small group of lawyers who spent their Thursday evenings studying abstruse legal problems and discussing the relative merits of the feudal system and Rousseau.

Into this quiet pool, as elsewhere in the colonies, the Stamp Act descended with disruptive violence. It "has raised and spread through the whole continent a spirit that will be recorded to our honor with all future generations," Adams wrote in his diary. "The people, even to the lowest ranks, have become more attentive to their liberties and more determined to defend them than they were ever known to be. Our presses have groaned, our pulpits have thundered, our legislatures have resolved, our towns have voted."[17] Parliament's bid to tax all colonial papers and documents had created an agitation that came close to revolution. In that agitation the hitherto circumspect Adams played a leading role.

"A man ought to be very cautious what kinds of fuel he throws into

a fire, when it is thus glowing in the community," Adams told himself.[18]
Still, he was determined to do his share in making the people "more
attentive to their liberties." Writing under the erudite title "Disserta-
tion on the Canon and Feudal Law," he discussed the rights and liberties of the colonies. Through that explosive August of 1765, in four
successive issues, the Boston *Gazette* printed Adams' learned attack on
arbitrary power. Man's natural rights, he said, were "antecedent to all
earthly government" and could not be "repealed or restrained by human laws." One of the great forces behind the "peopling" of America
had been a "love of universal liberty." Their forefathers had been determined to establish a government "more agreeable to the dignity of
human nature," and, knowing that nothing could preserve their posterity from the encroachments of tyranny except "knowledge diffused
generally through the whole body of the people," they had set up a
uniquely general system of education.

Yet, despite this superior education, they had been afraid to "examine the grounds" of their privileges—the extent to which they had an
"undisputable right to demand them against all the power and authority
on earth." There seemed (and the Stamp Act confirmed it) a direct and
formal design on foot to "enslave" all America. The common image of
a "mother country and children colonies" he found "extremely falla-
cious." "Are we not brethren and fellow subjects with those in Britain,"
he asked, adding significantly, "only under a somewhat different
method of legislation, and a totally different method of taxation?" The
pulpit, the bar, the colleges—"every sluice of knowledge"—should be
set "a-flowing with the doctrines and sentiments of liberty."[19]

On August 15 the figure of Stamp Officer Oliver was hanged in effigy,
his home broken into, his family terrorized. Adams' deep abhorrence of
mob violence was stirred. It was, he wrote, a "very atrocious violation
of the peace, and of dangerous tendency and consequence." As far as
anyone knew, Oliver had never done "anything to injure the people."
His brother-in-law, Lieutenant Governor Hutchinson, was a different
matter—a "very ambitious and avaricious" man, who had "grasped four
of the most important offices in the province into his own hands" and
had left open to question his loyalty to the people of Massachusetts.[20]
When, on August 26, Hutchinson's home was vandalized, no indignant
criticism of the act appeared in Adams' diary.

Adams was now asked to prepare a set of instructions for Braintree's
representative to the General Court. The instructions appeared in a
mid-October issue of the *Gazette*. The Stamp Act was unconstitutional;
Americans would "never be slaves," Adams proclaimed.[21] His reputation as a patriot leader spread across the province, and in Boston he was
chosen, together with two prominent lawyers, to present a petition
against the act to the governor.

John Adams, Reluctant Revolutionary

The following spring the Stamp Act was repealed, and life in Massachusetts returned briefly to normal. Adams' mind turned to peaceful pursuits. In 1767 the Townshend Acts went into effect, but for more than a year Adams refused to become embroiled in the resistance against them. Now in his thirties, he was very well known. He had been chosen a selectman in Braintree and could see that his career as a lawyer was assured. Eager for the wider opportunities available in Boston, he moved his home there early in 1768.

Almost at once he was offered the post of Advocate General in the Court of Admiralty. The office was considered a mark of royal favor—the open sesame to preferment. But Adams had already gone on record as an opponent of the autocratic Admiralty Courts. He refused the post, his answer politely implying the suspicion of bribery. He felt that the British government was "persevering in a system wholly inconsistent with" all his ideas of right and justice, and so he could not place himself in a situation in which his duty and his inclinations would be "so much at variance."[22] It had been, he thought in retrospect, a definite choice made, a Rubicon crossed. He had not yet openly associated himself with the people's party, but he had rejected the alternative path.

Still, he could not forever hang suspended between two courses. Sooner or later a final commitment must be made. "What is the end and purpose of my studies, journeys, labors?" he asked himself.

Am I grasping at money or scheming for power? Am I planning the illustration of my family or the welfare of my country? These are great questions. In truth, I am tossed so from post to pillar that I have not tranquillity enough to consider distinctly my feelings.

I am mostly intent, at present, upon collecting a library, and I find that a great deal of thought and care, as well as money, are necessary to assemble an ample and well chosen assortment of books. But, when this is done, it is only a means, an instrument. Fame, fortune, power, say some, are the ends intended by a library. The service of God, country, clients, fellow men, say others. Which of these lie nearest my heart?[23]

So Adams had come to think of the dangerous course of political criticism and opposition as the path of patriotism. With his Puritan conscience so clearly allied against it, how could the quiet pursuit of fortune long hold out against "duty"? Still he refused to become too openly tied to the popular cause: "I was solicited to go to the town meetings and harangue there. This I constantly refused. That way madness lies."[24]

During the summer of 1768, however, he was drawn obliquely into the patriot camp when the case of his client, John Hancock, developed into a *cause célèbre*. As a result of the tightening of customs enforcement under the Townshend Acts, Hancock's sloop, the *Liberty,* had been seized by the Board of Customs Commissioners. The resentful populace retaliated by assaulting the persons and property of the commissioners, who, in turn, responded by calling for military support. Early in the fall two regiments of British troops descended upon the rebellious town. Adams took a forceful public stand against their presence and voiced his personal irritation and his forebodings in his diary:

Through the whole succeeding fall and winter, a regiment was exercised directly in front of my house. The spirit-stirring drum and the ear-piercing fife aroused me and my family early enough every morning, and the indignation they excited, though somewhat soothed, was not allayed by the sweet songs, violins and flutes, of the serenading Sons of Liberty under my windows in the evening.

My daily reflections at the sight of those soldiers before my door were serious enough. Their very appearance in Boston was a strong proof to me that the determination in Great Britain to subjugate us was too deep and inveterate ever to be altered by us; for everything we could do was misrepresented, and nothing we could say was credited. On the other hand, I had read enough in history to be well aware of the extravagances of which the populaces of cities were capable when artfully excited to passion, even when justly provoked by oppression.[25]

On the evening of March 5, 1770, the eruption that Adams had anticipated occurred. At about nine o'clock he and other members of the Sodality were interrupted in their discussion by the ringing of alarm bells. Hurrying into the street, they were told that British soldiers had "fired on the inhabitants."[26] Adams hastened home to be with his wife and to ponder whether the crisis had not been "intentionally wrought up by designing men" and whether it would not be better "for the whole people to rise in their majesty and insist on the removal of the army and take upon themselves the consequences than to excite such passions between the people and the soldiers."[27]

After entertaining these seditious thoughts, Adams proceeded next morning to agree to help defend the British captain involved in this "Boston Massacre." A "great clamor" arose at his decision.[28] Adams explained that the captain could get no counsel (for Crown lawyers were afraid to handle the case) and that any man was entitled to a defense. It soon became evident that, among freeholders at least, Adams' prestige had not suffered, for, in the midst of the agitation, he was nominated and elected as a Boston representative to the General Court. Now at last he was thrust into a position where his political views would be constantly before the public. Furthermore, in those troubled times the post was virtually a full-time occupation. He received the news grimly:

I had never been at a Boston town meeting and was not at this one until messengers were sent to inform me that I was chosen. I went down to Faneuil Hall and in a few words expressive of my sense of the difficulty of the times, the importance of the trust, and my own insufficiency to fulfill the expectations of the people, I accepted the choice. Many congratulations were offered, but they gave no joy to me. I considered the step as a devotion of my family to ruin, and myself to death.[29]

At the very least he seemed to be throwing away a promising career. After performing "endless labor" and rising in his profession until he had "more business at the bar than any man in the province," he stood to lose it all—and that for nothing, except what was in the last analysis everything: his sense of duty. The legislative session that followed was "fatiguing." Adams served as legal adviser to the "Boston seat," the most powerful delegation in the General Court.[30]

By the following spring (1771) Adams had convinced himself that the "air of the town of Boston" was not favorable to him and that the "constant obligations to speak in public" had "exhausted" his health. He retired to Braintree, his "native spot, with the fine breezes from the sea on one side and the rocky mountains of pine and savin on the other." "Calm, happy Braintree," he rhapsodized. "I shall have no more General Court to attend, but shall divide my time between Boston and Braintree, between law and husbandry. Farewell, politics."[31] The Townshend Acts (with the single exception of the tea tax) had been repealed. The continent settled down to a last interlude of general acquiescence to British rule.

But Adams could not take off his political garments; they had become a part of him. He spent many pleasant evenings discussing "the state of affairs" at the home of cousin Sam Adams (Sam who had devoted his life to the art of fomenting revolution).[32] And he spent many unpleasant moments fuming at Britain and at the unbounded ambition of Governor Hutchinson. Once he burst out that there was "no more justice left in Britain than there was in hell" and that he wished for war.[33] Going home that night, he chastised himself:

I cannot but reflect upon myself with severity for these rash, inexperienced, boyish, raw, and awkward expressions. A man who has no better command over his tongue and temper is unfit for everything but children's play. Such flights of passion, such starts of imagination, though they may strike a few of the fiery and inconsiderate, yet they lower, they sink a man with the wise. They expose him to danger, as well as familiarity, contempt, and ridicule.[34]

By the beginning of 1773 Adams was beginning to hope he had

things on an even keel. He greeted the New Year with unaccustomed optimism:

> I never was happier in my whole life. I feel easy and composed and contented. The year to come will be a pleasant, a cheerful, a happy and a prosperous year to me. My resolutions to devote myself to the pleasures, the studies, and the duties of private life, are a source of comfort to me that I scarcely ever experienced before. Peace, be still, my once anxious heart.[35]

Before the month of January was out, that peace was shattered, and by March he was writing, "I have never known a period in which the seeds of great events have been so plentifully sown."[36]

First came the announcement that Lord North had decided to "reform" the courts of Massachusetts: henceforth her judges were to receive their pay from the Crown. This move to make the justices virtually independent of the province brought Adams out of his "retirement." In a series of ponderous letters to the *Gazette* he expatiated on the traditional dependence of English justices upon funds voted at regular intervals by the legislators.[37] Sam Adams' prompt suggestion that "Committees of Correspondence" be formed to air grievances was taken up, and letters expressing the general anger at the Crown's action began to circulate across Massachusetts. An embryonic network of government, independent of Britain, had come into being. Soon there would issue from the Virginia House of Burgesses the suggestion that the Committees of Correspondence be made intercolonial.

In the midst of Adams' series of letters, Governor Hutchinson decided to come to the defense of the mother country by laying before the House all the reasons why Parliament might make laws for the colonies and impose on them any taxes that it saw fit. "No line can be drawn between the supreme authority of Parliament and the total independence of the colonies," he told the representatives.[38] In one inept move he had ripped off the binding that moderates had long been applying to the wound. The governor himself had admitted it. There was no middle stand—the alternatives were total subservience to Parliament or total independence. "I stand amazed," said Adams, "that the Governor should have forced this controversy." His reasoning, he observed with pleasure, "instead of convincing the people that Parliament had sovereign authority over them in all cases whatsoever, seemed to convince all the world that Parliament had no authority over them in any case whatsoever."[39]

A legislative committee set to work drafting a reply, laboring over it with a full sense of its significance. The vital issue had been broached by the opposition; they would make the most of it. The draft was brought to Adams for revision. He found it, he recalled later, "full of those elementary principles of liberty, equality and fraternity which have since made such a figure in the world—principles which are founded in nature and eternal unchangeable truth, but which must be well understood and cautiously applied. There was no answer nor attempt to answer the Governor's legal and constitutional arguments, such as they were."[40] Adams wrestled with himself briefly. If he joined in the challenge to the Governor in this essential matter, he would irrevocably be embroiled in the political turmoil.

Can I describe to you [he wrote a friend] the state of my mind at that time? I had a wife—and what a wife! I had children—and what children! In this situation I should have thought myself the happiest man in the world if I could have retired to my little hut and forty acres which my father left me in Braintree and lived on potatoes and sea-weed for the rest of my life. [!] But I had taken a part, I had adopted a system, I had encouraged my fellow-citizens, and I could not abandon them in conscience nor in honor.[41]

He sat down with the committee, discussed the reply paragraph by paragraph, "modestly suggested the expediency of leaving out many of those popular and eloquent periods," and "introduced those legal and historical authorities which appear on the record" (including the assertion that no precedent existed which precluded the coexistence of two legislatures within one empire).[42]

As he feared, he was elected in May to the important post of councilman. When Governor Hutchinson refused to confirm him because of the "conspicuous part" he had been taking in the opposition, Adams replied that he was proud to have Hutchinson's veto.[43]

Early in the summer, through the offices of Benjamin Franklin, a packet of valuable letters came into the dextrous hands of Sam Adams —letters written by Governor Hutchinson to friends in England, in which he advocated an "abridgment of what are called English liberties" in the provinces. Hutchinson's career was virtually at an end. John Adams joined in the attack. The changes Hutchinson favored would, he said, be the ruin "not only of the colonies, but of the empire."[44]

But the most crucial blunder of all in that fateful year of 1773 came when Parliament granted to the East India Company a monopoly over the American colonies for the marketing of all tea. Suspecting that this act represented the first step toward a complete monopoly of their trade, colonial merchants came over in a body to the side of the patriots. Consignees of the tea in New York and Philadelphia agreed not to accept the shipments when they arrived, but those in Boston refused to cooperate, despite threats of tar and feathers.* Everyone waited

*These consignees were the sons of Governor Hutchinson. The tea crisis so impaired

tensely for the "bainfull weed" (as Abigail Adams called it) to arrive. In December three ships laden with choice Bohea tea sailed into Boston port. "The flame is kindled and like lightning it catches from Soul to Soul," said Abigail.[45] With the patriots refusing to allow the tea ashore and the governor determined not to give it clearance to return to England, tensions mounted. Then, on the night of December 16, several hundred "Mohawks" descended upon the ships and dumped their cargoes into the harbor.

Adams' reaction was immediate and decisive. Here was no cry against the tyranny of the mob or the destruction of property, but a shout of glee worthy of his cousin, Sam. "The die is cast," he said. "The people have passed the river and cut away the bridge."[46]

Last night, three cargoes of Bohea tea were emptied into the sea. This is the most magnificent movement of all. There is a dignity, a majesty, a sublimity, in this latest effort of the patriots, that I greatly admire. The people should never rise without doing something to be remembered. This destruction of the tea is so bold, so daring, so intrepid, and it must have so important consequences that I cannot but consider it as an epoch in history.

This, however, is but an attack upon property. Another similar exertion of popular power may produce the destruction of lives. Many persons wish that as many dead carcasses were floating in the harbor as there are chests of tea. A much smaller number of lives, however, would remove the causes of all our calamities.

What measures will the Ministry take in consequence of this? Will they dare to resent it? Will they punish us? How? By quartering troops upon us? by annulling our charter? by laying on more duties? by restraining our trade? by sacrifice of individuals? or how?[47]

When Parliament's answer came, it was clearly all that Adams had anticipated and more. The Port of Boston was to be closed until such time as the recalcitrant province agreed to pay for the tea that had been destroyed. Judges and councilmen were to be appointed by the governor, and jurors by the sheriffs. Town meetings could be held only under the supervision of the governor. A military governor (General Gage) was appointed and given power to quarter soldiers in occupied dwellings. Persons involved in incendiary activity might be transported out of the province (to England or elsewhere, at the governor's discretion) for trial.

Boston responded to these "Intolerable Acts" with spirit. In the brief

---

Hutchinson's status that he shortly retired to England and to permanent exile from his native land.

time that remained before her punishment was to take effect, she charted a firm course of resistance. The *Gazette* published the terms of

Parliament's decree, and beside them it printed the call "Britons arise! And know you have the virtue to be mov'd."[48] From the Committee of Correspondence went out a plea for united colonial action in an embargo against England. The legislature convened hastily in the town of Salem and heard Sam Adams place a motion that a General Congress be called to meet at Philadelphia and discuss a common course of action for the protection of colonial liberties. While a Tory member rushed to the governor with news of the rebellious meeting, the assemblage passed the motion, named the delegates, and began to consider the financing of the journey. A messenger arrived and began pounding on the locked doors. Getting no response, he shouted out the governor's proclamation that the meeting was dissolved.[49] The men within continued their discussion, voted 500 pounds for the delegates' expenses, and then adjourned. No Massachusetts legislature would ever again be convened by the King of England.

"There is a new and a grand scene open before me," Adams wrote when he was notified of his appointment as a delegate. "This Congress will be an assembly of the wisest men upon the continent, who are Americans in principle, that is against the taxation of Americans by authority of Parliament."[50]

So it had come about, thought Adams, as the coach neared Philadelphia. So he had come to be "American in principle"—to feel that American liberties must be defended at all costs.

Numerous "carriages and gentlemen" came out from the city to meet them, and the education of John Adams began anew—again a maze of personalities to be assessed; again the strong forces of conservatism and the deep suspicion toward New England to be combatted.[51] "We have had numberless prejudices to remove here," Adams wrote as the session "spun out" interminably. "We have been obliged to act with great caution, to keep ourselves out of sight, to feel pulses and sound depths, to insinuate our sentiments and designs by means of other persons, sometimes of one province and sometimes of another."[52]

Often Adams despaired of their ever reaching an accord. The "diversity of religions, educations, manners, interests" made it seem "almost impossible to unite in one plan of conduct," he wrote disconsolately.[53] But from the start there were strong allies in the cause. I am "not a Virginian, but an American," affirmed Patrick Henry.[54] Richard Henry Lee urged a resolution demanding the repeal of the Intolerable Acts. And Washington, Adams was told, had sworn to raise and equip a thousand men and "march at their head for the relief of

Boston" if necessary.[55] The "gentlemen from Virginia," Adams decided, were especially "spirited and consistent."[56]

When the delegates went home in November, it was with a substantial list of accomplishments to their credit: a boycott declared, an Association formed to enforce it, and a call issued to the separate colonies to form their own militias and establish their own legislatures. And they had decided to reconvene the following year to consider the shape of things.

By the time the Second Continental Congress met in the fall of 1775, Lexington and Concord had hardened colonial resistance, and the delegations were somewhat less conservative—their tone more to Adams' liking. But still the delegates "nibbled and quibbled" and "spun out" their debates.[57] Reading in each dispatch from home how his family in Braintree lay under constant threat from British raiders, how ragged and ill-equipped patriot soldiers passed through the town, and how refugees, miserable "beyond the power of language to describe," streamed out of Boston, Adams chafed at the delay, thinking relief would never come.[58] He threw himself into the struggle obsessively, became known as the workhorse of the Congress. He was out in the open now, advocating a well-defined and radical program "publicly and privately, without reserve." Congress should urge Americans everywhere to seize all Crown officials and hold them as hostages for the people of Boston, and it should declare the colonies "free, sovereign, and independent states."[59]

As the months went by, the British—blockading, harassing, propagandizing—continued to drive increasing numbers of colonists to the belief that the alternatives were total subjection or complete independence. Finally, on July 4, 1776, came the long-sought agreement, the declaration that it had, in the course of human events, become necessary to dissolve the political bands that had tied them to England—that, in fact, the "good people" of the "United States of America" were "free and independent."

Like the nation he had helped midwife, Adams had come a long way from the provincialism of two years before. Observing the "immensity of time" spent unnecessarily while the "refined geniuses" of whom he had stood in such awe displayed their "wit, sense, learning, acuteness, subtlety, eloquence, &c.,"[60] and realizing that he himself had contributed so outstandingly to the final result, Adams had concluded that he too had much to offer to the making of these new United States. It would be many tormented years before he could return to Braintree. He had been called to the "ordeal path among red hot ploughshares."

Lithograph by P. Haas, 1843. Courtesy Library of Congress.

13

Mosaic of Freedom

Yet think not thirst of glory unsheaths our vengeful swords
To rend your bands asunder and cast away your cords.
'Tis Heaven-born Freedom fires us all and strengthens each brave son,
From him who humbly guides the plough to god-like Washington!
—Anonymous song[1]

In the fall of 1777 a Philadelphia minister wrote to General Washington urging him to reconsider his course and lead the colonies back to Britain. No one of any substance was left in Congress, he said, and the army was a mob of the "lowest of the people, without principle and without courage."[2] He begged Washington to lay down arms and concede that the Declaration of Independence had been hasty and ill advised. If Washington would only do this, he predicted, thousands who had prayed for such a step would declare their loyalty to England.

Furthermore, the Loyalists were not alone in undermining the Revolution. Profiteering (even among statesmen and officers of the rebellion) was so flagrant that Washington advocated "hunting down" these "murderers" of the cause.[3] The Governor of New Jersey charged that American officers were trafficking with the enemy:

. . . [Constant] communication and commercial intercourse has for a considerable time past been [going on] . . . supported by means of flaggs and passports obtained from divers officers of the Army. . . . Under colour of their flaggs . . . [persons] of dubious political characters . . . have been sent over; provisions for the aid and comfort of the British troops furnished; a pernicious and unlawful traffic carried on; the little specie left among us collected with the greatest avidity to maintain this execrable trade; and the

Continental currency by that means further depreciated; opportunities afforded the enemy for circulating their counterfeit bills, and the disaffected of conveying to them intelligence of every movement and designed operation of our troops; the confidence of the people in the integrity of our officers diminished, and a universal murmuring excited among the friends of the common cause.[4]

Inflation skyrocketed to such heights that a pint of rum cost 1,200 paper dollars. Cavalry hero Allen McLane wrote in his journal: "The labouring part of the City [Philadelphia] . . . [is] desperate from the high price of the necessaries of life."[5] So precarious was the financial situation of the revolution makers that, when a messenger brought news to the Continental Congress of the British capitulation in the final Battle of Yorktown, there was not enough "hard money" in the Treasury to pay his expenses, and each member of Congress contributed one dollar to cover the deficit.[6]

Yet, despite the internal conflicts, the disorganization, and the desperate financing, the Revolution *was* won. It was won in part in the diplomatic halls of France and the garrets of the Sons of Liberty. It was won by the masses of determined patriot troops (too generally armed and too widely dispersed for the professional armies of Britain to subdue) and by individual acts of courage and inspirational leadership.[7] From two fine collections of Revolutionary writings that record this "Spirit of '76" comes the following reading, demonstrative of the mood that stirred the young nation to victory.

The quiet heroism of American spy Nathan Hale inspired his fellow rebels and became a legend. In the following account a patriot officer tells how the news of Hale's martyrdom first reached the Americans.

[A British] officer came to our camp, under a flag of truce. . . . He said that Captain Hale had passed through their army, both of Long Island and York Island. That he had procured sketches of the fortifications, and made memoranda of their number and different positions. When apprehended, he was taken before Sir William Howe, and these papers, found concealed about his person, betrayed his intentions. He at once declared his name, his rank in the American army, and his object in coming within the British lines. Sir William Howe, without the form of a trial, gave orders for his execution the following morning. . . .

"On the morning of his execution," continued the officer, "my station was near the fatal spot, and I requested the Provost Marshal to permit the prisoner to sit in my marquee, while he was making the necessary preparations. Captain Hale entered: he was calm, and bore himself with gentle dignity, in the consciousness of rectitude and high intentions. He asked for writing materials, which I furnished him." . . . He was shortly after summoned to the gallows. But a few persons were around him, yet his characteristic dying words were remembered. He said, "I only regret that I have but one life to lose for my country."[8]

Another Revolutionary legend was Molly Hays, a Pennsylvania Dutch girl who brought so many pitchers of water to the thirsty soldiers at the Battle of Monmouth that they called her "Molly Pitcher." Molly took up the station of her wounded husband, and manned his cannon under fire, thus earning a place in American lore. The following little episode, recorded by an admiring soldier, points up the spirit that won the Revolution.

While . . . reaching a cartridge and having one of her feet as far before the other as she could step, a cannon shot from the enemy passed directly between her legs without doing any other damage than carrying away all the lower part of her petticoat. Looking at it with apparent unconcern, she observed that it was lucky it did not pass a little higher, for in that case it might have carried away something else.[9]

No period in the American Revolution more completely exemplifies the Spirit of '76 than the winter at Valley Forge. The sufferings and the fortitude of that dreary winter are starkly portrayed in the personal letters of the men who endured it. The journal of an army surgeon describes the hardships entailed in setting up the winter quarters: the cold, the hunger, the disaffection, and the dying.

Dec. 12th [1777]—A bridge of wagons made across the Schuylkill last night, consisting of 36 wagons, with a bridge of rails between each. Some skirmishing down the river. Sun set—We are ordered to march over the river—it snows—I'm sick—eat nothing—no whiskey—no baggage—Lord—Lord—Lord. The army were till sunrise crossing the river.

Dec. 14th—Prisoners & deserters are continually coming in. The Army, who have been surprisingly healthy hitherto, now begin to grow very sickly from the continued fatigues they have suffered this campaign. Yet they still show a spirit of alacrity & contentment not to be expected from so young troops.

There comes a soldier—his bare feet are seen thro' his worn out shoes —his legs nearly naked from the tatt'red remains of an only pair of stockings—his breeches not sufficient to cover his nakedness—his shirt hanging in strings—his hair dishevell'd—his face meagre—his whole appearance pictures a person forsaken & discouraged. He comes and cries with an air of wretchedness & despair.

Mosaic of Freedom

Dec. 21st—A general cry thro' the camp this evening—"No meat! No meat!" What have you for dinner, boys? "Nothing but fire cake & water, Sir."

Dec. 22nd—What have you got for breakfast, lads? "Fire cake and water, Sir." I am ashamed to say it, but I am tempted to steal fowls if I could find them—or even a whole hog—for I feel as if I could eat one. But the impoverish'd country about us affords but little matter to employ a thief. At 12 of the clock at night, Providence sent us a little mutton—with which we immediately had some broth made & a fine stomach for same. Ye who eat pumpkin pie and roast turkies—and yet curse fortune for using you ill —curse her no more.

Dec. 25th, Christmas—We are still in tents—when we ought to be in huts—the poor sick suffer much in tents this cold weather.

Dec. 28th—Yesterday, upwards of fifty officers in General Green's Division resigned their commissions—six or seven of our regiment are doing the like today. All this is occasion'd by officers' families being so much neglected at home on account of provisions. When the officer has been fatiguing through the wet & cold and returns to his tent where he finds a letter directed to him from his wife, fill'd with the most heart-aching, tender complaints a woman is capable of writing, acquainting him with the incredible difficulty with which she procures a little bread for herself & children [he cannot but listen as] she begs him to consider that charity begins at home.

Sunday, Jan. 4th [1778]—I was called to relieve a soldier tho't to be dying—he expir'd before I reach'd the hut. He was an Indian—an excellent soldier—and an obedient good natur'd fellow. He engaged for money doubtless as others do—but he has serv'd his country faithfully. What a frail, dying creature is man.[10]

Like all wars, the American Revolution yielded its quota of humor in the midst of suffering. A private wryly recorded the drastic measures he and his fellows took to rid themselves of a common camp scourge—the itch:

When I was inoculated with the smallpox, I took that delectable disease, the itch. It was given us, we supposed, in the infection. We had no opportunity, or at least we had nothing to cure ourselves with during the whole season. I had it to such a degree that by the time I got into winter quarters I could scarcely lift my hands to my head. Some of our foraging party had acquaintances in the artillery, and by their means we procured [some] sulphur. Accordingly, we made preparations for the general attack upon it.

We commenced the action by mixing a sufficient quantity of brimstone and tallow, which was the only grease we could get, at the same time not forgetting to mix a plenty of hot whiskey toddy, making up a hot blazing fire and laying down an oxhide upon the hearth. Thus prepared with arms and ammunition, we began the operation by plying each other's outsides with brimstone and tallow and the inside with hot whiskey sling. Had the animalcule of the itch been endowed with reason, they would have quit their entrenchments and taken care of themselves when we made such a formidable attack upon them; but as it was, we had to engage, arms in hand, and we obtained a complete victory, though it like to have cost some of us our lives. Two of the assailants were so overcome, not by the enemy, but by their too great exertions in the action, that they lay all night naked upon the field. The rest of us got to our berths somehow, as well as we could; but we killed the itch and we were satisfied. This was a decisive victory, the only one we had achieved lately.[11]

In February the Baron von Steuben arrived and set about making soldiers out of the ragged rebels. Beginning at six o'clock each morning, the men were drilled and instructed in the use of firearms. Evenings the officers received instruction in maneuvers and techniques of command. By May, when word reached the camp of the alliance between France and the United States, the army was prepared to greet it in appropriate style.

After the Chaplains had finished their discourses, and the cannon was fired, the troops began their march. Each Major General conducted the first brigade of his company to the ground; the other brigades were conducted to their commanding officers in separate columns. But this arrangement can convey no adequate idea of their movements to their several posts—of the appearance of his Excellency, during his circuit around the lines—of the air of his soldiers—the cleanliness of their dress—the brilliancy and the good order of their arms, and the remarkable animation with which they performed the necessary salutes as the General passed along. Indeed, during the whole of the review the utmost military decorum was present. The French gentlemen of rank and distinction seemed peculiarly pleased with this public approbation of our alliance with their nation. The General himself wore a countenance of uncommon delight and complacence.[12]

Washington's complacency was understandable, for these soldiers, who had endured so well the travail of Valley Forge, were in the fullest sense "his." The adulation with which his men followed him and the deep respect accorded him by his contemporaries are evident in their writings. Typically, an aide to the French commander Rochambeau described him as "the most illustrious man of our century," adding:

Mosaic of Freedom

His majestic, handsome countenance is stamped with an honesty and a gentleness which correspond well with his moral qualities. He looks like a hero; he is very cold, speaks little, but is frank and courteous in manner; a tinge of melancholy renders him, if possible, more interesting.[13]

A sergeant under Washington at Princeton wrote:

Three or four days after the victory at Trenton, the American army recrossed the Delaware into New Jersey. At this time our troops were in a destitute and deplorable condition. The horses attached to our cannon were without shoes, and when passing over the ice they would slide in every direction and could advance only by the assistance of the soldiers. Our men, too, were without shoes or other comfortable clothing; and as traces of our march towards Princeton, the ground was literally marked with the blood of the soldiers' feet. . . . While we were at Trenton . . . the time for which I and most of my regiment had enlisted expired. At this trying time General Washington, having now but a little handful of men and many of them new recruits in which he could place but little confidence, ordered our regiment to be paraded, and personally addressed us, urging that we should stay a month longer. He alluded to our recent victory at Trenton; told us that our services were greatly needed, and that we could now do more for our country than we ever could at any future period; and in the most affectionate manner entreated us to stay. . . . A few stepped forth, and their example was immediately followed by nearly all who were fit for duty. . . .

Leaving our fires kindled to deceive the enemy, we decamped that night and by a circuitous route took up our line of march for Princeton. . . . As we were descending a hill through an orchard, a party of the enemy who were entrenched behind a bank and fence rose and fired upon us. Their first shot passed over our heads. . . . Our fire was most destructive; their ranks grew thin and the victory seemed nearly complete when the British were reinforced. Many of our brave men had fallen, and we were unable to withstand such superior numbers of fresh troops.

I soon heard Gen. Mercer command in a tone of distress, "Retreat!" He was mortally wounded and died shortly after. I looked about for the main body of the army which I could not discover, discharged my musket at part of the enemy, and ran for a piece of wood at a little distance where I thought I might shelter. At this moment Washington appeared in front of the American army, riding towards those of us who were retreating, and exclaimed, "Parade with us, my brave fellows! There is but a handful of the enemy, and we will have them directly." I immediately joined the main body, and marched over the ground again.

. . . The British were unable to resist this attack, and retreated into the

College, where they thought themselves safe. Our army was there in an instant, and cannon were planted before the door, and after two or three discharges a white flag appeared at the window, and the British surrendered.[14]

If veneration for General Washington was one great force for victory in the Revolution, another was the enthusiastic cooperation of French leaders such as Lafayette. The story of the events leading to the final, decisive Battle of Yorktown, as told in the letters of the time, indicates the crucial contribution the French made to the defeat of the British. In January, 1781, Lafayette wrote home to French Foreign Minister Vergennes, pleading for strong naval support:

With a naval inferiority it is impossible to make war in America. It is that which prevents us from attacking any point that might be carried with two or three thousand men. It is that which reduces us to defensive operations, as dangerous as they are humiliating. The English are conscious of this truth, and all their movements prove how much they desire to retain the empire of the sea.

Since the hour of the arrival of the French, their inferiority has never for one moment ceased, and the English and the Tories have dared to say that France wished to kindle, without extinguishing, the flame. This calumny becomes more dangerous at a period when the English detachments are wasting the South; when, under the protection of some frigates, corps of fifteen hundred men are repairing to Virginia without our being able to get to them. . . .

The result sir, of all this is that . . . it becomes, in a political and military point of view, necessary to give us, both by vessels sent from France and by a great movement in the fleet in the islands, a decided naval superiority for the next campaign.[15]

Within a few months a powerful fleet under the command of the Comte de Grasse set sail for the West Indies with instructions to cooperate with the allied armies. In May the Comte de Rochambeau and Washington concerted a plan for a combined attack (supported by the French fleet) on the British stronghold at New York. Washington wrote to Lafayette in Virginia detailing the project and inviting him to participate. This strategic letter was intercepted. The British commander (Clinton) was now convinced that the offensive would come against New York. Meanwhile, from the South, Lafayette wrote Washington urging that he shift his assault to Lord Cornwallis at Yorktown, Virginia. Preliminary skirmishes around New York made it clear that the British were preparing a stiff defense there. De Grasse sent word that it would be necessary for him to return to the West Indies in two months and that he was sailing to the Chesapeake. Furthermore, the northern colonies were failing to furnish the quotas of men needed for the New York plan. Faced with all these deterrents, Washington began to consider a move against Yorktown instead. Once he had made the decision, the plans were carried out with meticulous secrecy, though speculation was rife. An army doctor wrote in his journal:

[Aug. 15, 1781]—General orders are now issued for the army to prepare for a movement at a moment's notice. The real object of the allied armies in the present campaign has become a subject of much speculation. Ostensibly an investment of the city of New York is in contemplation —preparations in all quarters for some months past indicate this to be the object of our combined operations. The capture of this place would be a decisive stroke . . . [but] New York is well fortified both by land and water and garrisoned by the best troops of Great Britain. . . .

General Washington and Count Rochambeau have crossed the North River, and it is supposed for the purpose of reconnoitering the enemy's posts from the Jersey shore. A field for an extensive encampment has been marked out on the Jersey side, and a number of ovens have been erected and fuel provided for the purpose of baking bread for the army. From these combined circumstances we are led to conclude that a part of our besieging force is to occupy that ground. But General Washington possesses a capacious mind, full of resources, and he resolves and matures his great plans and designs under an impenetrable veil of secrecy. . . .

22nd.—Resumed our line of march. . . . We have now passed all the enemy's posts and are pursuing our route with increasing rapidity toward Philadelphia; wagons have been prepared to carry the soldiers' packs, that they may press forward with greater facility. Our destination can no longer be a secret. The British army under Lord Cornwallis is unquestionably the object of our present expedition. . . . The deception has proved completely successful; a part of Cornwallis' troops are reported to have returned to New York. His Excellency General Washington, having succeeded in a masterly piece of *generalship*, has now the satisfaction of leaving his adversary to ruminate on . . . the perilous fate which awaits his friend Lord Cornwallis.[16]

Rushing southward, Washington sent word ahead to Lafayette on September 2 that he was worried because the French fleet had not yet made an appearance:

. . . [My] dear Marquis, I am distressed beyond expression, to know what is become of the Count de Grasse, and for fear the English Fleet, by occupying the Chesapeake (towards which my last accounts say they were steering) should frustrate all our flattering prospects in that quarter.[17]

Washington need not have worried. For once the synchronization of forces was exemplary. By the time the allied armies arrived, the French fleet was in the harbor. A colonel of the Virginia militia wrote jubilantly to his wife on September 5:

Hear then . . . from me what perhaps you have not heard yet from good authority. About the middle of last week twenty-nine ships of the line and four frigates arrived in our bay, with four thousand land forces sent to our assistance by Louis the Great. Besides these there are three thousand marines to be landed in case of an emergency. . . .

Our troops lie from four miles beyond this town to near James Town; so that Cornwallis is . . . effectually hemmed in . . . Nor is this all, for, to my great surprise and pleasure, I was this morning informed from undoubted authority that General Washington is at the Head of Elk with five thousand troops. . . .

If after such a torrent of good news I could wish to add another article, it would be that Lord Cornwallis, with his whole army, were in our possession. But this I hope . . . will be the subject of some future letter.[18]

Within a matter of days De Grasse drove off an English rescue fleet and sealed the harbor. It remained only to tighten the noose. Virginia General Weedon wrote delightedly to General Greene: "The business with his Lordship in this State will very soon be at an end, for suppose you know e'er this that we have got him handsomely in a pudding bag."[19]

Blocked from escape by sea, pressed back on all flanks by converging siege lines of the allies, Cornwallis surrendered in October, 1781. With that defeat the war came essentially to a close, although peacemaking dragged on for nearly two years. The leaders of the young nation now turned their thoughts to winning the peace. Writing to Lafayette in 1783, Washington voiced the challenge that faced the victorious rebels:

We are placed among the nations of the earth . . . and have a character to establish, but how we shall acquit ourselves time must discover.[20]

The Celebration in New York City Following the Ratification of the Federal Constitution on July 26, 1788

14

E Pluribus Unum

'Tis done. We have become a nation.

When the founding fathers inscribed their names to the Constitution at the close of the great Convention, they handed down to the separate states a momentous obligation. With those thirteen states now rested the final decision as to the shape of the new nation. The proposed Constitution would create a government very different from what they had known or expected. If they were to accept this new charter of unification, they would first have to overcome local prejudices and suspicions as deep as their long separate traditions and as old as their colonial past. They would be called upon to fly a new flag above the old and to entrust a giant new organ of government with the care of their widely divergent economic interests.

Through the winter of 1787–88 and into the spring the contest raged. People of many persuasions, backgrounds, and temperaments debated and clashed over the issue. By June, after months of manipulations, pressures, exploration of basic principles, and dedicated effort, eight of the necessary nine ratifications had been won. Conventions were then concurrently weighing the question in Virginia, New York, and New Hampshire. As it transpired, New Hampshire became the ninth state to approve the Constitution and thereby set the new government in motion. But without the great states of Virginia and New York, real union would have been unachievable, and it is the drama of those two crucial conventions that the following accounts highlight.

While New Hampshire met and adjourned and delayed, Virginia was holding her convention at Richmond, in the new Academy on Shockoe Hill.

The country looked to the Old Dominion, wondering which way she would go. Virginia's territory reached to the Mississippi; it included the District of Kentucky and West Virginia. Her population was a fifth of the population of the entire Union. Should Virginia ratify, she would be the ninth state, or so she thought; New Hampshire's final vote was still three weeks away. If Virginia refused, New York, North Carolina and Rhode Island would doubtless follow her lead.

This was to be the ablest of all the ratification conventions and the best prepared, a gathering studded with stars, with names and faces known throughout the state and beyond—well-speaking gentlemen on both sides, well-dressed, well-born.

Washington was not present but remained at Mount Vernon, receiving and sending letters, messages. All that month of June the driveway was busy with express riders. The General had not put himself forward for nomination, nor had it been urged on him by Federalist leaders. His absence did not detract from his influence; the nation knew of his approval.

Toward the rear of the hall sat the fourteen Kentuckians, wearing pistols and hangers [short swords]; to reach here they had ridden through Indian country. The Antifederalist ranks were very strong, led by such men as Benjamin Harrison, John Tyler (father of the President), James Monroe and Richard Henry Lee. Washington, pondering over their names, said it was "a little strange that the men of large property in the South should be more afraid that the Constitution will produce an aristocracy or a monarchy, than the genuine democratical people of the East." Chief among Antifederalists was Patrick Henry, tall, thin, stooped, and at fifty-two looking on himself as aged and broken in health. He wore spectacles, concealed his reddish-brown hair by a brown wig, not too well-fitting. His blue eye was still keen, his long face alive with feeling; the old magic waited to be called up at will. "I fear that overwhelming torrent, Patrick Henry," wrote [one Federalist].

From the first day, Henry was the nerve center of the room. "The Henry-ites," they called his followers. Every Federalist came girded against them. And the Federalist ranks were impressive. One of them, Judge Edmund Pendleton, served as presiding officer. White-haired, painfully crippled, he struggled to his feet on crutches; his hip had been dislocated by a fall from a horse. Pendleton's dress was elegant; his infirmity only added somehow to the dignity of his bearing. "The Confederation did not carry us through the war," he said. "Common danger and the spirit of America did that."

When the convention went into the Committee of the Whole, another Federalist presided. Everybody in Richmond knew [Chancellor Wythe]. Wythe had taught law to Madison's father and to Thomas Jefferson; Henry Clay would one day be his pupil. Behind a bald forehead, thick gray hair fell loose to his neck. He was a small man and brisk, his carriage erect, graceful.

Madison was present, hair powdered, ending in a long queue, "hand-

Chapters from the American Experience

somely arrayed in blue and buff. His low stature" [wrote the Honorable Hugh Blair Grigsby] "made it difficult for him to be seen from all parts of the house; his voice was rarely loud enough to be heard throughout the hall. He always rose to speak as if with a view of expressing some thought that had casually occurred to him, with his hat in his hand and his notes in his hat; and the warmest excitement of debate was visible in him only by a more or less rapid and forward see-saw motion of his body." Madison, as always masterful in debate, called the meeting back to earth from the impassioned flights of Henry.

James Monroe, Antifederalist, at thirty came almost unknown to this assembly. He was the son of a Scotch carpenter; his demeanor appeared stiff, a little awkward.

John Marshall, now in his thirty-third year, was a great strength to the Constitutionalists. Ruddy and handsome, with wild black hair, a piercing dark eye, as a concession to the occasion he had draped his tall frame in a new coat which however had cost but a pound and looked it. The assembly knew Marshall, respected him for his soldierly record in the Revolution and loved him for his sociability—which, says Grigsby primly, at times verged on excess.

With such dramatis personae, the Virginia convention could not lack color. Always, one is conscious of the fourteen Kentuckians, sitting watchful, biding their time.

Clause by clause, the Virginians went through the Constitution. A federal bench would swallow up and destroy the state courts; the tax power should not be used by the federal government until requisitions first were tried. "I will never give up that *darling* word, requisitions," said Henry, and the reporter underlined it. Madison lost patience. In his own state, among his intimate friends, Madison used a different tone, different arguments than in Philadelphia. There were here strong local loyalties to combat, and a local feeling, a deep proud provinciality. John Tyler, whose estate, Greenway, lay on the James River, one day declared mournfully that should Constitutionalists prevail, then ships, as they passed his door on foreign voyages, would carry another flag than Virginia's—that pennant which in a day of doubt and dread he had seen when it was first hoisted above the Capitol at Richmond.

Antifederalists brought up the old argument that the nation was too big, too widely extended for a central government as proposed: congressmen from New Hampshire would never understand or sympathize with the needs of Virginia or the Carolinas. Madison replied soothingly, and with a touch of his prophetic gift: "Let it not be forgotten there is a probability that that ignorance which is complained of in some parts of America will be continually diminishing. Does not our own experience teach us that the people are better informed than they were a few years ago? The citizen of

Georgia knows more now of the affairs of New Hampshire than he did, before the Revolution, of those of South Carolina. When the representatives from the different states are collected together they will interchange their knowledge with one another, and will have the laws of each state on the table."

Madison seemed tired, edgy. Once he interrupted Henry in full flight, and twice in a single day the reporter wrote that Madison's voice failed him: "Here Mr. Madison spoke of the distinction between regulation of police and legislation, but so low he could not be heard. Mr. Madison made several other remarks, which could not be heard." After one strenuous debate, Madison fell ill and went to bed for three days.

It was Edmund Randolph who supplied the prime shock and surprise of the convention. The handsome young Governor was much beloved in his state. The great part he had played in Philadelphia was known to many; his refusal to sign the Constitution had become common knowledge. But since then, Randolph had begun to waver.

On June fourth the Governor rose and made his declaration. It took him some time to reach his point. Plainly on the defensive, Randolph said he had not come hither to apologize. He was not a candidate for popularity. If the Constitution were put before him as in Philadelphia—wholly to adopt or wholly to reject—he would again refuse his signature. But Massachusetts had urged amendments to be enacted by Congress *after* full ratification. For himself, he had originally been for *previous* amendments, to be approved by the several states before they ratified. But the postponement of this convention to so late a date made this impossible, "without inevitable ruin to the Union." Eight states had adopted the Constitution; they could not recede. He stood, then to express his earnest endeavors for a firm, energetic government, and to concur in any practical scheme of amendments. Randolph, in short, was for the Constitution.

Randolph had spoken convincingly; a convert's argument is always heartfelt. But Patrick Henry had no intention of letting his adversary off without a challenge as to this change of front. The gentleman's alteration of opinion, Henry said, "was very strange and unaccountable. Something extraordinary must have operated so great a change in his opinions."

Randolph and the convention understood Henry's hints very well, with their implication that Washington's persuasion—or worse, Washington's promise of future favors under the new government—had brought about this change. Much later, when Washington named Randolph as United States Attorney General, Randolph would be at pains to defend himself from this same charge. Furiously, Randolph answered Patrick Henry. He disdained the honorable gentleman's aspersions and insinuations. "If our friendship must fall," said Randolph, "let it fall like Lucifer, never to rise again! He has accused me of inconsistency. Sir, if I do not stand on the bottom of integrity and pure love for Virginia, as much as those who can be most clamorous, I wish to resign my existence." Hereafter, Randolph was superb in debate, forgot personal feuding and gave what was surely the best performance of his life.

On June twenty-fourth, by prearrangement with his supporters, Chancellor Wythe moved a resolution for ratification, with a bill of rights and subsequent amendments, thus forestalling Patrick Henry, who had come to the assembly that day with his own very different resolution to present. Wythe, rising to speak, "looked pale and fatigued," says Grigsby, and so agitated that even those near him could not understand what he said. Patrick Henry, for his part, showed "a fierce humor, strangely mixed with grief and shame." *Subsequent* amendments, Henry said, were a novelty and an absurdity. To enter into a compact of government, and then afterward to settle the terms of this compact was an idea dreadful, abhorrent to his mind.

Only one day of debate remained. The Virginia legislature was due to assemble, and required the Academy hall. Each night for the past three weeks, both sides had made careful, detailed estimates of the votes they could count upon, the changes that a day's work might have caused. The fourteen Kentuckians were a source of jealous contention. With the vote running so close, even two of them might turn the tide. Throughout the convention, Patrick Henry had been extremely effectual on the great issue of the Mississippi River, though he was aware, he said, that he had been accused of "scuffling for Kentucky votes." [He reminded] delegates that only two years ago John Jay had urged Congress to surrender the Mississippi to Spain for a generation.

Under the new Constitution [there] was danger that navigation of the river might be sacrificed. Henry's picture of the Mississippi Valley, prosperous and happy under a future Confederacy, ruined and deserted under the Constitution, dismayed the assembly. In the end, however, four out of the fourteen Kentuckians voted on the Federalist side.

On Wednesday, June twenty-fifth, shortly before the vote was taken, Patrick Henry spoke his last word. If he should find himself in the minority, he would have, he said, those painful sensations which arise from a conviction of being overpowered in a good cause. But he would be a peaceful citizen. "I wish not to go to violence, but will wait with hopes that the spirit which predominated in the Revolution is not yet gone, nor the cause of those who are attached to the Revolution not yet lost. I shall therefore wait in expectation of seeing that government changed, so as to be compatible with the safety, liberty and happiness of the people." Randolph spoke next, very briefly, and his last word did not equal Henry's.

The Constitution was now put to the vote, including a Declaration of Rights which contained twenty articles, and subsequent amendments to the same number. By eighty-nine to seventy-nine the Constitution won. That night angry Antifederalists, determined to create measures for resisting the new system, held a mass meeting in Richmond, with Patrick Henry presiding. But Henry told his wrathful colleagues that he had done his best against the Constitution "in the proper place [the Convention]." The question, said Henry, was now settled; "as true and faithful republicans you had all better go home."[1]

Word of the Federalist victory in Virginia went out by fast post to New York. Meanwhile, at Poughkeepsie, the delegates of New York State debated and maneuvered. Here too emotions ran high, each faction convinced of the justice of its cause and the vital importance of the issue. Alexander Hamilton, principal spokesman for the Federalists, admitted that "on no subject" had his "breast filled with stronger emotion, or more anxious concern,"[2] and Melancton Smith, debate leader for the Antifederalists, spoke of "all the apprehensions of danger from the new government" that agitated his associates.[3]

As John Jay wrote complacently to his wife, the Federalists represented the preponderance of wealth and of "Shineing Abilities."[4] Besides Jay (then Confederation Secretary of Foreign Affairs), their delegation included the state's chancellor and its chief justice, the mayor of the city of New York, and brilliant young Hamilton—all elected from New York City. Among the Antifederalists, only Governor George Clinton could compare in eminence. The bulk of the "Antis" were "country lawyers who had no greater distinction than a few terms in the state legislature."[5] Melancton Smith was as plain in appearance as Hamilton was resplendent:

He was not handsome. His hair was unpowdered and curled down the back of a thick neck; his head was large and his features irregular. While Hamilton dressed like a courtier, Smith was known for his "prepossessing plainness." And while Hamilton was disliked even by some members of his own party because of the haughtiness that occasionally crept into his manner, Smith was held in warm regard even by men who abhorred his politics.[6]

But, although the Federalists enjoyed this superiority in prestige, they were at a great disadvantage numerically. When the Convention opened, the ratio among delegates stood at 46-19 against the Constitution. Even Alexander Hamilton despaired; writing Madison he expressed the "fear" of "eventual disunion and civil war."[7] An Antifederalist exulted:

Notwithstanding the Eclat with which the Federalists left the City . . .
and the Impressions on their Minds of their Weight and Importance, yet I
believe there has not been a time since the Revolution in which the *Well*
Born, who are the Leaders of that Party, have felt and appeared so uninflu-
ential, as they feel and appear at this Time and Place.[8]

Fortunately for the Federalist cause, however, the delegates had not
been pledged in advance. "Their constituents expected them to delib-
erate, to listen to the arguments of the opposition, and then to decide
the issue accordingly to their best judgments."[9] To the task of swaying
that decision and those judgments the Federalists directed their highly
skilled efforts.

Faced with such overwhelming numerical odds, the Federalists
adopted a strategy of delay, waiting for word of a Constitutional victory
in either Virginia or New Hampshire to turn the tide in their favor. A
motion was put through deferring any vote on the Constitution until
after it and proposed amendments had been "considered Clause by
Clause," and the Convention settled down to prolonged debate.[10]

Hamilton consumed hours in recapitulating the arguments he had set
forth under the name Publius in the *Federalist Papers,* and much time
was also spent in suave recrimination and misrepresentation.

. . . It was not remarkable that the debate made no converts, for . . . the
participants rarely directed their remarks to meeting the objections of the
opposition. The Federalists spoke as if they suspected the Antis of designs
against the Union and the Antis spoke as if the Federalists were aristocratic advocates of tyranny—though the language was politer as suited
face-to-face discussion.

. . . On Saturday, 21 June, Hamilton so badly misconstrued some of
Clinton's remarks that the governor protested. "The gentleman has attempted to give an unjust and unnatural coloring to my observations. I am
really at a loss to determine whence he draws his inference. I declare that
the dissolution of the Union is, of all events, the remotest from my wishes.
That gentleman may wish for a consolidated, I wish for a federal republic.
The object of both of us is a firm, energetic government. . . .

A pleasing contrast to Hamilton's . . . orations was the single recorded
speech that John Jay made during the formal debate, in which he expressed pleasure at the general agreement "that a strong, energetic federal government is necessary for the United States." . . . In contrast to
[those] . . . who enjoyed twisting the remarks of the opposition whenever
an ill-phrased comment gave them the opportunity, Jay politely turned to
Melancton Smith to ask whether he was stating his views properly.[11]

The Antifederalists "continued to vote in a bloc," and the Federalists continued to rely heavily on the impact of a Constitutional victory in New Hampshire or Virginia.[12] Writing to the president of the New Hampshire ratifying convention, Hamilton urged that the greatest possible speed be exercised in transmitting any favorable news to New York:

> You will no doubt have understood that the Antifederal party has prevailed in this State by a large majority. It is therefore of the utmost importance that all external circumstances should be made use of to influence their conduct. This will suggest to you the *great advantage* of a speedy decision in your State, if you can be sure of the question, and a prompt communication of the event to us. With this in view, permit me to request that the instant you have taken a decisive vote in favor of the Constitution, you send an express to me at Poughkeepsie. Let him take the *shortest route* to that place, change horses on the road, and use all possible diligence. I shall with pleasure defray all expenses, and give a liberal reward to the person.[13]

When tidings of victory finally arrived from New Hampshire, the results disappointed the Federalists. Melancton Smith voiced the attitude of his party when he announced that his views were unchanged. He had "long been convinced that nine states would receive the Constitution." Writing to a friend, while Hamilton spoke from the floor, Governor Clinton said confidently: "I steal this Moment while the . . . little Great Man [is] employed in repeating over Parts of Publius to us, to drop you a line. The News from New Hampshire has not had the least Effect on our Friends at this Place."[14]

Nor did the news arriving shortly thereafter that strategic Virginia had joined the ranks of the Constitutionalists have the expected effect on the opposition. The Federalists stopped their verbal fireworks and set about determining exactly what the Antifederalists wanted and whether any compromise could be reached that would bring New York into the fold.

It then became clear that many of the Antifederalists "had every intention of ratifying the Constitution and coming into the new Union" if they could insist upon certain amendments that would, in their opinion, make the document a more worthy charter of government.[15] These proposed amendments were now examined in detail and substantially agreed upon. The issue became one of presentation. Should the amendments be made a condition of ratification, as the Antifederalists insisted, or should they be appended as a sort of rider to acceptance, with the request that the new nation subsequently adopt them? The Federalists took the position that they had agreed to the amendments and that the Antifederalists should "compromise" on the degree of insistence with which New York presented them.

During this negotiating phase the Federalist leadership shifted to John Jay, whose talents lay in the direction of conciliation and persuasion. It began to appear that the most the Antifederalists were going to concede would be ratification with the proviso that, unless the amendments were agreed upon by the country as a whole within a certain period, New York would withdraw from the Union. The Federalists warned them that the Union would not accept New York under those terms. If they persisted, said Jay, New York might be deprived of the right to share in organizing the new government. "These are not threats," he asserted. "This is prudence."[16] From Virginia, James Madison wrote that, in his opinion, a ratification on the condition that amendments be adopted later would not be acceptable. "It does not make N. York a member of the New Union," he said, "and consequently . . . she could not be received on that plan."[17] These arguments had an effect. For the first time the Federalists could see their opponents weakening. Meanwhile, pressures were being exerted from New York City.

. . . For many years New York had profited from the presence of the Continental Congress in the City. John Jay estimated that Congress was worth 100,000 pounds a year. . . . If New York rejected the Constitution or if Congress refused to accept the form of ratification adopted by the state, the City would lose a valuable source of income. The fear of losing Congress was shared by City Feds and Antis alike, and as the weeks passed without any decisive action by the Poughkeepsie Convention, Antifederalists in the City grew concerned that their party would be blamed if Congress decided to make its residence elsewhere when the new government went into operation. "The Anxiety of the Citizens, is probably greater than you would imagine," [wrote a New Yorker to Melancton Smith]. . . . "If New York should hold out, the Opposition will have all the Blame laid at their Door for forcing Congress to leave this City." [He warned that, on Smith's return to New York City] "it needs not the Spirit of Prophecy to foretell that your Reception will not be very cordial."[18]

The suggestion was put forth that, if the state proved adamant, New York City might "abandon New York, and cling to the confederacy."[19] The Antifederalists became increasingly convinced that, if New York was to have a firm and assured place in the new nation, unqualified ratification was necessary. On July 25, the necessary num-

E Pluribus Unum

ber of them (led by Melancton Smith) capitulated. By the narrow margin of 30 to 27, the Convention ratified the Constitution, and New York became the eleventh state to join the Union.

As elsewhere in the country, it had been a bitterly contested fight marked by deep emotions, self-examination, and often reappraisal. At the end many remained unconvinced. Remarking on a Union parade in hilly Boston, an Antifederalist newspaper quipped bitterly:

> There they went up, up, up,
> And there they went down, down, downy,
> There they went backwards and forewards,
> And poop for Boston towny![20]

But on the whole the spirit of conciliation prevailed. The opposition had served a function that was to become traditional in American political life. Washington commented: "Upon the whole the opposition to the Constitution has called forth in its defence, abilities . . . that have thrown new light upon the science of Government, given the rights of man a full and fair discussion, and explained them in so clear and forcible a manner, as cannot fail to make a lasting impression."[21]

Following Patrick Henry's illustrious example, the Antifederalists accepted defeat—for the most part—graciously. The young nation bound up its wounds and celebrated. Oxen were roasted, toasts were drunk, and parades swept through the large cities. Popular features of these processions were full-rigged ships—the *Federal Constitution*, the *Union*, the *Hamilton*—drawn on wagons by eight or ten horses each and flying the banners of the ratifying states.

[Philadelphia's] celebration outdid all the rest. At sunrise a full peal of bells rang out from Christ Church steeple; the ship *Rising Sun*, anchored off Market Street, discharged her cannon in salute to the day. At the wharves all vessels were decorated, and along the harbor from South Street to the Northern Liberties ten ships were ranged, each bearing at its masthead a broad white flag inscribed with the name of a state in gold: *New Hampshire, Massachusetts, Pennsylvania.*

A brisk south wind, coming up with the dawn, fluttered the pennants all day.

All along Third Street, up Callowhill to Fourth and west on Market Street went the Grand Procession, a mile and a half of it. Spectators crowded the footways, stood at open windows and on the roofs of the houses, gazing down at the tramping bright lines of marchers.

Afterward, people remarked upon the spectators' silence while the procession passed. Benjamin Rush the Philadelphia physician, signer of the Declaration of Independence, called it a "solemn silence." The sight of the Federal ship *Union* complete in all its parts and moving upon dry land conveyed emotions that cannot be described. The union effected in less than ten months, under the influence of local prejudices, opposite interests, popular arts, and even the threats of bold and desperate men, is a solitary event in the history of mankind. " 'Tis done," Rush wrote. "We have become a nation."[22]

Thomas Jefferson

Painting by Rembrandt Peale.
The White House Collection.

Painting by John Trumbull.

The Metropolitan Museum of Art,
gift of Henry G. Marquand, 1881.

Alexander Hamilton

15

A Pendulum Is Set
In Motion:
Hamilton and Jefferson

We are all republicans—
We are all federalists.

"A bloodless revolution," Jefferson called the election of 1800—and if not quite that, it was certainly a highly significant shift in power. The forces that accomplished it were widespread and complicated, at once general and narrowly personal. Two of the greatest men to move through the tangle of events culminating in that election were Alexander Hamilton and Thomas Jefferson—Hamilton the financial genius, the brilliant organizer of national strength, a man of tremendous drive and single purpose; Jefferson the democratic aristocrat, the statesman-philosopher, a man of many facets and magnificent talents. Called to New York to serve in Washington's first Cabinet, they brought with them political philosophies as divergent as their personalities and characters.

From the spacious porticoes of Monticello, Jefferson had looked out over broad valleys to the mountains of the west and had been sure that in this virgin land lay an opportunity to evolve a form of government more perfect than any that had been possible in the crowded, corrupt cities of Europe. Here, with each man close to the simple virtues, America might, through enlightened education, develop her people to something nearer their potential. "Man's mind is perfectible to a degree of which we cannot as yet form any conception," he wrote.[1] "This corporeal globe, and everything upon it, belong to its present . . . inhabitants, during their generation. They alone have a right to direct what is the concern of themselves alone, and to declare the law of that direction; and this declaration can only be made by their majority."[2] Eternal vigilance must be exercised to ensure that control of the government should never slip from the majority. "Sometimes it is said that man cannot be trusted with the government of himself. Can he, then, be trusted with the government of others? Or have we found angels in the forms of kings to govern him? Let history answer this question.[3] The needs and rights of the minorities, however, must also be respected. The key to the entire riddle of government—its whole justification for being—is the protection of the rights of the individual.

Returning from his ministry in France to become the first Secretary of State, early in 1790, Jefferson found that the Congress, faced with monumental tasks of organization, had been preoccupied for weeks in sober debate over a question of protocol: What should be the title of the chief executive?

[Jefferson's] old friend John Adams . . . had espoused the cause of titles with great earnestness in the Senate, over which . . . [he] was presiding. The Senate had resolved to designate the chief executive as "His Highness the President of the United States and Protector of Their Liberties," but had been forced to yield to the House of Representatives, where Madison was at work, and call him simply "The President of the United States." Jefferson, who had recently reported the fall of the Bastille and rejoiced in the humbling of a king, thought the proposal of the Senate the most ridiculous thing he ever heard of; and it was then that he repeated Franklin's now-famous characterization of John Adams as always an honest man, often a great one, and sometimes absolutely mad.[4]

In the weeks that followed, Jefferson was shocked to see an elaborate ritual of official life developing in the capital city. Washington "never rode out without six horses hitched to his carriage, four servants, and two gentlemen before him," and at his regular formal levees he made it a point not to shake hands with his guests but only to bow stiffly. Jefferson, who venerated the President, attributed the latter habit to the infirmities of age and joined Madison in blaming the pomp on those around Washington who "had wound up the ceremonials of government to a pitch of stateliness which nothing but his personal character could have supported."[5]

No such pomp and circumstance characterized the dinners that Jefferson gave, although the food and wine were excellent and the conversation delightful. Superficially, Jefferson's appearance reflected little of his background in patrician Virginia and the court of France, foretold little of his political eminence and power.*

The gruff Maclay [radical Senator from Pennsylvania], on seeing Jefferson for the first time, was disappointed with his slender frame, the looseness of his figure, and the "air of stiffness in his manner," while pleased with the sunniness of his face. He was of imposing height, being more than six feet, and slender without being thin. His [red] hair was combed loosely over the forehead and at the side, and tied behind. His complexion was light, his eyes blue and usually mild in expression, his forehead broad and high. Beneath the eyes, his face was rather broad, the cheek-bones high, the chin noticeably long, and the mouth of generous size. The casual glance discovered more of benevolence than force, more of subtlety than pugnacity. Nor, in that day of lace and frills, was there anything in his garb to proclaim him of the élite. His loose carpet slippers and worn clothes [evoked comment].

As some found fault with his dress, others criticized a slovenly way of sitting—"in a lounging manner, on one hip commonly, with one of his shoulders elevated much above the other." [Maclay also was] disappointed to find that "he had a rambling vacant look, and nothing of that firm collected deportment which should dignify the presence of a Secretary or Minister." Another found that "when speaking he cast his eyes toward the ceiling or anywhere but at the eye of his auditor."[6]

Nevertheless, many disinterested and even hostile observers admitted that, on talking with him, one soon became aware that "he was in the presence of one who was not a common man." A French nobleman noted that Jefferson's conversation was "most agreeable" and that it revealed "a stock of information not inferior to that of any other man," and the wife of Federalist leader Bayard Smith found "something in his manner, his countenance and voice that at once unlocked" her heart.[7]

Alexander Hamilton, on the other hand, was one of the most elegant young men in the Washington court:

We have one striking picture of him in a blue coat with bright buttons with a white waistcoat, black silk small-clothes, white silk stockings; another in fine lace ruffles. It is quite impossible to think of him as unfit for an instant summons to a court levee or a ladies' drawing room.

*Material from Claude G. Bowers' *Jefferson and Hamilton: The Struggle for Democracy in America* is used in condensed form, by permission of the publisher, Houghton Mifflin Company.

A Pendulum Is Set in Motion

It was his head and features that denoted the commander. His head was well-shaped, massive, and symmetrical with its reddish fair hair turned back from his forehead, powdered and collected in a queue behind. His well-moulded lips could be firm and stern, and the soft, mirthful eyes could freeze and flash. If women were to observe the softer nature, the politicians were to note the man of relentless will disclosed in the firm, strong jaw.[8]

Hamilton's driving ambition had manifested itself early in life when (at thirteen) he chafed at the future that seemed to lay before him as an obscure clerk in the West Indies and swore that he "would willingly risk his life but not his character to elevate his station."[9] His dreams of greatness were not limited to himself. He also conceived of "great destinies" for the young nation and envisioned it as "majestic, efficient and operative of great things."[10] He had little confidence in the masses, regarding man as "ambitious, vindictive, and rapacious" by nature.[11] The poor, being generally ungifted intellectually (or they would not be poor), seldom entertained large visions of public welfare. They were best off governed by a small group of leaders who might, through imagination and talent, identify their own natural ambitions with the welfare of the nation. These leaders would logically be drawn from the moneyed class, whose loyalty must be carefully cultivated through special privileges designed to give them a financial stake in the government. The powers granted by the Constitution to the federal government, Hamilton felt, should be expanded. The strength of the executive branch particularly should be increased. He would do everything in his power to stabilize and dignify his government, both at home and abroad.

From the first, Hamilton, as Secretary of the Treasury, wielded more power than either of his two colleagues in the Cabinet. He exerted a great influence over Washington. In addition, the Congress had stipulated that the Treasury head report to it periodically on financial programs, and this was all the leverage Hamilton required to extend his influence to the legislative branch.[12] Within two years he had driven through a program that laid a solid foundation for national solvency and power.

That Hamilton and Jefferson could have worked together in the first Cabinet as long as they did was in part a tribute to the personal magnetism of Washington. It was also a manifestation of a conviction that he and Jefferson shared—the conviction that the precarious position of the young nation demanded the talents and cooperation of her best leaders. But by 1791 Jefferson was coming to the conclusion that greater perils than disunity threatened the new government.

Hamilton was at the high tide of his popularity and power. His funding system had established the Nation's credit, and the genius and daring of the brilliant young man of thirty-three were on every tongue. Among the merchants and people of wealth and property he was acclaimed the savior of the State.

And, in the saddle, he was riding hard. He thought of himself as the Prime Minister. The other members of the President's official family were his subordinates. His policies were the policies of the Government, and to question them was hostility to the State. In the Cabinet meetings his manner was masterful. He felt no delicacy about interfering in the departments of his colleagues. Even Knox [Secretary of War and a strong Hamiltonian] resented his determination to make all the purchases for the Department of War.[13]

Jefferson had acquiesced in Hamilton's early financial program, and, although he opposed the Bank Bill, he at first restricted his criticism of it to a written opinion requested by Washington. As he grew increasingly dissatisfied with the aristocratic leanings of the Secretary of Treasury and with the speculation and favoritism that accompanied Hamilton's program, his feelings were reflected in his private correspondence and conversation. But he continued to be circumspect in his public remarks, believing that propriety forbade any open airing of his views as long as he was a member of the official family.

In the summer of 1791, however, his opinion on the growing issue of the French Revolution was splashed over the nation's press. An alignment was already taking shape in America that, during the next two years (as the excesses of the French Revolution mounted and the French and English came into conflict), would split the nation into "Francophiles" and "Anglophiles." Like many of his countrymen, Jefferson looked on the French Revolution as a continuation of a worldwide struggle for the rights of man that had begun with the American Revolution. He "deplored as much as anybody" that the innocent had suffered with the guilty, but he regarded them as "fallen in battle." "The liberty of the whole earth was depending on the issue of the contest, and was ever such a prize won with so little innocent blood?"[14]

Hamilton, on the other hand, spoke for most Federalists when he said that the "bloody scenes" of the French Revolution were violating man's basic right of property, "ravishing the monuments of religious worship," and proving to all not blinded by prejudice that there was "no real resemblance" between the cause of America and that of France—that the difference was as great as that "between liberty and licentiousness."[15] Hamilton found a much more suitable model in the moderation and rule of law of England.

In 1791 these feelings were formulating rapidly, and the time was inopportune for a Secretary of State who prized discretion to have his opinions on this issue blazoned before the country. Early in the year Thomas Paine had published in England his famous pamphlet, *The Rights of Man.* One of the first copies to reach America was rushed to Jefferson by a friend, with the request that he in turn forward it to the printer who was going to distribute it throughout the country. Before he sent it on, Jefferson attached a little note saying: "I am extremely pleased to find it will be reprinted here, and that something is at length to be publickly said against the political heresies which have sprung up among us."[16] When the pamphlet appeared, Jefferson's provocative comments were printed with it, as a preface. It was evident to many that the heresies he had in mind were especially those of his good friend John Adams, whose undemocratic *Discourses on Davila* had been running for several months in a Philadelphia newspaper. "I am afraid the indiscretion of a printer has committed me with my friend Mr. Adams, for whom, as one of the most honest & disinterested men alive, I have a cordial esteem," Jefferson explained to Washington. "I certainly never made a secret of my being anti-monarchical, & anti-aristocratical; but I am sincerely mortified to be thus brought forward on the public stage."[17] Whether he liked the publicity or not, his name was now intimately associated with the cause of democracy in the minds of the American people.

Popular antagonism to the Federalist program mounted as speculation in bank stocks contributed to an economic crisis that involved many leaders and sent the Assistant Secretary of the Treasury to prison. "What do you think of this scrippomony?" Jefferson wrote a friend, and he made caustic private comments on the "corrupt squadron of the First Congress" and its subserviency to Hamilton.[18]

In the spring of the next year (1792) the split in the official family became noisily public with a newspaper free-for-all in which identities of combatants were thinly disguised and feelings ran high. Vitriolic accusations by Hamilton appeared under such pseudonyms as "An American," "Amicus," and "Scourge," and Jefferson's friends retaliated with equal vehemence. By August the controversy had become so acrid that Washington sent letters of rebuke to his two Secretaries.

In reply, Hamilton admitted that he "had some instrumentality" in the newspaper recriminations and added that he found himself unable to "recede for the present." His attack was justified, he said, for clearly "there was a formed party deliberately bent upon the subversion of measures, which in its consequences would subvert the government." When he saw that the "avowed object of the party" was the undoing of his financial system, he "considered it as a duty to endeavor to resist the torrent, and, as an effectual means to this end, to draw aside the veil from the principal actors."[19]

Jefferson, replying the same day, insisted that he had never criticized the Secretary of the Treasury in public, despite his conviction that Hamilton's system "flowed from principles adverse to liberty and was calculated to undermine and demolish the republic." He expanded his criticism to include the members of Congress who had reaped personal profit from their advance knowledge of the funding, assumption, and bank programs. The first fruits of Hamilton's influence over the legislature had been "the establishment of the great outlines of his project by the votes of the very persons who, having swallowed his bait were laying themselves out to profit by his plans."[20]

He had determined from the first, he said, not to "inter-meddle" with the legislature at all, and with his codepartments as little as possible. At this point Jefferson felt called upon to explain the "deal" whereby he had gone along with Hamilton's assumption program in return for the shifting of the capital to Washington. Unconvincingly, he claimed that, on this occasion of his "first and only" meddling with the legislature, Hamilton had "duped" him and made him a "tool for forwarding his schemes, not then sufficiently understood."[21]

On the other hand, said Jefferson, Hamilton had frequently caballed with members of the legislature and persistently interfered in the affairs of the State Department. At a time of most delicate relations with England and France, for instance, Hamilton had engaged in unauthorized conferences with the ministers of those two nations and was "on every consultation, provided with some report of a conversation with the one or the other of them, adapted to his views."[22]

Hamilton had been criticizing Jefferson publicly for hiring as staff translator the journalist Philip Freneau and for encouraging him to establish a paper of opposition in the capital. Jefferson now pointed out to Washington that the Secretary of the Treasury was in no position to cast stones:

I have never enquired what number of sons, relations and friends of Senators, representatives, printers or other useful partisans Colo Hamilton has provided for among the hundred clerks of his department, the thousand excisemen, custom-house officers, loan officers &c, &c, &c. appointed by him, or at his nod, and spread over the Union; nor could ever have imagined that the man who has the shuffling of millions backwards and forwards from paper into money and money into paper, from Europe to America, and America to Europe, the dealing out of Treasury-secrets among his friends in what time and measure he pleases, and who never slips an occasion of making friends with his means, that such an one I say would have brought forward a charge against me for having appointed the poet Freneau translating clerk to my office, with a salary of 250. dollars a year.[23]

Jefferson concluded with the statement that he was eagerly planning an early retirement. In the interim he would continue to avoid public discussion of his views. Thereafter, however, he would speak up if necessary to clear his name, "clouded by the slanders of a man whose history, from the moment at which history can stoop to notice him, is a tissue of machinations against the liberty of that country which has not only received and given him bread, but heaped its honors on his head."[24]

Thus were the lines of battle drawn and the personal antipathies sharpened. The newspaper war went on, and the more Hamilton castigated Jefferson, the more Jefferson, despite his public silence, became the symbol of the opposition. While the Jefferson image crystallized, resentment against Federalist measures and methods grew more and more general. Through the remainder of his term as Secretary of State and during the three years of retirement at Monticello that followed, Jefferson continued to extend his influence at the leadership level through correspondence and personal contact. His talents as a political leader came into full sway.

When a measure was passed or a policy adopted in Philadelphia, he knew the reactions in the woods of Georgia without waiting for letters and papers. In every community he had his correspondents with whom he communicated with reasonable regularity, doing more in this way to mould and direct the policies of his party than could have been done in any other way. Seldom has there lived a more tireless and voluminous letter-writer. With all the powerful elements arrayed against him, he appreciated the importance of the press as did few others. "If left to me," he once wrote, "to decide whether we should have a government without newspapers, or newspapers without a government, I should not hesitate for a moment to prefer the latter."

In his personal contacts he was captivating—a master of diplomacy and tact, born of his intuitive knowledge of men. [Of a newly appointed Minister from France, he wrote to Madison] "De M. is remarkably communicative. With adroitness he may be pumped of anything. His openness is from character, not affectation. An intimacy with him may, on this account, be politically valuable."[25]

These skills Jefferson now devoted to criticizing the party in power and making clear his own views. He charged that under the Federalists the features of the government were being "monarchized" by "the forms of its administration." The Hamiltonians intended, he said, to "conciliate a first transition to a President and Senate for life, and from that to an hereditary tenure of these offices, and thus to worm out the elective principle."[26] He favored avoiding entanglements in the "quarrels and slaughters of Europe." Angry at the "atrocious depradations" the French had been committing on American commerce, he insisted that he had no "fibre of attachment" to any country except his own.[27] As for the Whiskey "Rebellion," no incident connected with it, as far as he knew, had been "anything more than riotous." The people of the West had exercised admirable restraint in the face of the repressive expedition the government had sent against them—an expedition in which Hamilton had so eagerly participated.[28]

Jefferson reappeared on the public scene with the election of 1796. In that election Hamilton (underestimating Republican strength and wishing to see Charles C. Pinckney elevated to the Presidency above Adams) juggled Federalist votes, with the unexpected result that Adams' lead was reduced to an uncomfortably narrow margin and Jefferson became Vice-President. Jefferson improved the moment of uncertainty before the final decision was known to remind Adams of Hamilton's treachery to him. He was sure Adams would be elected, he said. "Indeed it is impossible that you may be cheated of your succession by a trick worthy the subtlety of your arch-friend of New York who has been able to make of your real friends tools to defeat their and your just wishes."[29] His sympathy and admiration for the crusty old New Englander were genuine, however, for he wrote Madison at the same time: "If Mr. Adams can be induced to administer the government on its true principles, and to relinquish his bias to an English constitution, it is to be considered whether it would not be on the whole for the public good to come to a good understanding with him as to his future elections. He is perhaps the only sure barrier against Hamilton's getting in."[30] Nothing came of this thought, for the deterioration of relations with France widened party differences and made any link between Adams and the Republicans impossible.

In 1798 the nation was seized with hysterical fear of subversion as a result of the undeclared naval war with France. From this hysteria emerged the Alien and Sedition Acts, regarded by many—and certainly by Jefferson—as the capstone of Federalist perfidy. Freedom of speech was effectually stifled, and opposition presses were closed down. In defying these laws, Jefferson proceeded with even more caution than usual. As Vice-President he stood in real danger of being charged with sedition himself for criticizing the Federalists. Preparing a strongly worded set of resolutions (advocating resistance by state governments), he forwarded them to a trusted friend, who in turn gave them to John Breckinridge of Kentucky. Breckinridge took the resolutions to his state, where, slightly modified, they were passed by the legislature. The secret of their origin was carefully guarded for many years, but these resolutions and the ones that Jefferson encouraged Madison to draw up for Virginia became clarion calls to the party whose very existence the laws threatened.[31]

Thus Jefferson's power steadily increased. As the election of 1800 approached, his position as leader of the Republican Party was unchallenged.

Meanwhile, Hamilton had been losing ground among the Federalists. His "retirement" early in 1795 had been in name only. For the balance of Washington's administration, Hamilton continued as a powerful force behind the scenes. His correspondence with Washington is studded with references to this influence: "The evening I had last the pleasure of seeing you, you asked my opinion whether any and what measures might be taken with the Senate with reference to the treaty."[32] "I had the honor to receive yesterday your letter of the 22d. The course you suggest has some obvious advantages, and merits careful consideration."[33] On more than one occasion he coached the President on the exact tone and manner his diplomacy should take:

It is all-important to us—first, if possible, to avoid rupture with France; secondly, if that cannot be, to evince to the people that there has been an unequivocal disposition to avoid it. Our discussions, therefore, ought to be *calm,* and when remonstrance and complaint are unavoidable, carrying upon the face of them a *reluctance* and *regret,* mingling a steady assertion of our rights and adherence to principle with the language of moderation, and, as long as it can be done, of friendship. I am the more particular in these observations, because I know that Mr. Pickering [Secretary of State], who is a very worthy man, has nevertheless some thing warm and angular in his temper, and will require much a vigilant, moderating eye.[34]

"As to your resignation, sir," he wrote to Washington in the summer of 1796, "you should really hold the thing undecided to the last moment."[35] Washington put off his farewell address until three months before the election—a source of great frustration to the Republicans, who were thus deprived of time to wage an effective campaign.

After Washington's retirement Hamilton's influence still made itself felt through Adams' Cabinet, in which all three secretaries were under his sway. To Secretary of State Pickering he frequently wrote in the following vein: "I have this moment received your two favors of the

25th; I am delighted with their contents, but it is impossible for me to reply particularly to them so as to reach you *tomorrow* as you desire."[36]
To his "dear friend" Secretary of War McHenry he sent instructions imperious in tone: "Take my ideas and weigh them of a proper course for our Administration in the present juncture."[37] And Wolcott, his one-time assistant in the Treasury Department who succeeded him as secretary, he coached as follows: "The sentiment [expressed by President Adams] is intemperate and revolutionary. . . . Some hint must be given. . . . Enclosed is a sketch of some ideas which have run through my mind."[38]

As long as Hamilton's views, passed on to Adams as their own by these secretaries, coincided with the convictions of the President, the Federalist ship held an even course. Hamilton had developed the judgment that Adams was a weakling whom he could without difficulty control—"one of the worst miscalculations of Hamilton's career," says biographer John C. Miller.[39]

Many such psychological errors marred his career. Although he had been regarded for years as a demigod by large numbers of Federalists, Hamilton antagonized many besides Adams. His arrogant manner, his intolerance of opposition, and his misjudgment of the potential force of public opinion all contributed to a gradual weakening of his position. So, too, did the revelation that he had been involved (in 1791) in a sordid affair with a blackmailer—a discovery of which the Republicans made full capital. To his credit (but not to the improvement of his relations with his party) he took a stand that differed radically from that of most Federalists on the emotion-charged Alien and Sedition Laws:

There are provisions in this bill, which appear to me highly exceptionable, and such as, more than any thing else, may endanger civil war. I hope sincerely the thing may not be hurried through. Let us not establish a tyranny.[40]

The wound in the Federalist Party occasioned by the Hamilton-Adams rift in 1796 was precariously taped up in view of the crisis with France, but it was soon set festering over the issue of Hamilton's role in the new standing army (created in the face of that crisis). Hamilton had always been obsessed by a passion for military glory, and now, against Adams' wishes, he exerted obvious pressure to force himself into the position of Second-in-Command under Washington. Having urged Washington to accept the appointment as Commander in Chief, Hamilton wrote him:

It is a fact of which there is a flood of evidence that a great majority of leading Federal men were of opinion that in the event of your declining the command of the army, it ought to devolve upon me, and that in case of your

acceptance, which everybody ardently desired, the place of second in command ought to be mine. It is not for me to examine the justness of this opinion.[41]

Washington insisted on Hamilton's appointment, and Adams was privately furious. It remained for the events leading to the election of 1800 to precipitate a noisy and undignified final break between the two Federalist leaders and to bring about a rupture from which their party never recovered.

An early omen of Republican victory came in the spring of 1800, with the election of state legislators in New York. Since these legislators would in turn choose the state's Presidential electors, the contest was of national significance. Hamilton assumed personal control of the campaign. However, his aversion to Adams colored his choice of candidates, and he selected a weak slate in order to be certain that there were no pro-Adams men among them. Meanwhile, meeting in their little "Wigwam" (which the Federalists scornfully called the "Pig Pen"), the Tammany opposition assembled a ticket of the most prominent Republicans in the state and went on to a victory that shook the Federalists across the nation.[42] Stunned, Hamilton resorted to a dubious and unsuccessful stratagem.

The next night he presided over a secret meeting of Federalists where it was agreed to ask Governor Jay to call an extra session of the Legislature to deprive that body of the power to choose electors. Hamilton approached Jay in a letter. "In times like these," he wrote, "it will not do to be over-scrupulous." Jay read the letter with astonishment, made a notation that it was a plan to serve a party purpose, and buried it in the archives.[43]

The Republicans jubilantly rewarded their New York leader, Aaron Burr, with the Vice-Presidential nomination. Furious at the defeat in that key state, Adams took the long-overdue step of dismissing Pickering and Wolcott from his Cabinet. The rift between Adams and Hamilton was now complete. In letter after letter Hamilton campaigned against the President in favor of the other Federalist candidate, Charles Pinckney. Finally he wrote a highly critical pamphlet maintaining that Adams "did not possess the talents adapted to the administration of government," and that his "extreme egotism" and "ungovernable temper" rendered him unfit for office. This diatribe was intended for limited circulation among Federalist leaders, but Burr obtained a copy and publicized (at the height of the campaign) the fact that Mr. Hamilton opposed the candidate of his party and doubted "the solidity of his understanding."[44] Federalists were appalled; even the staunch Hamiltonian George Cabot warned Hamilton:

All agree that the execution is masterly, but I am bound to tell you that you are accused by respectable men of egotism; and some very worthy and sensible men say you have exhibited the same vanity in your book which you charge as a dangerous quality and great weakness in Mr. Adams.[45]

For the balance of the election struggle, Hamilton played a surprising and admirable role. Foreseeing the defeat of both Federalist candidates, he exerted such influence as remained to him in favor of Jefferson and against Burr. Hamilton had long mistrusted Burr, had said of him, as early as 1792, "If we have an embryo-Caesar in the United States, 't is Burr. . . . I feel it to be a religious duty to oppose his career."[46] Now he termed him "as unprincipled and dangerous a man as any country can boast," a man who would "certainly attempt to reform the government *à la Bonaparte.*" Furthermore, Hamilton wrote to one party leader: "If Jefferson is President, the whole responsibility of bad measures will rest with the Anti-federalists. If Burr is made so by the Federalists, the whole responsibility will rest with them. The desire of mortifying the adverse party must be the chief spring of the disposition to prefer Mr. Burr."[47] It would be far better, he urged, to "obtain from Jefferson assurances on some cardinal points":

1st. The preservation of the actual fiscal system.

2nd. Adherence to the neutral plan.

3rd. The preservation and gradual increase of the navy.

4th. The continuance of our friends in the offices they fill, except in the great departments, in which he ought to be left free.[48]

"If there be a man in the world I ought to hate," he wrote again, "it is Jefferson. With Burr I have always been personally well. But the public good must be paramount to every private consideration."[49] Finally, in desperation, he sent a long letter to James Bayard (Federalist Representative from Delaware) in which he said that it was too late for him to become Jefferson's apologist, nor had he the disposition to do so. Jefferson's politics were "tinctured with fanaticism," he had been "a mischievous enemy" to the principal measures of their administration, and he was "crafty and persevering in his objects" and "not scrupulous about the means of success."[50] Nevertheless, Hamilton went on:

It is not true, as is alleged, that he is an enemy to the power of the

Executive. It is a fact that, while we were in the administration together, he was generally for a large construction of the Executive authority and not backward to act upon it in cases which coincided with his views. Nor is it true that Jefferson is zealot enough to do anything in pursuance of his principles which will contravene his popularity or his interest. To my mind a true estimate of Mr. Jefferson's character warrants the expectation of a temporizing rather than a violent system. And there is no fair reason to suppose him capable of being corrupted.

(Very, very confidential.—In my opinion Mr. Burr is inferior in real ability to Jefferson. It is past all doubt that Burr has blamed me for not having improved the situation I once was in to change the government [by grasping more power]. That when answered that this could not have been done without guilt, he replied, "Great spirits seldom trouble themselves with petty morals"; that when told the thing was never practicable from the genius and situation of the country, he answered, "That depends on the estimate we form of the human passions, and of the means of influencing them.")[51]

Appropriately, the final scene for the victory of democratic republicanism was set in the new capital of Washington, rather than in fashionable Philadelphia or New York. As the lawmakers convened to choose, by states, between the two tied Republican candidates, they were appalled at the primitive unreadiness of the "city." Federalist Gouverneur Morris wrote a French princess: "We only need here houses, cellars, kitchens, scholarly men, amiable women, and a few other such trifles to possess a perfect city" Abigail Adams recorded that she had made of the "great unfinished audience [East] room . . . a drying room . . . to hang up the clothes in."[52]

Pennsylvania Avenue, stretching from the President's house to the Capitol, bordered by miasmic swamps, did not at this time boast a single building. From the steps of the Capitol one could count seven or eight boarding-houses, one tailor's shop, one shoemaker's, one printing establishment, the home of a washwoman, a grocery shop, a stationery store, a dry-goods house, and an oyster market. And this was all. At the wharf, not a single ship. From the President's house to Georgetown living conditions were better because of immunity from swamps, but the wretched roads made it all but prohibitive as a place of residence for members of Congress. Six or seven of the more fastidious braved the distance and found comfortable quarters; two or three found lodgings near the President's house; but the remainder crowded into the boarding-houses on Capitol Hill. In the best of these, by sharing a room one could have attendance, wood, candles, food, and an abundance of liquor for fifteen dollars a week. However, the fare was unsatisfactory, the beef not good, and vegetables hard to get.[53]

Arriving in Washington to await the outcome of the House vote, Jefferson went to Conrad's boardinghouse, where, being late, he took a place at the foot of the table, farthest from the fire. A Senator's wife suggested that he be placed at the head of the table, but he refused. Amid rumors of a usurpation of power by the Federalists and of military preparations by the Republicans, the House convened and began voting.[54]

The House balloted nineteen times on February 11 and again after midnight. It balloted thirty-five times during five days, with no change except a few indecisive ones within state delegations. The tally always stood eight states for Jefferson and six for Burr, two being divided and therefore not voting. . . . On the thirty-sixth ballot the Federalists in the two divided states of Vermont and Maryland abstained, giving the vote of these to Jefferson, who thus had ten. Delaware and South Carolina also abstained, being recorded as not voting. . . .

The breaking of the deadlock was directly attributable to the actions of Bayard . . . the sole representative of [Delaware] . . . Perhaps Bayard was influenced by Hamilton to some extent and got from him the idea of seeking . . . guarantees from Jefferson. Whether . . . [Jefferson received these overtures or not] was afterwards a disputed question. . . . There is no evidence that he made any sort of deal. Jefferson believed, as his friends did, that the vast body of Federalists around the country approved the outcome of this contest. And few will now question the calm statement of the *National Intelligencer* that the voice of the people had prevailed.[55]

The election had taken so long that only about two weeks remained until inauguration day. As it approached,

great crowds began to pour into the drab little capital from the surrounding country. The thunder of artillery ushered in the day. That morning Jefferson remained quietly at Conrad's receiving friends. At noon, dressed plainly, with nothing to indicate the dignity of his position, Jefferson stepped out of Conrad's, accompanied by citizens and members of Congress, and walked to the Capitol. As he passed the threshold, there was a thunder of artillery. When he entered the little Senate Chamber, the Senators and Representatives rose—all standing until Jefferson sat down in the chair he had occupied until a week before.[56]

It seems doubtful that this triumphal entry was as unstudied as it appeared. The stark contrast to the pomp and ceremony of Federalist occasions of state bears the marks of stagecraft. The inaugural address that Jefferson then delivered also bespoke the skilled politician. He was, he said, conscious that the task was above his talents; he looked to the gentlemen of the legislature for guidance and support, and he asked their indulgence for his errors. But amid the soporifics of the politician arose the voice of the philosopher-statesman as he summarized his beliefs on government and enjoined his fellow countrymen to unity under liberty:

We are all republicans—we are all federalists. If there be any among us who would wish to dissolve this Union or to change its republican form, let them stand undisturbed as monuments of the safety with which error of opinion may be tolerated where reason is left free to combat it.[57]

While the victor thus held out a conciliatory hand to the Federalists, Alexander Hamilton, in New York City,

was tasting the bitter fruits of victory he had fought to win for his greatest opponent. From his window he could see the marching men and he could hear the paeans of triumph. The brilliant party he had moulded was in ruins —his leadership scorned. A little while and he would write Morris, "What can I do better than withdraw from the scene? Every day proves to me more and more that this American world was not made for me." Some years more, and a visitor to the home of the retired sage of Monticello would see in the hall a marble bust of Hamilton—the tribute of one great man to another.[58]

It is difficult to conceive of the American story without either of them. Each had been guilty of excesses—Hamilton in looking on criticism of his program as subversion against the nation, and Jefferson in allowing his devotion to liberty to carry him to extremes of Arcadian idealism. In the heat of campaigns, and to serve party ends, each had spoken of the other with extravagant exaggeration. Jefferson had pictured Hamilton as an archmonarchist; Hamilton had portrayed Jefferson as an anarchist of wild, unsettled persuasion. But in the end each grudgingly recognized the capabilities and integrity of the other.

Certainly theirs were the clear voices of two separate yet intertwining traditions in American thought—traditions which have, like the pans of a balance, risen and fallen in power, have had their ardent and sincere adherents in every generation, have softened each the harshness of the other. While Hamilton laid a brilliant and firm foundation for national solvency and power, Jefferson refused to allow the drive for that solvency and power to overshadow another quest—the quest for a way of life where each may rise to the measure of his ability, shielded by a government dedicated, above all, to the protection of individual rights. Without either of these traditions (and perhaps without either of these great protagonists) our history would have run a very different course.

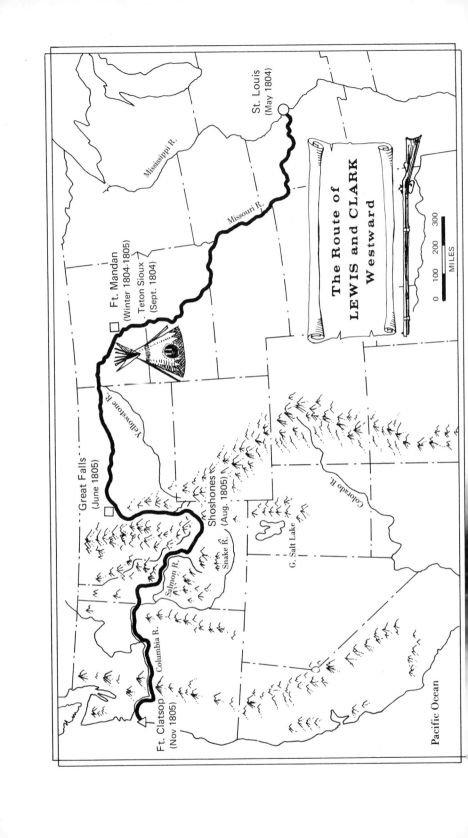

The Route of
LEWIS and CLARK
Westward

St. Louis
(May 1804)

Mississippi R.

Missouri R.

Ft. Mandan
(Winter 1804-1805)

Teton Sioux
(Sept. 1804)

Yellowstone R.

Great Falls
(June 1805)

Shoshones
(Aug. 1805)

Salmon R.

Snake R.

Colorado R.

G. Salt Lake

Columbia R.

Ft. Clatsop
(Nov 1805)

Pacific Ocean

0   100   200   300
MILES

16

Star of Empire

To bestride the mighty
and heretofore deemed endless Missouri.

"The object of your mission," wrote Jefferson to Meriwether Lewis in 1803, "is to explore the Missouri River, and such principal stream of it as by its communication with the waters of the Pacific Ocean, may offer the most direct and practicable water communication across the continent, for the purposes of commerce."[1] * Lewis and his party were to make careful observations of longitude and latitude along the entire route, study and prepare the Indians for the commerce and missionary work to come, and look into the possibilities of attracting the Northwest fur trade down the Missouri River to the United States. Only in one small paragraph did Jefferson list (as "other objects worthy of note") the general scientific data that had been the ostensible purpose of the expedition. The tone of imperialism was inescapable. If, as current geographical knowledge indicated, a navigable route to the Pacific Ocean existed up the Missouri, across one short portage and down the Columbia, the Americans intended to find and claim it.

Undisputed control of such a "Northwest Passage" would give them a secure Pacific base for their extremely lucrative triangular trade with China and for a fur-trade network to be developed over the Northwest. But, in these two commercial objectives, the Americans faced serious competition from the British, who also entertained visions of empire. Huge British monopolies had long been exploiting the fur lands of the north. British explorers were pushing down the rivers of western Canada in search of a route to the Pacific. Canadian imperialists were urging the extension of British sovereignty south to the 45th parallel—

*Material from Bernard DeVoto's *Journals of Lewis and Clark* is reprinted in condensed form, by permission of the publisher, Houghton Mifflin Company.

a boundary that would give them control of the entire Columbia River and access to the Mississippi at a point where canoe travel south was possible. It would, they promised, give Britain "the entire command of the fur trade of North America," except for Russian outposts along the coast. The American "adventurers" who had taken over the trade with China would "instantly disappear" before a "well-regulated" British trade.[2]

While Lewis was preparing for the expedition, word came from France of the Louisiana Purchase, whereby New Orleans, the Mississippi, and an indefinite expanse of wilderness to the north and west (larger than the entire United States) would be transferred to the young nation. It now became the explorers' added duty to convince the Indians along the route (and such representatives of Britain as they met) that America intended to take a firm hold of her new lands.

Both Lewis and the man he selected for his co-leader brought remarkable qualifications to the task. Meriwether Lewis, who had been Jefferson's private secretary, was well educated and intellectually curious; William Clark, a genial extrovert, possessed a deep understanding of the frontier, its people, and its challenges. Both were experienced river men and natural leaders—intelligent, compassionate, highly perceptive of potential trouble, and quick and courageous in meeting it.

Jefferson had suggested they take a company of only a dozen men. On reaching the Mississippi, however, they were warned by local frontiersmen that such a force would be inadequate. When they set out from St. Louis in mid-May, 1804, they numbered over 40, with more than a third of these planning to return after the first winter. By early fall they had sailed, rowed, and hauled their 55-foot keelboat and their two smaller pirogues up the treacherous Missouri to a spot (in present-day South Dakota) where the river they named the Teton flowed into "Old Muddy."*

There, on September 25, the explorers were confronted with a major crisis in Indian relations. They had been forewarned that the Teton Sioux, known as the "Pirates of the Missouri," had been blocking passage upriver to all white traders who would not pay exorbitant tribute. Clark undertook the crucial task of diplomacy. After entertaining the chiefs on the keelboat, he took them ashore in a pirogue. When the large canoe touched the banks, Indian warriors seized its rope and refused to let Clark return:

> The 2d Chief was very insolent both in words and gestures (pretended drunkenness and staggered up against me) declaring I should not go on, stating he had not received presents sufficient from us. His gestures were

---

*This river is today called the Bad River and flows into the Missouri at the city of Pierre. A pirogue was a canoelike boat.

of such a personal nature I felt myself compelled to draw my sword (and made a signal to the boat to prepare for action). At this motion Captain Lewis ordered all under arms in the boat. Those with me also showed a disposition to defend themselves and me. I felt myself warm and spoke in very positive terms.[3]

Unaccustomed to such a response, the Indians yielded. The Grand Chief took hold of the rope and ordered the young braves back, and he and the other chiefs went aboard the keelboat with Clark. Proceeding one mile upriver, they anchored off a willow island for the night. Although the Indians camped on the mainland, Clark set a careful watch on the island and on the boat. There followed two more days of tense parleying and two more nights of sleepless suspense. Delegations of natives toured the boat, and the white party was entertained with elaborate ceremonials, feasts of dog meat, and midnight dances by squaws decorated with "scalps and trophies of war."[4] Seeing several Mahar prisoners, Clark told the chiefs that they should return these captives and make peace if they "wished to follow the advice of their great father." The chiefs slept each night on the boat, constantly urging the party to remain just "one more" day. The expedition's bowman, who could speak Mahar, warned Clark that the prisoners had told him the Sioux did not intend to let them pass. The whites, pretending ignorance of any unfriendly design, remained on taut alert. "We kept a strong guard all night in the boat," wrote Clark. "No sleep."[5]

The final crisis came on September 28. Sergeant John Ordway described it in his journal:

We told them we could not wait any longer. They then did not incline to let us go on. They said we might turn back with what we had or remain with them, but we could not go up the Missouri any further. About 200 Indians were then on the bank. Some had fire arms. Some had spears. Some had a kind of cutlass, and all the rest had bows and steel or iron pointed arrows. Several of the warriors sat beside the rope by which our boat was tied. Captain Lewis asked the chiefs if they would leave the boat. They did not incline to. Then Captain Lewis came out and ordered every man to his place, ordered the sail hoisted. One man went out and untied the rope, which the warrior had in his hand; then 2 or 3 more of their warriors caught hold of the cord and tied it faster than before. Captain Lewis appeared to be angry and told them to go out of the boat, and the chief then went out and said, "We are sorry to have you go. But if you will give us one carrot of tobacco, we will be willing for you to go on and will not try to stop you." Captain Lewis gave it to them. The head chief said then that we must give him one more carrot of tobacco for his warriors who held the rope, and then we might go. Both of our Captains told him that we did not mean to be trifled with, nor would they humor them any more, but would give him one carrot more for the warriors, if he would be a man of his word. The chief said he was mad too, to see us stand so much for one carrot of tobacco. If we would give it, we might go on. Captain Lewis gave it to him. He then took the cord in his hand and gave it to us. We set off under a gentle breeze, which happened to be favorable.[6]

They continued up the river for almost another month. Then, among the friendly Mandans, they built a cottonwood fort for protection against marauding Sioux and settled down for the winter. In the months from late October until early April (1805), they improved their already good relations with the Mandans, sharing their ways and administering to their sick.

A Frenchman named Charboneau came offering his services as a translator. His wife, Sacajawea, was a native of the Shoshone, or Snake, tribe, whose lands lay near the crest of the Rockies and whose assistance would be vital in the crossing from the Missouri to the Columbia.

While they waited for the ice to clear from the river, they constructed dugout canoes of cottonwood, for it would now no longer be possible to continue upstream in the big keelboat. Toward the end of March there were indications that they could soon be underway. On the 25th Clark noted: "Saw swans and wild geese flying N.E. this evening."[7] And the next day the ice began to break up. Clark marveled at the dexterity with which the Indians leaped from one small, swiftly moving cake of ice to another in pursuit of buffalo.

On April 7, the men who had planned to return after the first winter steered the keelboat into the current and headed back down the Missouri, carrying voluminous notes for the government. On the same day the rest of the company set out upriver, to the north and west. As the weeks passed, the high grassy plain gradually gave way to occasional woodlands and then to mountainous terrain. The buffalo became scarce, and in their place came elk and deer, bears, trout, and panthers. High winds, rain, and snow flurries alternated with broiling hot days. They began to find the towline the "safest and most expeditious mode of traveling."[8] "The hills are high and rugged," wrote Clark in mid-May.[9] On the 26th, Lewis recorded that the promontories were "high and jutting in on both sides to the river in many places. The stones tumbling from these cliffs and down the rivulets became more troublesome."[10] Attempts to move along the high bluffs brought near disaster. On June 7, Lewis described their effort to follow an uncertain path 90 feet above the river:

I had scarcely reached a place on which I could stand with tolerable safety before I heard a voice behind me cry out, "God, God, Captain, what shall I do," and turning about I found it was Windsor, who had slipped and fallen about the center of this narrow pass and was lying prostrate on his belly, with his right hand, arm and leg over the precipice, while he was holding on with the left arm and foot as well as he could, which appeared to be with much difficulty. I discovered his danger, and the trepidation which he was in gave me still further concern, for I expected every instant to see him lose his strength and slip off; although much alarmed at his situation, I disguised my feelings and spoke very calmly to him and assured him that he was in no kind of danger, to take the knife out of his belt behind him with his right hand and dig a hole with it in the face of the bank to receive his right foot. This he did, and then raised himself to his knees. I then directed him to take off his moccasins and to come forward on his hands and knees, holding the knife in one hand and the gun in the other. This he happily effected and escaped. Those who were some little distance behind returned by my orders and waded the river at the foot of the bluff where the water was breast deep.[11]

Two days later they abandoned the larger pirogue and buried all excess heavy baggage. Four more days, and Lewis, scouting ahead, heard the sound of "a fall of water and advancing a little further saw the spray arise above the plain like a column of smoke."[12] It was the Great Falls of the Missouri. Here the remaining pirogue was left behind, and another three weeks were spent in laboriously portaging the goods and canoes around this barrier. On July 15, they were again on the river, which now had narrowed and grown more turbulent. Bighorn sheep appeared on the cliffs. Under the grueling effort the men began to fall ill and were treated for "tumors" (boils), sprains, toothaches, intestinal disorders, and fevers.

Toward the end of July they came to the Three Forks of the Missouri, almost 2,500 miles above St. Louis. Here the group rested while Clark reconnoitered. The thin soil was covered now with dry low sedge, and trees were scarce. On July 26, Clark recorded that, fatigued from the scorching heat, his feet blistered and cut by prickly pear, he had difficulty fording the river. Only from Lewis' account does it emerge that "here Charboneau was very near being swept away by the current, but Captain Clark risked himself and saved his life."[13]

They were beginning, Lewis noted, to "feel considerable anxiety" as to the whereabouts of the elusive Shoshone:[14]

If we do not find them or some other nation who have horses, I fear the successful issue of our voyage will be very doubtful. We are now several hundred miles within the bosom of this wild and mountainous country, where game may rationally be expected shortly to become scarce and subsistence precarious, without any information with respect to the country, not knowing how far these mountains continue, or where to direct our course in order to cross them and intercept a navigable branch of the Columbia. Even if we come upon such a branch, the probability is that we should not find any timber within these mountains large enough for canoes, judging from the portion of them through which we have passed.

However, I still hope for the best, and intend taking a tramp myself in a few days to find these [Indians] if possible.[15]

When they set out again, it was up the northernmost of the three forks—the one they named the Jefferson. They separated, with Clark taking the canoes and supplies upriver and Lewis scouting overland for the Shoshone. The mountain peaks were tipped with snow, but, in the valley, he and his men "nearly suffocated with the intense heat of the mid-day sun," while the nights were "so cold that two blankets" were no more than enough.[16] Their stores were now so reduced that they could eliminate one canoe. On August 8, Sacajawea recognized a spot where her tribe sometimes spent its summers. She was now able to tell them that a pass over the mountains lay ahead. Lewis determined to "proceed with a small party" to the source of the Missouri, cross the mountain pass to the Columbia, and descend that river until he found the Indians—Shoshones or any others with horses—if it took him "a trip of one month."[17]

Within two days he came to a place where the stream again forked. Lewis examined the two small forks and "readily discovered from their size that it would be vain to attempt the navigation of either any further."[18] As far as the canoes were concerned, he had reached the end of the Missouri.

Fastening to a willow stake a note telling Clark to wait for them there, he and his three companions investigated numerous Indian trails and tracks, all of which faded away into the mountains and the brush. The stream narrowed to such a point that one of the men "exultingly stood with a foot on each side of this little rivulet and thanked his God that he had lived to bestride the mighty and heretofore deemed endless Missouri."[19] Finally they came upon a single Indian.

I was overjoyed at the sight of this stranger and had no doubt of obtaining a friendly introduction to his nation provided I could get near enough to him to convince him of our being white men. When I had arrived within about a mile, he made a halt, which I did also and unloosening my blanket from my pack, I made him the signal of friendship known to the Indians of the Rocky mountains and those of the Missouri, which is by holding the mantle or robe in your hands at two corners, throwing it up in the air higher than the head, bringing it to the earth as if in the act of spreading it, and repeating this three times. This signal had not the desired effect; he still kept his position and seemed to view Drewyer and Shields, who were now coming in sight on either hand, with an air of suspicion. I hastened to take out of my sack some beads, a looking glass, and a few trinkets which I had brought with me for this purpose, and leaving my gun and pouch with

McNeal advanced unarmed towards him. He remained in the same stead-
fast posture until I arrived about 200 paces from him, when he turned his
horse about and began to move off slowly from me; I now called to him in
as loud a voice as I could command, repeating the word *tab-ba-bone*,
which in their language signifies "white-man." But looking over his shoulder he still kept his eye on Drewyer and Shields, who continued to advance. When I arrived within about 150 paces, I again repeated the word
tab-ba-bone and held up the trinkets in my hands and stripped up my shirt
sleeve to give him an opportunity of seeing the color of my skin and advanced leisurely towards him. But he did not remain until I got nearer than
about 100 paces, when he suddenly turned his horse about, gave him the
whip, leaped the creek, and disappeared in the willow brush.[20]

On the following day, August 12, 1805, Lewis found a large, plainly
marked Indian road paralleling the brook. Following it, he came shortly
to the source of the Missouri River,

that most distant fountain of the waters of the Mighty Missouri, in search
of which we have spent so many toilsome days and restless nights. After
refreshing ourselves we proceeded on to the top of the dividing ridge* from
which I discovered immense ranges of high mountains still to the West of
us with their tops partially covered with snow. I now descended the mountain about three-fourths of a mile, which I found much steeper than on the
opposite side, to a handsome bold running creek of cold clear water. Here
I first tasted the water of the great Columbia.[21]

Continuing along this tributary rivulet, down the western slope of the
Great Divide, the men saw a party of Indians on the hill ahead of them
but again were unable to entice them close enough to parley. Then,
threading a steep ravine, they came suddenly upon three Indian
women. The young woman fled, but the elderly one and the girl "seated
themselves on the ground, holding down their heads as if reconciled to
die."

I took the elderly woman by the hand and raised her up, repeated the
word *tab-ba-bone* and stripped up my shirt sleeve to show her my skin, to
prove to her the truth of the assertion that I was a white man, for my face
and hands, which have been constantly exposed to the sun, were quite as
dark as their own. They appeared instantly reconciled, and I gave them
some beads, a few moccasin awls, some pewter looking-glasses and a
little paint. I now painted their tawny cheeks with some vermillion, which
with this nation is emblematic of peace. I informed them by signs that I

*In crossing the Continental Divide, Lewis had followed the route known today as
Lemhi Pass, west of Armstead, Montana.

wished them to conduct us to their camp—that we were anxious to become acquainted with the chiefs and warriors of their nation. They readily

obeyed, and we set out, still pursuing the road down the river. We had marched about two miles when we met a party of about 60 warriors mounted on excellent horses, who came in at nearly full speed. When they arrived, I advanced towards them with the flag, leaving my gun with the party about 50 paces behind me. The chief and two others who were a little in advance of the main body spoke to the women, and they informed them who we were and exultingly showed the presents which had been given them. These men then advanced and embraced me very affectionately in their way, which is by putting their left arm over your right shoulder, clasping your back, while they apply their left cheek to yours and frequently vociferate the word *âh-hí-e, âh-hí-e,* that is, "I am much pleased."[22]

They communicated haltingly in sign language, sat down on antelope skins to smoke the ceremonial pipe, and shared the mountain Indians' meager fare of berry cake and dried choke cherries. One native took them aside to offer a carefully hoarded piece of dried salmon. Here Lewis got his first word of the virtual impassibility of the land ahead. The evening was spent in festivities. Despite this propitious beginning, as soon as they realized that Lewis wanted them to return with him to the forks of the Jefferson to meet the other white chief and his men, the Indians grew suspicious, fearing an ambush plot by their enemies, the Pahkees. Lewis appealed to their pride:

I told Chief Cameahwait that I was sorry to find they had put so little confidence in us, that among white men it was considered disgraceful to lie or trap an enemy by falsehood. I told him if they continued to think thus meanly of us that they might rely on it that no white men would ever come to trade with them or bring them arms and ammunition and that, if the bulk of his nation still entertained this opinion, I hoped that there were some among them that were not afraid to die, that were men and would go with me and convince themselves of the truth of what I had asserted. He told me that, for his own part, he was determined to go— he was not afraid to die. I had touched him on the right string; to doubt the bravery of a savage is at once to put him on his metal. He was joined by six or eight only, and with these I smoked a pipe and directed the men to put on their packs, being determined to set out with them while I had them in the humor. We had not proceeded far before our party was augmented by ten or twelve more, and before we reached the creek, it appeared to me that we had all the men of the village and a number of women with us.[23]

With his own supply of flour almost exhausted and the Indians obviously ravenous, Lewis sent ahead two of his men to search for food. He asked the chief to keep his young braves back with the main party so that their "whooping and noise" would not frighten the game.

So strongly were their suspicions excited by this measure that two parties of discovery immediately set out, one on each side of the valley, to watch the hunters and see whether they had not been sent to give information of their approach to an enemy. I saw that any further effort to prevent their going would only add strength to their suspicions and therefore said no more. After the hunters had been gone about an hour, we set out. We had just passed through the narrows when we saw one of the spies coming up the level plain under whip. The chief paused a little, somewhat concerned. I felt a good deal so myself and began to suspect that, by some unfortunate accident, some of their enemies had straggled hither at this unlucky moment; but we were all [relieved] to learn that the young man had come to inform us that one of the white men had killed a deer.

In an instant they all gave their horses the whip, and I was taken nearly a mile before I could learn what were the tidings. As I was without stirrups and had an Indian behind me, the jostling was disagreeable. I therefore reigned up my horse and forbade the Indian to whip him. He had given him the lash at every jump for a mile, fearing he should lose a part of the feast. The fellow was so uneasy that he dismounted and ran on foot at full speed. When they arrived where the deer was, they dismounted and ran in, tumbling over each other like a parcel of famished dogs, each seizing and tearing away a part of the intestines which had been previously thrown out.[24]

Two more deer and an antelope were killed and shared with the Indians, who were now in "a good humor." As they approached the spot of the rendezvous with Clark, however, the Indians halted and put around the necks of their guests "tippets" such as they wore around their own necks. Lewis, realizing that they intended in this way to camouflage the whites, played along with them:

To give them further confidence, I put my cocked hat with feather on the chief and, my overshirt being of the Indian type, my hair disheveled and skin well browned with the sun, I needed nothing more to make me a complete Indian in appearance. My men followed my example, and we were soon completely metamorphosed. We now set out and rode briskly within sight of the forks, making one of the Indians carry the flag, that our own party should know who we were. When we arrived in sight at the distance of about two miles, I discovered to my mortification that the party had not arrived. The Indians slackened their pace. I now scarcely knew what to do and feared every moment that they would halt altogether. I now determined to restore their confidence, cost what it might, and therefore gave the chief my gun and told him that, if his enemies were in those bushes before him, he could defend himself with that gun—that for my own part I was not afraid to die, and if I deceived him, he might shoot me. The men also gave their guns to other Indians, which seemed to inspire them with more confidence. They sent their spies before them at some distance. When I drew near the place, I thought of the notes which I had left and directed Drewyer to go with an Indian man and bring them to me. He did, the Indian seeing him take the notes from the stake on which they had been placed.

I now had recourse to a stratagem in which I thought myself justified by the occasion, but which I must confess set a little awkward. It had its desired effect. After reading the notes (which were the same notes I had left for Clark), I told the chief that they had been left here today and said that my brother chief was just below the mountains and was coming slowly up, and that I should wait here for him. I wrote a note to Captain Clark by the light of a willow brush fire and directed Drewyer to set out early, being confident that there was not a moment to spare. The chief and five or six others slept about my fire, and the others hid themselves in various parts of the willow brush. I now entertained various conjectures myself as to the cause of Captain Clark's detention. I knew that, if these people left me, it would be impossible to find them, and that they would spread the alarm to all other bands.

My mind was in reality quite as gloomy all this evening as the most afrighted Indian, but I affected cheerfulness to keep the Indians so who were around me. We finally laid down, and the chief placed himself by the side of my mosquito bier. I slept but little, as might be well expected, my mind dwelling on the state of the expedition, which I have ever held in equal estimation with my own existence, and the fate of which appeared at this moment to depend in a great measure upon the caprice of a few savages.[25]

Drewyer had been gone only about two hours when "an Indian who had straggled a short distance down the river, returned with a report that he had seen the white men only a short distance below." The Indians were "transported with joy, and the chief in the warmth of his satisfaction renewed his embrace of Captain Lewis, who was quite as much delighted as the Indians themselves."[26]

Meanwhile, Clark, coming upstream, had been surprised to see Sacajawea begin "to dance and show every mark of the most extravagant joy." Pointing to the approaching Indians, she sucked her fingers "to indicate that they were her native tribe."[27] A moment later Clark recognized Drewyer, dressed like an Indian, among the approaching braves. Learning of Lewis' position, Clark and his men hurried forward to the other camp, where a double reunion took place.

We soon drew near the camp, and, just as we approached it, a woman made her way through the crowds towards Sacajawea. Recognizing each other, they embraced with the most tender affection. They had been companions in childhood, in the war with the Minnetarees they had both been taken prisoners in the same battle. They had shared the rigors of captivity till one of them had escaped, with scarce a hope of ever seeing her friend freed. While Sacajawea was renewing among the women the friendships of former days, Captain Clark went on and was received by Captain Lewis and the chief, who, after the first embraces and salutations were over, conducted him to a sort of circular tent or shade of willows. Here he was seated on a white robe. Sacajawea was sent for, and she came into the tent, sat down, and was beginning to interpret when, in the person of Cameahwait, she recognized her brother. She instantly jumped up and ran and embraced him, throwing her blanket over him and weeping profusely. The chief was himself moved, though not in the same degree. After some conversation between them, she resumed her seat and attempted to interpret for us. But her new situation seemed to overpower her, and she was frequently interrupted by tears.[28]

The Shoshone carried the white men's supplies over the Divide, sold them horses, and earnestly advised them not to continue so late in the season over the hostile terrain ahead. The expedition nevertheless pressed on and for three months struggled through the tortuous defiles of the Rockies and down the wild Columbia to its sodden, treacherous mouth.

But the days with the Shoshone at the top of the Rockies represented a major climax for the expedition. Standing near the ridge of the Great Divide, looking out over the forbidding barrier of mountains stretching far ahead, hearing the Indians warn of impassable gorges and vast reaches of barren lava between him and the River of the West, Lewis must have known that the dream of a Northwest Passage was dead. Nor did any great river, flowing from the north, connect the Missouri with the rich fur trade of Canada.

But, although these hopes were stilled, another would soon pulsate with new life. Three more months, and the claim of the United States to the vast empire of the Columbia would transcend that of any other nation. Another spring and summer of arduous travel and exploration, and Lewis and Clark would be back in the United States, where meticulous maps and journals would lay before the American people the chart to that empire, replacing the fear of unknown dangers with the knowledge of specific surmountable hazards. The brilliant exploits of Lewis and Clark, together with the Louisiana Purchase, would assure that the new nation was not to be bound by the Mississippi—that it would stretch across the prairie, over the mountains, to the ocean of the West.

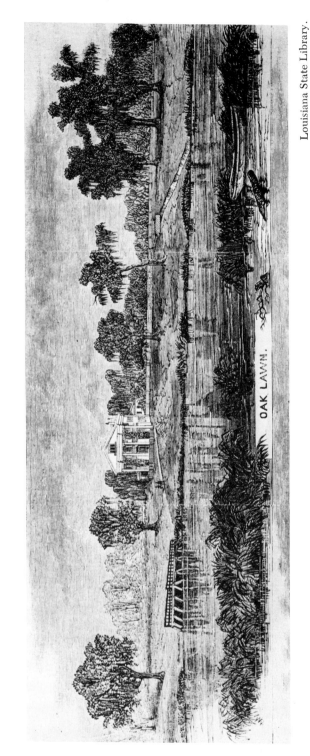

OAK LAWN.

17

The Defenders of
New Orleans

The enemy is near.
If he finds us contending among ourselves,
it will be for the prize of valor.

Indian summer, 1814—and the young nation again fought for its existence. New England, attacked by the British from the north and from the coast, was divided in its support of "Mr. Madison's War." Even after the victory on Lake Champlain, many there demanded peace at any price, and some talked of secession. The British had been repulsed at Baltimore, but the country still smarted at the humiliating ease with which Washington had been invaded and burned.

As discussions of peace terms proceeded at Ghent, the British assembled in Jamaica an armada of more than fifty ships and a large army of Napoleonic War veterans for an attack on New Orleans. At the very least, the conquest of that oft-contested gateway city would make it an added price of peace. New Orleans, drenched in the humid summer heat, pursued its drowsy way, unaware that the greatest hostile force the Gulf of Mexico had ever borne was converging upon it.

Just west of the point where the Mississippi wanders irresolutely into the Gulf, and separated from New Orleans by a maze of sluggish bayous and cypress swamps, lies the Bay of Barataria. One morning early in September the pirates who had made this bay their stronghold awakened to find a British brig-of-war standing just off the coast. The four officers who came ashore in a small gig explained to the outlaw leader,

Jean Lafitte, that the British had come to free the people of Louisiana from the "oppressions" of the Americans, that a "powerful British reinforcement" was on its way to New Orleans, and that they hoped the pirates would join in the conquest of that city.[1]

Lafitte, however, did not feel persecuted by his neighbors, who provided, in fact, a generous market for the booty he brought to Barataria Bay. To his swamp kingdom "resorted the merchants of New Orleans to buy the costly plunder of the world's commerce, which was conveyed with a show of secrecy to New Orleans, to be sold on a scale of profit that laid the foundation of many a great estate."[2] In the city itself the pirates maintained recruiting and sales agencies and operated warehouses to which they brought merchandise across the bayous by night. Involved in this illicit traffic were members of some of the most prominent families in New Orleans.

It was true that the authorities had of late taken a firmer stand with the pirates, had even arrested Lafitte's brother. But the rewards of the trade more than counterbalanced such occasional inconveniences. Lafitte was not interested in the British officer. His reaction was an exercise in skilled diplomacy. Escorting his guests to their boat, he requested a fortnight in which to put his affairs in order. If the British ship would return in two weeks, he and his men would "claim the reward of the services" they might render.[3]

As soon as the British were gone, Lafitte sent warning letters to the governor and to a prominent legislator at New Orleans, enclosing the documents the British had left with him. Governor Claiborne called a military council, which concluded that the documents were false and that the entire story had been concocted by Lafitte to get his brother out of jail. A force of men, dispatched to Barataria, attacked the pirate stronghold, capturing many of the outlaws and driving others, including Lafitte, into the swamps.

But, as word of Lafitte's message spread through the city, many citizens took his warning seriously. Fear of invasion grew, and demands arose for an effective program of defense. Mysteriously, Pierre Lafitte slipped out of prison one night. And Claiborne, feeling that the British documents might be bona fide, sent copies to the American commanding general, Andrew Jackson, at Mobile.

An attack on New Orleans was more than likely, Jackson believed, but it would not come directly by sea. Military common sense, he felt, dictated that, if the British came, they would land somewhere on the Spanish Gulf Coast—probably at Mobile—and proceed overland in a sweeping arc to Baton Rouge. From this position, upriver from New Orleans, they could cut off the city's food supply and starve it into submission. Therefore Jackson could not be persuaded to hurry to New

Orleans until he had set up strong fortifications on Mobile Bay. As for the pirates, Jackson rebuked Claiborne for not having long since suppressed the "hellish banditti."[4] The general did, however, send proclamations to the people of the Southwest, entreating them to "leave their peaceful homes" and hasten to the "point where the honor of the Republic" was threatened. To New Orleans he sent a dispatch urging the men there to join together to protect their city and inviting colored freemen of Louisiana to "cooperate with their white brethren in the defense of a common country."[5]

But New Orleans was not yet ready for cooperation. Factionalism had long roiled the city, for New Orleans bore the stamp of her varied past. Parvenu Americans controlled the administration under Governor Claiborne, haughty French Creoles dominated the legislature, and earlier residents of Spanish origin resented both.

Americans questioned the loyalty of the Creoles, and the Creoles "could not believe that the new settlers would risk their lives for the defense of a soil whereon they had so recently pitched their tents." Both distrusted the "foreign population" (new French immigrants and Irish), and all resented Jackson's having called up the New Orleans Negroes.[6]

Into the city thus enervated by petty antagonisms, General Jackson came on December 2. He was so ill with fatigue, anxiety, and dysentery that he could hardly sit on his horse. He came with no display of power, accompanied only by a party of five or six aides. At the old Spanish villa north of the city where he first stopped, his hostess, a proud Creole matron, refused to believe that the weary, unkempt, jaundiced man with the unshined boots could really be the famous General Jackson. "Ah," she expostulated indignantly, "I worked myself almost to death to prepare a splendid déjeûner, and now I find that all my labor is thrown away upon an ugly, old Kaintuck-flatboatman, instead of a grand General."[7]

If Jackson did not measure up to the Creole lady's standard of a grand general in "plumes and epaulettes," he did bring the comforting voice of authority and assurance to many humbler citizens of the threatened city. His first address to the people, which was translated into French, produced an "electric effect" on the crowd beneath his balcony.[8] His bearing in polite society, too, proved much less boorish than his first hostess had feared. That evening at a formal dinner reception, the general appeared resplendent in a light-blue and buff uniform, carrying himself with such stately charm that he captivated the American faction of New Orleans society, which attended in force. The sensibilities of the city's Creoles, however, were offended because they had not been asked to this affair and because the invitation that their leader had extended Jackson to use his lovely home as general headquarters had not been accepted. But Jackson had other concerns than the city's tangle of social rivalries.

First, there was room for doubt as to how many sacrifices the people of New Orleans would make to keep their city in the Union it had so recently joined.

The population of the city was a new and mixed one, composed of people of all nations and races. Besides, there was a vast amount of valuable property, merchandise and produce accumulated in the storehouses, which would be in danger of destruction in case of an attempt to repel the invader. To save this property would be a strong inducement to surrender the city.[9]

Certainly no concerted defense had as yet been put into effect. Furthermore, few cities in the world lay so vulnerable to enemy attack. Built on a small crescent of firm land 9 feet above sea level in the midst of the vast flat delta of the Mississippi, New Orleans possessed no natural fortifications.

The banks of the Mississippi in the Delta were higher than the swamps adjacent. Thus the scene along the river could be divided into four parts: first, there was the river itself, half a mile wide; secondly, the narrow levee, or river bank; thirdly, a strip of arable rich land a mile wide, where lay the vast plantations that were the wealth of the area; and fourthly, the swamp, a dismal amphibious region of trembling morass.

Water lay not only on, under and in the earth, but in the air also. In the winter months, fogs of the densest description frequently overspread the river and the line of plantations—coming and going with the south wind.

The river offered a smooth approach to New Orleans from either below or above. And, close behind the city, like twin daggers at its spine, lay two large shallow bays, Lake Pontchartrain and Lake Borgne.[10]

Nor did the encircling swamps offer a secure barrier to invasion. If most of the bayous that threaded them wandered aimlessly through impassable terrain, still many—especially along the 6-mile strip between the river and Lake Borgne—were navigable to flat-bottom barges, and these bayous had accumulated uncertain banks of silt along which lines of troops might pass.

Against all these threatening fingers of possible attack, Jackson's available forces were desperately inadequate. He sent small companies of men and a few artillery pieces to each of the old Spanish fortresses that guarded the city—on the roads to Lakes Pontchartrain and Borgne and on the Mississippi above and below the town. Shallows blocked large ships from entry into Lake Pontchartrain, and, for the 60 miles nearest the city, Lake Borgne also was too shallow for men-of-war to pass, so Jackson felt no need to deploy a sizable force there. The six small American gunboats stationed in Lake Borgne would, he believed, bring word of any attack from that direction before the British could transport men and equipment ashore. The general ordered skeletal guards stationed on the navigable bayous and trees felled to block passage up them. Invaluable information as to the hidden passageways of the lower delta came to him indirectly from the pirates, but still he refused their open assistance.[11] The desperate nature of the situation grew on him as he and Major Latour (an ex-Napoleonic officer and Chief Engineer of New Orleans) prepared a strategic map of the area and tallied the available forces.

The troops then in or near New Orleans, and its sole defenders as late as the middle of December, were these: two half-filled, newly-raised regiments of regular troops; a high-spirited battalion of uniformed volunteers (mostly Creole youths of prominent families); two regiments of state militia, badly equipped and some without arms, all imperfectly disciplined; and a battalion of free men of color. Two vessels-of-war lay at anchor in the river—the immortal little schooner *Carolina* and the ship *Louisiana*.

General Coffee, with Jackson's army, was approaching the city from the East by slow marches. Nearly a tenth of his forces were sick with fever, dysentery, and exhaustion. But he was coming.

From the North, General Carroll was coming too. Burning with zeal to join his old friend and commander, he had raised a volunteer force in Tennessee early in the autumn, composed of men of substance and respectability, and, after incredible exertions and many delays, had got them afloat upon the Cumberland River. The state of Tennessee had already been so stripped of arms that Carroll's regiment had less than one weapon to every ten men. An unusual flooding of the Cumberland had enabled General Carroll to make swift progress into the Ohio and thence into the Mississippi, where another piece of good fortune befell him, so important that it may almost be said to have saved New Orleans. He overtook a boatload of muskets coming slowly down-river. This priceless load had been sent by the government, but for economy's sake the captain had been permitted to stop at towns along the river to trade.

Two thousand Kentuckians were also on their way down the Mississippi —the worst-provided body of men, perhaps, that ever went fifteen hundred miles from home to help defend a sister state. A few rifles they had among them, but no clothing suitable for the season, no blankets, no tents, no equipage. In a flotilla of boats hastily patched together on the banks of the

The Defenders of New Orleans

Ohio, they had started on their voyage, carrying provisions for exactly half the distance. They too overtook a boat, this one loaded with flour, and went on their way ragged but rejoicing.

Such was General Jackson's situation as late as the middle of December—two or three thousand troops in the city; four thousand more within ten or fifteen days' march; six gunboats on Lake Borgne; two armed vessels on the river; small garrisons of regulars at strategic forts; the obstruction of the bayous still in progress.[12]

On December 14, as Jackson was returning to New Orleans from a tour of inspection, a courier rushed up with the crushing news that British ships had entered Lake Borgne, overcome the six American gunboats there, and taken command of the lake. "They give no quarter, but in four days will enter the city," a witness wrote in hurried warning to his sister in New Orleans. "Retire to the swamp. It is the city they are aiming for."[13] Panic seized New Orleans. Jackson declared martial law and rushed reinforcements to the defenses on the lake roads. Letters went out to all the commanders of American troops moving toward the city: "You must not sleep until you reach me."[14] Now, in the city, recruits of many nations and races flocked to the defense. And the pirate leader of Barataria made a final and—at last—successful effort to offer his services.

At this point Jean Lafitte reappeared upon the scene. A large number of his band were in prison; others were concealed in the city and its vicinity. Forgetting in the excitement of those hours that Jackson had stigmatized the Baratarians as "hellish banditti," Lafitte sought an interview with the General and tendered his services. Leading citizens all uniting in recommending the acceptance of his offer, the General consented, and the whole band was formed into two most efficient companies of artillerymen. So destitute was the city of the munitions of war that the very flints of these privateers' pistols were received as a precious prize, and transferred to muskets.[15]

A week of frantic preparation passed. The reinforcements that Jackson had so urgently summoned began coming in: Hinds' Mississippi dragoons first, followed closely by 800 men from Jackson's army under General Coffee. These veterans of the campaigns in Spanish Florida (although already exhausted by a march of close to a thousand miles through the wilderness) had left their sick and baggage behind when they heard the news and had covered the

150 miles to New Orleans in just two days.* Watching them file into the city, many a Creole lady found it hard to believe these were skilled soldiers:

In their woollen hunting-shirts of dark dingy color and copperas-dyed pantaloons made—both cloth and garments—at home by their wives, mothers, and sisters, with slouching wool hats, some of raccoon and fox skins, with belts of untanned deer-skin in which were stuck hunting knives and tomahawks, with their long unkempt hair and unshorn faces—Coffee's men were not calculated to please one accustomed to regard neatness and primness as essential virtues of the good soldier.

But their superb skill with the rifle soon won them respect, and a friendly rivalry developed between them and Beale's New Orleans sharpshooters, a corps of trim volunteers from the merchant and professional classes of the city.

Coffee's men were hardly established in camp before Carroll arrived at the levee before the city, with a number of barges and flatboats full of Tennessee militia.[16]

On December 18, a prominent American of the city delivered, in the general's name, an impassioned speech to the soldiers of New Orleans:

Inhabitants of an opulent and commercial town, long strangers to the perils of war, you have shown that you are resolved to deserve the blessings of fortune by bravely defending them. You have forgotten the difference of language and prejudices of national pride. Natives of the United States! It is the oppressors of your infant political existence, the men your fathers conquered, whom you are to oppose. Descendants of Frenchmen! They are the English, the hereditary eternal enemy of your ancient country! Men of color; soldiers! I knew you loved your native land, but you surpass my hopes. The enemy is near. His sails cover our lakes. But the brave are united. If he finds us contending among ourselves, it will be for the prize of valor.[17]

Then, two days before Christmas, the British struck. Searching among the reed-choked bayous, their scouts had found one passageway left unguarded and unobstructed. A reconnaissance party had stolen up this Bayou Bienvenue to the edge of the Villeré plantation, where a village of Spanish and Portuguese fishermen perched on stilts above the swamp. From these fishermen the British scouts had bought both information as to the weakness of the city's defenses and clothing in which

*According to Walker, there had been "no march to equal this in the history of modern warfare."

The Defenders of New Orleans

to disguise themselves and reconnoiter the plantation. Based on their report, an attack was launched which, on the morning of December 23, brought a large British force up the bayou to the Villeré plantation.

Major Gabriel Villeré was sitting on the front gallery of the house looking toward the river and quietly enjoying his cigar while his brother cleaned a fowling piece. Suddenly he observed some men in red coats running toward the river. Immediately he leaped from his chair and rushed into the hall, with a view to escaping by the rear of the house, only to encounter at the back door several armed men. The young Creole surrendered, but in a short while, he saw a desperate chance to escape. Springing suddenly from the group of soldiers, he leaped through the window and, throwing down several of the British who stood in his way, ran towards a high picket fence which enclosed the yard. Clearing this at a bound, in the presence of some fifty British soldiers, several of whom discharged their arms at him, he made for the woods. The British immediately started in hot pursuit under orders to "Catch or kill him." Villeré plunged into the cypress forest where he hid in a tree until the British relinquished pursuit. Then, slipping down, he stole to a neighboring plantation, whence he hurried to Jackson's headquarters.[18]

"By the Eternal, they shall not sleep on our soil!" exclaimed Jackson when he heard the report. "We must fight them tonight."[19] It was then 1:30 in the afternoon. Issuing instructions to pull in forces from the outlying stations, Jackson ate a frugal dinner of rice and coffee (all that his system could tolerate in those days of crisis and illness) and lay down for a nap—the last sleep he was to have for over seventy hours. By three o'clock he was mounted and on his way to the battlefield. So quickly had his commanders moved that, by nightfall, 2,131 defenders—more than half of whom had never seen battle—were lined up behind the Rodriguez Canal, two miles above the Villeré plantation.

Meanwhile, the British had made the fatal mistake of halting their advance at the plantation instead of pressing on in the early afternoon, before Jackson's forces could have been drawn in from their posts. Prisoners captured by the British had consistently reported a force of 12,000 to 20,000 men defending New Orleans, and the British commander, General Keane, hesitated, not knowing whether to believe them or the Spanish and Portuguese fishermen. In twelve hours the number of his soldiers would be doubled; in twenty-four hours, trebled; in forty-eight, quadrupled. He decided to wait.

As the early winter darkness came to the Villeré plantation, the British completely unaware that the enemy was drawn up just two miles above and preparing for battle, had set numerous bonfires blazing, had eaten their evening meal, and were about to retire for the night. They numbered approximately 1,600—for the only time in the entire invasion, a force inferior to that of the defenders.

By six o'clock the American General-in-Chief had completed his plans. Coffee, with his own riflemen, Beale's New Orleans sharpshooters, and Hinds' Mississippi dragoons, was to leave the river road, march across the plain to the cypress swamp, turn down toward the enemy, wheel again, attack them in the flank, and crowd them to the river. Guiding General Coffee was Colonel De la Ronde, owner of one of the plantations in the circle of operations. Jackson, with the main fighting strength of the army, was to keep closer to the river and open an attack directly upon the enemy's position.[20]

As planned, the little schooner *Carolina* slipped downriver, anchoring off the British encampment. At 7:30 a loud voice called from her deck, "For the honor of America," and immediately a barrage of grapeshot and musket balls swept the levee and the British camp.[21] After a delay to allow the British to swing their armament around toward the schooner, Jackson opened fire along the line. The battle that followed was evenly contested, fierce, and disorderly. It was a "war of detachments and duels" in the dark. During the night British reinforcements arrived, giving them a substantial numerical advantage.[22] Under cover of a heavy fog, Jackson drew back to Rodriguez Canal. In the days that followed, the Americans threw up a rampart of mud, fence rails, and cotton bales to convert that broad, shallow ditch into a line of defense of variable strength. The *Carolina* and the *Louisiana* harassed the British camp so incessantly that the men withdrew to a village of Negro huts back from the river. Heavy British reinforcements continued to work their way up the bayou, and Major General Sir Edward Pakenham arrived to take over command. During the night of December 26, the British managed to haul two howitzers and a mortar across the swamp, and at dawn they blasted the little schooner out of the river and sent the *Louisiana* scuttling out of range.

By the morning of December 28, Jackson could see through his telescope that a British advance was imminent. The crew of the martyred *Carolina* arrived to man one of the few cannon that had been mustered. Red-shirted, bewhiskered Baratarians, under their artillery expert, Dominique You, took charge of another. The *Louisiana*, manned by a "motley crew taken from the streets of New Orleans not a fortnight before," lay ready for action.[23]

The battle that followed culminated in a clear defeat for the British. One of their soldiers later recorded his chagrin after the encounter: "In

The Defenders of New Orleans

spite of our sanguine expectations of sleeping that night in New Orleans, evening found us occupying our Negro hut at Villeré's, nor was I sorry that the shades of night concealed our mortification from the prisoners and slaves."[24]

A week and a half passed before the final confrontation—a time spent by both armies in strengthening their positions. The fighting had disclosed a weakness on Jackson's left flank, and he now remedied it by extending the line well into the swamp. The Tennessee bushfighters, whom the British called the "Dirty Shirts," improved the time by slipping through the woods and picking off British stragglers and sentries.[25] On New Year's Day an exchange of artillery fire took place in which Dominique You played a leading role, "standing exposed on the edge of the embankment, shouting French imprecations to his scarred warriors." This exchange cost the British much of their artillery and took a heavy toll of their morale. Two more regiments joined the British, but, at the same time, the long-awaited Kentucky militia arrived in New Orleans—most of them with only one shirt apiece, only a third of them armed, and these with fowling pieces and old muskets. "I don't believe it," Jackson exploded. He had never in his life seen a Kentuckian, he said, "without a gun, and a pack of cards, and a bottle of whiskey."[26] As they marched through the streets holding their tattered garments together, the citizenry was deeply moved and, within a few days, had subscribed $16,000 for blankets and warm clothing, which were quickly distributed.

On January 6, Jackson received intelligence that the British were deepening a canal from the swamp to the river and bringing up heavy equipment and boats. Clearly he could expect a British attack on the west bank of the river. Jackson ordered the few troops already stationed there, under General Morgan, to move up to the levee, from behind which they could decimate a landing force. On January 7, scouts reported that the British were improvising scaling ladders of sugarcane stalks. Their principal force, then, would be coming against his main line there on the east bank, Jackson concluded. Soon after dark, noises of preparation in the British camp came distinctly across the field, and the Americans set about making ready for the last great defense. Arms were cleaned and loaded, flints adjusted, and piles of scrap metal gathered beside the cannon. "If you sleep," warned Jackson, "sleep on your arms."[27]

At about one o'clock in the morning, a courier arrived from General Morgan and urgently requested more troops. Jackson replied that the main attack would come on the already established battlefield, that he could not spare more men, and that Morgan should hold his line "at all hazards."[28] Nevertheless, the general sent 500 Kentuckians to help man the west-bank defenses. Morgan failed to deploy his force as Jackson had suggested, but instead drew up a line along one of the canals back from the levee—a position untenable for his small body of 800 poorly equipped militia.

Jackson set out down the American line for a final review of the defenses. From the river, across the plantation land, and to the swamp he moved, studying the emplacement of the thirteen artillery pieces (which ranged from a single large thirty-two pounder to a small brass carronade with a defective carriage) and reexamining the disposition of his men. First, near the river, came Beale's New Orleans riflemen. Then, across the field, the regular artillery, the New Orleans dragoons, the crew of the *Carolina*, U.S. infantry, the pirates of Barataria, French privateers, the Battalion d'Orleans, the colored freedmen, a company of Creole artillerymen, and U.S. marines. From the point where the line struck the forest until it angled back into the swamp, the Tennessee militiamen under Generals Carroll and Coffee were posted. Because Jackson expected the heaviest assault here, he had ordered the Kentucky reserves drawn up behind them. In reserve, besides the Kentuckians, stood the Mississippi and Louisiana cavalries. Finally, farther out in the swamp lay a contingent of Choctaw Indians under a half-French leader. The entire force totaled 4,000 or 5,000 men, against about twice that number of attackers.[29]

In the predawn fog the British forces moved out of their encampment in long, trim columns of red. The advance companies came to a stop within 400 or 500 yards of the American line. Here they remained, listening anxiously for the sound of firing from across the river, for this was to be their signal to attack. Dawn came, but the fog continued to lay a protective cover over them. Still no firing broke the silence from the other side of the river, for the troops in flatboats had been swept downstream by the current and had not yet worked their way up to the American lines there. Then, suddenly, a capricious breeze shredded the fog, disclosing the ranks of redcoats to the watchers on the American parapet.

All the batteries in the American line began at once to hurl a tornado of iron missiles into the scarlet column, which shook and oscillated like a huge red ship on an angry sea.

The band of the Battalion d'Orleans struck up "Yankee Doodle." "Stand to your guns," cried Jackson. "Don't waste ammunition—see that every shot tells. Give it to them, boys. Let's finish the business today."[30]

The main attack (under General Gibbs) came, as Jackson had anticipated, against the Tennesseans along the edge of the swamp. The

Kentucky reserves moved up to the line, and the ranks of backwoodsmen sent a merciless relay fire smashing into the red line.

The men had previously calculated the range of their guns, and their bullets swept through the British column, cutting down men by the scores. Nor did the fire come in several volleys followed by intervals, but was kept up without interruption—the front men firing and falling back to load, while the next rank moved up and fired. Thus did the four lines—two Tennesseans and two Kentuckians—share the labor and glory of the most rapid and destructive fusillade ever poured into a column of soldiers. The British halted, wavered. Then General Pakenham himself came up, rallying and inspiring the men by appeals to their ancient fame. At this moment Pakenham's bridle arm was struck by a ball, and his horse killed by another. He then mounted a small black pony of his aide and pressed forward. But the column had advanced now as far as it could get. Most of the regimental officers were cut down. There were not enough to command, and the column began to break into detachments, some pushing forward to the ditch, but the greater parts falling back to the rear and to the swamp. Keane now wheeled his line into a column and pushed forward. Encouraged by their example, the remnant of Gibbs' brigade again came up, with Pakenham on their left and Gibbs on the right. They had approached within a hundred yards of the line. At this instant there was a terrible crash. The contents of one of the big guns of the Americans had fallen on the spot, killing and wounding nearly all who were near. Pakenham fell—a grapeshot had struck him in the thigh and passed through his horse, killing it immediately. Some of the men raised the General; another ball struck him in the groin. Dying, he was borne to the rear, where in a few minutes he breathed his last. Gibbs, desperately wounded shortly afterwards, lingered many hours in agony. Keane also fell badly wounded. There were now no field officers to rally the broken column. A handful reached the American breastwork, where they cowered under the protection of the entrenchment, enjoying a momentary respite. One mortally wounded man reached the top of the parapet. The remainder of the column, broken and panic-stricken, retired in confusion, leaving two thirds of its men dead or wounded on the field. In less than twenty-five minutes the main attack of the British was thus most violently repelled.[31]

The fighting on the rest of the field was not so bloody, but the rout was complete. By eight o'clock—two hours after the action had begun—only a few desultory shots followed the stragglers in retreat, and soon the cease-fire order passed down the lines. Jackson left his position to walk down the entrenchment, commending his men. As he went, a band struck up *Hail, Columbia,* and prolonged cheers greeted the chieftain.

Chapters from the American Experience

Jackson, concerned about the west bank, where the British had clearly won a decisive victory, set about organizing a strong relief force to rush across the river. It was an unnecessary precaution. The new British commander, surrounded by disaster, concluded that the advance position could not be held and ordered a withdrawal to the east bank.

While the British prepared an orderly retreat to their ships, the city of New Orleans erupted in celebration. And, almost a month later, when the news reached the Atlantic seaboard, men, women, and children paraded in the streets despite heavy snows. The "ALMOST INCREDI-BLE VICTORY" which the *National Intelligencer* announced in its largest headlines was just that. It bound up the country's wounded pride and fired a cult of hero worship that carried Jackson, fourteen years later, to the White House. Although fought more than two weeks after the treaty of peace was signed, the Battle of New Orleans, which the British had hoped would split America in two, had a very different result. Faced with a choice between easy surrender to the British and an "almost incredible" defense against impossible odds, the people of New Orleans—her Creoles, her Americans, her "new population," her Negroes, her pirates, her Indians—had joined together with Jackson and his heroic backwoodsmen to set the greatest armada the region had ever seen reeling back. It was a triumph of unity and courage that the young nation would not soon forget.

Jackson, concerned about the west bank, where the British had clearly won a decisive victory, set about organizing a strong relief force to rush across the river. It was an unnecessary precaution. The new British commander, surrounded by disaster, concluded that the advance position could not be held and ordered a withdrawal to the east bank.

Washington and Lee University.

John Marshall

18

The Man Behind
the Robes

The constitution, since its adoption, owes more to Chief Justice Marshall
than to any other single mind, for its true interpretation and vindication.
—Justice Joseph Story[1]

For America, 1819 was a year of crisis. After the close of the War of
1812, the nation had enjoyed a brief prosperity and a surge of proud
nationalism. It had been a time of dynamic development, with the
economy burgeoning and settlers in unprecedented numbers thrusting
out into the new areas west of the Appalachians and along the Gulf. The
Federalist Party, already under a cloud for its negative role in the war
and bound to the narrow interests of the Atlantic seaboard, had failed
to adjust to the needs of the new age and had slipped into the limbo
of history. The Republican Party had held an ascendancy unparalleled
since the early days of Federalism, as partisan rivalries melted in an Era
of Good Feeling.* But the Republican Party proved unequal to the task
of coping with the problems of the new age, although it did establish
a tariff to protect young American industry and charter a Second Bank
of the United States in an attempt to stabilize the country's currency
and credit.

The depression that struck suddenly in the opening weeks of 1819
undercut the nation's newfound unity and set the divisive forces of

* The Republican Party of this period was, of course, the Jeffersonian party, rather than
that which bears the name today.

sectionalism to work. In the Northeast, manufacturers brought pressure to bear for higher tariff protection, while shippers and the agrarian South voiced resentment at the tariff already in effect. Commercial interests of the Northern seaboard pressed for internal improvements that would help open up trade with the West, but the South balked at costly road and canal building at federal expense. The new agricultural areas of the South and West, suffering from the curtailment of the European market for their cotton and wheat and feeling the depression more sharply than any other section, turned on the Second Bank of the United States as the primary cause of their problems. By tightening credit and forcing the state banks to redeem their notes in gold, the branches of the national bank had compounded the difficulties of these pioneer farmers, who now vented their anger on that institution and on the business leaders of the Eastern seaboard who held most of its stock.

The sectional fears thus raised by the depression were deepened by the slavery question, as the struggle over Missouri roiled the South and stirred there the growing conviction that the section's best interests would be served not by nationalism but by states' rights.[2]

In that crucial year of 1819, as depression and the clash of sectional and economic interests undermined the solidarity of the nation, John Marshall, Chief Justice of the United States, seized the opportunity presented by several cases brought before him to strike at the power of the states and to declare in unmistakable, broad terms the philosophy of nationalism. Marshall's courageous stand in these cases was in perfect keeping with his beliefs and with his long career on the bench. The Virginian had been appointed by President Adams in the last months of his administration to serve on the Supreme Court as a bulwark of conservatism against the rising Republican tide. For thirty-four years he led that tribunal in every sense of the word—shaping it to his will, putting the stamp of his enduring Federalism on the governmental structure, justifying history in calling him the "Great Chief Justice." Even after the Court became predominantly Republican in personnel, it continued so completely under his sway that it was known as "Marshall's Court."

The tremendous influence Marshall wielded over his associates on the bench—both Federalist and Republican—is at first difficult to understand. His appearance was anything but impressive. Countless tales from his hometown of Richmond indicate that he was looked on with deep regard but also with a certain affectionate amusement.*

---

*Material from Albert J. Beveridge's *Life of John Marshall* is reprinted in condensed form, by permission of Houghton Mifflin Company, the publisher.

The tall, ungainly, negligently clad Chief Justice, ambling along the street, his arms laden with purchases, was a familiar sight. He never would hurry, and habitually lingered at the market-place, chatting with every- body, learning the gossip of the town, listening to the political talk that in Richmond never ceased. . . . The humblest and poorest man in Virginia was not more unpretentious than John Marshall.

No wag was more eager for a joke. One day, as he loitered on the outskirts of the market, a newcomer . . . offered him a small coin to carry home for him a turkey just purchased. Marshall accepted, and, with the bird under his arm, trudged behind his employer.[3]

Other stories added to the Marshall legend. A relative's wife once mistook him for the butcher and sent him around to the stable. Again, carrying a jug of whiskey out to the farmhands on his land near Richmond, he used his thumb for a stopper to replace a lost cork, amusing neighbors who delighted in telling how they saw the Chief Justice plodding along with his thumb immersed in a jug. On another occasion, driving his gig to Raleigh, he ran over a sapling, wedging it between a wheel and the shaft of the carriage. One of the slaves at work in a nearby field came over,

held down the sapling with one hand, and with the other backed the horse until the gig was free. Marshall tossed the negro a piece of money and asked him who was his owner . . . [The slave gave his master's name.] "He is an old friend," said Marshall; "tell him how you have helped me." . . . When the negro told his master . . . [the owner] said, "That was the . . . biggest lawyer in the United States." The slave smiled and answered, . . . "He may be the biggest lawyer in the United States, but he hasn't got sense enough to back a gig off a sapling."[4]

Anyone approaching the city of Richmond might see him riding along home from a day at the farm, with one hitchhiking youngster in front of him and another behind—or might see the Justice and his friends pitching horseshoes with exuberant zeal:

He was . . . [an] enthusiastic . . . attendant of the meetings of the Quoit Club . . . under the trees . . . on the outskirts of Richmond. . . . When he won . . . [said an observer] "the woods would ring with his triumphant shout." . . . [Once] a dispute arose between two players "as to the quoit nearest the meg." Marshall was agreed upon as umpire. "The Judge bent down on one knee and with a straw essayed the decision of this important question . . . frequently biting off the end of the straw" for greater accuracy.[5]

The Man Behind the Robes

Thomas Jefferson, Marshall's distant cousin and arch political antagonist, insisted that the Chief Justice's humble ways were a great sham. The philosophically democratic sage of Monticello found it difficult to reconcile Marshall's warm, folksy manner with his seemingly cold judicial decisions outlawing relief to debtors and consistently favoring the vested economic interests. But those who knew Marshall best considered honesty to be one of his most fundamental qualities. He believed that the business community was the stabilizing factor in American life, that sanctity of contract was the keystone to dynamic economic development. No real inconsistency existed between this philosophy in action and the portrait of the Chief Justice playing marbles with a small boy to put him at his ease or frolicking boisterously at one of his famous bachelor dinners. The men with whom he played quoits and talked on the street corners might one day avail themselves of the promise of America. He wished them all well. He shared their problems and their laughter; he loved their children. His radiant good health and enthusiasm for life touched all he knew and met an answering chord in the hearts of the folk of Richmond and in those of his associates on the bench. His gentle care for his distracted wife, who suffered from a nervous malady that became progressively worse, evoked the reverent regard of his neighbors.

It was a common thing for the Chief Justice to get up at any hour of the night and, without putting on his shoes lest his footfalls . . . further excite his wife, steal downstairs and drive away . . . a cow, a pig, a horse . . . whose sounds had annoyed her. Even upon entering his house during the daytime, Marshall would take off his shoes and put on soft slippers in the hall.

She was . . . unequal to the management of the household. When the domestic arrangements needed overhauling, Marshall would induce her to take a long drive. . . . The carriage out of sight, he would throw off his coat and vest, roll up his shirt sleeves, twist a bandana . . . about his head, and gathering the servants, lead them . . . in dusting the walls and furniture, scrubbing the floors and setting the house in order.[6]

During the six to eight weeks out of each year when he was in Washington for the sessions of the Supreme Court, Marshall's appearance and manner were the same as they had been in Richmond.

If he reached the court-room before the hour of convening court, he sat among the lawyers and talked and joked as if he were one of them; and, judging from his homely, neglected clothing, an uninformed onlooker would have taken him for the least important of the company. Yet there was about him an unconscious dignity. . . . When . . . the time came for him to open court, a transformation came over him. Clad in the robes of his great office, with the Associate Justices on either side of him, no king on a throne ever appeared more majestic than did John Marshall.[7]

Marshall's wit was gentle, even when it embodied a reproof. One young man (later a prominent jurist) coming to the Chief Justice for advice, tried to flatter him with the comment that he had "reached the acme of judicial distinction." "Let me tell you what that means, young man," broke in Marshall. "The acme of judicial distinction means the ability to look a lawyer straight in the eyes for two hours and not hear a damned word he says."[8]

Most eloquent among the Associate Justices in attesting the influence of Marshall's personality over his fellow magistrates was Joseph Story. Appointed to the Court as a Republican, Story wrote of the great Federalist, "I love his laugh . . . it is too hearty for an intriguer—and his good temper and unwearied patience are equally agreeable on the bench and in the study. . . . I am in love with his character, positively in love."[9]

Washington was still a "dismal" place, as Daniel Webster described it, and the Justices did not bring their wives to the malaria-infested capital but lived together in a single boardinghouse, in a communal sort of existence where Marshall played the role of the genial patriarch. As Story describes this life, the pervasive nature of Marshall's influence over his fellow Justices becomes evident.

"We live very harmoniously and familiarly," writes Story, . . . "with a mutual esteem which makes even the labors of Jurisprudence light." Sitting about a single table at their meals, or gathered in the rooms of one of them, these men talked over the cases before them. . . . "The Judges live here with perfect harmony," Story reiterates, . . . "and our social hours . . . are passed in gay and frank conversation." . . .

This "gay and frank conversation" of Marshall and his associates covered every subject—the methods, manners, and even dress of counsel who argued before them, the fortunes of public men, the trend of politics. . . . "Two of the Judges are widowers," records Story, "and of course objects of considerable attraction among the ladies of the city. We have fine sport at their expense, and amuse our leisure with some touches at match-making. We have already ensnared one of the Judges, and he is now (at the age of forty-seven) violently affected with the tender passion."

Thus Marshall, in his relation with his fellow occupants of the bench, was at the head of a family as much as he was Chief of a court. Although the discussion of legal questions occurred continuously at the boarding-

The Man Behind the Robes

house, each case was much more fully examined in the consultation room at the Capitol. There the court had a regular "consultation day" devoted exclusively to the cases in hand. Yet, even on these occasions, all was informality, and wit and humor brightened the tediousness. These "consultations" lasted throughout the day and sometimes into the night; and the Justices took their meals while the discussions proceeded. . . .

"We are great ascetics, and even deny ourselves wine except in wet weather," Story dutifully informed his wife. "What I say about the wine gives you our rule; but it does sometimes happen that the Chief Justice will say to me, when the cloth is removed, 'Brother Story, step to the window and see if it does not look like rain.' And if I tell him that the sun is shining brightly, Judge Marshall will sometimes reply, 'All the better, for our jurisdiction extends over so large a territory that the doctrine of chances makes it certain that it must be raining somewhere.' "

When, as sometimes happened, one of the Associate Justices displeased a member of the bar, Marshall would soothe the wounded feelings of the lawyer. Story once offended [a Virginia counselor] . . . by something said from the bench. "On my return from court yesterday," the Chief Justice hastened to write the irritated Virginian, "I informed Mr. Story that you had been much hurt at an expression used in the opinion he had delivered. . . . He expressed . . . surprise and regret . . . and declared that the words which had given offense were not used by him in an offensive sense. He assented without hesitation to such modification of them as would render them in your view entirely unexceptionable."[10]

Whether as the "king" among them in open court, or as their father confessor or jocular playmate in the consulting room or boardinghouse, Marshall thus exerted a powerful personal influence over his associates. The men who worked with him during their epochal sessions in Washington deeply admired his integrity, his "imperturbable temper," his open humor, his "unassuming simplicity and sincere gentleness." But Marshall's fellow justices were men of intelligence, and his personality alone could not have sufficed to account for his command. He also brought to bear upon them a penetrating mind, a driving will, and a deep sense of conviction.

For Marshall was a man with a message. "I had grown up at a time when . . . 'united we stand, divided we fall' was the maxim of every orthodox American," he said; "and I had imbibed these sentiments so thoroughly that they constituted a part of my being. I carried them with me into the [Revolutionary] army, where I found myself associated with brave men from different states, who were risking life and everything valuable in a common cause . . . and where I was confirmed in the habit of considering America as my country and congress as my government."[11]

Marshall came to the Supreme Court with a vivid recollection of the hardships the army had suffered because of a weak central government and with a deep distrust of the general trend among Americans to put loyalty to their states above loyalty to the nation. Through more than three decades on the bench, he used his position to strengthen the power of the central government.* Whenever the doctrine of national power could be implied in a case, he did so, expanding his decision into a declaration of fundamental principles that, in the end, shaped the course of government as surely as had the makers of the Constitution he interpreted.

And, less directly, throughout his tenure, he sought to swell the national power by enhancing the prestige of the judiciary. When he assumed office, the Supreme Court was so weak—relative to the executive and legislative branches—that retired Chief Justice John Jay (offered the position before Marshall) declined reappointment to it, saying, "I left the bench perfectly convinced that under a system so defective it would not obtain the energy, weight, and dignity which are essential to its affording due support to the national government."[12] Marshall, too, saw that the Constitution had left the status of the Court rather nebulous. But by the end of his term no one questioned the "energy, weight, and dignity" of the supreme tribunal. Assessing his contribution, Justice Frankfurter says that Marshall "gave institutional direction to the inert ideas of a paper scheme of government." His achievement, Frankfurter adds, testifies to an "uncompromising devotion" to the ideal of nationalism.[13]

Marshall's prime opportunity to propound this doctrine came in the case of *McCulloch* v. *Maryland* in March, 1819. The particular issue involved was Maryland's right to tax the notes issued by the Baltimore branch of the Second Bank of the United States. Maryland also raised the question of whether the federal government had any right to charter a bank and set up branches in competition with the state banks. Here was a clear conflict of national and state powers, and Marshall's ruling constituted a ringing affirmation, in Hamiltonian terms, of the nationalistic creed.

The federal government had indeed the right to establish a national bank with branches in the states, Marshall ruled. Then he moved magisterially on to fundamental principles. The Constitution was the instru-

---

*It should be pointed out, however, that, in cases involving neither the power of the national government nor the sanctity of contract, Marshall sustained the power of the state.

ment of the people of the United States, not a compact among states. It had been "ordained and established" in the name of the people, not of the separate states. "The government of the Union" he declared, "though limited in its powers, is supreme within the sphere of its action. . . . It is the government of all; its powers are delegated by all; it represents all and acts for all. . . . [The] people have in express terms decided it by saying, 'this constitution and the laws of the United States which shall be made in pursuance thereof . . . shall be the supreme law of the land.' "[14]

The Constitution was necessarily a brief and general document, he pointed out; it could not specifically encompass all possible situations that might arise. It was "intended to endure for ages to come and consequently to be adapted to the various *crises* of human affairs" as they occurred. In stating that the Congress shall have the right to make all laws "necessary and proper" for carrying out the general powers given it, the makers of the Constitution meant to "remove all doubts" respecting the right of Congress to "legislate on that vast mass of incidental powers which must be involved in the constitution" if that instrument is not to be merely a "splendid bauble." In determining which specific powers rest, by implication, with the general government, Marshall laid out a simple rule: "Let the end be legitimate, let it be within the scope of the constitution, and all means which are appropriate" and consistent with "the letter and spirit of the constitution" are constitutional.[15]

As for Maryland's taxing the national bank, the separate states could not tax any instrument of the federal government. The bank, the mail, the mint, the customhouses—none of these were either created by the constituents of the states, as such, or subject to them. For they were the creatures of that supreme government which had been erected by the people of *all* the states. "The states," he concluded, "have no power, by taxation or otherwise, to retard, impede, burden, or in any manner control, the operations of the constitutional laws enacted by congress to carry into execution the powers vested in the general government."[16]

These tenets of nationalism are today established pillars of the American way. They were not so when Marshall pronounced them. At a time when depression and the pull of antagonistic sectional interests strained at the foundations of the young nation, he voiced a confident, exuberant nationalism. With the country moving toward the "irresistible conflict that would come close to tearing it apart, Marshall spoke out authoritatively to shore up the edifice against the whirlwind. Marshall's economic conservatism was a direct reflection of the old Federalist Party creed, but his nationalism went beyond its seaboard provincialism and beyond the vague expansionist dreams of the old Republicans to a program of national strength that could render such visions a permanent reality. To the furtherance of this great goal, he concentrated the full efforts of a luminous mind, a driving conviction, and a magnetic personality.

Home of Abraham Lincoln in Spencer County, Indiana

Engraving by R. Hinshelwood. Indiana Historical Society.

19

Pioneers
of the Old Northwest:
The Lincoln Family

It is a great piece of folly to attempt to make anything out of my early life.
It can all be condensed into a single sentence from Gray's Elegy—
"The short and simple annals of the poor."
—Abraham Lincoln

When Abraham Lincoln assumed the presidency, he brought from Illinois two young men who worked closely with him as his personal secretaries throughout his administration. A quarter of a century later these men, John Nicolay and John Hay, collaborated in publishing a biography which, despite all the extensive studies that have intervened, is still read for its colorful depiction of the world through which the great president moved.[1] The following reading is condensed from a chapter of that work portraying Lincoln's boyhood and adolescence in Indiana and the harsh realities of pioneer life in the Old Northwest during the second and third decades of the nineteenth century.

By the time the boy Abraham had attained his seventh year, the social condition of Kentucky had changed considerably from the early pioneer days. Life had assumed a more settled and orderly course. [Caught up in a dispute over his right to the land he had been cultivating] Thomas Lincoln concluded that Kentucky was no country for a poor man and decided to seek his fortune in Indiana. He built a rude raft, loaded it with his kit of tools and four hundred gallons of whisky, and trusted his future to the winding water-courses. On his way, his raft capsized in the Ohio River, but he fished up his kit of tools and most of the ardent spirits, and arrived safely at the place of a settler named Posey, with whom he left his odd inventory of household goods, while he started on foot to look for a home in the dense forest. He selected a spot which pleased him in his first day's journey. He then walked back to Knob Creek, Kentucky, and brought his family on to their new home. No humbler cavalcade ever invaded the Indiana timber. Besides his wife and two children, his earthly possessions were of the slightest, for the backs of two borrowed horses sufficed for the load. Insufficient bedding and clothing, a few pans and kettles, were their sole movable wealth. They relied on Lincoln's kit of tools for their furniture, and on his rifle for their food. At Posey's they hired a wagon and literally hewed a path through the wilderness to their new habitation near Little Pigeon Creek, in a rich and fertile forest country.

Thomas Lincoln, with the assistance of his wife and children, built a temporary shelter of the sort called in the frontier language "a half-faced camp"—merely a shed of poles, which defended the inmates on three sides from foul weather, but left them open to its inclemency in front. For a whole year his family lived in this wretched fold, while he was clearing a little patch of ground for planting corn, and building a rough cabin for a permanent residence. They moved into the latter before it was half completed, for by this time the Sparrows [relatives of Mrs. Lincoln] had followed the Lincolns from Kentucky, and the half-faced camp was given up to them. But the rude cabin seemed so spacious and comfortable after the squalor of "the camp," that Thomas Lincoln did no further work on it for a long time. He left it for a year or two without doors, or windows, or floor. The battle for existence allowed him no time for such superfluities. He raised enough corn to support life; the dense forest around him abounded in every form of feathered game; a little way from his cabin an open glade was full of deer-licks, and an hour or two of idle waiting was generally rewarded by a shot at a fine deer, which would furnish meat for a week, and material for breeches and shoes. His cabin was like that of other pioneers. A few three-legged stools; a bedstead made of poles stuck between the logs in the angle of the cabin, the outside corner supported by a crotched stick driven into the ground; the table, a huge hewed log standing on four legs; a pot, kettle, and skillet, and a few tin and pewter dishes were all the furniture. The boy Abraham climbed at night to his bed of leaves in the loft by a ladder of wooden pins driven into the logs.

Old settlers reminiscing about the "happy, healthy" pioneer days in this area tend to see by the flattering light of distance the time of their youth. Dennis Hanks [Lincoln's cousin, who was raised with him], speaking of his

Chapters from the American Experience

days in the half-faced camp, says, "I tell you, I enjoyed myself better then than I ever have since." But, existence was a constant and precarious struggle. The rank woods were full of malaria, and strange epidemics from time to time ravaged the settlements. In the autumn of 1818 the little community of Pigeon Creek was almost exterminated by a frightful pestilence called the milk-sickness. It is a mysterious disease which seems to have been a malignant form of fever—attributed variously to malaria and to the eating of poisonous herbs by the cattle—attacking cattle as well as human beings, attended with violent retching and a burning sensation in the stomach, often terminating fatally on the third day. In many cases those who apparently recovered lingered for years with health seriously impaired. Among the pioneers of Pigeon Creek, with their poor diet and primitive housing, there was little prospect of recovery from such a grave disorder. The Sparrows, husband and wife, died early in October, and Nancy Hanks Lincoln followed them after an interval of a few days. Thomas Lincoln made the coffins for his dead "out of green lumber cut with a whipsaw," and they were all buried, with scant ceremony, in a little clearing of the forest. This was the dreariest winter of young Abraham's life.

Before the next December came, his father had brought from Kentucky a new wife, who was to change the lot of all the desolate little family very much for the better. Sarah Bush had been an acquaintance of Thomas Lincoln before his first marriage; she had, it is said, rejected him to marry one Johnston, who had died, leaving her with a boy and two girls. When Lincoln's widowhood had lasted a year, he went to Kentucky to begin again the wooing broken off so many years before. He wasted no time in preliminaries, but promptly made his wishes known, and the next morning they were married. It was growing late in the autumn, and the pioneer probably dreaded another lonely winter on Pigeon Creek. Mrs. Johnston had a store of household goods which filled a four-horse wagon borrowed of Lincoln's brother-in-law, to transport the bride to Indiana. It took little time for this energetic and honest woman to make her influence felt, even in those discouraging surroundings. The lack of doors and floors was at once corrected. She dressed the children in warmer clothing and put them to sleep in comfortable beds. With her slight addition to their resources the family were much improved in appearance, behavior, and self-respect.

Thomas Lincoln joined the Baptist church at Little Pigeon in 1823. The family became known as active and consistent members of that community. Lincoln was himself a good carpenter when he chose to work at his trade. As for education for the children, they made use of the scanty opportunities the neighborhood afforded. "It was a wild region," writes Abraham Lincoln, in one of those rare bits of autobiography which he left behind him, "with many bears and other wild animals still in the woods.

Pioneers of the Old Northwest: The Lincoln Family

There were some schools so-called, but no qualification was ever required of a teacher beyond 'readin', writin', and cipherin' to the Rule of Three.' If a straggler supposed to understand Latin happened to sojourn in the neighborhood, he was looked upon as a wizard. There was absolutely nothing to excite ambition for education." But in the case of this ungainly boy there was no necessity of any external incentive. A thirst for knowledge as a means of rising in the world was innate in him. All the little learning he ever acquired he seized as a tool to better his condition. He learned his letters that he might read books and see how men in the great world outside of his woods had borne themselves in the fight for which he longed. Had it not been for that interior spur, his schooling could have done little for him; for, counting his attendance in Kentucky and in Indiana, it amounted to less than a year in all. The schools were much alike. They were held in deserted cabins of round logs, with earthen floors, and small holes for windows, sometimes illuminated only by such light as could penetrate through panes of paper greased with lard. Young Abraham's last schooldays were passed at a distance of four and a half miles from the Lincoln cabin. The nine miles of walking doubtless seemed to Thomas Lincoln a waste of time, and the lad was put at steady work and saw no more of school.

Still, in all the intervals of his work and when his daily tasks were done, he read, wrote, and ciphered incessantly. Studying became the chief pleasure of his life. Books were among the rarest of luxuries in that region and time, but Lincoln devoured everything he could lay his hands on—the *Bible, Aesop's Fables, Robinson Crusoe, The Pilgrim's Progress,* a history of the United States, and Weem's *Life of Washington.* These he read over and over till he knew them almost by heart. He would sit in the twilight and pore over a dictionary as long as he could see. He used to go to the town constable's and study the *Revised Statutes of Indiana.* Of the books he did not own he took voluminous notes, filling his copy-book with choice extracts, and going over them until they were fixed in his memory. He could not afford to waste paper upon his original compositions. He would sit by the fire at night and cover the wooden shovel with essays and arithmetic exercises, which he would then shave off so he could begin again.

John Hanks says, "When Abe and I returned to the house from work, he would go to the cupboard, snatch a piece of cornbread, take down a book, sit down, cock his legs up as high as his head, and read." The habit remained with him always. Some of his greatest work in later years was done in this grotesque Western fashion—"sitting on his shoulder-blades."

Otherwise his life at this time differed little from that of ordinary farm-hands. His great strength and intelligence made him a valuable laborer, and his good temper and flow of rude rustic wit rendered him the most agreeable of comrades. It was considered an eccentricity that he hated

Chapters from the American Experience

and preached against cruelty to animals. Some of his comrades remember still his bursts of righteous wrath, when a boy, against the wanton murder of turtles and other creatures. His was a happy and united household, brothers and sisters and cousins living peacefully under the gentle rule of the good stepmother, but all acknowledging from a very early period the goodness and cleverness of their big brother Abraham. Mrs. Lincoln, not long before her death, gave striking testimony to his character. "I can say what scarcely one mother in a thousand can say. Abe never gave me a cross word or look, and never refused in fact or appearance to do anything I asked him. His mind and mine—what little I had—seemed to run together. I had a son John, who was raised with Abe. Both were good boys, but I must say, both now being dead, that Abe was the best boy I ever saw or expect to see."

We are making no claim of early sainthood for him. One of his employers faithfully remembers that young Abe liked his dinner and his pay better than his work. It is also reported that he sometimes slowed harvest operations with burlesque speeches or comic sermons from the top of some tempting stump, to the delight of the hired hands and the exasperation of the farmer. His budding talents as a writer were not always used discreetly. He was too much given to scribbling coarse satires and chronicles. From this arose occasional heart-burnings and feuds, in which Abraham bore his part according to the custom of the country. Despite his natural love of peace, he was no practitioner of non-resistance, and when he once entered upon a quarrel, the opponent usually had the worst of it. Brawling was common in the state of society that prevailed among the people with whom Lincoln's lot was cast in these years.

In most respects there had been little moral or material improvement since the early settlement of the country. Their houses were usually of one room, built of round logs with the bark on. Their dress was still mostly of tanned deer-hide, a material to the last degree uncomfortable when the wearer was caught in a shower. Their shoes were of the same, and an authority on the subject calls a wet moccasin "a decent way of going barefoot." About the time, however, when Lincoln grew to manhood, garments of wool and coarse thread began to be worn, dyed with the juice of butternut or white walnut, and the hides of neat-cattle began to be tanned. But for a good while it was only the women who indulged in these novelties.

There was little public worship. Occasionally an itinerant preacher visited a county, and the settlers for miles around would go nearly in mass to the meeting. If a man was possessed of a wagon, the family rode luxuriously; but as a rule the men walked and the women went on horseback with the little children in their arms. It was considered no violation of the sanctities of the occasion to carry a rifle and take advantage of any game

Pioneers of the Old Northwest: The Lincoln Family

which might be stirring during the long walk. Arriving at the place of meeting, which was some log cabin if the weather was foul, or the shade of a tree if it was fair, the assembled worshipers threw their provisions into a common store and picnicked in neighborly companionship.

There were few other social meetings. Men came together for "raisings," where a house was built in a day; for wolf-hunts, where a tall pole was erected in the midst of a prairie or clearing, and a great circle of hunters, sometimes of miles in diameter, gradually contracted with shouts and yells and drove all the game in the woods together at the pole for slaughter; and for horse-races, which bore little resemblance to those magnificent exhibitions which have since become the boast of Kentucky. In these affairs the women naturally took no part; but weddings, which were entertainments scarcely less rude and boisterous, were their own peculiar province. These festivities lasted rarely less than twenty-four hours. The guests assembled in the morning. There was a race for the whisky bottle; a midday dinner; an afternoon of rough games and outrageous practical jokes; a supper and dance at night, interrupted by the successive withdrawals of the bride and of the groom, attended with ceremonies and jests of more than Rabelaisian crudeness; and a noisy dispersal next day.

The one point at which they instinctively clung to civilization was their regard for law and for courts of justice. Yet these were of the simplest character. An early jurist of the country writes: "I was Circuit Prosecuting Attorney at the time of the trials at Fall Creek. Four of the prisoners were convicted of murder, and three of them hung, for killing Indians. The court was held in a double log cabin, the grand jury sat upon a log in the woods, and the foreman signed the bills of indictment upon his knee; there was not a petty juror that had shoes on; all wore moccasins, and were belted around the waist, and carried side-knives used by the hunters." Yet amidst all this apparent savagery we see justice done, despite the bitter prejudice of the pioneers against Indians.

Many pioneers were full of strange superstitions. The belief in witchcraft survived far into the Nineteenth Century in Kentucky and lower Indiana and Illinois—touched with a peculiar tinge of African magic. Veterinary practice was mostly by charms and incantations, and luck was an active divinity. A dog crossing such a hunter's path spoiled his day, unless he instantly hooked his little fingers together, and pulled till the animal disappeared. A vague and ignorant astronomy governed their plantings and sowings, the breeding of their cattle, and all farm-work. They must fell trees for fence-rails before noon, and in the waxing of the moon. The moonless season was the proper one for planting potatoes and other vegetables whose fruit grows underground; but those which bear their product in the air must be planted when the moon shone.*

---

*The impression, of course, should not be conveyed that all pioneers deserted their

Among these people, Abraham Lincoln passed his childhood and youth. He was not remarkably precocious. His mind was slow in acquisition, and his powers of reasoning and rhetoric improved constantly to the end of his life. But there was that about him, even at the age of nineteen years, which might well justify his admiring friends in presaging for him an unusual career. He had read every book he could find, and could "spell down" the whole county at their contests. By dint of constant practice he had acquired an admirably clear and serviceable handwriting. He occasionally astounded his companions by giving them such scientific information as that the world is round and that the sun is relatively stationary. He wrote, for his own amusement and edification, essays on politics, of which gentlemen of standing said with authority at the cross-roads grocery, "The world can't beat them." One or two of these compositions got into print and vastly increased the author's local fame. Also, his generosity, courage, and capability of discerning two sides to a dispute, were remarkable. But perhaps, after all, the thing which gained and fixed his mastery over his fellows was to a great degree his gigantic stature and strength. He attained his full growth, six feet and four inches, two years before he came of age. He rarely met with a man he could not easily handle. One of his employers says, "He could sink an axe deeper into wood than any man I ever saw."

In 1828 an opportunity offered for a little glimpse of the world outside, and the boy gladly embraced it. He was hired by a Mr. Gentry, an entrepreneur in the neighboring village, to accompany his son with a flat-boat of produce to New Orleans and intermediate landings. The voyage was made successfully, and Abraham gained great credit for his management and sale of the cargo. The only important incident of the trip occurred a few miles below Baton Rouge. The young merchants tied up for the night and were asleep in a cabin when they were aroused by shuffling footsteps, which proved to be a gang of marauders, coming to rob the boat. Abraham instantly attacked them with a club, knocked several overboard and put the rest to flight.

The next autumn, John Hanks went to Illinois. He settled in Macon County and was so well pleased with the country, and especially with its admirable distribution into prairie and timber, that he sent repeated messages to his friends in Indiana to come out and join him. In 1830, Thomas Lincoln handed over his farm to Mr. Gentry, sold his crop of corn and hogs, packed his household goods and those of his children and sons-in-law into

cultural heritage or their wits when they moved West—as evidenced by Lincoln's own life. Their reactions to the environment varied, as did those of Lincoln's father and stepmother. See Ray Allen Billington, *America's Frontier Heritage* (New York: Holt, Rinehart & Winston, Inc., 1966).

Pioneers of the Old Northwest: The Lincoln Family

a single wagon, drawn by two yoke of oxen (the combined wealth of himself and Dennis Hanks), and started for the new state.

Two weeks of weary tramping over forest roads and muddy prairie, and the dangerous fording of streams swollen by the February thaws, brought the party to John Hanks' place near Decatur. Hanks had already selected a piece of ground for them a few miles from his own, and had the logs ready for their house. They numbered men enough to build without calling in their neighbors, and immediately put up a cabin on the north fork of the Sangamon River. The family thus housed and sheltered, one more bit of filial work remained for Abraham, now 21, before assuming his independence. With the assistance of John Hanks he plowed fifteen acres and split, from the tall walnut trees of the primeval forest, enough rails to surround them with a fence.

Little did either dream, while engaged in this work, that the day would come when the appearance of John Hanks in a public meeting, with two of these rails on his shoulder, would electrify a State Convention and kindle throughout the country a contagious and passionate enthusiasm, whose results would reach to endless generations.[2]

Illustration by E. Boyd Smith for an early twentieth-century edition of Richard Henry Dana's *Two Years Before the Mast.* The Granger Collection.

20

Before the Mast

I vowed that I would do something
to redress the grievances
of that poor class of beings.

"There is a witchery in the sea, its songs and stories, and in the mere sight of a ship, especially to a young mind, which has done more to man navies and fill merchantmen than all the press-gangs of Europe," wrote Richard Henry Dana in his immortal *Two Years Before the Mast.* "Many are the boys, in every seaport, who are drawn away, as by an almost irresistible attraction, from their work and schools and hang about the decks and yards of vessels with a fondness which, it is plain, will have its way."[1] The romantic pull of the sea was especially strong in the nineteenth century, as the tall, stately Indiamen, the whalers, the sleek clippers, and the square-rigged brigs set out on seemingly glamorous adventures to the ends of the earth. Nowhere was that pull stronger than in Boston Harbor. In the summer of 1834 young Dana, whose vision had been temporarily impaired by illness, left his studies at Harvard to sail in one of these Yankee ships, a small brig manned by a crew of eight and bound, via treacherous Cape Horn, for the remote coast of California. Its hold was filled with a wide variety of finished goods, and it sought in return a cargo of cattle hides and tallow.

Ever since Mexico had opened the ports of California to American trade in the early 1820s, Yankee vessels had been tempting the people of that pastoral land with the products of civilization. The only substantial commodity that the rancheros had to exchange for such merchandise was hides. These they priced so high that the profit to the vessel owners lay almost entirely in the sale of the manufactured goods brought West. Before midcentury this commerce, becoming increasingly unprofitable and being disrupted by the Mexican War and the Gold Rush, dwindled to a trickle. But, between 1826 and 1848, approximately a million hides were taken out of California, largely in Yankee vessels. This trade stimulated American manufacturing and shipping and stirred an interest in California that contributed to its admission into the Union.[2]

However, like other merchantmen of the sailing era, the ships of the "hide-droghing" trade offered a harsh school for young men who took up the life of the sea. Long before Dana returned to Boston, he had lost his romantic notions about that way of life. "All who have followed me in my narrative must be convinced that the sailor has no romance in his everyday life to sustain him," he wrote. "If I have not produced this conviction, I have failed in persuading others of what my experience has most fully impressed upon myself."[3] Dana's classic account of his voyage won immediate acclaim and became one of the first of many literary works to expose the monotonous drudgery, the daily hardships, and the ever-present threat of irresponsible tyranny which were the lot of nineteenth-century seamen.

The fourteenth of August, 1834, was the day fixed upon for the sailing of the brig *Pilgrim* on her voyage from Boston round Cape Horn to the western coast of North America. As she was to get under way early in the afternoon, I made my appearance on board at twelve o'clock, in full sea-rig. The change from the tight dress coat, silk cap and kid gloves of an undergraduate at Cambridge, to the loose-bottomed duck trousers, checked shirt and tarpaulin hat of a sailor having been made, I supposed that I should pass very well for a jack tar. But I was, no doubt, known for a landsman by everyone on board as soon as I hove in sight. A sailor has a peculiar way of wearing his clothes which a green hand can never get. The low-crowned, well varnished black hat worn on the back of the head with half a fathom of black ribbon hanging over the left eye and the peculiar tie to the black silk neckerchief, along with sundry other little things, set the seaman apart. Besides, my complexion and hands were enough to distinguish me from the regular *salt,* who, with sunburnt cheek, wide step, and rolling gait, swings his bronzed and toughened hands athwartships, half open, as though just ready to grasp a rope.

We hauled out into the stream and came to anchor for the night. The next day was employed in preparations, and on the following night I stood my first watch. I remained awake nearly all the first part of the night for fear that I might not hear when I was called. And when I went on deck, so great were my ideas of the importance of my trust that I walked regularly fore and aft the whole length of the vessel, looking out over the bows and taffrail at each turn, and was not a little surprised at the coolness with which the old salt who took my place stowed himself snugly away under the long boat for a nap. That was sufficient lookout, he thought, for a fine night, at anchor in a safe harbor.

The next morning was Saturday, and, being delayed by adverse winds, we remained in harbor through the day and part of the night. About midnight the wind became fair, and in a short time everyone was in motion, the sails loosed, the yards braced, and we began to heave up the anchor which was our last hold on Yankee land. I could take but little part in all these preparations. Unintelligible orders were so rapidly given and so immediately executed, there was such a hurrying about, and such an intermingling of strange cries and stranger actions that I was completely bewildered. The noise of the water thrown from the bows began to be heard, the vessel leaned over from the damp night breeze and rolled with the heavy ground swell. We had actually begun our long, long journey.

The first day we passed at sea was the Sabbath. When we were called aft to be divided into watches, I had a good example of the ways of a sea captain, for he gave a short characteristic speech, walking the quarter deck with a cigar in his mouth, and dropping the words out between the puffs.

"Now, my men, we have begun a long voyage. If we get along well together, we shall have a comfortable time; if we don't we shall have hell afloat.—All you've got to do is to obey your orders and do your duty like men—then you'll fare well enough. —If you don't, you'll fare hard enough —I can tell you."

When eight bells were struck, we went below. I now began to feel the first discomforts of a sailor's life. The steerage in which I lived was filled with coils of rigging, spare sails, old junk and ship stores, which had not been stowed away. Moreover, there had been no berths built for us to sleep in. The vessel was rolling heavily, everything was pitched about in grand confusion, and we were allowed no light to find anything with. I began to feel strong symptoms of sea-sickness and, giving up all attempts to collect my things together, lay down upon the sails. Shortly I heard the rain drops falling on deck, thick and fast, and the loud and repeated orders of the mate, the trampling of feet, the creaking of blocks, and all the accompaniments of a coming storm. In a few minutes the slide to the hatch was thrown back and the loud cry of "All hands, ahoy" saluted our ears. When I got up on deck, the winds were whistling through the rigging, loose ropes flying about, loud orders rapidly executed, and the sailors "singing out" at the ropes in their hoarse and peculiar strains. In addition to all this, I was now dreadfully sick, with hardly strength to hold on to anything, and it was "pitch dark." This was my state when I was ordered aloft for the first time to reef topsails.

How I managed I cannot now remember. I "laid out" on the yards and held on with all my strength. I could not have been of much service, for I remember having been sick several times before I left the topsail yard.

Before the Mast

When all the sails were snug, we were allowed to go below again. This I did not consider much of a favor, for the confusion of everything below and that inexpressible sickening smell caused by the shaking up of the bilge water in the hold made the steerage but an indifferent refuge from the cold wet decks. In addition to every other evil, I could not but remember that this was only the first night of a two years' voyage.[4]

Dana quickly "got his sea legs on," and the ship now enjoyed a long spell of fine weather "without an incident to break the monotony" of the days. The young landsman had time to learn the ways of a sailing vessel and to observe the beauties and the awesomeness of the sea—the iridescent grace of a dolphin moving a few feet below surface on a bright day, the "perpendicular fierceness of the tropic sun," the "melancholy first grey streaks of dawn across the face of the deep," the brilliance of the Southern Cross.

Rounding the Horn, the little brig plunged abruptly into a "tremendous head sea, which rushed in through the bow-ports and over the bows, and buried all the forward part of the vessel." For more than a week the *Pilgrim* and her crew battled their way westward. Then they turned north and, leaving the albatross and the howling winds behind, headed for the equator and the coast of California. The cargo was to be cleared with the Mexican authorities at the port of Monterey, and there the *Pilgrim* came to anchor in late January, 1835, after a voyage of more than five months.

The next day being Sunday, which is the liberty-day among merchantmen, the sailors were already disputing who should ask to go ashore when we found that the topmast, which had been sprung, was to come down at once and a new one to go up. If there is anything that irritates sailors and makes them feel badly used, it is being deprived of their Sabbath, which is their only day of rest. They are often necessarily deprived of it by storms and unavoidable duties, so, to take it from them when lying quietly in port stirs much resentment. The only reason in this case was that the captain had determined to have the custom officers on board on Monday and wished to have his brig in order. Jack Tar is a slave aboard ship, but still he has many opportunities to thwart his master. When he is well treated, no one can work faster than he. But the instant he feels that he is kept at work for nothing, no sloth could make less headway. He must not refuse his duty, but all the work that an officer gets out of him, he is welcome to. This morning everything went in this way. Send a man below to get a block, and he would capsize everything in finding it, then not bring it up till an officer had called him twice, and take as much time to put things in order again. Marline-spikes were not to be found, knives wanted a prodigious deal of sharpening, and generally three or four were waiting round the grindstone at a time. When a man got to the mast-head, he would come slowly down again to get something which he had forgotten. When the mate was out of sight, nothing was done. At eight o'clock, when we went to breakfast, things were nearly where they were when we began.

During our short meal, the matter was discussed. One proposed refusing to work. But that was mutiny and of course was rejected at once. After breakfast, it leaked out, through the officers, that if we would get through with our work quickly, we might have a boat in the afternoon and go fishing. This bait took with several who were fond of fishing. Accordingly, things took on a new aspect, and before two o'clock the work was done, and five of us went fishing in the jolly boat.

The next day, the cargo having been entered in due form, the Californians came aboard, and we began trading. A trade-room was fitted up in the steerage and furnished out with specimens of the cargo. A young crewman who had been a clerk in a Boston counting house was taken out of the forecastle and made supercargo's clerk. For a week or ten days all was life on board. The Mexicans came to look and to buy, and we were continually going in the boats, carrying goods and passengers. A new ship was an important event in the pastoral lives of these people. They must dress up (in silks and figured calico, the men with rich waistcoats and red sashes, the women with high combs and mantillas) and come aboard, if only to buy a paper of pins. Our cargo was an assorted one. We had spirits of all kinds (sold by the cask), teas, coffee, sugars, spices, raisins, molasses, hardware, furniture, kitchenware, clothing of every sort—shoes, calicoes and cottons from Lowell, shawls, jewelry and combs—everything from Chinese fireworks to English cart wheels. Things sell, on an average, at an advance of nearly three hundred per cent over the Boston prices.

These people have no credit system, no banks, and no circulating medium but silver and hides—which the sailors call "California bank notes." Everything that they buy they must pay for in one or the other of these things. The hides they bring down dried and doubled, in clumsy ox-carts, or upon mules' backs, and the money they carry tied up in a handkerchief—fifty or a hundred dollars and half dollars.

After a few days, finding the trade beginning to slacken, we hove our anchor up, set our topsails, ran the stars and stripes up to the peak, fired a gun (which salute was returned) and left the little town astern, bearing down the coast for Santa Barbara. Here and in other towns along that remote coast, we continued the long task of clearing the hold of Boston goods and reloading it with hides.

I had never studied Spanish while at college, and could not speak a word, but I borrowed a grammar and dictionary from the cabin, and soon put a vocabulary together and got the name of a great linguist. So I was always sent by the captain to get provisions or to carry messages. I was often sent for something I could not tell the name of to save my life; but

Before the Mast

I liked the business and never pleaded ignorance but contrived to get along. This gave me opportunities of seeing the customs, characters, and domestic arrangements of the people. . . .

Monterey is the most civilized-looking place in California. In the center is an open square, surrounded by four lines of one-story plastered buildings, with half a dozen cannon in the center. This is the "Presidio," or fort. There were several officers at Monterey with long titles, and about eighty soldiers, poorly paid, fed, clothed, and disciplined. The governor-general lives here, which makes it the seat of government. In addition to him, Monterey (like every other town) has a commandant, who is the chief military officer, and two or three alcades, or civil officers, elected by the inhabitants. Courts and jurisprudence they have no knowledge of. Small municipal matters are regulated by the alcades, and everything relating to the general government by the commandant.

The houses are made of sun-hardened clay bricks, the windows generally grated and without glass, though some of the more wealthy have glass windows, board floors, and red tile roofs. The Indians do all the hard work, two or three being attached to each house; and the poorest Mexicans can keep one at least, for they have only to feed them and give them a small piece of coarse cloth and a belt for the males and a coarse gown without shoes or stockings for the females.

In every town there are a number of English and Americans. They usually keep shops, in which they retail the goods purchased from our vessels and also send a good deal into the interior, taking hides in pay, which they again barter with our vessels. The people are generally suspicious of foreigners, and they would not be allowed to remain, were it not that they become good Catholics, and by marrying natives and bringing up their children as Catholics and Mexicans and not teaching them the English language, they quiet suspicion, and even become popular and leading men. The chief alcades in Monterey and Santa Barbara were both Yankees by birth.

It was only over a period of time that I observed these things, for our harbor duties were heavy. All hands were called at the first grey of morning, and the crew rigged the head pump and washed down the decks until eight o'clock, when breakfast was ordered. After breakfast, for which half an hour was allowed, the boats were lowered, and the crew turned to on their day's work.

When the surf was not high, we landed goods and took off hides. The goods were taken away by Indians in large clumsy ox-carts with the yoke on the ox's neck instead of under it, and with small solid wheels. We carried the hides back to the ship in "California style," wading out with them through the breakers and tossing them into the boat just outside the surf. We provided ourselves with thick Scotch caps, which would be soft to the head and at the same time protect it, for we soon found that "head-work" was the only system for the task.

Chapters from the American Experience

The captain told us that it was "California fashion" to carry two hides on the head at a time, and we did so for the first few months. But, after falling in with a few other "hide-droghers" and finding that they carried only one at a time, we "knocked off" the extra one and thus made our duty somewhat easier. After we had got our heads used to the weight and had learned how to toss a hide, we could carry off two or three hundred in a short time. But it was always wet work and, if the beach was stony, bad for our feet, for we always went barefoot on this duty, as no shoes could stand such constant wetting with salt water. Then too, we had a long pull to the ship, and with a loaded boat this often took a couple of hours.

In addition to boating, there was always a good deal to be done in the hold—goods to be broken out and cargo shifted to make room for hides or to keep the trim of the vessel. Also, the usual work on the rigging had to be done. Some religious captains give their crews Saturday afternoons to do their washing and mending in, so that they may have their Sundays free. We were glad if we got Sunday to ourselves, for, if any hides came down on that day we were obliged to bring them off, which usually took half a day. Also, we now lived on fresh beef alone and ate one bullock a week, and the animal was almost always brought down on Sunday, so we had to go ashore, kill it, dress it, and bring it aboard.

But all these little vexations and labors would have been nothing—they would have been passed by as the common evils of sea life—had it not been for the uncertainty which hung over us as to the length of our voyage. Here we were in a little vessel, with a small crew, on a half-civilized coast at the ends of the earth. When we left Boston we supposed that it was to be a voyage of eighteen months, or two years at most. But, on arriving on the coast, we learned more about the trade and found that, with the scarcity of hides (which was yearly greater and greater), it would take us a year at least to collect our cargo. A ship which was then preparing to depart had been nearly two years on the coast before it was fully loaded. Further, during the passage, we had heard rumors, which had leaked out from the captain and mate, that a large ship belonging to the same firm as ours was following us and that we would be required to act as her tender. We had dismissed these rumors as mere "yarns," but, when we arrived, they were confirmed by letters we had brought from the owners to their agents in California. We were to collect all the hides we could and deposit them at San Diego. Then the new ship—the *Alert,* a well-known Indiaman which would carry forty thousand hides—was to be filled by us and sent home. After that, we would begin anew and collect our own cargo. Here was a gloomy prospect indeed. A cloud seemed to hang over the crew. Hints were thrown out about three and four years. This was bad enough for the others, but still worse for me, who did not mean to be a sailor for life. Three or four years would make me a sailor in every respect, mind and

Before the Mast

habits as well as body, and would put all my companions so far ahead of me that college and a profession would be in vain to think of.

Perhaps partly as a consequence of this state of things, there was trouble brewing on board the vessel. The captain was a vigorous, energetic fellow, made of steel and whalebone. During all the time that I was with him, I never saw him sit down on deck. He was always active and driving, severe in his discipline. The mate not being enough of a driver for him, he began to interfere in everything. He drew the reins taughter and became suspicious of the crew. Seeing that everything went wrong, that nothing was done "with a will," he attempted to remedy the difficulty by severity, and only made everything worse. We felt that our situation called upon our superiors to give us occasional relaxations and to make our yoke easier. But the contrary policy was pursued. We were kept at work all day when in port, and when we were at sea, sailing from port to port, instead of giving us "watch and watch," as was the custom, we were all kept on deck and at work, rain or shine. All hands were called to "come up and see it rain," and kept on deck hour after hour in a drenching rain, standing around the deck so far apart as to prevent our talking with one another, with our tarpaulins and oilcloth jackets on, picking old rope to pieces, or laying up gaskets and spun yarn. This is called "hazing" a crew.

The captain now took on board a short, red-haired, round-shouldered, vulgar-looking fellow, who had lost one eye and squinted with the other. Introducing him as *Mr.* Russell, he told us he was to be an officer on board. This was bad. We had lost overboard on the passage one of the best of our number; another had been taken from us and appointed clerk. Instead of shipping some hands to make our work easier, he had put another officer over us, to watch and drive us. We now had four officers and only six of us in the forecastle.

For several days the captain seemed very much out of humor. Nothing went right or fast enough for him. He had a dispute with the mate and quarrelled with the cook, threatening to flog him for throwing wood on deck. However, his displeasure was chiefly turned against a large, heavy-moulded fellow from the Middle States called Sam. This man hesitated in his speech and was rather slow in his motions, but he was a pretty good sailor, and always seemed to do his best. The captain took a dislike to him, thought he was surly and lazy, and found fault with everything he did.

We worked late Friday night and were turned-to early Saturday morning. About ten o'clock the captain ordered our new officer, Russell (who by this time had become thoroughly disliked by all the crew), to get the gig ready to take him ashore. John, the Swede, was sitting in the boat alongside, and Russell and myself were standing by the main hatchway, waiting for the captain, who was down in the hold, where the crew were to work, when we heard his voice raised in violent dispute, and then came blows and scuffling. I ran to the side and beckoned to John, who came up, and we leaned down the hatchway. Though we could see no one, yet we knew that the captain had the advantage, for his voice was loud and clear—

"You see your condition! Will you ever give me any more of your jaw?" No answer; and then came wrestling and heaving, as though the man was trying to turn him. "You may as well keep still, for I have got you," said the captain. Then came the question, "Will you ever give me any more of your jaw?"

"I never gave you any, sir," said Sam; for it was his voice that we heard, though low and half choked.

"That's not what I asked you. Will you ever be impudent to me again?"

"I never have been, sir," said Sam.

"Answer my question, or I'll make a spread eagle of you! I'll flog you, by G-d."

"I'm no slave," said Sam.

"Then I'll make you one," said the captain; and he came to the hatchway and sprang on deck, threw off his coat, and, rolling up his sleeves, called out to the mate, "Seize that man up! Seize him up! Make a spread eagle of him. I'll teach you all who is master aboard!"

The crew and officers followed the captain up the hatchway, and after repeated orders the mate laid hold of Sam and carried him to the gangway.

"What are you going to flog that man for, sir?" said John, the Swede, to the captain.

Upon hearing this, the captain turned upon him, but knowing him to be quick and resolute, he ordered the steward to bring the irons, and calling upon Russell to help him, went up to John.

"Let me alone," said John. "I'm willing to be put in irons. You need not use any force." And putting out his hands, he let the captain slip the irons on. Sam by this time was seized up, that is, placed against the shrouds with his wrists made fast to the shrouds, his jacket off, and his back exposed. The captain stood on the break of the deck, a few feet from him and a little raised, so as to have a good swing at him. He held in his hand the bight of a thick, strong rope. The officers stood round, and the crew grouped together in the waist. All these preparations made me feel sick and almost faint, angry and excited as I was. A man—a human being, made in God's likeness—fastened up and flogged like a beast! A man, too, whom I had lived with and eaten with for months, and knew almost as well as a brother. The first and almost uncontrollable impulse was resistance. But what was to be done? The time for it had gone by. The two best men were fast, and there were only two beside myself, and a small boy of ten or twelve years of age. And besides, what is there for sailors to do? If they resist, it is mutiny; and if they succeed and take the vessel, it is piracy. If they ever yield again, their punishment must come; and if they do not yield, they are pirates for life. Bad as it was, it must be borne.

Swinging the rope over his head and bending his body so as to give it

Before the Mast

full force, the captain brought it down upon the poor fellow's back. Once, twice—six times. "Will you ever give me any more of your jaw?" The man writhed with pain, but said not a word. Three times more. This was too much, and he muttered something which I could not hear; this brought as many more as the man could stand; when the captain ordered him to be cut down.

"Now for you," said the captain, making up to John and taking his irons off. When he was seized up, John turned to the captain, who stood rolling up his sleeves and getting ready for the blow, and asked him what he was to be flogged for. "Have I ever refused my duty, sir? Have you ever known me to hang back, or to be insolent, or not to know my work?"

"No," said the captain, "it is not that that I flog you for. I flog you for your interference—for asking questions."

"Can't a man ask a question here without being flogged?"

"No," shouted the captain; "nobody shall open his mouth aboard this vessel but myself." And he began laying the blows upon his back, swinging half round between each blow, to give it full effect. As he went on, his passion increased, and he danced about the deck, calling out as he swung the rope. "If you want to know what I flog you for, I'll tell you. It's because I like to do it—because I like to do it.—It suits me! That's what I do it for!"

The man writhed under the pain, until he could endure it no longer, when he called out, "Oh, Jesus Christ! Oh, Jesus Christ!"

"Don't call on Jesus Christ," shouted the captain; "he can't help you. Call on Captain T_____, he's the man! He can help you! Jesus Christ can't help you now!"

At these words, which I never shall forget, my blood ran cold. I could look on no longer. Disgusted, sick, I turned away and leaned over the rail and looked down into the water. Rapid thoughts of my situation and of the prospect of future revenge crossed my mind, but the falling of the blows and the cries of the man called me back at once. At length they ceased, and, turning round, I found that the mate had cut him down. Almost doubled up with pain, the man walked slowly forward and went down into the forecastle. Everyone else stood still at his post while the captain, swelling with rage and with the importance of his achievement, walked the quarterdeck, and at each turn, as he came forward, calling out to us—"You see your condition! You know what to expect. Now you know what I am. —I'll make you toe the mark, every soul of you, or I'll flog you all, fore and aft, from the boy up! —You've got a driver over you! Yes, a slave-driver! I'll see who'll tell me he isn't a slave."

Soon after, John came aft, with his bare back covered with stripes and wales in every direction and dreadfully swollen. He asked the steward to ask the captain to let him have some salve or balsam to put on it. "No," said the captain, who had heard him. "Tell him to put his shirt on. —That's the best thing for him—and pull me ashore in the boat. Nobody is going to lay-up on board this vessel." He then called to Mr. Russell to take those two men and two others in the boat and pull him ashore. I went. The two men could hardly bend their backs, and the captain called to them, but finding they did their best, he let them alone. The agent was in the stern sheets, but during the whole pull—a league or more—not a word was spoken. We landed. The captain, agent, and officer went up to the house, and left us with the boat. John and Sam walked slowly away and sat down on the rocks. They talked some time together, but at length separated, each sitting alone. I had some fears of John. He was violently tempered and suffering. He had his knife with him, and the captain was to come down alone to the boat. But nothing happened, and we went quietly on board.

After the day's work was done, we went down into the forecastle and ate our plain supper; but not a word was spoken. It was Saturday night; but there was no song—no "sweethearts and wives." A gloom was over everything. The two men lay in their berths, groaning with pain, and we all turned in, but for myself, not to sleep. A sound coming now and then from the berths of the two men showed that they were awake, as awake they must have been, for they could hardly lie in one posture a moment; the dim, swinging lamp of the forecastle shed its light over the dark hole in which we lived; and many and various reflections and purposes coursed through my mind. I thought of our situation, living under a tyranny; of the character of the country we were in; of the length of the voyage, and of the uncertainty attending our return to America; and, if we should return, of the prospect of obtaining justice and satisfaction for these poor men. And I vowed that, if God should ever give me the means, I would do something to redress the grievances and relieve the sufferings of that poor class of beings, of whom I then was one.[5]

Through influence at home, Dana was transferred to the *Alert* when she arrived from Boston. On May 8, 1836, her hold bulging with hides, the Indiaman cleared port and stood sluggishly off to sea. By sunset the coastline of California had faded over the horizon, and they were "once more upon the ocean, where sky and water meet."[6]

On his return to Boston, Dana completed his education. Through a long and brilliant career as a lawyer and writer, he devoted much of his life to relieving the sufferings of American sailors, with whom he had spent those two memorable years before the mast.

Watercolor and cut-out silhouette by J. H. Whitcomb. Museu
of Fine Arts, Boston. M. and M. Karolik Collectio

Our President, Old Hickory

21

Enter the Self-made
Man and the Machine

Planting hickory trees!
Odd nuts and drumsticks!
What have hickory trees to do
with republicanism and the great contest!

The campaign that led to the election of Andrew Jackson as President in 1828 put a new face on American politics. The Jacksonian victory of that year has frequently been called a "revolution" marking the "rise of the common man." In a limited sense, it was. The label, however, should not be interpreted to mean that the "common man," having a well-defined vision of his own needs and interests, suddenly took over the government of the nation—or that the candidate clearly represented those interests or was himself a "common man."

In fact, General Jackson was, in 1828, a highly exceptional man. Tall and specter thin, he moved with the grace of assurance, his masterful bearing a constant reminder that he was the savior of New Orleans. His white hair rose like a mane above eyes that commanded respect, and even antagonists conceded that his presence was magnetic. "General Jackson's manners are more presidential than those of any of the candidates," Daniel Webster admitted in 1824, "My wife is for him decidedly." A Boston merchant, waiting to see the "dangerous monster" pass his window, was so impressed by the "natural grandeur" of the general that he called to his family, "Do some one come here and salute the old man!" And Josiah Quincy testified to the charisma of this man who "wrought a mysterious charm upon old and young."[1]

Nor did the voters who put him in the White House have any logical reason to expect, on the basis of his past record, that he would act in the interest of the "common man." Richard Hofstadter, in his *American Political Tradition*, describes this aspect of Jackson's background.

... Andrew Jackson ... has often been set down as typical of the democratic frontiersman; but ... many ... facts about his life fit poorly with the stereotype. From the beginning of his career in Tennessee he considered himself to be and was accepted as an aristocrat, and his tastes, manners, and style of life were shaped accordingly. True, he could not spell, he lacked education and culture, but so did most ... aristocrats in the old southwest. ...

Jackson was born in 1767 on a little farm in the Carolinas some months after the death of his father. He enlisted in the Revolution at thirteen, was captured and mutilated by British troops at fourteen, and lost his entire family in the war when one brother was killed, another succumbed to smallpox in prison, and his mother was carried off by "prison fever" while nursing captured American militiamen. From his family he inherited a farm-size plot of land in North Carolina. ... For six months Jackson was apprenticed to a saddler. Then ... he turned for a brief spell to school-teaching. When a relative in Ireland left him a legacy of over three hundred pounds, he moved to Charleston, where, still in his teens, he aped the manners of the seaboard gentry and developed a taste for gambling, horses, and cock-fighting. When he was not playing cards or casting dice for the rent with his landlord, Jackson studied law. At twenty ... he was admitted to the bar of North Carolina. ...

Before long Jackson made what he intended to be a brief visit to the growing settlement of Nashville. The one established lawyer in the vicinity was retained by a syndicate of debtors, leaving creditors legally helpless. Jackson went to work for the creditors, collected handsome fees, and earned the gratitude and friendship of local merchants and money-lenders. From a fellow Carolina law student he also accepted an appointment as public solicitor. He soon fell in with the machine of William Blount, a powerful territorial land speculator and political patron, and began to consolidate his position among ... the owners of slaves and horses, the holders of offices and titles. With his salary and fees he began to buy land and Negroes. ...

Offices, chiefly appointive, came quickly and easily to Jackson in the territory and youthful state of Tennessee. He was a solicitor at twenty-two, United States Attorney at twenty-three, a Congressman at twenty-nine, a United States Senator at thirty, and justice of the Supreme Court of Tennessee at thirty-one. . . .

. . . In 1821, when General William Carroll ran for the governorship of the state on a democratic economic program, Jackson supported Carroll's opponent . . . a wealthy planter. . . . Carroll was elected, and proceeded to put through a program of tax revision and constitutional and humanitarian reform, which has many elements of what historians call "Jacksonian" democracy. At the moment when Jackson was pitting himself against Carroll in Tennessee, his friends were bringing him forward as a presidential candidate.[2] . . .

Thus, while he was still in his thirties, Jackson had won political laurels from his fellow Westerners. And, disproving the notion that the spirit of the frontier was leveling in nature, he had won them by virtue of his membership in the mercantile and planting aristocracy. Of political success in the early American West, Hofstadter says:

The frontier, democratic in spirit and in forms of government, was nevertheless not given to leveling equalitarianism. The ideal of frontier society . . . was the self-made man. And the self-made man generally received a measure of casual deference from the coonskin element, which itself was constantly generating new candidates for the local aristocracies. Keen class antagonisms were not typical of frontier politics. . . . Frontiersmen may have resented alien Eastern aristocrats—as Jackson did himself—but felt otherwise about those bred in their own community, as they thought, out of competitive skill rather than privilege. Even in those states and territories where suffrage was broadly exercised, men who owned and speculated in land and had money in the bank were often accepted as natural leaders, and political offices fell to them like ripe fruit.[3]

This idealization of the self-made man, which contributed so substantially to Jackson's political success, was not limited to the West or to men of democratic persuasion. Without necessarily articulating it, Americans everywhere and of all stations subscribed to the creed that it was one of their "inalienable rights" to rise as high as their individual abilities enabled them. In the process of developing that creed, Americans had gradually widened the electoral base. By 1828 in the large majority of states property qualifications for voting had

Enter the Self-made Man and the Machine

been either eliminated or reduced, and the voters had taken over from the legislatures the task of choosing presidential electors.[4]

The tool for expressing a political opinion was in the hands of the "common man," and for a decade that opinion had been in the process of formation. The Depression of 1819 had awakened in the public an interest in local government as an agency of social reform.* It had also, as Calhoun put it, caused a "general mass of disaffection to the Government, not concentrated in any particular direction, but ready to seize upon any event and looking out anywhere for a leader."[5] Industrialization, too, was creating social dislocations and restiveness.

Above all, in 1828 the "common man" was fed up with top-level management. A great self-perpetuating dynasty of the wellborn and well prepared had dominated the presidency from the beginning, regarding that office as its special trust. The old system had given the country some great leaders. But the pressure for change had risen steadily. The Era of Good Feelings proved inadequate to contain or channel divergent views and conflicting personal ambitions. In 1824, when Monroe failed to name his successor, the neat line of continuity broke, and a scramble ensued among the various princelings of the dynasty. As a result, General Jackson, a political outsider from Tennessee, almost captured the presidency. Only by grace of the House of Representatives (which chose Adams when none of the candidates received a plurality of electoral votes) was the New Englander able to salvage the office for the old order. This operation was carried out at the cost of widespread resentment. The presidential caucus as a nominating device came under heavy fire, as did the "aristocratic clique" that had maintained control of the government despite popular pressure for change.

The administration of John Quincy Adams compounded the general grievances. Although Adams was a man of integrity and considerable vision, he moved in the world of practical politics with amazing ineptness. He immediately named Henry Clay as his Secretary of State, and, since Clay's influence as Speaker of the House had contributed materially to the election of Adams, the cry of "corrupt bargain" arose at once. Above the din came the injured rhetoric of the general: Clay, "the *Judas* of the West, has closed the contract and will receive the thirty pieces of silver."[6] Throughout his administration, feeling against Adams grew as the earnest little New Englander blundered from one crisis to an-

---

*Legislation calculated to relieve the debtors (e.g., laws to eliminate imprisonment for debt and various inflationary measures) was common during the 1820s.

other. As George Dangerfield puts it, Adams "misunderstood democracy."

He believed that he could bring about a marriage between the democratic theory of equality and his scientific plans for collective administration. The American people believed that it was not a marriage but a rape. His planned economy—his policy of conservation—was out of place in those simple and expanding times. In spite of his high ideals and his pure motives, he . . . announced himself the President, not of the whole country, but of its industrial and financial classes.[7]

Clearly a change was indicated. A new base of power was emerging. Grievances against the old order of special political and economic privilege were mounting. And a potential leader of great force stood ready in the wings. The possibilities inherent in this dramatic situation were not lost upon numerous leading figures in Washington. Alienated by the President's obstinate pursuit of disaster, weary of standing interminably in line for an office that now seemed earmarked for Clay, and seeing the handwriting on the wall, various heirs apparent of the old dynasty began to defect. By 1827 leaders from every part of the nation had joined them. One by one they climbed on the Jackson bandwagon— Calhoun, the brilliant, gaunt Vice-President (from South Carolina); Thomas Ritchie, the vitriolic editor of the Richmond *Enquirer*; William Crawford, adroit but incapacitated presidential candidate of 1824; and other Southern Radicals; silver-tongued Thomas Hart Benton of Missouri; hard-hitting Duff Green of the United States *Telegraph* in Washington; the influential Pennsylvanian James Buchanan; and, above all, Martin Van Buren, master organizer, the "Little Magician" from New York.

They brought a formidable array of talent to the Jackson camp. But they also brought an unwieldy assortment of political beliefs. Aside from a rather general dislike of federal power, Jackson's supporters had little in common—except a resolve to put him in the White House in 1828. Here they were in complete agreement, and to this end they set about creating, in a single campaign, the basic paraphernalia of the modern political machine.

It began with organization. An "understanding" had long existed between Van Buren's following in New York and the states-rights "Radicals" of Virginia. Now a new element joined the combine—the Nashville Junto, dedicated to the cause of Andrew Jackson. In Congress, where leaders of all three groups conferred regularly, a central committee was formed to serve (with that in Nashville) as a nerve center of the whole organization. Between these two central bodies and among all levels of the growing party, a flood of cordial communication began to flow. "In N. York I saw many of your friends in various parts of the State." "I wish you would communicate my views to . . . " "I have visited our friends every where."[8] So effectively did the disparate elements of the new leadership work together that the administration press wailed, of Van Buren, "The masterspirit with his magic wand cast a spell over the heterogeneous mass, and the wolves and kids mingled together in peace and love!"[9]

Across the country a network of state organizations began to mushroom. In each state a typical pattern emerged. At the local level "Hickory Clubs" held demonstrations and parades, served barbecues, and organized rallies wherever a crowd was likely to be gathered. "Get up a meeting . . . on some court day," a local leader was instructed; "mount Edward on a rostrum [and have] the ablest men set about to make the necessary arrangements."[10] Supervising these groups were the county committees—the shirtsleeved grubbers of the structure—who raised funds, carried on tireless correspondence, propagandized, and sent representatives to state conventions. These conventions in turn declared eloquently for Jackson and set up central committees to control the state organizations and keep in touch with the central organs in other states.

As the new juggernaut developed, it set about a task which also was new to American political experience: it initiated a colossal program of "image making," an undertaking made easy by the already heroic dimensions of its candidate. Horatio Alger had not yet begun his tales of men rising from humble beginnings to greatness. Abraham Lincoln had not yet emerged from log-cabin obscurity. Jackson was America's first self-made man in presidential politics, and as such he had an appeal that the image makers did not neglect. But the aspect of Jackson's background which really glowed with possibilities was his record as the Great Hero of New Orleans. The image of the hero-general has become a staple of American politics. But in 1828 the image as a gimmick was new, and the machine exploited it to the hilt.* Also, the defeat of the Hero in a

*The military prowess of Washington had been utilized by the Federalists, but voters in 1789 needed little convincing that the venerable Father of their Country was the man of the hour. In 1828 it was considerably less evident that the candidate whose reputation in many quarters was that of a hot-tempered Indian fighter represented the leadership the nation needed. A selling job was indicated, and the machine's primary sales pitch was the hero image.

conniving House of Representatives brought the added dimension of martyrdom.

Many of the tricks of mass manipulation that have since proved so serviceable to American vote getters sprang full-grown from the hydra head of this first great national political machine. The Twentieth Congress, which the Jacksonians dominated, enacted a series of laws calculated to win friends in undecided and electorally important states. In a day when internal improvements at federal expense were generally frowned upon, appropriations for "harbor installations, lighthouses, public buildings, and roads" glided effortlessly through the Congress, and generous land grants fell to such key states as Illinois and Ohio.[11]

A newspaper web of unprecedented proportions was spread over the country. Pamphlets and propaganda of all kinds rolled from the presses in such abundance that the literate members of the party were kept busy writing for them and the grass-roots workers were hard pressed to distribute them all.

To finance this massive print production and the many other projects under way, party members at all levels extended themselves personally, used every persuasion to induce others to contribute, and cut some corners ethically. Robert Remini describes two of the financial stratagems employed by the Jacksonians and then goes on to discuss the campaign they waged.

The campaign's largest single expense, running into the hundreds of thousands, was ingeniously shifted to the United States Government through the franking privilege. The delivery of franked newspapers alone cost the federal government 40,000 dollars each year in allowance to postmasters. Hundreds of newspapers circulated freely throughout the country. Representatives and Senators were hounded by confederates at home to mail every scrap of campaign literature that crossed their desks. Thomas Ritchie happily noted that many enterprising Jacksonians were also franking wrapping paper, which they then turned over to local committees in their states to be used as needed. Even buttons, banners, and insignias went through the mails under the frank.

Next, there was the state government on which to saddle election expenses. Wherever the Democrats* controlled the legislative and executive branches of a particular state, they awarded the position of state printer to the editor of their official organs. To provide additional revenue, editors

*The group Remini refers to as "Democrats" were actually a faction of the Jefferson Republican Party. The Democrats did not crystallize as a distinct political party until 1832.

Enter the Self-made Man and the Machine

were sometimes given minor offices that did not consume much time or interfere with their primary responsibility of running a newspaper.

The improved electioneering methods that the Jacksonians developed to manipulate votes on a mass scale were the most obvious signs of the "great political revolution in progress."

Thoughtful discussion was virtually discarded in favor of more effective tactics, such as barbecues, tree planting, parades, public rallies, dinners, jokes, cartoons, and propaganda guaranteed to induce mass enthusiasm. This was the first election in which "gimmicks" were extensively employed to arouse and maintain popular interest in the activities of the party.

Since the Hero was already known as "Old Hickory," hickory brooms, hickory canes, hickory sticks shot up across the country, at crossroads, on steeples, on steamboats, in the hands of children.

"Planting hickory trees!" snorted the opposition press. "Odd nuts and drumsticks! What have hickory trees to do with republicanism and the great contest!" Predictably, the Democrats did not stop their planting to tell them.

Barbecues were advertised where the voters were told they could eat beef and pork and swill hard liquor "under the shadow of a hickory bush."

"Considerable pains were taken," remarked one organizer "to bring out the people; flags were made and sent to different parts of the county, and the people came in in companies with the flag flying at their head." To whip up enthusiasm prior to a public meeting, local committees frequently sent out squads of men on horseback "with labels on their hats" to identify their party and their candidate. In the Baltimore 12th Ward these riders threw small coins among the crowds that gathered, and called to the boys "to huzza for Jackson" as they rode by.

To prove the Hero's unrivaled popularity, the Democrats began conducting public opinion polls. Militias, grand juries, readers of certain newspapers, bridal parties, and other groups were asked to state their preference. And, as politicians soon learned, published polls had a tendency to create votes.[12]

Nor was a trick lost when it came to election day. "To the Polls!" the voter was enjoined. "The faithful sentinel must not sleep—Let no one stay home, and all will triumph in the success of JACKSON and LIBERTY." Voters were gathered together in companies of fifty or sixty and marched to the polls under a banner, "JACKSON AND REFORM." The fact that Jackson racked up a 178–83 electoral victory while only winning fifty-six percent of the popular vote demonstrates how skillfully the party put its efforts in the right places.[13]

Chapters from the American Experience

In recognition of the broadened suffrage, the campaign was pitched deliberately to the people. "Our true object," Duff Green reminded his party, "is to induce all aspirants for office to look to the people for support."[14]

Very early in this campaign the Hero made it clear that he regarded himself as the candidate of the people, as a man "taken up" by the electorate to defend justice and virtue, as a popular champion sent against an entrenched elite who viewed the government as a private operation restricted to certified gentlemen.

The Democrats offered Andrew Jackson as the symbol of a rising popular democracy. John Quincy Adams, on the other hand, was the candidate of the aristocracy who conducted himself like a king.

To prove the Administration's "royal extravagances," the Jacksonians whipped up a great storm over an account of White House expenditures submitted to the Congress. The report stated that public funds had been used to equip the East room with gambling furniture, in particular a billiard table, cues and balls, and a set of expensive chessmen made of ivory. Although Adams later showed that he paid for these games out of his own pocket, and the Treasury Department [confirmed it], the Jacksonians did not alter a single accusation.[15]

A program was initiated to draw the votes of many special-interest groups. Immigrants were reminded:

that John Adams was the well-known "author" of the Alien and Sedition Acts, and that there was always a distinct possibility that John Quincy Adams might revive them—apparently for no other reason than that he was the son of John Adams and, as everyone said, like father like son. The Dutch in New York, New Jersey, Pennsylvania, and Delaware were solemnly assured that the friends of the [Adams-Clay] Coalition "have heretofore spoken of the Dutch, calling them *the Black Dutch,' 'the Stupid Dutch.'*" The Hero, naturally, "revered" the Dutch for their many virtues.

In Boston, the leaders [proclaimed] Jackson as an Irishman. "General Jackson, it is well known," [wrote Duff Green] "is the son of honest Irish parents. Mr. Adams," he charged, "denounced the Roman Catholics as bigots, worshippers of images, and declared that they did not read their bibles." In the West, poor Adams was accused of hobnobbing with Catholics, conversing in Latin with nuns and priests. Meanwhile in puritan New England [a report was published] that the President was seen "tra-

Enter the Self-made Man and the Machine

velling through Rhode Island and Massachusetts on the Sabbath, in a ridiculous outfit of a jockey."

The gentle Quakers were told that the Hero of the Battle of New Orleans, when a member of the Tennessee constitutional convention, advocated a proposition "to exempt Quakers from military duty."

The most concentrated Democratic propaganda, however, was aimed at the vast numbers of farmers and yeomen throughout the nation. Jackson was described to them as a man of the soil who dropped his tools in the field like Cincinnatus of old and instantly responded to his country's call to duty. But that scion of the House of Braintree, that aristocrat, he never worked a day in his life, never toiled, never knew suffering and hardship. As long as he remained President his corrupting influence would spread like a disease over the land.[16]

Partly in response to the scurrilous campaign against Jackson's wife, Rachel, the Jacksonians went far afield to smear Adams and his wife, despite Jackson's own efforts to dissuade his lieutenants from such tactics.

In what now seems like the funniest joke ever recounted in campaigning history—funny because it is so totally incredible—the Jacksonians claimed that President John Quincy Adams of Massachusetts was once a practicing pimp. It was stated that Adams, while Minister to Russia, procured an American girl for Tsar Alexander I. The facts behind this libel, as reported by the President in his diary, were obviously quite different. A chambermaid to Mrs. Adams wrote letters back home which recounted the Tsar's reputed love affairs.

They were intercepted by Russian postal authorities and turned over to Alexander who, amused, expressed a wish to see the girl [which he did for ten minutes in the company of his wife]. That anyone would believe John Quincy Adams a procurer is an extraordinary commentary on American politics in 1828. In the West the Democrats mocked the President as "The Pimp of the Coalition" whose fabulous success as a diplomat had at last been explained.

Operating on the principle that one "dirty" story deserved another, the Democrats charged that Mrs. Adams had had premarital relations with the President. Later, they said that she was illegitimate.

There can be no question that this election splattered more filth in more different directions and upon more innocent people than any other in American history.[17]

Many of the Jacksonians began to chafe at being restricted by tradition from displaying their candidate. Several state committees urged Jackson to appear at rallies in his own behalf, but he declined, not wishing to risk criticism for violating the customary reticence of presidential candidates. He was, however, lured away from this policy on the occasion of New Orleans' annual celebration of his great victory.

Surely no one could criticize him for taking part in a patriotic affair. But, as one committee member subtly reminded him, "The effect thro the Union would be such as would dispose all to feel grateful for your manifold services." Louisiana was a "doubtful and troublesome state" whose vote had been split in 1824. It behooved him to "concentrate" it.

The Louisiana Committee assured him that he would be "hailed with enthusiastic demonstrations of respect and regard." To lessen the inconvenience of the journey, they would dispatch the ship *Pocahontas* to convey him to New Orleans.

In accepting the invitation, Jackson laid down one condition: the celebration must be completely nonpolitical. The committee replied that they were more than happy to abide by his terms. Nevertheless, they went right ahead with their plans to secure national attention in the event.

Once these preliminary problems were out of the way, the Hero notified the Nashville Junto to begin preparations for the trip and to schedule a stop at Natchez, Mississippi, on the way down. He wanted to "receive the [Jackson] committee" in that city, he said, though he had every intention of avoiding "the appearance of electioneering." Then he added a postscript to his letter: "Have Judge Overton informed of the arrangements."

Not only Overton, but the entire city of Natchez, was informed. And the schedule of events programmed by the Tennessee, Mississippi, and Louisiana state committees for the Hero's two personal appearances could not have been more elaborate.

Late in December, Jackson boarded the *Pocahontas* and headed south. With him on this "nonpolitical" trip were Judge Overton, John Coffee, William Carroll, Houston, Lewis, and deputations from the Ohio, Kentucky, New York, Pennsylvania, and Mississippi state delegations. When the group finally arrived at Natchez, a great crowd turned out to greet the warrior; cannons boomed; a public dinner and ball were given; and Jackson heard himself called the benefactor of his country whose services could never be forgotten.

January 8, 1828, dawned cloudy and dark over New Orleans, a chilly day that threatened to ruin in an instant what had taken months to prepare. But at ten o'clock, as though on signal, the thick mist that had covered the

Enter the Self-made Man and the Machine

land and water rose into great clouds. The sun broke through and bathed the scene in brilliant light.

On that "never to be forgotten day" the city was packed with people from as far away as New Hampshire. They crowded along the river bank, hung from windows and balconies, and stood on the roofs of their homes. The tops and riggings of ships at the wharves were alive with spectators. As they waited they saw a flotilla of steamboats get under way to serve as an escort. In all, eighteen ships of the" first class" maneuvered into position. Finally, the *Pocahontas* rounded the bend of the river and came into sight, preceded by "two stupendous boats, lashed together." The flotilla signaled its presence with a continuous fire of artillery, answered by several ships in the harbor and from the shore.

Then the crowds saw him standing on the fantail of the *Pocahontas,* his head uncovered. They let loose with wild screams. They waved to him, shouted his name, and finally in unison set up a cry: "Huzza! Huzza! Huzza!"

At the precise moment that General Jackson's foot touched the shore a signal was given. Artillery blazed away. The fearsome noise "thundered from the land and the water" as the erect commander strode forward to meet the welcoming committee. Generals Planché and Labaltat with soldiers of the Revolution and the remnants of the "old New Orleans Battalion" stood stiffly at attention, forming a line in his honor. The governor moved forward and greeted the Hero with a long laudatory address. Then the General reviewed the troops, his shoulders squared, chin high, looking every inch the proud commander and savior of his country.

That night a magnificent dinner was tendered the General and his lady. Men from every section of the country proposed extravagant toasts in his honor. When the shouting, drinking, speechmaking, and huzzahing were over, the members of the Central Committee congratulated themselves for organizing what was probably "the most stupendous thing of the kind that had ever occurred in the United States."[18]

Hoopla, ballyhoo, imagery, smears—anything but issues. Early in the campaign the party organizers had decided that the motley nature of their constituency made it undesirable to take a stand on controversial matters. Meeting in Washington, the central committee argued out its policy, and Thomas Hart Benton conveyed its decisions to other party workers.

"I have talked to V. B. & others and they think as I do." If a "friend" should ask about Jackson's views on internal improvements, that "friend" should be made to realize that "there is no necessity for any public answer." If an "enemy" should ask, and do so in such a "respectable" way as to make an answer "indispensable," put him off by referring to Jackson's record in the Senate.

Senator Eaton, the "party's circulating medium," had a bag full of assurances, which he blithely distributed as he toured the several states [each answer tailored to regional needs].

Certain leaders simply ignored national questions in favor of "local, state, and regional problems."

As for the General himself, when asked specifically about certain issues, he responded by following one of several alternatives: either he took Benton's advice and referred to his voting record in the Senate, or he refused a direct answer on the ground that it might be interpreted as electioneering, or he wrote long, highly ambiguous replies that could be interpreted several ways, or he ignored the question and simply struck a pose as the Hero of New Orleans cheated of the presidency in 1825.

The Indiana legislature pressed Jackson for a more precise declaration [on the tariff], but the General refused to be drawn out. "Not, sir, that I would wish to conceal my opinion from the people upon any political, or national subject, but I am apprehensive that my appearance before the public, at this time, may be attributed to improper motives."

[In insisting on saving some land in Georgia for the Creek Indians, Adams had infuriated the voters of that area.] Jackson unreservedly endorsed the policy of total removal. "Say to them [the Indians]," he wrote, "their Father, the President will lay off a country of equal extent, transport them to it, and give them a free [sic] simple title to the land." But, as the General's friends in Georgia understood only too well, it was less important to tell the Indians anything than it was to assure the electorate of the Hero's commitment to removal.

No sooner did Calhoun and Van Buren draw close to him than Jackson began repeating that he was much too old and ill to serve *two* terms as President. (He was sixty in 1827, the same age as John Quincy Adams.) Four years as chief executive was all he wanted; then he would turn the reins of government over to younger men. His protestations of feebleness had Calhoun—to say nothing of Martin Van Buren—quivering with anticipation. Perhaps the Hero meant what he said; but whether he did or not, his words were perfectly calculated to swell the loyalties of several important and ambitious men in Washington.[19]

So Jackson offered his party a nearly perfect candidate—a warrior statesman who avoided delicate issues, who carefully seemed to conform to the tradition that a presidential candidate did not stoop to electioneer, while still encouraging the extravaganza at New Orleans, and who consistently embellished the image of himself as the great military hero robbed by an arrogant oligarchy of his just reward.

Adams, on the other hand, contributed in almost every possible way to the difficulties of his campaign managers. Against the general's imposing figure he offered a short, squat physique topped by a belligerent bald head, with somewhat peevish lips and rheumy eyes.[20] Instead of skillfully avoiding controversial issues, he met them head on and with such consummate lack of tact that he managed to appear on the wrong side of everything. He carried the traditional reticence to such an extreme that his supporters could not ascertain whether he even wanted the office. And, in the face of calumny, instead of striking back and making capital of his wounds, he shrank into a stony introversion and refused to vindicate himself. Rather, he "spilled his hurt and bitterness over the secret pages of his diary. Seated at his desk, in the quiet of his study, writing furiously, he dispatched his tormenters with the business end of his pen, calling them all 'skunks of party slander.' "[21]

By the time the machine had finished its work, Adams had been reduced, in the eyes of many, to a wizened, corrupt vestige of a bygone day, and Jackson had emerged as the symbol of America's future. And, as far as Jackson was concerned, the machine's propaganda was right: he represented a new force in the country's political life. As Hofstadter points out:

> ... [At] the beginning of the Jackson era, Daniel Webster had observed: "Society is full of excitement: competition comes in place of monopoly; and intelligence and industry ask only for fair play and an open field." No friend of Jacksonian democracy expressed more accurately than this opponent the historic significance of the Jackson movement. With Old Hickory's election a fluid economic and social system broke the bonds of a fixed and stratified political order. Originally a fight against political privilege, the Jacksonian movement . . . broadened into a fight against economic privilege, . . . and by the time of his death in 1845 the "excitement" Webster had noticed had left a deep and lasting mark upon the nation. "This," exulted [one contemporary] . . . "is a country of self-made men, than which there can be no better in any state of society."[22]

The election of 1828 brought into sharper focus a scale of values inherent in American life. The tradition of individual rights came to its natural fruition with the announcement that the "common man" intended to select his own national leaders and to open the office of

President to the self-made man. And it marked out a new cut for the American political cloth: the two-party system was here to stay, and so was the machine. Henceforth the pattern of the 1828 campaign would be repeated every four years, by parties of all persuasions—the same cheap, effective tactics, sometimes even bigger and louder and, with the advent of improved communication media, even more widespread. But this was the beginning. If 1828 would go down as the election that saw the "rise of the common man," the price was on the line: a quadrennial Saturnalia of smear, cheer, and beer—and the end of a system that had yielded a dynasty of responsible (if not always responsive), well-prepared (if not always well-equipped) statesmen. For this price America had bought the chance for a self-made man to rise to the highest office. And she had bought a government more nearly "of" and "by" the people than any that had gone before. Henceforth the "common man" would be taken into account, would be recognized as a fact of American political life.

Andrew Jackson

Portrait by Asher B. Durand. Courtesy The
New York Historical Society, New York City.

22

Storm Warning
in South Carolina

Disunion by armed forces is treason.
Are you really ready to incur its guilt?

For almost half a century before the Civil War, periodic crises erupted in the nation—ominous warnings of the "irrepressible conflict." One of the most violent of these confrontations took place in South Carolina during the fall and winter of 1832–33 over the issue of nullification. For several months the angry state threatened secession, insisting on her right to declare the protective tariff of the previous summer unconstitutional. In Washington, President Jackson marshaled all his power to prevent a complete rupture of the Union.

A tumultuous political campaign and menacing military preparations had kept the state in an uproar through the hot Carolinian summer. Old friendships and even family ties had disintegrated as "young hotheads brawled in the alleys or . . . shot at each other on the dueling ground, according to their social caste."[1] In October Nullifiers swept the state elections. Immediately the governor ordered an extraordinary session of the legislature, which in turn called a convention to determine means of resisting the tariff. After brief deliberation, this convention issued an ordinance declaring the Tariffs of 1828 and 1832 null and void and prohibiting collection in South Carolina of duties levied under them. Defiantly the decree went further. It forbade any appeal of tariff cases to the Supreme Court and warned that, if the federal government undertook to apply force, South Carolina would secede from the Union. Within three days the state legislature enacted the laws needed to put the ordinance into effect and added its own belligerent note by ordering the state militia reorganized for protection against federal coercion.[2]

A stunned nation asked itself why South Carolina had exploded quite so violently. Most Southern Congressmen had found the new tariff a sufficient improvement over that of 1828 to vote for it. South Carolina had a long tradition of patriotism to the Union. As late as the War of 1812 her nationalist fervor outshone that of many states. The tariff alone hardly accounted for the hostility or the angry threat of secession. Since the first emphatically protective tariff in 1816, South Carolinians had been resentful. By 1832 a high tariff could no longer be justified on the ground that it furnished needed revenue, for the national debt was almost entirely repaid. The federal government clearly intended to pursue a policy of high protection for Northern industry, despite the hardships that such a policy inflicted on the South. If the Union would no longer protect the interests of the South, then South Carolina would.

Yet, real as the issue of the tariff was in 1832, another, even more basic, problem infuriated the South Carolinians: the problem of slavery. Just a decade and a half before, their Congressman, John C. Calhoun, had called slavery an "odious traffic."[3] Now he was proclaiming it equally beneficial to blacks and to whites. In this abrupt reversal, Calhoun spoke for his state. The propelling force behind this about-face was the boom in the cotton industry which followed the invention of the cotton gin. In 1790 the entire country had produced only 3,000 bales of the fiber. Three decades later the figure had skyrocketed to 400,000. As cotton fields spread over the humid South, the demand became vociferous for cheap slave labor. Slavery had seemed on its way to extinction following the Revolution. The Constitution had provided that the control of African slave importation should pass from the states to Congress in the year 1808. Considerably before that time all states had passed laws forbidding the traffic. But, between 1803 and 1807, South Carolina alone reopened her doors to the slavers, who deluged Charleston with many thousands of African captives.[4]

Coastal South Carolina was a vast marshland, broken by many rivers, along which great plantations thrust occasional fingers into the swamps. There the moss-hung cypress had been cleared to make way for fields of rice and fine "sea-island" cotton. Such crops and such a land did not encourage small growers. These crops required large labor crews for efficient operation, and the fertile land was far too expensive and too unhealthy to attract small entrepreneurs. So deadly were these swamps that absentee ownership prevailed; such owners as did reside on their plantations betook themselves each year, with the advent of the malaria season, to Europe or the North or to the more salutary uplands of the interior. As a result, the coastal area suffered a staggering racial imbalance—as high as eight Negroes to one white in some districts even during the winter, when the plantation owners were in residence. "No other area in the Old South," says Freehling, "contained such a massive, concentrated Negro population."[5] Wrapped in the distinctive customs of their native Africa, speaking a Gullah dialect that most whites could not understand, separated from their masters by the long malaria season, these slaves represented to the whites an incomprehensible, threatening culture. The coastal planters, engulfed in this alien sea, developed a culture of their own, baronial and rigidly exclusive.

Imbued with a social code which required cultivated gentility, the lowcountry gentry despised manual labor, detested moneygrubbers, and hated penny-pinching. In the years before the American Revolution, great planters had often been great merchants. But in the early nineteenth century foreigners from the North and from Europe captured control of the Charleston countinghouses. After that even wealthy new merchants usually failed to attain the top rank in the social hierarchy. . . . "The town bourgeoisie is so odious!" [said a typical planter]. . . .

Planters only looked down on merchants; they reserved their most cordial contempt for white "mechanics" [skilled laborers]. . . . The only sort of mechanic that planters could stomach was a well-groomed, dressed-up master mechanic who, with gloves carefully pulled over his hands, directed a gang of slaves. . . .

An idle aristocracy which sometimes found its own profession distasteful, lowcountry planters had time to engage in politics, to study, to write. . . . At best it was a cultivated, dignified life—a round of books, of music, of rich conversation. At worst it was a dissipated one, filled only with the chase, the duel, and the table.[6]

The South Carolina uplands to which many coastal lords came each summer were dominated by another breed of planter. The clay soil of the rolling Piedmont country, being less expensive and less hazardous to cultivate, offered an opportunity for small-scale operation. Here a man with a few slaves could profitably work a little plantation of cheap short-staple cotton. In time he might expand his holdings and join the upland gentry. Between these *nouveaux riches* and the grandees of the lowlands, a cordial relationship existed, based on the recognition by the upland planters of the social superiority of their summer visitors. The two groups mingled freely and sometimes intermarried. They discussed their problems and developed a solidarity of interest that left little room in the control of state politics for the merchants of the coast or the yeomen of the uplands.[7]

Although they differed in the relative emphasis they placed on the two grievances, both groups of planters agreed that the tariff offered a more acceptable justification for complaint than did slavery. They had not yet rationalized their position on that issue to the extent that they found it easy to live with. Some years would pass before they could affirm, with Calhoun, that, although many Southerners had "once believed that slavery was . . . evil," they saw it now "as the most safe and stable basis for free institutions in the world." Carolinians in 1832 did not like to discuss their "peculiar institution." When the Virginia legislature deliberated for an entire month on the desirability of abolishing slavery, South Carolinians were appalled. The tariff was an "exorbitant burthen," said one Nullifier, but it was perhaps "the least of the evils" they faced. "Our dispute involves questions of the most fearful import to the institutions and tranquility of South Carolina," he said. "I fear to name them. The bare thought of these is enough to rouse us to resistance."[8] Astute observers from other sections of the country sensed that, with many South Carolinians, slavery was the underlying issue. Congressman John Davis of Massachusetts said, in the course of House debate: "The discontent of the South has deeper root than the tariff and will continue when that is forgotten." And Senator Thomas Hart Benton added that Davis' fear that "South Carolina would not be satisfied with the overthrow of the protective policy" was shared by "many others" and was confirmed by subsequent events.[9]

The beautiful English actress Fannie Kemble, visiting in Charleston during the 1830s captured in her journal the fear that was too deep for South Carolinians to name.

The colored people are not allowed to go out without passes after nine o'clock. . . . This explained to me the meaning of a most ominous tolling of bells and beating of drums, which, on the first evening of my arrival in Charleston, made me almost fancy myself in one of the old fortified frontier towns of the Continent, where the tocsin is sounded, and the evening drum beaten, and the guard set as regularly every night as if an invasion were expected. In Charleston, however, it is not the dread of foreign invasion, but of domestic insurrection, which occasions these nightly precautions; and, for the first time since my residence in this free country, the curfew (now obsolete in mine, except in some remote districts, where the ringing of an old church bell at sunset is all that remains of the tyrannous custom) recalled the associations of early feudal times, and the oppressive insecurity of our Norman conquerors. But truly it seemed rather anomalous hereabouts, and nowadays; though, of course, it is very necessary where a large class of persons exists in the very bosom of a community whose interests are known to be at variance and incompatible with those of its other members. And no doubt these daily and nightly precautions are but trifling drawbacks upon the manifold blessings of slavery (for which, if you are stupid, and cannot conceive them, see the late Governor's speeches); still I should prefer to sleep without the apprehension of my servants' cutting my throat in my bed.[10]

In the fall of 1832 it seemed quite likely that throats would be cut. Abolitionists had begun in earnest the agitation that would drive the South to distraction, and several actual insurrections had already terrorized the planter community.

On New Year's Day, 1831, William Lloyd Garrison had inaugurated his *Liberator* and had proclaimed to the nation that his views would be heard. Less than eight months later, Nat Turner burned a trail of destruction across the Virginia countryside. For weeks South Carolina communities were paralyzed with fear as wild tales of uprisings spread throughout the state. . . .

In the first eight months of 1832, planters thought they saw evidence that at least some Carolina slaves were taking Garrison's pronouncements to heart. Roving bands of Negro desperadoes were loose in the lowcountry swamps; at one point three runaways emerged and strangled . . . [an] overseer. A slave in the Marion district murdered his master; another in Lancaster killed his master's daughter; and a Charleston slave ran amok, slashing two white men before he was subdued. The most frightening incident involved a slave cook who poisoned a feast in Sumter on July 4, 1832, killing several celebrants and leaving two hundred others desperately ill.[11]

A confusion of motives thus gripped South Carolina's ruling caste during the months of the nullification crisis. They felt an angry frustration at the "imbalance" in the federal government and at its inequitable protective tariffs. And, weaving these irritations together into a fabric

Storm Warning in South Carolina

of fear was the constant threat to their peculiar institution. Though some South Carolinians still abhorred slavery, increasing numbers were beginning to defend it. It was an uneasy defense as yet, compounded of their economic and psychic needs and physical fears on the one hand and their lack of a plausible justification on the other. Yet, in varying degrees, they still loved the nation to which they had given such unstinting loyalty. It would have taken a seer of extraordinary perception to foretell which way the Carolinians, caught in this tangle of emotions, would move in the emerging crisis.

On the other hand, the response of President Andrew Jackson did not long remain in doubt. Receiving private word of the nullification decree, he noted on his memo pad: "South Carolina has passed her ordinance. As soon as it can be had in authentic form, meet it with a proclamation. Nullification has taken deep root in Virginia, it must be arrested by a full appeal to the good sense of the people."[12]

He had already made military preparations, as the controversy raged through the summer and fall. Troops long stationed in Charleston were replaced by others as yet uncharmed by Southern hospitality. Naval forces at Norfolk were kept on alert, and those in the harbor of Charleston had instructions to defend their posts "to the last extremity." Jackson maintained close touch with events in the rebel state through its Unionist leaders. In all these precautions, however, the President took great care to ensure that no overt action on the part of federal forces precipitated an armed clash. If the central government was to enlist the cooperation of the other states, any hostilities must be initiated by South Carolina. Privately he warned the South Carolinians that he would not brook open rebellion:

"They can talk and write resolutions and print threats to their hearts' content. But if one drop of blood be shed there in defiance of the laws of the United States I will hang the first man of them I can get my hands on to the first tree I can find." South Carolina's senior Senator expressed a doubt as to whether the President would go that far. "I tell you, Hayne," [responded Senator Benton of Missouri] "when Jackson begins to talk about hanging, they can begin to look for the ropes."[13]

While Jackson waited for official written verification of the South Carolina Ordinance of Nullification before issuing his proclamation, he took further steps to strengthen the government's military position by sending a small fleet of seven revenue cutters and a battleship to Charleston Harbor.

Chapters from the American Experience

They anchored off the Battery, their guns commanding the fashionable waterfront lined with the homes and brick-walled gardens of the city's elect. General Scott strengthened [federal] harbor defenses against attack from the land side. With the Charleston post office in the hands of Nullifiers, a courier service was established to keep Jackson in constant touch with Joel Poinsett. "No state or states," the President wrote the leader of the Unionists, "has a right to secede. Nullification therefore means insurrection and war; and other states have a right to put it down. I am assured by all the members with whom I have conversed that I will be sustained by Congress. If so, I will have the leaders arrested and arraigned for treason. In forty days I can have within the limits of So. Carolina fifty thousand men, and in forty days more another fifty thousand."

Elsewhere than in South Carolina anxious eyes turned toward Andrew Jackson. "Those who but yesterday," [said a Pennsylvania Senator] "opposed your re-election with ferocity now loudly profess their reliance on your saving the Union."

Congress convened amid great excitement, which the President's message did little to allay. This document seemed poor company for the martial alarms and even more threatening private assertions of General Jackson. Its tone was conciliatory. Further tariff reductions were recommended. "The message," remarked John Quincy Adams, "is a complete surrender to the nullifiers." Nullifiers took heart. Randolph of Roanoke wrote the President: "You are now in a situation to recede with [dignity]."*

There was no recession. On the day the message was read to Congress, Edward Livingston [now Secretary of State and Jackson's literary alter-ego] was engaged on Jackson's answer to the country's question, with Old Hickory peering over the Secretary's shoulder as he worked. "I submit [this] as the conclusion of the proclamation," prompted the President. "Let it receive your best flight of eloquence: The Union must be preserved at all hazards and at any price."

The Proclamation [appeared] on December 10, 1832. The words [were] Livingston's, the initiative, the thought and the spirit Jackson's. By skillful blending of argument, entreaty and warning the Executive addressed himself to the intelligence, the pride, the interests and the fears

---

*In thus assuming that Jackson's speech indicated a determination not to take a strong hand in South Carolina, these commentators were ignoring the warning that the President went on to issue. If the "proceedings" there continued, he cautioned, he would have to ask Congress for extraordinary powers to meet them. See Thomas Hart Benton, *Thirty Years' View, or, A History of the Working of the American Government for Thirty Years, from 1820 to 1850*, Vol. I (New York: D. Appleton and Company, 1854), p. 303.

of the citizens of South Carolina; and he sought to unite the rest of the nation against the recalcitrant State.

Nullification was branded an "impractical absurdity." "If this doctrine had been established at an earlier day, the Union would have boon dissolved in its infancy. Admit this doctrine and every law for raising revenue may be annulled."

The right of secession was categorically denied. "The Constitution forms a *government* not a league. To say that any State may at pleasure secede from the Union is to say that the United States is not a nation." Relief from burdens of which South Carolina complained was foreshadowed by the "approaching payment of the public debt." But meanwhile the laws would be enforced.

"Fellow-citizens of my native State, let me admonish you. I have no discretionary power on the subject. Those who told you that you might peaceably prevent [the execution of the laws] deceived you. Their object is disunion. Disunion by armed force is treason. Are you really ready to incur its guilt? If you are, on the heads of the instigators of the act be dreadful consequences. [Your] first magistrate cannot, if he would, avoid the performance of his duty."

Bonfires blazed, bells rang, men paraded. Military volunteers offered themselves, state legislatures denounced nullification. John Quincy Adams and Daniel Webster joined the President promptly and cordially.

The story in South Carolina was different. "Gen. Jackson's extraordinary proclamation has just reached me," wrote an editor to Robert Y. Hayne, who had resigned his Senate seat for the governorship of the embattled State. "Upon the timid and ignorant of our party I fear it will have great influence." The Governor [issued a counter-proclamation in which he] promised to maintain the sovereignty of South Carolina or perish "beneath its ruins." Proffers of military service poured upon the state Executive. Union men refused to be overawed. Poinsett continued to arm his men and to drill them at night.

John C. Calhoun quit these tense scenes to start north with the intention of resigning the vice presidency and taking the place in the Senate vacated by Hayne. The journey required courage. Friends of years' standing turned their backs. The curious gathered at every stage stop to stare at the man who, rumor said, would enter Washington a prisoner under charge of treason. Pale but determined, the South Carolinian walked into the Senate chamber on January 4, 1833, and swore to uphold and defend the Constitution of the United States.

Jackson chartered a direct course. "I am now waiting," he apprized Van Buren, "for the [official] information from the assembly of So. Carolina of their having passed their laws for raising an army to resist the execution of the laws, which will be a levying of war, and I will make a communication to Congress ask[ing] power to call upon volunteers to serve. If the Assembly authorizes twelve thousand men to resist the law, I will order thirty thousand to execute [that law]." Leaders of nullification would be seized wherever found "regardless of the force that surrounds them, [and] tried for treason."

Vice President-elect [Van Buren] moved subtly to modify the chieftain's Draconian impulses. "You will say I am on my old track—caution—caution—caution: but my Dr. Sir I have always thought that considering our respective temperaments there was no way perhaps in which I could better render you service." [He] went so far as to "regret" the inclusion in the famous proclamation of certain "doctrinal points," meaning, at bottom, Jackson's flat denial of the right of a state to secede. He said this was borrowing trouble. It had offended Virginia. Besides, "South Carolina has not and will not secede." Even if she did, would not the question of bringing her back by force be better decided by Congress than by the Executive? The letter closed with an intimation that a gesture toward tariff reduction might pave the way to a happy solution of everything.

To South Carolina's surprise and discomfiture the high-hearted words of the proclamation [met with silence from most states' righters elsewhere]. Then came the parade of resolutions from state legislatures which, under pressure from Administration sources where necessary, soon were to isolate South Carolina from the declared support of a single state.

These circumstances constituted a salutary triumph for Jackson's leadership, a triumph which made things look better for him than they really were. The President was able to cheer Poinsett with the assurance that "the national voice from Maine to Louisiana declares nullification and secession consigned to contempt and infamy." But to a confidential friend he wrote: "There are more nullifiers here than dare avow it," and it was true. Virginia incurred Jackson's wrath by coupling to her resolution a proposal to mediate between South Carolina and the general government. New York legislators sat on their hands until a stiff letter from Jackson moved them to act. General John Coffee, wintering with his old comrade in the White House, wrote a relative in Memphis, "Nullification will be put down, but it has taken deeper root in the Southern States than any one could have supposed."

While moving to cut off South Carolina from outside sympathy and succor, the President permitted an extension of the olive branch. In the last days of December, Representative Verplanck of New York laid before the House a hastily drawn bill calling for heavy reductions of the tariff duties. This was in keeping with a promise implied in the proclamation.

Storm Warning in South Carolina

[Senator] Silas Wright [sent Van Buren] further disturbing details of the presidential state of mind. "He does not expect that [anything can] prevent an open rupture." Before a room filled with company, Wright had heard Jackson tell of a steamer sailing from Charleston with the stars and stripes upside down. "'Sir,' said [Jackson] for this indignity to the flag she ought to have been instantly sunk, no matter who owned or commanded her.'"

In the same crowded drawing room, the President spoke of the advisability of "disciplining" Calhoun and Hayne as an object lesson to others. General Jackson could be something of an artist at dropping apparently unguarded expressions. Flying from tongue to tongue in the nervous capital, such threats grew with repetition. In the fullness of time, Congressman Letcher of Kentucky, so one story goes, called at the White House to learn the President's true intentions. Old Hickory said that "if one more step was taken he would try Calhoun for treason and, if convicted, hang him as high as Haman." In the middle of the night the South Carolina Senator is said to have been called from his bed to hear this not improbable tale.

Beyond doubt Jackson had them scared—Nullifiers and near-Nullifiers alike, along with political tight-rope performers. And not in Washington alone did knees shake behind facades of bravado. In December the President had said he would suspend positive action awaiting officially certified copies of the acts of the South Carolina Legislature giving effect to the ordinance of nullification. When these failed to arrive Jackson shot off a courier to fetch them. Ten days passed without word from the courier. It was January 16, 1833. Fifteen days remained until February 1, when the ordinance and supporting decrees were to go into force. Jackson waited no longer. Acting without the official copies, he asked Congress for authority to use military force to collect the customs.

But what if Congress, in that short time, should fail to convey the power requested? Andrew Jackson was ready for the contingency. He would take unto himself the power, stretching the Constitution to suit the needs of the case. "The preservation of the Union is the supreme law." On January 24 seven days remained in which to act before the first of February. The inability of Congress to agree on a bill seemed imminent. A hurried scrawl to Poinsett left Washington by night.

"Should Congress fail to act, [and should South Carolina] oppose the execution of the revenue laws [with] an armed force, I stand prepared to issue my proclamation warning them to disperse. I have a tender of volunteers from every state in the union. I can if need be, which god forbid, march two hundred thousand men in forty days to quell any and every insurrection that might arise. I repeat to the union men, fear not, *the union will be preserved.* Keep me well advised."

Chapters from the American Experience

On the next day the President's proclamation was ready. So were preparations to call on the governors for thirty-five thousand men "ready to march at a moment's warning."

But the proclamation was never issued; the requisitions on the governors never sent. The courier who bore the President's letter of January 24 to Poinsett passed a messenger hurrying northward with news that South Carolina had yielded. Jackson's awesome mobilization had been too much for the Nullifiers' nerves. On January 21 they had suspended their belligerent ordinance pending the outcome of the tariff debate. Old Hickory had outmaneuvered his foemen at every point and, sword in hand, faced them down.

The sword having had its vital hour, the time had come for the pen, and for many tongues. The major responsibility shifted to the halls of Congress, where Verplanck's tariff bill, weighed down with amendments, made little headway. But the president insisted on the enactment, without one barb blunted, of the "Force Bill," as opponents called the measure authorizing the use of the military to collect the Government revenue. The demand unleashed an oratorical onslaught. "I proclaim," [said Calhoun], "that should this bill pass it will be resisted at every hazard—even that of death."

Jackson refused to give an inch. He insisted on the passage of the Force Bill. The last ten days of February were at hand, and on March 2 Congress must adjourn. The votes to pass the Force Bill were pledged. Only something akin to a miracle could relieve John C. Calhoun of the unpleasant option of capitulating or of [making good] his menacing words.

The situation afforded Henry Clay, a practiced dispenser of parliamentary miracles, the opportunity that he sought. The tariff was Clay's specialty, and in this field he saw a number of serviceable possibilities: reconciliation between South Carolina and the general government; Calhoun rescued from his perilous position; something of a protective system saved from the devastations of the Verplanck Bill; Henry Clay in the role of pacifier instead of Martin Van Buren, as would be the case should Verplanck's measure go through. The outcome was a bewildering maneuver which Clay counted on Calhoun's desperation to crown with success. As an independent "compromise," he introduced a bill which in ten years would lower tariffs by twenty per cent. The Verplanck Bill would cut them that much in two years or less. Notwithstanding the fact that the Administration bill embodied the more liberal terms, Calhoun, sweating blood, was dragooned into supporting Clay's measure on the strange ground that it was a compromise to which South Carolina could accede with dignity.

This metaphysical proposition agreed to, the Force Bill was called up for a vote in the Senate. Mr. Calhoun and all his supporters except one left

Storm Warning in South Carolina

the chamber. Irate John Tyler of Virginia stayed and cast the only negative vote. Jackson ordered his congressional captains to drive the bill on through the House ahead of Clay's tariff. Skillfully the Kentuckian spread the meshes of delay, and Jackson's captains failed. On the last day but one of the session, the two measures—Jackson's Force Bill and Clay's tariff—finished their legislative journeys together and at the same hour came to the President's desk. South Carolina would make the most of the opportunity to accept peace from the hands of Mr. Clay rather than from those of General Jackson. But veto the bill he could not; that would be pushing Calhoun too far.

On Old Hickory's sixty-sixth birthday, March 15, 1833, South Carolina rescinded her ordinance of nullification. Snatched from the brink of civil war, the nation gave way to rejoicing that lifted Andrew Jackson's popularity to a pinnacle.

General Jackson regarded the demonstrations with sober mien. "Nullification and secession are for the present, I think, effectively, and I hope forever put down. But the coalition between Clay and Calhoun, combined with a few nullifiers in Virginia and Poindexter [of Mississippi] and his coadjutors in the south and southwest, portends no good, but much evil." But the late crisis had ended more tamely than Jackson had reckoned on. "I thought I wd. have to hang some of them & [I] wd. have done it."

Charleston gave a "victory ball" for volunteers who had taken up arms against "the invader." It was easy to smile at the face-saving device; too easy. The President observed and reflected deeply. He knew the real issue to be slavery—as yet untouched and almost unavowed. From the shadow of the gallows John C. Calhoun emerged with a new and sinister prestige. In Virginia John Tyler responded to the toast, "Nullification the rightful and, as it proved, the efficient remedy." Andrew Jackson saw that the viper he had set out to kill was only scotched. "The nullifiers in the south intend to blow up a storm on the slave question. This ought to be met, for be assured these men would do any act to destroy this union and form a southern confederacy."[14]

Thus was the final conflict deferred. The forces of rebellion in the remainder of the South were not yet sufficiently well organized, the other Southern states not yet sufficiently alarmed. But the challenge had been made. In rescinding her ordinance, South Carolina had not yet retracted her assertion that, as a state, she had the right to nullify federal legislation. Resentments in many Southern hearts had been aggravated. In the North fears had been stirred that would not be quieted. An uneasy watchfulness would henceforth characterize the attitudes of the two sections. The fateful wedge had been driven.

Ralph Waldo Emerson

Etching, 1905.
The Granger Collection.

23

Emerson: A Voice for America

Whoso would be a man,
must be a noncomformist.

"Time and nature yield us many gifts, but not yet the timely man, the
new religion, the reconciler, whom all things await."[1] When Ralph
Waldo Emerson issued this call, he was in his early forties, and his
penetrating, epigrammatic wisdom had captivated American audiences
across the land and brought him to a position of leadership among the
intellectual elite of New England. Yet, deeply as he felt the need for a
new religion, a reconciler, Emerson did not consider himself the timely
man whom all things awaited. Perhaps the reasons for that reticence lay
buried in his childhood.

From his earliest days Emerson was driven by the imperatives of his
background. He was less than a week old when his maiden Aunt Mary
promised him, and herself: "We'll make a minister of you, my dear."
"Ralph Waldo Emerson," she savored the words. "It's a good name. May
you make it shine among men."[2] As a matter of family precedent, it was
almost certain that either Emerson or one of his five brothers would
follow the ministry. Nearly two centuries had passed since the first
Emerson crossed the Atlantic in 1638; with one exception, each generation after him had contributed at least one pastor to a New England
flock.

The preparation for this station was grueling. When Emerson was three years old, his father, the minister of Boston's First Church, expressed dissatisfaction with the boy's progress in reading and urged his

wife to keep him more diligently at his studies. As in most prominent New England families, the Emerson boys learned their letters and a battery of prayers and biblical verses before the age of three. At that time or a little before, they were enrolled in "infant school," where they sat through long class hours in "stiff little rows," with the teacher, switch in hand, "rebuking even a smile."[3] Through the grammar and Latin schools that followed, attendance was required six days a week, all seasons of the year, with few holidays. Sundays were consumed in lengthy church services and religious exercises.

Nor were the fragments of time left by this rigid program devoted to childish pleasures. Work, discipline, training in self-discipline, the sense of a high calling—these filled the days of Emerson and his brothers. Overt display of affection was frowned upon, and both parents maintained a reserved distance from their children.

When Emerson was eight years old, his father died of a "consuming marasmus," probably tuberculosis. The family settled down to a regimen of poverty, with the mother taking in boarders and the boys working in the early morning and after school was dismissed at five o'clock. Meals were frequently inadequate, and, with the advent of the War of 1812, the struggle became even more difficult. Through the harsh New England winter Emerson and his older brother shared an overcoat, to the mocking amusement of their classmates. When the pinch of hunger occupied their minds, Aunt Mary regaled them with accounts of the first colonists' suffering and fortitude.

By 1814 their hardships had become so pressing that they moved to the home of their grandmother and their step-grandfather Ripley, who was the pastor of the Church in Concord. A year of relative ease now passed in the Old Manse, where the boys often heard stories of their heroic ancestors—especially of their grandfather Emerson and his stand at Concord bridge in April, 1775. "There was your grandfather in his minister's robes," they were told with pride, "standing straight as any pine tree, and calling aloud upon the Lord."[4]

The years of poverty, the incessant intellectual force-feeding, the predominance of female influence in his life, the constant pressure for achievement to match that of the family's past were telling on Emerson. The sturdy baby had become a thin, pale boy. Try as he might to repress it, he had developed an overwhelming tendency to giggle at critical moments. His half uncle observed with concern that his peers tormented and jeered at him. "Is there anything wrong in that?" asked his grandfather Ripley. "They are going to grow up to be merchants and farmers; he's to be a minister." "Solitude," said Aunt Mary, "is to genius the stern friend, the cold obscure shelter where moult the eagle wings which will bear one farther than the suns and stars."[5] In his later years, remembering the frustration of his youthful search for a friend, Emerson would write:

The youth longs for a friend; when he forms a friendship he fills up the unknown parts of his friend's character with all virtues of man. The lover idealizes the maid, in like manner. The virtues and graces with which they thus attribute, but fail to find in their chosen companions are only really ripened, here one, and there the other, in scattered individuals.[6]

With the conclusion of the war the family returned to Boston. Again the scrimping, the boarders, the chores, and now Emerson was the eldest at home, for his brother had gone to Harvard. On the death of his baby sister, it fell to the eleven-year-old boy to read the prayers over her coffin. Though tears streamed down his cheeks, his clear voice remained unbroken, firmly disciplined.

When his preparation at the Latin school was completed, Emerson entered Harvard as the "president's freshman," or messenger—an appointment that would pay his room and board. In addition, he would earn a little money tutoring the president's nephew, and his father's old congregation pledged a yearly sum of ten pounds. Small grants from the college and part-time work as a waiter would eke out his financial necessities, but throughout his years of training he would never escape what he later called the "goading, soul-sickening sense of extreme poverty."[7]

On the threshhold of the educational adventure for which he had so carefully been groomed, the fourteen-year-old boy wrote his brother: "My college life begins, *Deo volente*, and I hope and trust will begin with determined and ardent pursuit of real knowledge that will raise me high in the class while in college, and qualify me well for stations of future usefulness."[8] Disillusionment came swiftly, both for him and for those guiding spirits who had breathed their fervor into him. Mathematics—not Emerson's forte—was heavily stressed, tradition hemmed his studies into a narrowly defined path, and rote recitation made work in all areas tedious. Emerson's mind drifted away. He found a much more congenial atmosphere in the well-equipped library, where he spent hours in what he guiltily called his "cardinal vice of intellectual dissipation—sinful strolling from book to book."[9] As a senior he recorded in his *Journal* the conflict that raged between his natural inclinations and his driving sense of duty:

I find myself often idle, vagrant, stupid, and hollow. This is somewhat appalling and, if I do not discipline myself with diligent care, I shall suffer severely from remorse and the sense of inferiority hereafter. All around me are industrious and will be great: I am indolent and shall be insignificant. Avert it, heaven! avert it, virtue![10]

When he graduated, he stood twenty-ninth in a class of fifty-nine. He was selected class poet—but only after six other boys had refused the honor.

To help finance graduate work at the Divinity School, he began at once to teach; but the profession held no charms for him. "School-keeping is a dreary task," he would write in later years, "only relieved by the pleasure the teacher takes in two or three bright pupils."[11] At eighteen, surveying his life to date and finding it barren, he flailed himself with blame:

In twelve days I shall be nineteen years old; which I count a miserable thing. Has any other educated person lived so many years and lost so many days?

I have not the kind affections of a pigeon. Ungenerous and selfish, cautious and cold, I have not sufficient feeling to speak a natural, hearty welcome. There is not one being to whom I am attached with warm and entire devotion, not one whose interests I have nearly and dearly at heart; and this I say at the most susceptible age of man—a true picture of a barren and desolate soul.[12]

In the years that followed, tragedy added its mellowing influence. One brother had already died in boyhood, and another, being mentally incompetent, had been sent away to spend his life on a farm. Both of his two brilliant and beloved younger brothers now died of tuberculosis, one of them having first suffered a nervous breakdown that reduced him for a time to the status of a "maniac." In his early twenties Emerson himself felt the ominous "little mouse gnawing" in his chest and fled to the South, where Florida's sun cured his illness and where the indolent life relaxed a few of the tensions that the compulsive years had built up within him. On his return he met and married a beautiful young girl, and within two years she also succumbed to the "white plague." For five days his journal was silent, and then came the entry: "I shall go again among my friends with a tranquil countenance. Again I shall be amused. I shall stoop again to little hopes and little fears. But there is one birth and one baptism and one first love."[13]

Meanwhile, Emerson had become pastor of Old North, the Second

Unitarian Church of Boston. The long years of poverty, of depending on the charity of others seemed at an end. On the whole, his preaching was acceptable to his congregation. The older members might question his emphasis on ethics rather than dogma, but the younger ones were drawn to him. But within the young minister's own mind dissatisfactions arose that would not be quieted. "Suicidal," he wrote in his *Journal* in July, 1831, "is this distrust of reason; this fear to think; this doctrine that 'tis pious to believe others' words, impious to trust entirely to yourself."[14] And at the same time he recorded in his *Journal* the beginning of heresy: "If thou canst bear strong meat of simple truths, then take this fact into thy soul—God dwells in thee."[15]

He chafed at the ties of form and custom that bound him, yearning to speak instead of "the great circling truths" that were shaping into a pattern within him—a pattern alien to the dogma of the institution to which he was tied.[16] "I meditate, now and then, total abdication of the profession, on the score of ill health," he had written his Aunt Mary when doubts first began to assail him. But, he asked, "how to get my bread? Shall I commence Author? Of prose or verse?"[17] Now economic necessity could no longer restrain him. In the fall of 1832 Emerson resigned his position with the church. He could not, he told his congregation, observe the Lord's Supper. "Jesus," he said, "was a Jew, sitting with his countrymen, celebrating their national feast."[18] He would not have wanted that simple occasion to have been developed into an institutional ritual. The shocked parishioners let him go. And so did Aunt Mary, though she voiced her disappointment to another nephew: It is "far sadder than the translation of a soul by death of the body to lose Waldo as I have lost him."[19]

In December he boarded a cargo vessel and sailed to Europe to rest and formulate his thoughts. Five-and-a-half weeks later he landed in Malta. Syracuse, Naples, Rome, Florence, Venice followed, and the constricting bands of the past began to loosen. Viewing the beauties of Rome, he wrote, "It is vain to refuse to admire; you must in spite of yourself."[20] In England he talked with the rebellious Romantic poets, Wordsworth and Coleridge, and in Scotland formed a lasting friendship with the gruff Carlyle. God, he wrote, had shown him the men he had wished to see and had "thereby comforted and confirmed" him in his convictions.[21]

Returning to America, Emerson was asked to lecture on his travels, and he did so with such success that invitations to speak on many topics followed. On these circuits around the country, Emerson could discuss, without restriction, the philosophy he had been developing. The old insecurities continued to drop away; his rich baritone voice took on the firmness of conviction. Emerson had found his natural medium—and he had found himself.

The matured philosophy that Emerson had evolved with such travail pivoted around the concept of man's essential goodness. When man's heart and mind are "opened," he said, he learns that he is born "to the good, to the perfect." Even in a nation where Calvinism had spread so broadly, this was not very revolutionary. Many intellectuals had moved consciously away from the doctrine of predestination, and a much larger number of Americans had rejected it subconsciously. But Emerson went further. Not only did man carry within him the seed of perfection, but the good within him represented a portion of the universal good which was God. "If a man is at heart just, then in so far is he God," he said. "Speak the truth, and all things alive or brute are vouchers, and the very roots of the grass underground there do seem to stir and move to bear you witness. The world is of one will, of one mind; and that one mind is everywhere active, in each ray of the star, in each wavelet of the pool." This universal good is the absolute force. Evil is not absolute but is only the absence of good; "it is like cold, which is the privation of heat. All evil is so much death." Insofar as a man is benevolent, just that far has he life. "For all things proceed out of this same spirit, which is differently named love, justice, temperance, in its different applications, just as the ocean receives different names on the several shores which it washes."[22] Each individual bears in him the spark of divinity that permeates all nature. In the wonders of evolution may be seen an all-pervading purpose.

Now we learn what patient periods must round themselves before the rock is formed, then before the rock is broken, and the first lichen race has disintegrated the thinnest external plate into soil, and opened the door for the remote Flora and Fauna to come in. How far off yet is the trilobite! how far the quadruped! how inconceivably remote is man! All duly arrive, and then race after race of men. It is a long way from granite to the oyster; farther yet to Plato, and the preaching of the immortality of the soul. Yet all must come, as surely as the first atom has two sides.

Motion or change and identity or rest, are the first and second secrets of nature: Motion and Rest. The whole code of her laws may be written on the thumbnail. Every shell on the beach is a key to it. A little water made to rotate in a cup explains the formation of the simpler shells. So poor is nature with all her craft, that, from the beginning to the end of the universe, she has but one stuff. Compound it how she will, star, sand, fire, water, tree, man, it is still one stuff, and betrays the same properties. That identity makes us all one, and reduces to nothing great intervals on our customary scale.

Chapters from the American Experience

The astronomers said, "Give us matter and a little motion, and we will contruct the universe. It is not enough that we should have matter, we must also have a single impulse, one shove to launch the mass. We cannot bandy words with nature, or deal with her as we deal with persons. If we measure our individual forces against hers, we may easily feel as if we were the sport of an insuperable destiny. But if, instead of identifying ourselves with the work, we feel that the soul of the workman streams through us, we shall find the peace of the morning dwelling in our hearts, and the fathomless powers of gravity and chemistry, and, over them, of life, pre-existing within us in their highest form. And the knowledge that we traverse the whole scale of being, from the centre to the poles of nature, and have some stake in every possibility, lends that sublime lustre to death, which philosophy and religion have too outwardly and literally striven to express in the popular doctrine of the immortality of the soul. The reality is more excellent than the report. Here is no ruin, no discontinuity, no spent ball. The divine circulations never rest nor linger. Nature is the incarnation of a thought, and turns to a thought, again, as ice becomes water and gas. The world is mind precipitated, and the volatile essence is forever escaping again into the state of free thought. Man imprisoned, man crystallized, man vegetative, speaks to man impersonated. That power which does not respect quantity, which makes the whole and the particle its equal channel, delegates its smile to the morning, and distils its essence into every drop of rain.[23]

If man thus holds within him a divine spark which is part of the universal good, then it follows that he must search within himself, not in ritualistic institutions, for the answer to what is right and good. Christianity, being the "established worship of the civilized world," held "great historical interest." Its "blessed words" had been "the consolation of humanity." But it had done harm in downgrading the position of man in the total scheme of things—had, for example, misinterpreted the relationship between Jesus and God.

Jesus Christ belonged to the true race of prophets. He saw with open eye the mystery of the soul. Alone in all history, he estimated the greatness of man. He saw that God incarnates himself in man, and evermore goes forth anew to take possession of his world. He spoke of miracles; for he felt that man's life was a miracle, and all that man doth, and he knew that this daily miracle shines, as the character ascends. But the word "miracle," as pronounced by Christian churches, gives a false impression; it is "monster." It is not one with the blowing clover and the falling rain. Historical Christianity has fallen into the error that corrupts all attempts to communicate religion. It is not the doctrine of the soul, but an exaggeration of the personal, the ritual. It has dwelt, it dwells, with noxious exaggeration about the *person* of Jesus. The soul knows no persons. It invites every man to expand to the full circle of the universe. By his holy thoughts Jesus serves us, and thus only. The stationariness of religion; the assumption that the age of inspiration is past, that the Bible is closed; the fear of degrading the character of Jesus by representing him as a man—indicate with sufficient clearness the falsehood of our theology. It is the office of a true teacher to show us that God is, not was. In the soul, then, let the redemption be sought.[24]

Emerson's words shocked many listeners, but he remained serene in the determination to speak what must be spoken. He would, in the years ahead, analyze and pass judgment on almost every subject of significance to his time. But, veining all his teachings would run this basic theme: the freedom of the individual soul (as an integral part of the great universal "Oversoul" that pervades all nature) to seek out the good, the true, and the beautiful, and in so doing to come ever nearer perfection.

The practical application of this doctrine was the call to "Self-Reliance," and on this subject Emerson wrote his most famous essay. If the religious theme of the soul failed to stir most Americans, this message of self-reliance was one to which they were highly attuned. To a young nation pushing its way across a continent, and building an industrial colossus, these words set bells of affirmation ringing:

Trust thyself: every heart vibrates to that iron string. To believe your own thought, to believe that what is true for you in your private heart is true for all men—that is genius. In every work of genius we recognize our own rejected thoughts; they come back to us with a certain alienated majesty. Great works of art have no more affecting lesson for us than this. They teach us to abide by our spontaneous impression with good-humored inflexibility, then most when the whole cry of voices is on the other side. Else tomorrow a stranger will say with masterly good sense precisely what we have thought and felt all the time, and we shall be forced to take with shame our own opinion from another.

Whoso would be a man, must be a nonconformist. He who would gather immortal palms must not be hindered by the name of goodness, but must explore if it be goodness. Nothing is at last sacred but the integrity of our own mind. Absolve you to yourself, and you shall have the suffrage of the world.

What I must do is all that concerns me, not what the people think. This rule, equally arduous in actual and in intellectual life, may serve for the whole distinction between greatness and meanness. It is the harder because you will always find those who think they know what is your duty better than you know it. It is easy in the world to live after the world's opinion; it is easy in solitude to live after our own; but the great man is he who in the midst of the crowd keeps with perfect sweetness the independence of solitude.

The other terror that scares us from self-trust is our consistency. A foolish consistency is the hobgoblin of little minds, adored by little statesmen and philosophers and divines. With consistency a great soul has simply nothing to do. If you would be a man speak what you think today in words as hard as cannon balls, and tomorrow speak what tomorrow thinks in hard words again, though it contradict every thing you say today. Ah, then, exclaim the aged ladies, you shall be sure to be misunderstood! Is it so bad then to be misunderstood? Pythagoras was misunderstood, and Socrates, and Jesus, and Luther, and Copernicus, and Galileo, and Newton, and every pure and wise spirit that ever took flesh. To be great is to be misunderstood.

Man is timid and apologetic; he is no longer upright; he dares not say "I think," "I am," but quotes some saint or sage. These roses under my window make no reference to former roses or to better ones; they are for what they are.

In the Will work and acquire, and thou hast chained the wheel of Chance, and shalt always drag her after thee.[25]

This was heady stuff. It offered the exploiter and the self-seeking a rationale for the most rugged individualism. And many Americans heard only this element of the great essay—failed to heed the warp-thread of morality that ran through it, or its concluding warning:

And now at last the highest truth on this subject remains unsaid; probably cannot be said. When good is near you, when you have life in yourself, you shall not discern the footprints of any other; the way, the thought, the good, shall be wholly strange and new. The soul is raised over passion. It seeth identity and eternal causation. It is a perceiving that Truth and Right are. Hence it becomes a Tranquillity out of the knowing that all things go well. This is the ultimate fact which we so quickly reach on this, as on every topic, the resolution of all into the ever-blessed ONE. Virtue is the governor, the creator, the reality.

He who knows that power is in the soul, that he is weak only because he has looked for good out of him and elsewhere, and, so perceiving, throws himself unhesitatingly on his thought, instantly rights himself, stands in the erect position, works miracles.

Emerson: A Voice for America

Nothing can bring you peace but yourself. Nothing can bring you peace but the triumph of principles.[26]

Years later Emerson would stress even more explicitly the moral obligation so basic to self-reliance and to acquisition:

Hitch your wagon to a star. Do the like in your choice of tasks. Let us not fag in paltry selfish tasks which aim at private benefit alone. Let us work rather for those interests which the gods honour and promote: justice, love, utility, freedom, knowledge.

A man for success must not be pure idealist—then he will practically fail; but he must have ideas, he must obey ideas, or he is a brute.[27]

Against the brute aspects of his America, Emerson declared war. In a materialistic society, he charged, the best thinking had been diverted from "the temple" to "the senate or the market." Literature had become "frivolous," and science, "cold." "Public and private avarice make the air we breathe thick and fat," he asserted. "Young men of the fairest promise, who begin life upon our shores, inflated by the mountain winds, shined upon by all the stars of God, find the earth below not in unison with these, but are hindered from action by the disgust which the principles on which business is managed inspire, and turn drudges or die of disgust."[28]

The many reformers of the time, who sought solutions of every sort for the nation's growing pains, took him to their hearts and sought his endorsement of their criticisms and their plans. But, if he generally agreed with their complaints, he seldom participated in their projects for improvement. The reformers, he warned, wanted simple, one-sided solutions to ills that affected every aspect of society. The attack should move equally on all fronts, and above all on the individual man, for any lasting reform must come through the improvement of the individual. "Society gains nothing while a man not himself renovated, attempts to renovate things around him."[29]

From one great crusade of his time, however, Emerson could not stand aloof. The institution of slavery represented to him such a crime against nature that his determination not to be drawn into any "movement" gave way, and he became an ardent abolitionist. "Just now," he wrote, "the supreme public duty to all thinking men is to assert freedom."[30] When the Fugitive Slave Law went into effect, he said, with unaccustomed vehemence, "I will not obey it, by God." With the coming of war and early Northern defeats, he recorded his confidence in the ultimate "triumph of principles": "I look on the Southern victories as due to fanaticism, to the petulance and valour of a people who had nothing else and must make a brilliant onset. But ideas and their slow massive might are irresistible at last."³¹ He came to favor an all-out prosecution of the war. It was madness, he insisted, "to bargain or treat at all with the rebels, to make arrangements with them about exchange of prisoners, or hospitals, or truces to bury the dead." As for any final peace, "every arrangement short of forcible subjugation of the rebel country," would be "flat disloyalty."³² England's role in the war, he felt, was inexcusable. She had freed her own slaves in the West Indies but had refused to help the North in its struggle against the infamous institution—had, in fact, given aid and comfort to the South. England, in sum, was waxing old and fat and unprincipled. America was well rid of any vestigial tie to her:

We are coming (thanks to the war) to a nationality. Put down your foot and say to England, I know your merits and have paid them in the past the homage of ignoring your faults. I see them still. But it is time to say the whole truth—that you have failed in an Olympian hour, that when the occasion of magnanimity arrived, you had it not—that you have lost character; your insularity, your inches, are conspicuous.³³

In thus allowing himself to become so bitterly involved, Emerson did violence to his own conception of the scholar's high role in civilization. The function of the scholar, he had said, is to "guide men by showing them facts amidst appearances." He should ply the "slow, unhonored, and unpaid task of observation." And, when he has collected all these facts and acquainted himself with "whatsoever oracles the human heart in all solemn hours, has uttered as its commentary on the world of actions," then whatever "new verdict Reason from her inviolable seat pronounces on the passing men and events of today—this he shall hear and promulgate." To fulfill this exalted function, it was necessary for the scholar to remain objective and remote from the particular frays of the moment.*³⁴

In addition to this ultimatum to the scholar to "be a university of knowledges" and to find slumbering in himself "the whole of Reason" wherewith to voice new truths, Emerson made special demands on the scholars of his own young nation.³⁵

*Perhaps Emerson was right in abstaining as long as he did from active involvement in "causes." Although he was only in his mid-fifties when the war broke out, it seems to have marked the end of his creativity. See Saul K. Padover, *The Genius of America: Men Whose Ideas Shaped Our Civilization* (New York: McGraw-Hill Book Company, 1960), p. 194.

This confidence in the unsearched might of man belongs by all motives, by all prophecy, by all preparation to the American Scholar. We have listened too long to the courtly muses of Europe. The spirit of the American freeman is already suspected to be timid, imitative, tame. The scholar is decent, indolent, complaisant. What is the remedy? If the single man plant himself indomitably on his instincts, and there abide, the huge world will come round to him. We will walk on our own feet; we will work with our own hands; we will speak our own minds. The study of letters shall be no longer a name for pity, for doubt, and for sensual indulgence. A nation of men will for the first time exist, because each believes himself inspired by the Divine Soul which also inspires all men.[36]

As Emerson called for scholars to speak for and guide America, so also he made an impassioned plea for a poet to record and interpret the moving panorama of American life.

I look in vain for the poet whom I describe. We do not with sufficient plainness, or sufficient profoundness, address ourselves to life, nor dare we chant our own times and social circumstance. If we filled the day with bravery, we should not shrink from celebrating it. We have yet had no genius in America [who] knew the value of our incomparable materials, and saw, in the barbarism and materialism of the times, another carnival of the same gods whose picture he so much admires in Homer. Banks and tariffs, the newspaper and caucus, methodism and unitarianism, are flat and dull to dull people, but rest on the same foundations of wonder as the town of Troy, and the temple of Delphos, and are as swiftly passing away. Our logrolling, our stumps and their politics, our fisheries, our Negroes, and Indians, our boats, and our repudiations, the wrath of rogues, and the pusillanimity of honest men, the northern trade, the southern planting, the western clearing, Oregon, and Texas, are yet unsung. Yet America is a poem in our eyes; its ample geography dazzles the imagination, and it will not wait long for metres.[37]

Almost every American who read, or heard, or heard of Emerson's words—and those who did not were few—found there the verbalization of some inner conviction of his own. It was an age of affirmation, and Americans of all levels acclaimed his clear, sure optimism. They shared his love of nature and glowed in response to his demand for self-reliance and for Americanism. Reformers welcomed his criticism of society. Walt Whitman heard his cry for a poet to sing America. Intellectuals, particularly the Transcendentalists, were stirred by his "new religion," and gifted disciples spread his word, saw in him a reconciler of new needs with an old morality.

In the last analysis, then, it was Emerson himself who, in those yeasty times which knew so many eloquent voices, spoke most tellingly for and to the young nation. Much of what he said expressed their own aspirations. And, if some of his words—the ones nearest his heart, those of the spirit—came through less clearly than he would have wished, they too shared in the shaping of American thought. Emerson sang in lyrical prose of the eager, self-reliant youth of America. But also, he exemplified and glorified the highly moral life, appealing to a deep strain of idealism in his fellow countrymen and softening their brash materialism with an overlay of spiritual values. Emerson called for a voice to stir the nation to better things, and the voice that answered was his own.

Brook Farm

24

Pitchforks
and Panaceas

Persons of marked individuality—crooked sticks,
as some of us might be called—
are not exactly the easiest to bind up into a fagot.
—Hawthorne[1]

One of the most valiant experiments in American history got under way at Brook Farm, Massachusetts, in the spring of 1841. That the effort at communal living initiated then ultimately failed is not so important as whether it was inevitable that it should have failed. To that question observers have offered answers that run the spectrum, depending on their optimism as to man's perfectibility and their views on the means by which such a goal, if feasible, might best be achieved.

The ferment of reform which in the 1840s stirred every segment of the nation worked with particular fervor in New England. There a galaxy of intellectuals defied the established order, condemning the poverty, ignorance, and crime that they insisted it had spawned. Nor did they limit themselves to negative criticism. They envisioned a brotherhood of men lifting one another toward almost infinite perfection. And so reform movements of every kind sprang up. The lyceum circuit hummed as lecturers and eager audiences examined the ills of the world and possible remedies. And here and there enthusiastic activists embarked on experiments in communal living.

Of all these pilot programs to a better world, Brook Farm evoked perhaps the most general interest—although that interest was often curious rather than constructive. When George Ripley, a distinguished graduate of Harvard and a Unitarian minister, founded the "Farm" near

Boston, he hoped to attract to it his fellow members of that city's famed Transcendentalist Club, and especially Ralph Waldo Emerson. To Emerson he outlined his plans:

> Our objects, as you know, are to insure a more natural union between intellectual and manual labor than now exists; to combine the thinker and the worker, as far as possible, in the same individual; to guarantee the highest mental freedom, by providing all with labor, adapted to their tastes and talents, and securing to them the fruits of their industry; to prepare a society of liberal, intelligent, and cultivated persons, whose relations with each other would permit a more simple and wholesome life, than can be led amidst the pressure of our competitive institutions.
>
> To accomplish these objects, we propose to take a small tract of land, which, under skillful husbandry, uniting the garden and the farm, will be adequate to the subsistence of the families; and to connect with this a school or college, in which the most complete instruction shall be given, from the first rudiments to the highest culture. Our farm would be a place for improving the race of men that lived on it; thought would preside over the operations of labor, and labor would contribute to the expansion of thought.
>
> I can imagine no plan which is suited to carry into effect so many divine ideas as this. If wisely executed, it will be a light over this country and this age.[2]

The light that Ripley sought to cast needed no explaining to Emerson, who knew already that the Brook Farm experiment stemmed from disgust with their society and from a dream of human betterment. Confronted with the materialism and inequities of his time—the mass unemployment, the slums, the exploitation—Ripley had long been an active reformer. He had been particularly interested in the democratization of the church and in the individualizing of education. His reforms rose naturally out of his Transcendentalist belief in the divinity (and hence the worth) of the individual.

By the beginning of the 1840s Ripley had concluded that these attempts to strengthen the individual did not suffice. If America were to attain her promise, if all men were to have an opportunity to realize their individual potentialities, if the rich were to be kept from exploiting the poor—society must be reformed into a structure wherein men worked and lived together in a spirit of brotherhood.

Association must replace competition, so that each man might fulfill himself. Brook Farm would point the way to a new order in America —communal in nature, but always protective of individual rights. Brook Farm would, of course, practice religious freedom. The old and disabled would be cared for, and the strong would bear the burden of the society. No ranks or titles would discriminate among members. Men from all walks of life might join in the experiment. On this point Ripley wanted to be very clear with Emerson: Brook Farm could not be exclusively a haven for cultured intellectuals. After all, their Transcendentalist creed taught that the most "degraded, ignorant, and obscure" of men possessed a faculty to "perceive spiritual truth when distinctly presented."

I recollect you said [his letter to Emerson went on] that if you were sure of compeers of the right stamp you might embark yourself in the adventure: as to this, let me suggest the inquiry, whether our Association should not be composed of various classes of men? If we have friends whom we love and who love us, I think we should be content to join with others, with whom our personal sympathy is not strong, but whose general ideas coincide with ours, and whose gifts and abilities would make their services important. For instance, I should like to have a good washerwoman in my parish admitted into the plot. She is certainly not a Minerva or a Venus; but we might educate her two children to wisdom and varied accomplishments, who otherwise will be doomed to drudge through life. The same is true of some farmers and mechanics, whom we should like with us.[3]

Pondering the matter, Emerson concluded that Brook Farm was not for him. He could "get the same advantages at home without pulling down" his house. Broadly speaking, he still had "some remains of skepticism in regard to the general practicability of the plan." Doubts ran through his mind as to the possibility for individual self-fulfillment in such a communal society. Nevertheless, "of all the philanthropic projects" he had examined, he found Ripley's the "most pleasing," and, if it was carried out in the spirit in which it was begun, he would "regard it with lively sympathy & with a sort of gratitude."[4] Other prominent Transcendentalists also limited their participation to moral and occasional financial support. "Association may be the great experiment of the age," conceded the brilliant Margaret Fuller. "Still it is only an experiment. It is not worth while to lay such stress on it; let us try it, induce others to try it—that is enough." Theodore Parker, gifted minister and ardent voice in the emancipation struggle, watched the experiment with interest but did not join in it.[5]

Disappointed but not discouraged, Ripley stayed with his plans. He had faith that a benevolent God governed the universe and that mankind could "look forward to a more pure, more lively, more divine state of society than was ever realized on earth."[6] He would make the deed one with the word. He would devote his fine energies to the realization of a better life on this earth, or at least in one small corner of it. Brook Farm would be a "beacon to the world."[7] A fellow Brook Farmer later summarized Ripley's attitude:

> He was in his fortieth year. He was neither too young nor too old. A few years of life he could possibly spare for the experiment. He would then be only in his prime. He had no children. He could give all his strength of body and mind to it. He loved the country life. It was to be the fulfilling of what he had preached so long—the Christian life. People would laugh at him! I doubt if that gave him one disturbing thought. It was *right*; as it was right he would do it.[8]

Ironically, although New England teemed with great literary figures of an optimistic bent, the most eminent man of letters to share in the great experiment personally was one who later would write so tellingly of the evil in men's hearts—Nathaniel Hawthorne. Young Hawthorne was among the first twenty to settle at the Farm. His *Note-book* records the alternate enthusiasm and gloom with which he viewed the project during his brief association with it. Long eager to escape his confining job at the custom house, he had written, a year before, "What a beautiful day was yesterday! My spirit rebelled against being confined in my darksome dungeon. I was kept a prisoner till it was too late to fling myself on a gentle wind, and be blown away into the country. When I shall be again free I will go forth and stand in a summer shower, and all the worldly dust that has collected on me shall be washed away at once."[9] In April, 1841 (in the midst of a storm), he arrived at Brook Farm, and the process of washing away the worldly dust began. His letters to his fiancée, Sophia Peabody, recapture the first months of the Brook Farmers' venture and throw light on the complex personality of a great artist.

> Apr. 13th, 1841.—Here I am in a polar Paradise! I have not yet taken my first lesson in agriculture, except that I went to see our cows foddered, yesterday afternoon. I intend to convert myself into a milkmaid this evening, but I pray Heaven that Mr. Ripley may be moved to assign me the kindliest cow in the herd, otherwise I shall perform my duty with fear and trembling.
>
> I like my brethren in affliction very well; and could you see us sitting round our table at meal-times, before the great kitchen fire, you would call it a cheerful sight.

Chapters from the American Experience

April 14th, 10 A.M.—I did not milk the cows last night, because Mr. Ripley was afraid to trust them to my hands, or me to their horns, I know not which. But this morning I have done wonders. Before breakfast, I went out to the barn and began to chop hay for the cattle, and with such "righteous vehemence," as Mr. Ripley says, did I labor, that in the space of ten minutes I broke the machine. Then I brought wood and replenished the fires; and finally went down to breakfast, and ate up a huge mound of buckwheat cakes. After breakfast, Mr. Ripley put a four-pronged instrument into my hands, which he gave me to understand was called a pitchfork; and he and Mr. Farley being armed with similar weapons, we all three commenced a gallant attack upon a heap of manure. I shall make an excellent husbandman—I feel the original Adam reviving within me.

———— makes the rest of us laugh continually. He keeps quoting innumerable scraps of Latin, and makes classical allusions, while we are turning over the gold-mine [the manure pile]; and the contrast between the nature of his employment and the character of his thoughts is irresistibly ludicrous.

April 22d.—What an abominable hand do I scribble! but I have been chopping wood, and turning a grindstone all the forenoon; and such occupations are likely to disturb the equilibrium of the muscles and sinews. It is an endless surprise to me how much work there is to be done in the world.

May 1st.—My cold has almost entirely departed. Were it a sunny day, I should consider myself quite fit for labors out of doors; but as the ground is so damp, and the atmosphere so chill, and the sky so sullen, I intend to keep myself on the sicklist this one day longer, more especially as I wish to read Carlyle on Heroes.

May 4th.—There is nothing so unseemly and disagreeable in this sort of toil as you could think. It defiles the hands, indeed, but not the soul. This gold ore is a pure and wholesome substance, else our mother Nature would not devour it so readily, and derive so much nourishment from it, and return such a rich abundance of good grain and roots in requital of it.

The farm is growing very beautiful now,—not that we yet see anything of the peas and potatoes which we have planted; but the grass blushes green on the slopes and hollows.

I do not believe that I should be patient here if I were not engaged in a righteous and heaven-blessed way of life. When I was in the Custom House I was not half so patient.

June 1st.—I have been too busy to write a long letter, for I think this present life of mine gives me an antipathy to pen and ink, even more than my Custom House experience did. In the midst of toil, or after a hard day's work in the gold-mine, my soul obstinately refuses to be poured out on paper. That abominable gold-mine! Of all hateful places that is the worst, and I shall never comfort myself for having spent so many days of blessed

sunshine there. It is my opinion that a man's soul may be buried and perish under a dung-heap, or in a furrow of the field, just as well as under a pile of money.[10]

By mid-July, Hawthorne's spirits had ebbed to the point where he discouraged an inquirer who was considering joining the association. Quickly remorseful, Hawthorne wrote the man and tried to give a more balanced picture of the situation. Mr. Ripley had never forced any of the Farmers to labor more than they felt inclined to, he said. It was just that the tasks to be done were staggering for so few hands. Still, he should not have sounded so despairing; actually, his hopes tended to "vary somewhat" with his state of mind. What worried him and others most was that Mr. Ripley's zeal would not "permit him to doubt of eventual success," even in the face of mounting financial difficulties. Nevertheless he was determined not to dishearten Mr. Ripley by expressing his dissatisfactions but would "give his experiment a full and fair trial." If Ripley's many hopes were to be frustrated, Hawthorne did not want to have cause to feel that the failure might have stemmed from lack of effort on his part.[11]

Try as he would, however, the constant drudgery became increasingly difficult to bear. On August 12, as the heaviest season of farm labor drew to a close, he wrote Sophia:

Joyful thought! in a little more than a fortnight I shall be free from my bondage, free to enjoy Nature—free to think and feel! Even my Custom House experience was not such a thraldom and weariness; my mind and heart were free. Oh, labor is the curse of the world, and nobody can meddle with it without becoming proportionably brutified! Is it a praiseworthy matter that I have spent five golden months in providing food for cows and horses? It is not so.

August 22d.—Since I last wrote, we have done haying, and the remainder of my bondage will probably be light. It will be a long time, however, before I shall know how to make a good use of leisure, either as regards enjoyment or literary occupation. I am becoming more and more convinced that we must not lean upon this community. Whatever is to be done must be done by my own undivided strength. I shall not remain here through the winter, unless with an absolute certainty that there will be a house ready for us in the spring. Otherwise, I shall return to Boston—still, however, considering myself an associate of the community, so that we may take advantage of any more favorable aspect of affairs.

September 22d, 1841 [after a brief absence].—Here I am again, slowly adapting myself to the life of this queer community, whence I seem to have been absent half a lifetime,—so utterly have I grown apart from the spirit and manners of the place. I have a friendlier disposition towards the farm, now that I am no longer obliged to toil in its stubborn furrows.

I doubt whether I shall succeed in writing another volume while I remain here. I have not the sense of perfect seclusion which has always been essential to my power of producing anything. It is true, nobody intrudes into my room: but still I cannot be quiet. Nothing here is settled; everything is but beginning to arrange itself, and though I would seem to have little to do with aught beside my own thoughts, still I cannot but partake of the ferment around me. My mind will not be abstracted. I must observe, and think, and feel, and content myself with catching glimpses of things which may be wrought out hereafter. Perhaps it will be quite as well that I find myself unable to set seriously about literary occupation for the present. It will be good to have a longer interval between my labor of the body and that of the mind. I shall work to the better purpose after the beginning of November. Meantime I shall see these people and their enterprise under a new point of view, and perhaps be able to determine whether we have any call to cast in our lot among them.

September 25th.—One thing is certain. I cannot and will not spend the winter here. The time would be absolutely thrown away so far as regards any literary labor.

September 27th.—I was elected to two high offices last night,—trustee and Chairman of the Committee of Finance! My accession to these august offices does not at all decide the question of my remaining here permanently.[12]

The enchantment was gone, and no high office could hold him. Hawthorne lingered on for a few weeks, absorbing the beauties of the New England Indian summer—philosophizing on the fate of a little calf he had befriended and a squirrel that capered above him in the trees—recording the delights of a "lonesome glade," a company of mushrooms that had sprung up in the road overnight, the freshened "grass-verged" brook that spoke of spring (save that its chill waters reflected the orange-reds of a dying season).

The next fall he returned to tender his formal resignation. Though no longer a "brother" in their "band," he would always take the "warmest interest" in their progress, he promised.[13] Later he would write: "No sagacious man will long retain his sagacity, if he live exclusively among reformers and progressive people. It was now time for me, therefore, to go and hold a little talk with the conservatives, the writers of the *North American Review*, the merchants, the politicians, the Cambridge men, and all those respectable old blockheads who still, in this intangibility and mistiness of affairs, kept a death-grip on one or two ideas which had not come into vogue since yesterday morning."[14] Baldly stated, Hawthorne was "sick to death of playing at philanthropy and progress."[15]

But if, as historian Vernon Parrington put it, Utopia became, for Hawthorne, "only the shadow of a dream"[16] in the face of the reality of evil, it was—and remained—something much more substantial for many who shared in it. New members arrived steadily during the seasons that followed, and the individual work load lightened a little. Financial difficulties persisted, but there were carefree hours of boating, dancing, singing, rich intellectual table talk, and long private excursions into the woods to commune with the nature they loved with such romantic passion.

The school that the Brook Farmers had set up during their first summer quickly earned a fine reputation and prospered modestly. Pupils worked for their board and lodging, with boys and girls studying and working together in a manner unorthodox at the time. The girls further celebrated their emancipation by wearing bloomers under short skirts and by freeing their locks from the conventional buns, or "pugs."[17] Complete freedom existed as to church attendance; some walked to Theodore Parker's parish in the nearby village, while others roamed alone in the woods' hidden glades or joined a visiting minister at the "picnic rock." Yet, despite these daring breaks with convention, no breath of scandal touched the Farm, and the pupils not only profited from the combination of labor and study, but also absorbed the gentility and wit of the cultured intellectuals around them.

The agricultural activities of Brook Farm, however, proved another matter. The gradual increase in the number of members and students depleted the milk surplus that had at first been marketed. Droves of visitors swarmed over the Farm every pleasant day, consuming its produce and diverting its labor from the fields. And the "mechanical" or industrial component (which included such trades as carpentry, printing, and shoemaking) was an undisguised failure. Under a regimen where each member labored at will, the bulk of the work soon devolved on the more conscientious. The countryfolk, commented Emerson dryly, "naturally were surprised to observe that one man plowed all day, and one looked out the window all day, and perhaps drew his own picture, and both received at night the same wages."[18]

By the close of 1843 the directors of the association were casting about for a way to pull the Farm out of the red. Such a plan seemed to offer itself in the program of Charles Fourier, the French social philosopher. Fourierism had spread rapidly in America since its introduction by Albert Brisbane early the previous year. Like the Brook Farmers, Fourier and Brisbane held that "Association" offered a solution to the evils of industrial society, and they too spoke in terms of "combining full and unrestricted individual liberty with associated effort."[19] But, practically, they imposed many more restrictions and specific requirements on the individual than did the Farmers. The "Phalanx," or operating unit of Fourierism, applied "scientific" methods to the ordering of society. In keeping with the "noble idea" of "Attractive Industry," each member ideally would choose the spheres of labor that appealed to him. Then, to avoid boredom, he would shift from one to another of these preferred tasks every few hours. But he would do his full share of the work, including the onerous duties that no one found "attractive." All workers should live together in one giant "Phalanstery," where cooperative buying could offer great savings and household chores could be efficiently disposed of by an organized labor force to which this type of work was "attractive."[20] Studying the elaborately devised plan, Emerson said caustically, "Our feeling was that Fourier had skipped no fact but one, namely, Life."[21]

But to the men struggling at Brook Farm the scheme seemed to hold out a chance for survival. After much discussing and soul-searching, they initiated the change, and Ripley set about reorganizing the faltering industrial section at once.

Their new constitution announced a change in policy of admission. Brook Farm had hitherto been essentially a private experiment. The time had now come to bring it before the public. The convenient and beautiful location, the established, successful school connected with it, the experience already gained there—all made the Farm a logical choice for those interested in association. Men and women accustomed to labor and "ready to consecrate themselves" to the cause were urged to join. In return they would be guaranteed "freedom from pecuniary anxiety and the evils of competitive industry, free and friendly society, and the education" of their children. If they would come and work with the Brook Farmers, they might share in demonstrating the certain truth that "human life shall yet be developed, not in discord and misery, but in harmony and joy, and that the perfected earth shall at last bear on her bosom a race of men worthy of the name."[22]

The constitution differed from the original pact in several ways. Most significantly, it laid out very specific labor requirements for its members:

Three hundred days shall be considered a year's labor. The hours of labor shall be from the first of October to the first of April at least eight hours daily, and from the first of April to the first of October at least ten hours daily, and no person shall be credited for labor beyond that time.[23]

So that nothing might diminish the efficiency of the workers, no public meetings—for business or for pleasure—were to be "protracted beyond the hour of ten P.M."

The campaign brought many new members. John Thomas Codman, who had come to Brook Farm the spring before and who leaned decidedly toward the new school, described the change: "In the place of the Transcendentalists came other men and women, new and untried, with not so much of Greek and Latin, not so much suavity of manners, not so much 'cultivation,' but warm of heart and brave of purpose."[24] As these newcomers joined the Phalanx, many old Brook Farmers withdrew, and others were filled with misgiving. One of the latter, Georgianna Bruce, who had been with the group almost from the beginning, wrote of her own contradictory feelings, raising the same questions Ripley had put to Emerson at the beginning. Should only those "attracted by strong personal interests" join together in such an effort? Or might not other ideas "legitimately unite" them? She had long believed the former and had "with grief " seen their membership increased to include those less congenial. Now, after much thought, she had concluded that this "narrow" view set a "limit to God's love." And then this young girl asked herself two further questions—questions whose relevance will be clear as long as the underprivileged and the ghetto exist:

Why should I be so intolerant as to shut out from my heart (as I have done) the ignorant, the coarse, the unspiritual, by denying them also the benefits of a better external arrangement? Am I to wait till the millions of crushed beings have attained superior ideas of truth, or shall I now say to them, "Come, if you will work with me, we will share and share alike"?— Thus immediately taking away one great, nay, many great hindrances to the perfection of soul and body.[25]

The literary tone that had been the pride of the Transcendental period disappeared. Codman noted with pleasure:

Many persons who have heard of the Community life at Brook Farm have idealized it into a little coterie of choice spirits who sat around the study lamp at early eve, after the light toil of the day had ceased, and discussed the intellectual problems of the German philosophers. But this was only partially true.

Mr. Ripley at first endeavored to instruct the assembly and impart to them some of his own intellectual enthusiasm. Evening classes were formed; readings took place from some of the prominent poets—Goethe, Schiller, Shakespeare; from Carlyle and Cousin as well as Kant; but when the industrial period began he had his hands more than full, and he laid his books on the shelf. They were his tools—they were the ladders on which he had mounted to his high estate. Why should he worship them? To work! To begin to shape society to higher ends! That was indeed the worthiest end in life, and his worthiest homage to the writers and their books.[26]

Emerson no longer called at the Farm; nor did Margaret Fuller. Only Theodore Parker continued his regular visits, drawn by his fondness for Ripley. Codman recorded a revealing little exchange between the two friends:

Rev. Theodore Parker['s] afternoon walk every few days was over to the Farm and back for exercise, and to converse with Mr. Ripley. At the close of their chat you would see them coming down the hill towards the barn, where Mr. Ripley's duties as milkman took him at that time of day, when they would part.

Theodore Parker had not then become famous, but preached in a little square, wooden church, to his small country congregation, and once on a time a friend (we will call him Smith for convenience sake) asked Mr. Parker how Mr. Ripley was getting along with his "Community." "Oh," said the faithless Parker, "Mr. Ripley reminds me, in that connection, of a new and splendid locomotive dragging along a train of mud-cars."

Soon after Mr. Ripley heard what Mr. Parker had said of him, and resolved to pay him in his own coin. So he held him that day in pleasant, lively conversation until he reached the farmyard by the barn, and the unsprung joke was running all around the pleasant lines of his face and twinkling in the corners of his brilliant eyes. Towards the close of the conversation, as Mr. Parker was about to leave, Mr. Ripley casually said that he had met Mr. Smith, and he had spoken of Mr. Parker and his church.

"Indeed," said Mr. Parker, "and what did he say of me?"

"Well, if you must know," Mr. Ripley replied, "he said that you and your little country church, with its few dozen of farmers, reminded him of a new and splendid locomotive dragging along a train of mud-cars."

It would have been worth a month of an ordinary lifetime to be there when Mr. Ripley exploded his joke, to hear his merry peal of laughter, whilst his sides shook again, and his reverend friend stood confounded.[27]

Even the emphasis in entertainment shifted. In place of intellectualized evenings with the German Romantic composers, the country barn dance took over, with a neighboring fiddler imported to play and call the dances.

Crises and steady financial strain continued to plague those in charge of the Farm. Money persisted in eluding them. Brisbane, who had encouraged them to serve as torchbearers for Associationism, became interested in a bigger project (the North American Phalanx in New Jersey) and refused to help raise much-needed funds. Smallpox swept through the Farm, striking one-third of the population and causing many parents to withdraw their children permanently from the school.

The crowning blow came in the spring of 1846, when fire razed the most important building on the Farm. Bachelor accommodations in an exposed loft had always been primitive, and family housing was grossly inadequate. Hopes had come increasingly to be placed in the mammoth new Phalanstery, which the Farmers had been building since 1844. One hundred seventy-five feet long and three stories high, it would house all members of the community. It was to have a commodious communal kitchen, a gigantic dining hall, various living rooms, and a chapel, as well as comfortable partitioned dormitories and three-bedroom family apartments. When the Phalanstery was completed, they told themselves, the difficult times would pass. Then, when thousands of dollars and incalculable energy had brought the edifice near completion, a fire broke out and completely demolished the unplastered structure. Ripley published an account of the disaster:

The alarm of fire was given at about a quarter before nine, and it was found to proceed from the "Phalanstery"; in a few minutes, the flames were bursting through the doors and windows of the second story; the fire spread with almost incredible rapidity throughout the building; and in about an hour and a half the whole edifice was burned to the ground. The members of the Association were on the spot in a few moments, and made some attempts to save a quantity of lumber that was in the basement story; but so rapid was the progress of the fire, that this was found to be impossible.

On the Saturday previous to the fire, a stove was put up in the basement story for the accommodation of the carpenters, who were to work on the inside; a fire was kindled in it on Tuesday morning, which burned till four o'clock in the afternoon; at half past eight in the evening, the building was visited by the night watch, who found every thing apparently safe; and at about a quarter before nine, a faint light was discovered in the second story. Smoke at once showed that the interior was on fire. The alarm was immediately given, but almost before the people had time to assemble, the whole edifice was wrapped in flames. From a defect in the construction of the chimney, a spark from the stove pipe had probably communicated with the surrounding wood work; and from the combustible nature of the materials, the flames spread with a celerity that made every effort to arrest their violence without effect.

As it was not yet in use by the Association no insurance had been effected. The calamity is felt to be great. In our present infant state, it is a severe trial of our strength. We cannot now calculate its ultimate effect. It may prove more than we are able to bear. Whatever may be in reserve for us, we have an infinite satisfaction in the true relations which have united us, and the assurance that our enterprise has sprung from a desire to obey the divine law.[28]

In the months that followed, the story told by the Farmers' correspondence is one of gallantry in defeat—desperate attempts to raise funds and to persuade creditors to reduce interest rates, talk of possible ways of retrenching, whistling in the dark, gradual defection on the part of the membership. "If the wise, the good, and true think it their duty to quit, how or what shall I hope for Brook Farm?" wrote one young girl.[29] As the end approached, those remaining at the Farm held a day of fasting. Finally, while the auctioneers hammered their great adventure out of existence, they fled to the woods to avoid the sight.

The experiment was at end. Hawthorne, the erstwhile hopeful Nay Sayer, had given it up after a few months. Emerson, the dedicated optimist, had consistently avoided any deep commitment and in the end dismissed it with crushing finality as "an Age of Reason in a patty-pan."[30] But even Hawthorne would say, in later years, "Whatever else I may repent of, let it be reckoned neither among my sins nor follies that I once had faith and force enough to form generous hopes of the world's destiny—yes!—and to do what in me lay for their accomplishment."[31] And, for many of the men and women who shared in its struggle over a period of years, Brook Farm would remain what Ripley had hoped it would be for all men—a beacon by which to light their lives. Again and again, in their memoirs and their letters, they would raise the question "Is man indeed too frail for such a dream?"

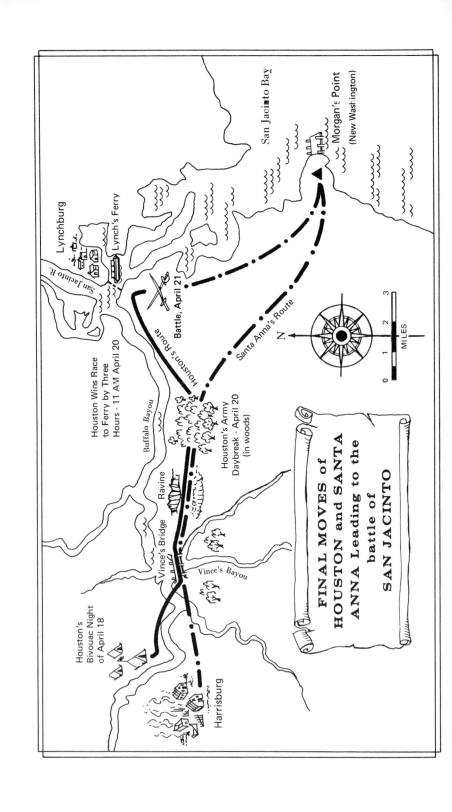

FINAL MOVES of HOUSTON and SANTA ANNA Leading to the battle of SAN JACINTO

Lynchburg

Lynch's Ferry

San Jacinto R.

San Jacinto Bay

Morgan's Point
(New Washington)

Houston Wins Race to Ferry by Three Hours - 11 AM April 20

Battle, April 21

Houston's Route

Santa Anna's Route

Buffalo Bayou

Ravine

Houston's Army Daybreak - April 20 (in woods)

Vince's Bridge

Vince's Bayou

Houston's Bivouac Night of April 18

Harrisburg

N

MILES
0 1 2 3

25

A Lone Star

It was the moulding period of life,
when the heart,
just charmed into the feverish hopes and dreams of youth,
looks wistfully around
on all things for light and beauty.

Sam Houston once wrote that Americans should listen to the old men of Kentucky and Tennessee, for they could spin unexcelled "legends of heroism and adventure."[1] From beginning to end, Houston's own life created such a legend of the Westward movement—a roistering tale of high drama, rich with the romance of the moving American frontier.

Houston's great-grandfather came to upland Virginia from Scotland early in the eighteenth century—came with silver buckles on his shoes and with an ample enough keg of gold coins to acquire broad holdings and slaves to work them and to establish himself as a first citizen of the community. But Houston's father (who chose the army for a career because it was a "gentleman's occupation") lived sufficiently above his means to dissipate most of the family wealth by the time he died late in 1806. He had been making plans to move West, had actually begun negotiations for a land grant in eastern Tennessee, when death overtook him.

As soon as the estate was liquidated, his widow and nine children set out over the Alleghenies and into the Tennessee wilderness, to the site Major Houston had selected under the Big Smoky Mountains. They patented 419 acres and set to work building a home. From the beginning, their venture prospered.

They bought slaves. They acquired an interest in a general store in Maryville. They enlarged the family residence.

But for [fourteen-year old] Sam the romantic part of the migration ended when the family began to clear the farm. Of Elizabeth Houston's six sons, Sam seemed to take after his father the most in one respect: his talents did not incline to agriculture. Frontier farming was an occupation involving much commonplace labor in order to eat not any too well. Sam perceived flaws in this scheme.

He was a likable culprit, though, fair and tall, with wavy chestnut hair and friendly blue eyes that looked from a head full of droll humor and long words he saw in books. He would disappear for days—usually with a book, but the stories that came drifting back were often difficult to reconcile with the pursuit of literature. There were reproofs from mother which Sam took with his tongue in cheek, but the bossing by his brothers stirred him to rebellion.

At length it was conceded that Sam was not cut out to be a planter, and so he was placed behind the counter of the store in Maryville. But his lapses increased, and he got the name of a wayward boy.

One morning he did not show up for work at the store. Weeks passed, and there was a great search and stir. Finally the family heard that its black sheep had crossed the Tennessee River into the Indian country and was living with the Cherokees. [His brothers] James and John went to bring him back. They were directed to the wigwam of the chief.

Chief Oo-loo-te-ka's council house [was] on an island that parts the current of the Tennessee where the yellow Hiwasse boils into it from the Big Smokies. The brothers paddled up to find the runaway lying under a tree, scanning lines of the *Iliad.* He was invited to return home. Sam relates that he stood "straight as an Indian," and (with a creditable touch of Cherokee imagery for a beginner) replied that he "preferred measuring deer tracks to tape" and "the wild liberty of the Red Men [to] the tyranny of his own brothers." He begged to be excused from saying more as "a translation from the Greek" claimed his interest and he desired to "read it in peace." He got his wish.[2]

With brief interludes at home, Houston spent the next three years with the Cherokee, absorbing their lore and their way of life.

Chief Oo-loo-te-ka adopted Sam as a son and christened him Co-lon-neh —The Raven. The name was a revered one, with associations in Cherokee mythology. The young braves taught him the green corn dance, the hoop and pole game.

Sam preferred these diversions to those on the civilized side of the Tennessee. He reveled in the wealth of legend with which Cherokee life abounded.

In the evenings Sam sat about the fires where the long pipe was passed, filling his mind with the maxims of the headmen and the picturesque idioms of the Indian speech, which time never eradicated from his vocabulary.

Headman Rogers [who was part Scot and an ancestor of actor Will Rogers] had two wives and many children, including two boys named, singularly enough, John and James. They were The Raven's fast friends.

These years were a permanent influence on Sam Houston's life. They left him with an attachment for the wilderness and a faith in primitive fellowships.

"It was the moulding period of life," he wrote, "when the heart, just charmed into the feverish hopes and dreams of youth, looks wistfully around on all things for light and beauty."

This was the school in which Sam Houston learned to practise the arts of courtship, "wandering," he wrote, "along the banks of streams, side by side with some Indian maiden, sheltered by the deep woods, making love and reading Homer's *Iliad.*" Enchanted island.[3]

Decades later, when Houston had "seen nearly all in life there is to live for," he would say there was "nothing half so sweet to remember as this sojourn among the untutored children of the forest."

Echoes—on the American frontier—of the great French Romantic, Jean Jacques Rousseau, who rebelled against his society, preached a return to nature and glorified the noble savage. Without giving it a name, Houston had arrived at the temperament pattern that was to shape his life—the pattern of Romanticism. Many men of his generation and of the one before had found their answers to the conundrums of life in pretty much the same set of values. So many, in fact, that the age has become known as the Romantic Era. Houston's brand of Romanticism was not that of Edgar Allan Poe—murkily delving in caverns measureless to man*—nor did it embrace the mysticism of the New England Transcendentalists. It was, rather, the lusty, energetic, earthy Romanticism of the American frontier. And its focus was the Bunyanesque figure of the American folk hero.

*This phrase, which comes so readily to mind in connection with Poe, is from the poem "Kublai Khan," by the English Romantic poet Samuel Taylor Coleridge.

A Lone Star

The boy who withdrew from the workaday world, who, lying on forested banks of wilderness streams, dreamed of Grecian demigods assaulting the walls of Troy, lived to create a vast empire for America and to become one of the great folk heroes of his age.

Houston returned to the white community in the spring of 1812. To meet debts he had incurred on his visits back to civilization, he opened a private school. Although his own education had been negligible, the new "master" met with success, and his log benches soon were filled to capacity.

Years afterward, while swapping yarns on a steamboat crossing Galveston Bay, an old army comrade reminded General Houston that he had been the governor of one state, a United States senator from another, the commander-in-chief of an army and the president of a Republic. Which office had afforded him the greatest pride?

"Well, Burke," replied Sam Houston, "when a young man in Tennessee I kept a country school, being then about eighteen years of age, and a tall, strapping fellow. At noon after the luncheon, which I and my pupils ate together out of our baskets, I would go into the woods and cut me a 'sour wood' stick, trim it carefully in circular spirals and thrust one half of it into the fire, which would turn it blue, leaving the other half white. With this emblem of ornament and authority in my hand, dressed in a hunting-shirt of flowered calico, a long queue down my back, and the sense of authority over my pupils, I experienced a higher feeling of dignity and self-satisfaction than from any office or honor which I have since held."[4]

Autumn came, the pupils were called to harvest corn, and cold winds invaded the schoolhouse through the "window" hole that furnished the only light. Sam closed his school and returned briefly to the life of a student, his teacher finding him "the most provoking" pupil he had ever taught.[5]

One spring day soon after his twentieth birthday, listening to a group of soldiers recruiting for the army, Sam was enticed by the drums, the parade of colors, the soldiers' white pantaloons. He took a dollar from their drumhead and thereby enlisted to fight in the War of 1812. From his mother he received a musket, a little homily on courage, and a golden ring engraved with the word "Honor." Vowing that the homefolks would hear from him, he set out. At the Battle of Horseshoe Bend against the Creek confederates of Great Britain, his valor attracted the attention of General Andrew Jackson; it also caused him so many wounds that he was sent home to die.

Chapters from the American Experience

But Houston refused to die, and after the war, Jackson, remembering his outstanding courage, undertook to sponsor him in a political career. Following a six-month whirlwind conquest of the law, Houston became, in quick succession, prosecuting attorney, U. S. Congressman, and, in 1827, Governor of Tennessee. He began to be spoken of as a likely candidate for the presidency.

At this pinnacle Houston's private life exploded. His bride of less than three months left him, and speculation ran high as to which, if either, had "transgressed." Despite pressures from friends to satisfy his constituency with an explanation, Houston refused to discuss the matter. It was, he said enigmatically, "no part of the conduct of a gallant or a generous man to take up arms against a woman."[6]

When it became clear that the public would insist on having its pound of flesh, he resigned his office and disappeared again into the West. Another interlude ensued with the Cherokee (now "removed" to the Indian Territory in present-day Oklahoma) He became a tribal citizen, built a home for Tiana, the halfsister of his boyhood friends, John and James Rogers, and planted an apple orchard. But the pastoral life no longer satisfied. He arbitrated tribal quarrels and, attired in a spectacular native costume, interceded with President Jackson in behalf of the Indians. Such simple services, however, failed to fill the life of a man who had entertained dreams of greatness. Life's charm, wrote Houston, had been broken. As he later put it, he "buried his sorrows in the flowing bowl."[7] Even his drinking had an epic quality. The Indians gave him a new name: "Big Drunk."[8] To his angry amazement, his candidacy for a place on the Cherokee Council met with defeat. In an alcoholic stupor, he quarreled with Chief Oo-loo-te-ka, struck him, and was in turn beaten by furious braves. At thirty-eight, his useful life seemed at an end.

But the forces that made it impossible for him to find contentment among his Indian friends were at work effecting his regeneration. To Jackson he wrote:

When I left the world, I persuaded myself that I would lose all care, about the passing political events of the world, as well as those of my own country, but it is not so, for . . . I find that my interest is rather increased than diminished. It is hard for an old Trooper, to forget the *note* of the *Bugle!* [9]

And it was hard for the Romantic to forget the positive side of his nature. While Houston brawled and drank big, tasting the dregs of his weakness, he heard still the note of the bugle: If man is "wretched," he also carries in him the seed of "greatness."[10] Like many other Romantics, Houston was a Yea Sayer and a doer. And, like them, his great constructive dreams revolved around his country. Before America lay a continent to be won. Houston would have a share in that conquest. At the beginning of his self-exile, he had boasted vaguely that he would someday found a "Rocky Mountain Empire" or, with the help of the Indians, conquer the vast domain of Mexican Texas. From time to time after that, adventurers approached him on the subject of a Texas campaign, but—mindful that Jackson had decreed there should be no recruiting for such an undertaking within the United States—Houston avoided committing himself.

In the spring of 1832 he was back in Washington with a delegation of Indians. Before he left the capital, Houston had discussed financial backing for a Texas venture with Eastern land speculators and had been promised a passport to treat with the Comanche Indians in that country.

Toward the end of the year he set out alone on his first journey through Texas. By the time Houston completed this extensive tour in mid-February, he was wearing a bright-hued poncho and silver trappings—symbols of a new life for "Don Samuel." He had found Texas in a turmoil of resentment against Mexican control, the welcome smell of revolution in the air. He settled down to the practice of law in the east Texas town of Nacogdoches and at once became embroiled in politics. Events moved rapidly. In Mexico City "El Presidente" General Antonio López de Santa Anna assumed the power of a dictator. A prominent Texan who had been sent to the Mexican government to present protests was clapped in jail, and Santa Anna's brother-in-law, General Cos, descended upon the restive province of Texas to invoke military law. A chain of repressions and reactions followed. In Nacogdoches a Committee of Vigilance and Safety was formed, with Houston as its military leader.

Then, in October, 1835, a skirmish between General Cos and the people of Gonzales touched off the fuse. Texan leaders demanded war. "The morning of glory is dawning," declared Houston. To his friends in the States, he urged: "War . . . is inevitable in Texas. . . . Let each man come with a good rifle and one hundred rounds of ammunition, and . . . come soon."[11]

Early in November a convention met, established a provisional government, elected a Governor and Council, and chose Sam Houston commander in chief of the rebel army. Almost at once the council fell to bickering with the governor and refused to support Houston's appointment of officers for a regular army. Discouraging word drifted in to the frustrated leader. Several hundred volunteers had stormed the Álamo, where they captured General Cos and his men. But, unable to feed their prisoners, they had released them on the general's promise to return to Mexico. Many of the Texas volunteers had then gone home, while others had embarked on an erratic excursion across the desert into Mexico. Intelligence also reached Houston that, just south of the border, Santa Anna was rapidly gathering an army and preparing an attack. Furious at being hamstrung in his efforts to organize a regular army, he mustered such volunteers as he could. Certain that Santa Anna would direct his first assault against the Álamo, Houston advised the volunteers remaining there to abandon the fort and move south to form a flexible line of defense. He was convinced that an attempt to defend any one point against such superior forces could only end in disaster.

The year wore away and 1836 came. Still the council delayed, bickered, changed personnel, and finally made an open bid for uncontested control by defying the governor and removing Houston from his command. While the rebels squabbled, Santa Anna crossed the Rio Grande, marched quickly to San Antonio, and laid siege to the garrison still entrenched at the Álamo.

Meanwhile, word had come that the Cherokee in northeastern Texas, alienated by white land-grabbers, were considering joining the Mexican attack. On the governor's orders, Houston went with a commission to the Indians and persuaded his friends to negotiate a treaty of neutrality.

It was now near the end of February, and stirring cries began to emanate from the Álamo. The commanding officer, Colonel Travis, sent word that he and his men were besieged by an overwhelming force. They had sustained a "continual bombardment & cannonade," but they would "never surrender or retreat," for "God and Texas—Victory or Death!!"[12] Words of immortal courage, but Houston wished they would get out and live to fight another day for Texas.

Early in March a general convention met and hurriedly reappointed Houston commander in chief, assuring him of the full support of the new government they were establishing. Houston promised the convention that "if mortal power could avail," he would relieve the "brave men of the Álamo." In less than an hour he was on his way to meet an "army" of volunteers who had congregated at Gonzales. As he went, Houston meditated bitterly on his situation. "A general-in-chief, you would suppose," he wrote later, would be "at least surrounded by a staff of gallant men. . . . He was to produce a nation; he was to defend a people; he was

A Lone Star

to command the resources of the country; and he must give character to the army. He had two aides-de-camp, one captain, and a youth. This

was his escort in marching to the headquarters of the army, as it was called."[13] Houston also later recorded how, as he hurried toward Gonzales, he came to know that the Álamo had fallen:

At the break of day I retired some distance from the party and listened intensely. Colonel Travis had stated in his letters that as long as the Álamo could hold out against the invaders signal guns would be fired at sunrise. It is a well authenticated fact that for many successive days these guns had been heard at a distance of over one hundred miles across the prairie—and being now within reach of their sound, I anxiously waited for the expected signal. The day before, like many preceding it, a dull, rumbling murmur had come booming over the prairie like distant thunder. I listened with an acuteness of sense which no man can understand whose hearing has not been sharpened by the teachings of the dwellers of the forest, and who is waiting a signal of life or death from brave men. I listened in vain. Not the faintest murmur came floating on the calm, morning air. I knew the Álamo had fallen, and I returned to tell my companions. The event confirmed my convictions, for . . . at the very moment I was speaking in the Convention, those brave men were meeting their fate.[14]

Massacring the defenders, Santa Anna divided his army into three forces and sent them fanning eastward over Texas to drive the Americans from the country. Near Gonzales, Houston found 374 men "without organization and destitute of supplies."[15] Hearing that Santa Anna was approaching, Houston set his scarecrow forces into retreat. Always at least a river or a swamp ahead of the Mexicans, he moved to the east —playing for time, welcoming the reinforcements who straggled in, determined to engage the enemy only in such a situation as might ensure him some chance of success. Word spread that the commander in chief was afraid; his men grumbled mutinously as they floundered through rain-soaked bogs—always back, away from the enemy. But Houston kept his council, refusing to justify his tactics. "I consulted none," he wrote. "I held no councils of war. If I err, the blame is mine."[16] In brief rests here and there, his officers drilled their men and Houston wrote hurried letters—to the council begging them to stop running; to acquaintances in the United States seeking more volunteers; to his Indian friends, encouraging them to honor their treaty; to the Texans, stirring them to action.

He leaned heavily on two highly skilled scouts, Henry Karnes and

Erastus ("Deaf") Smith, to keep him informed of the enemy's movements. A pair of six-pound cannon arrived (a gift from the citizens of Cincinnati), and the delighted soldiers dubbed them the "Twin Sisters." A group of mutineers who refused to break camp on empty stomachs were told to go "plumb to hell" and thrown out by Houston.[17] Morale improved a little.

Then, at last, as Houston had hoped, Santa Anna made a mistake. The president general decided to push on ahead of his army with a small unit and capture the Texas government at its temporary headquarters in Harrisburg. Houston put his army on forced march to intercept him. Santa Anna reached and burned Harrisburg on April 15 and then rushed on toward Galveston in pursuit of the fleeing Texas officials. As he neared his objective, his heavy artillery bogged down, slowing the advance. On the evening of the 18th, Deaf Smith captured a Mexican courier to Santa Anna. The dispatches he carried revealed that General Cos was "coming on with all possible speed to support His Excellency's advance."[18] The need for haste became even more apparent. Houston also knew that a larger force under Filisola was not far away. If, in the interval before too many reinforcements converged on the arena, the Texans could challenge and capture the Mexican ruler, they might free their country in one decisive battle.

On his soiled map Houston traced the situation of his quarry, not ten miles away, groping among the unfamiliar marshes that indented Galveston Bay and the estuary of a certain nebulous Rio San Jacinto. Sending his army to bed the Commander-in-Chief continued to pore over the chart. Two hours before dawn he slept a little.

After daybreak General Houston delivered a speech. "Victory is certain!" Sam Houston said. "Trust in God and fear not! And remember the Álamo!"

"Remember the Álamo!" the ranks roared back.[19]

A battle cry had been born.

Muffling their equipment, hiding in the woods by day, Houston's forces moved across Buffalo Bayou and along an easterly line roughly paralleling its course to the point where it merged into the San Jacinto River. There a ferry crossed the river to a town on the eastern bank, and toward this ferry, Houston learned, Santa Anna was advancing. The Mexican general had moved in a southerly loop and was now circling back up the river to the ferry. By his swift and direct march, Houston had gained the advantage of choosing the battlefield and his own posi-

A Lone Star

tion. He selected a stretch of open savannah separated from the river by treacherous swamp and commanded by a knoll covered with moss-draped oaks. Behind them to the west, enemy reinforcements (or retreat) would be slowed by a northerly flowing tributary to Buffalo Bayou, over which led a single span known as "Vince's Bridge." Houston posted his army in the oak grove on the hill and ordered the Twin Sisters loaded with broken horseshoes and wheeled out onto the prairie.

Santa Anna came up over a little rise and descended onto the savannah. Seeing the two six-pounders boldly confronting him across the plain, he halted, drew his army into a line, and ordered his two twelve-pounders to fire on the woods. Their shot cut into the upper branches of the trees, doing little damage to the army below. The Twin Sisters raked the enemy lines, and a Mexican infantry charge was repulsed. Santa Anna, deciding not to force an engagement, threw up hasty fortifications. The Texans ate and went to bed in eager anticipation of the next morning's fight. But, when reveille sounded at four A.M., they learned that their commander in chief was sleeping peacefully on a coil of rope and had left instructions not to be disturbed.

It was full day when Sam Houston opened his eyes—after his first sleep of more than three hours in six weeks.

The camp was in a fidget to attack. It could not fathom a commander who sauntered aimlessly under the trees in the sheer enjoyment, he said, of a good night's sleep. Deaf Smith rode up and dismounted. The lines of the old plainsman's leathery face were deep. Night and day he and Henry Karnes had been the eyes of the army.

"Santa Anna is getting reinforcements," [Smith called to the men] in his high-pitched voice. "I'm going to tell the general he ought to burn Vince's bridge before any more come up."

After a talk with Smith, Houston strolled past a gathering of soldiers remarking that it wasn't often Deaf Smith could be fooled by a trick like that—Santa Anna marching men around and around to make it look like a reinforcement. Smith returned from another gallop onto the prairie. "The general was right," he announced loudly. "It's all a humbug." But privately he informed Houston that the reinforcement numbered five hundred and forty men under Cos, which raised Santa Anna's force to the neighborhood of thirteen hundred and fifty. Houston's strength was slightly above eight hundred.

Houston later told Santa Anna that his reason for waiting for Cos was to avoid making "two bites of one cherry." But he did not care to see Filisola, who might turn up at any time with two or three thousand Mexicans. Handing . . . axes to Smith, Houston told him to destroy Vince's Bridge. "And come back like eagles, or you will be too late for the day."

Unaware of these preparations, the camp was working itself into a state. [Houston preferred not to tell them he was waiting for the siesta hour.]

At three-thirty o'clock, the Commander-in-Chief abruptly formed his army for attack. At four o'clock he lifted his sword. The drum and fife raised the air of a love-song, *Come to the Bower,* [the only tune they knew] and the last army of the Republic moved from the woods and slowly up the sloping plain of San Jacinto. [On a] big white stallion Sam Houston rode up and down the front.

"Hold your fire, men. Hold your fire. Hold your fire."

For ten of the longest minutes that a man ever lives, the single line poked through the grass. In front lay a barricade of Mexican pack-saddles and camp impedimenta, inert in the oblique rays of the sun.

"Hold your fire, men. Hold your fire."

Behind the Mexican line a bugle rang. A sketchy string of orange dots glowed from the pack-saddles and a ragged rattle of musketry roused up a scolding swarm of birds from the trees on the Texan's left. A few Texans raised their rifles and let go at the dots.

"Hold your fire! God damn you, hold your fire!" General Houston spurred the white stallion to a gallop.

The orange dots continued to wink and die. The white stallion fell. Throwing himself upon a cavalryman's pony, Houston resumed his patrol of the line.

"Fight for your lives! Vince's bridge has been cut down!" It was Deaf Smith on a lathered mustang. Rather inaccurately, the soldiers understood Vince's bridge to be their sole avenue of retreat.

Twenty yards from the works, Houston made a signal with his hat. A blast of horseshoes from the Twin Sisters laid a section of the fragile breastwork flat. The infantrymen roared a volley and lunged forward drawing their hunting knives. "Remember the Álamo!" "Remember the Álamo!"

They swept over the torn barricade as if it had not been there. Shouts and yells and the pounding of hoofs smote their ears. Through key-holes in a pungent wall of smoke they saw gray-clad little figures, with chin-straps awry, running back, kneeling and firing, and running back—toward some tents where greater masses of men were veering this way and that. The Texans pursued them. The pungent wall melted; the firing was not so heavy now as the Texans were using their knives and the bayonets of Mexican guns. The surprise lacked nothing. Santa Anna had thought Houston would not, could not, attack. In his carpeted marquee, he was enjoying

A Lone Star

a siesta when a drowsy sentinel on the barricade described the Texan advance. Cos's men were sleeping off the fatigue of their night march. Cavalrymen were riding bareback to and from water. Others were cooking and cutting wood. Arms were stacked.

When the barrier was overrun, Santa Anna rushed from his tent commanding everyone to lie down. A moment later he vaulted on a black horse and disappeared.

General Houston rode among the wreckage of the Mexican camp. He was on his third horse, and his right boot was full of blood. Fugitives plunged into the swamp and scattered over the prairie. "Me no Álamo! Me no Álamo!" Some cavalry bolted for bridgeless Vince's Bayou. The Texans rushed them down a vertical bank. A hundred men and a hundred horses, inextricably tangled, perished in the water.

As the sun set General Houston fainted. His right leg was shattered above the ankle. The other Texan casualties were six killed and twenty-four wounded.

The battle proper had lasted perhaps twenty minutes. The rest was in remembrance of the Álamo. This pursuit and slaughter continued into the night. The prisoners were herded in the center of a circle of bright fires. "Santa Anna? Santa Anna?" the Texans demanded until officers began to pull off their shoulder-straps. But no Santa Anna was found.

After a night of pain General Houston propped himself against a tree.

All day bands of scared prisoners were brought in. But no Santa Anna. This was more than vexing. Santa Anna might escape to Filisola and return with thrice the army Houston had just defeated. With the President of Mexico in his hands, however, Houston could rest assured that he had won the war, not merely a battle.

Toward evening a patrol of five men rode into camp. Mounted behind Joel Robison was a bedraggled little figure in a blue cotton smock and red felt slippers. The patrol had found him near the ruined Vince's Bayou bridge seated on a stump, the living picture of dejection. He said he had found his ridiculous clothes in a deserted house. He looked hardly worth bothering to take five miles to camp and would have been dispatched on the spot but for Robison, who was a good-hearted boy, and spoke Spanish. Robison and his prisoner chatted on the ride. How many men did the Americans have? Robison said less than eight hundred, and the prisoner said that surely there were more than that. Robison asked the captive if he had left a family behind. "Si, señor." "Do you expect to see them again?" The little Mexican shrugged his shoulders. "Why did you come and fight us?" Robison wished to know. "A private soldier, señor, has little choice in such matters."

Chapters from the American Experience

Robison had taken a liking to the polite little fellow and was about to turn him loose without ceremony among the herd of prisoners, when the captives began to raise their hats.

"*El Presidente! El Presidente!*"

[With] an air that left the Texan flat, the prisoner asked to be conducted to General Houston.

Sam Houston was lying on a blanket under the oak tree, his eyes closed and his face drawn with pain. The little man was brought up. He stepped forward and bowed gracefully.

"I am General Antonio López de Santa Anna, President of Mexico, Commander-in-Chief of the Army of Operations. I place myself at the disposal of the brave General Houston."

Raising himself on one elbow, Houston replied [in his stumbling Spanish] as words came to him.

"General Santa Anna!—Ah, indeed!—Take a seat, General. I am glad to see you, take a seat!"

"That man may consider himself born to no common destiny who has conquered the Napoleon of the West," [said Santa Anna], "and it now remains for him to be generous to the vanquished."

"You should have remembered that at the Álamo," Houston replied.[20]

The Battle of San Jacinto took its place among the most significant military contests of all time. Andrew Jackson wrote Houston that he considered the victory greater than that of New Orleans. At the site of the battle the Texans have erected a Texas-tall monument, which describes the effects of the victory without undue exaggeration:

Measured by its results, San Jacinto was one of the decisive battles of the world. The freedom of Texas from Mexico won here led to annexation and to the Mexican War, resulting in the acquisition by the United States of the states of Texas, New Mexico, Arizona, Nevada, California, Utah and parts of Colorado, Wyoming, Kansas and Oklahoma. Almost one-third of the present area of the American nation, nearly a million square miles of territory, changed sovereignty.[21]

And another man-myth giant had made lasting imprints upon the pages of America's history.

For months, Houston lay near death from his gangrenous wounds, but, on September 5, 1836, he was elected the first President of Texas. The extravagant youth of his Romanticism was over, but other great contributions to the nation were yet to come. He set to work erecting

A Lone Star

a constitutional government for the Lone Star Republic. For almost a decade he fought for annexation to the United States, and, when Texas entered the Union in 1845, he went to Washington as his state's first Senator. There he at once allied himself with the forces of Union. The years went by, and Houston again began to be spoken of as a presidential possibility.

But the flood of secession sentiment rose, destroying any such aspirations. For Houston was too Southern for the North and too Northern for the South. "Why need I want the Presidency?" he asked, and devoted all his energies to preserving the Union. So diligently did he work that leading Southern Democrats labeled him a "traitor-knave," and his Southern colleagues attacked him on the Senate floor.[22] In the spring of 1859 Houston retired from the Senate. Bidding his fellow solons farewell, he said:

I know the high and important duties that devolve upon Senators. . . . My prayers will remain with them, that . . . under their influence and their exertions the nation will be blessed, the people happy, and the perpetuity of the Union secured to the latest posterity.[23]

Still, by sheer force of his personality and his prestige, Houston was elected Governor of Texas in 1860. In that capacity he continued his dogged fight against secession. But Fort Sumter and secession came, and Houston was forced to watch his state, his friends, and his own son join in the Rebel cause. All Texas officials were ordered to take an oath of allegiance to the Southern Confederacy. Houston refused. Resigning, he wrote: "In the name of my own conscience and my own manhood I refuse to take this oath. I love Texas too well."[24] Houston went into retirement, dreaming of a counterrevolution but too old and tired to implement the dream. In July, 1863, he died of pneumonia, almost his last words being an allusion to the "wicked" Civil War.[25]

Houston died as he had lived—a Romantic. The pattern was complete. As a youth he had dreamed of heroic days, had escaped to a primitive interlude, and had returned to fight with reckless valor in the second war with England. As a man he had embraced the democratic faith of coonskin America, joining in the Jacksonian revolt. He had called up his training in the chivalric tradition of plantation life to protect his wife at the cost of his political career. He had sunk to Dionysian depths and had risen to the heights of gods. He had been a part of a shifting, restless world—a reaching out for the national domain that would soon be labeled "Manifest Destiny." He had led a ragtag army to victory over impossible odds, had founded an empire and given it to his country. And he had turned aside from the comforts and adulation of his patriarchal days to fight—once more against impossible odds —for the Union.

Matching the gargantuan strides of the land he loved, Houston had grown from a vagrant, self-indulgent boy to a responsible, heroic leader to a statesman of towering integrity—a rugged individual of Homeric qualities—Romantic America's giant of the West.

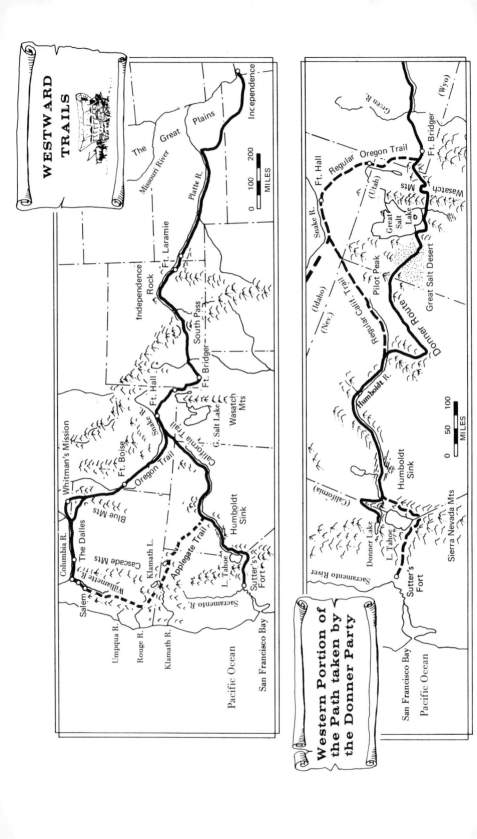

WESTWARD TRAILS

Incependence

The Great Plains

Missouri River

Platte R.

MILES
0   100   200

Independence Rock

Ft. Laramie

South Pass

Ft. Bridger

Wasatch Mts

G. Salt Lake

California Trail

Ft. Hall

Snake R.

Ft. Boise

Oregon Trail

Whitman's Mission

Blue Mts

The Dalles

Columbia R.

Salem

Willamette R.

Cascade Mts

Klamath L.

Applegate Trail

Humboldt Sink

L. Tahoe

Sutter's Fort

Umpqua R.

Rouge R.

Klamath R.

Sacramento R.

Pacific Ocean

San Francisco Bay

Green R. (Wyo)

Ft. Bridger

Regular Oregon Trail

(Utah)

Wasatch Mts

Ft. Hall

Snake R.

(Idaho)

(Nev.)

Great Salt Lake

Pilot Peak

Regular Calif. Trail

Donner Route

Great Salt Desert

Humboldt R.

(California)

Humboldt Sink

MILES
0   50   100

Donner Lake

L. Tahoe

Sierra Nevada Mts

Sacramento River

Sutter's Fort

San Francisco Bay

Pacific Ocean

Western Portion of
the Path taken by
the Donner Party

26

The Price of Empire:
The Donner Party

Westward the course of empire takes its way.
—George Berkeley[1]

In the sprawling train of "white tops" that streamed out from Independence, Missouri, in May, 1846, nothing marked the Donner Party as slated for disaster. The possibility of tragedy was a calculated risk that each member of that vast wagon train had willingly accepted. Whether a man and his family would reach the "golden shore" of the Pacific unscathed, chastened, or not at all rested on many factors of chance and human nature. No one could have foreseen that these factors would conspire to make the Donner crossing one of unprecedented horror.

True, the Donner group were tenderfeet. The pioneering they had done had not fitted them particularly for the passage across the plains or the mountain passes of the Far West. But in this they were not unique; of the many who would make that crossing safely, few were seasoned "mountain men." And certainly the equipage of this party was highly superior. The long, difficult trek to the Pacific was not a poor man's migration; the average family outfit cost between $700 and $1,500. But the luxuries that filled the Donner wagons, the spare yokes of oxen, the generous herds of cattle—all indicated wealth above the ordinary.

James Frazier Reed, from the first a leader of the party, was forty-six and of noble Polish birth. He had fought in the Black Hawk War with Abraham Lincoln, had settled in Illinois, and had prospered. With him came his young wife, their four children (Virginia, thirteen; Patty, eight;

James, five; and Thomas, three), and five employees. The Reeds had three wagons, one an outsized double-decker lined with bunks and fitted with a stove.

The heads of the Donner clan, George and Jacob, at sixty-two and sixty-five, were old men for the trail, but they were hardy pioneers of the earlier frontier—well fixed and highly responsible. The patriarchs had brought their wives and twelve children. George's wife, Tamsen (of New England origin), had been a teacher and a writer. With her went her scientific equipment, paints, supplies, and a great crate of books for a girls' school that she intended to found in California. Well secreted about the Donner wagons lay many thousands of dollars. Four young teamsters earned their passage by helping drive the family's six wagons.

Out of Independence the party found themselves toward the end of the giant white caterpillar—a position which, in that year of drought, meant a prolonged struggle to feed their herd along the dusty, grazed-out trail.

As it strung out across the plain, the unwieldy caravan began to break up into smaller, disorganized groups, whose ignorance of the craft of "living off the country, finding grass and water, managing the stock, making camp, reading buffalo sign and Indian sign" would cost them dearly. At night, after they had circled their wagons into a corral, they were exhausted.*

So their wagons were not kept up, horses and oxen strayed, and many hours, counting up to many days, were squandered. The movers dallied, strolling afield to fish or see the country, stopping to stage a debate or a fist fight, or just wandering like vacationists.

It was one of the great American experiences, this first stage of the trail in the prairie May. The ladies knitted or sewed patchwork quilts. They made spiced pickles of the "Prairie peas" and gathered wild strawberries to serve with fresh cream. They shook down into little cliques, with a chatter of sewing circles, missionary talk, and no charity for any nubile wench who might catch a son's eye. This was a fairy tale for children: bluffs to scale, coyote pups to catch and tame, the rich, exciting strangeness of a new life with school dismissed. Night camp was a deeper gratification still. The wagons formed their clumsy circle, within reach of wood and water. The squealing oxen were watered in an oath-filled chaos, then herded out to graze. Tents went up outside the wagons and fires blazed beside them. The most Methody of them were singing hymns. An incurable Yankeeness extemporized debates, political forums, and lectures on the

*Material from *The Year of Decision: 1846*, by Bernard DeVoto, is reprinted in condensed form, by permission of the publisher, Houghton Mifflin Company.

Chapters from the American Experience

flora of the new country or the manifest destiny of the American nation. This was the village on wheels, and the mind and habit of the village inclosed it.

Nevertheless, already something too subtle to be understood was working a ferment. Drenched blankets, cold breakfasts after rainy nights, long hours without water, exhaustion from the labor of double-teaming through a swamp or across quicksands or up a slope, from ferrying a swollen river till midnight, from being roused to chase a strayed ox across the prairie two hours before dawn, from constant shifting of the load to make the going better. Add the ordinary hazards of the day's march: a sick ox, a balky mule, the snapping of a wagon tongue, capsizing at a ford or overturning on a slope, the endless necessity of helping others who had fallen into the pits which your intelligence or good luck had enabled you to avoid. The unfit oxen sold to greenhorns at Independence were dying of heat. (What did you do when an ox died? If you had no spare, you yoked up a cow, when you had one; otherwise you threw out Mother's chest of drawers and went on.) But not only the oxen.[2]

A stone, a cross, an up-ended plank remained on the prairie to tell those who would follow that James Reed's mother-in-law, or Judge Bowlin's child, or someone else's, had died.

They did not know how to take care of themselves here. From the first days on, the emigrants are preyed upon by colds, agues, and dysenteries. All this has its part in the stresses put on human personality by emigration. Dissension that had simmered from the first boiled over. The train split in halves. The Oregon wagons formed their own train.

This division had more behind it than difference of destination. It had been preceded by a fist fight between two ordinarily peaceful men, and they drew knives before they could be separated. They were parted when the train split, but immediately there were fist fights and brandished knives and pistols in both halves.[3]

It was late June before the Donner Party straggled into Fort Laramie. Here, suddenly, they realized that time was moving too quickly. They scanned the map for the thousandth time and chafed at the long, time-consuming loop that the trail would take, from Fort Bridger 200 miles northwest to Fort Hall on the Snake River, in order to circle around the Wasatch Mountains and the Great Salt Desert. Many miles and, perhaps, many days could be saved if they made their way directly west-southwest through those mountains and across that desert, joining the established route at the point where it came curving down the Humboldt River in what is now the state of Nevada. Back home the Donners

The Price of Empire: The Donner Party

had pored over a guidebook to the Far West written by one Lansford W. Hastings—who dreamed of carving himself an empire of land and power in California and was not scrupulous as to how he enticed a following there. Hastings had confidently recommended the Wasatch-Salt Desert cutoff, although—and this he neglected to mention—he had not, at that time, attempted the route himself. Mountain man Jim Clyman warned the emigrants against the Wasatch. He had just come east on horseback by that way, had made it with difficulty, deemed it almost impassable to wagons. Most of those who heard decided for Fort Hall and the established trail. The Donner group would reserve judgment until Fort Bridger.

Across volcanic badlands now, up the long rise to South Pass, and on at last to Fort Bridger. By this time they had met a courier with a letter from Lansford Hastings (who was in the area trying to divert to California those headed for Oregon). The new route was easier, he urged, and would save at least 350 miles. The decision was made. The Donners would take the "shortcut." Others joined the party—among them William and Eleanor Eddy of Illinois and their two small children; the Fosters; Lewis Keseberg and his family from Germany; Antoine, a Mexican herder; Charles Stanton, a bachelor from New York; and the McCutchens, from Missouri. By the time the Graveses and Fosdicks from Illinois joined them in the Wasatch, they would total eighty-seven.

After resting their stock and repairing their wagons for four days at Fort Bridger, they headed for the Wasatch on July 31. A month earlier it had taken a small party on horseback six days to thread the maze of aimless canyons out into Salt Lake Valley. But the Donners were a wagon train. It was almost a month before they emerged on the western flank of the range.

They had had to make a road for wagons, by a route which no wagon had ever taken before. They had had to chop through aspen and popple and cottonwoods which choked the small canyons. They had to dig tracks and fell trees and level off centers high up on mountainsides, pry boulders out of their course, riprap swampy patches, sometimes bridge brooks that could not be crossed otherwise, grunt and strain and curse while the oxen heaved the wagons up inclines, over ridges, and around spurs of rock. Every ridge they topped showed a haze of further ridges beyond it. Every canyon that opened out closed in again.[4]

Resentment had flared against the weaker members of the train for not contributing their share. Antagonisms had risen against James Reed because of his aristocratic manner and because, as their guide for this stretch, he had had to make decisions—some of them wrong.[*]

*Reed had scouted ahead and had caught up with Hastings (who was "shepherding"

Five days out of the mountains they reached the eastern rim of the Great Salt Desert. Here they found another note from the irrepressible Hastings, allowing that he had underestimated the breadth of the desert —it would take two days and nights, instead of a single day.

It took them six days and they traveled all or most of every night. Twisting whirlwinds or high walls of salt blew past them. Mirages offered them lakes and streams or showed them fields of grass blowing in the wind. They strung out across the white hell, under sun or full moon, formless, disorganized, at random, the stock failing, men and women forced to observe the stoic, uncomprehending agony of the children. Reed rode ahead, passing most of the others. Some had abandoned their wagons, driving the teams toward the water that was somewhere ahead. At the end of the fourth day (if he had slept at all, it was during part of the first night) he got to Pilot Peak and its springs. William Eddy and the Graveses had got there before him. Eddy, taking water to an exhausted ox, went back a few miles with Reed, who again in the moon's unreality passed down the frayed line of specters. He met his own teamsters, who had unhitched the oxen and were trying to get them and his horses to water in time. Then the Donners, driving their stock and some wagons. Then an abandoned Donner wagon and at last, toward dawn, his wife and children and some employes. One of the employes took Reed's horse back. The others waited for the drivers and the oxen.

They sat there in the salt, under the sun, blistered by wind, all the next day. No oxen and no drivers came. The herd, maddened by thirst, had stampeded into the wasteland and would never be recovered. So at the end of the day, Reed carrying the three-year-old Tommy, the others packing some food from the wagons and the remaining gills of water, they started out to walk it. When the children could go no farther, they made a kind of camp. An insane ox charged them and they got up again and went on. Nearly everyone was getting to Pilot Peak now, some with their wagons, some with only their teams, some staggering in alone. The last day stretched out its agony, and with no one dead, they had crossed the Salt Desert in six days. September 8.

When at last they had finished [trying to round up stock], the extent of

---

another party to California) at the southern end of the Great Salt Lake. Hastings had earlier promised to come back and bring the Donners through the mountains, but he now refused to fulfill his promise. He did take Reed back to an eminence and point out a route which he now thought superior to the one he had recommended earlier. Reed returned to the Donners without him and piloted the party through the mountains by the new route. Significantly, it was this route that the Mormons followed to Salt Lake the next year. See George R. Stewart, *The California Trail* (New York: McGraw-Hill Book Company, 1962), pp. 167–68.

The Price of Empire: The Donner Party

disaster was clear. Reed abandoned two of his wagons. He still had one ox and a cow; he hired two oxen from others and yoked the two teams thus formed to his remaining wagon. The surplus food supplies he had carried were distributed among his companions, who would presently refuse to share them with his family. Jacob Donner also abandoned a wagon, and so did the opulent Keseberg.[5]

On the last day of September they reached the regular trail and started down the Humboldt. Their food supply had begun to show the ravages of delay, and they sent ahead two volunteers, Stanton and McCutchen, to seek help at Sutter's, on the California side of the Sierras. The Donners' equipment was in better shape than the others', and they pulled ahead. In the lagging section of the train a quarrel erupted into violence, in the course of which Reed was struck in the head by a bullwhip and, in turn, stabbed and killed his attacker, a member of the Graves party.

The Graveses demanded Reed's life. Keseberg, whom Reed had once insisted on temporarily banishing from the train for rifling an Indian grave and thus risking all their lives, propped up his wagon tongue—they were sufficiently veteran to know that this was how you hanged a man on the trail. Reed, supported by Eddy and Elliott, would not be hanged without some shooting first. When due fear of loaded guns had made itself felt above the blood lust, the party convened as a court. Sentence: on promise of the others to take care of his family, Reed must hereafter travel alone. And unarmed.

Such a verdict could not have been reached if the more stable Donners had been with this half of the party. They were depriving themselves of their strongest personality.

Prevailed on by his family, and by the thought that he might bring help to them all, Reed rode ahead the next day. Someone—either [his step-daughter] Virginia or William Eddy—defied the common will by taking his rifle to him and so giving him a chance to survive.[6]

More desert terrain now—across the desolate Humboldt Sink, with men dropping back to bury precious belongings they could no longer haul and with Digger Indians on their flanks stealing and killing their livestock. They had reached the base of the Sierras and had started threading up Truckee Canyon when Stanton returned from Sutter's with two Indians and seven mules loaded with supplies. Both McCutchen and Reed, he reported, had been exhausted by their passage over the mountains and were recuperating in California.

They struggled up toward the lake which—when their ordeal was done—would bear their name. Then, a Donner wagon's axle broke, and, in repairing it, Jacob was injured. Thus it was that, when the snows caught them, the party was split into two segments. October was spent by the time the advance group came up to the lake—three months out of Fort Bridger. (Four months should have sufficed for the entire journey from Missouri to California). Above them, shrouded in snow and forbidding clouds, lay the greatest barrier of all—the steep, boulder-strewn ascent to the pass. On November 3, they attempted it.

Even when there was no snow, wagons were taken up that terrible slope only by an all-out labor of man and beast, by doubling teams, prying with crowbars, blocking wheels with stones and drags, all hands manning ropes. Before they reached the ascent, before they had even passed the lake, they saw that [for the wagons] the snow was impassable. They abandoned the wagons, packed what they could on the backs of oxen, tied the now crippled Keseberg to a horse, shouldered the children, and drove the stock ahead of them, to pack down a trail through the snow.

Stanton and an Indian got to the divide and could have gone down the western slope. He came back, to help the others.

But they had reached the extremity and he could not rally them. Evening was coming up and they made a fire and stayed close to it, quarreling. So it came on to snow. The next morning, while the snow fell steadily, they straggled back to their abandoned wagons and on to the little cabin [they had found] at the lake.[7]

Farther back, caught by the same snow, the Donners made camp in Alder Creek Valley, throwing up brush huts for protection. And, on the western side of the mountains, that early November snow (which fell for eight days) turned back Reed and McCutchen from their attempt to reach their families, only 30 miles away, across a now insurmountable barrier. They would wait, they decided, until February. Their people were provisioned and could winter-in without excessive risk. But the supplies that the party had had when these men left them, as well as those Stanton had brought, were nearly gone. They could not wait until February.

They made several attempts on the mountain. On November 21, Eddy and Stanton got twenty of them up to the pass and over the divide. They had brought a few slices of thin beef for their food supply. The snow measured 25 feet deep. The mules that had broken trail for them were exhausted, and a treacherous descent lay ahead. They turned back. A week-long storm struck now, and, when it cleared, they found that the remaining livestock had been buried and lost in the snow. Another blizzard, and five men were dead, including old Jacob Donner.

The Price of Empire: The Donner Party

In desperation they began to make snowshoes of split oxbows and oxhide strips. On December 16, when enough snowshoes were ready, fifteen of the strongest set out—nine men, five women, and a boy—with the barest of rations for six days.

Stanton and his Indians and William Eddy were again the dominant spirits.

On December 17 they got over the divide, all but dead. They could go down the far slope now but they were eating an ounce of food a day and the sun gave them snow blindness. Their movement was slow and agonizing, the travel of the half dead. Stanton, besides being snow-blind, was weakening. On the march he fell behind, coming in to the campfire at night. There were brief, wild swirling snowstorms. Their feet froze. Mary Graves had a hallucination.

December 20. Stanton came in late to that campfire too. And Stanton was done.

December 21. That morning, going through his little pack, Eddy found half a pound of bear meat which, unknown to him, his wife, Eleanor, had put there, taking it from her own small store in order, her note said, to save his life in extremity. And when the others prepared to set out, Stanton sat quietly smoking a pipe. They asked him if he were coming. Yes, he said honorably, he would be along. He sat there, smoking.

It was up to William Eddy now.

On the day before Christmas the fourteen survivors labored in agony through snow that fell steadily all day long. Stanton had died three days before; since then they had depended on Sutter's Indians to find the landmarks that would take them down to safety. Without knowing it they had lost the trail and were wandering. Nine days out, they had eaten nothing since the last daily mouthful was used up two days before. All the men except Eddy anounced that they would go no farther.

Eddy insisted on continuing the effort while life was left to them. The two Indians agreed. So did all the women. "I told them," Mary Graves said, "I would go too, for to go back and hear the cries of hunger from my little brothers and sisters was more than I could stand. I would go as far as I could."

Mary Ann Graves, twenty years old, born in Illinois of parents who had emigrated there from Vermont. An undistinguished item in the year's migration, one dot of Manifest Destiny, who had set out to find the West with her [family]. A person of no moment making the western traverse. There is nothing remarkable about Mary Ann Graves, except that mankind can be staunch.

The will prevailed. But also it precipitated another decision. To go on they must live, to live they must eat, but there was no food. But there was food. Patrick Dolan voiced the thought which they had so far kept from voicing. Let them draw lots to see which one should be killed. In a moment the obvious became obvious to them. They were all near death. Someone would die soon. They groaned on through falling snow.

They stopped when dusk came and, with their single small axe, got wood for a fire—which they built on little logs on top of the deep, crusted snow. Now the Mexican herder, Antoine, died. Eddy knew that he was dead when he did not withdraw his hand, which had slumped into the fire. Suddenly, toward ten o'clock, the snowstorm changed into a blizzard. All the wood they had been able to cut was used up. Trying to cut more in the midnight blizzard, they lost their hatchet. The fire began to sink through the snow. It made a deep hole but they succeeded in keeping it going for a while, water welling up around their legs. Finally it went out and the yelp of the blizzard was round them.

Most of them were moaning or screaming in the dark, Uncle Billy Graves was dying, and all but Eddy were willing to die. He remembered an expedient of the mountain men in such storms as this. They had their blankets. Eddy spread some of them on the snow and had his companions sit on them in a circle. He tented them over with the remaining blankets and closed the circle himself. This was shelter of a kind. And presently the blizzard covered them over and they could live. But not Uncle Billy. He reminded his daughters of their mother and brothers and sisters at the lake, told them they must get through to Sutter's for their sake, bade them eat his body, and died.

In that mound of snow, Grave's corpse upholding its part of the tent, they stayed all through Christmas Day, while the blizzard howled on and made the mound bigger. That morning delirium came upon Patrick Dolan and, screaming, he broke his way through tent and snow. Eddy went out into the blizzard and tried to bring him back but could not. He came back after a while, and they held him down till he sank into a coma. As dusk seeped through the blizzard, he died.

The storm kept on through Christmas night, with two corpses in the mound now, and through the morning of the next day. In the afternoon the snow stopped. They crawled out of their mound, cut strips from the legs and arms of Patrick Dolan and roasted them. Eddy and the two Indians would not eat. Lemuel Murphy had been delirious for hours. The food could not revive him. That night he died, his head in the lap of Mrs. Foster, his sister.

The next day, December 27, they butchered the bodies of Graves, Dolan, Antoine, and Lemuel Murphy and dried at the fire such portions as they did not need now, packing them for the journey still to come. The Indians would eat this meat now, but Eddy still refused, though his strength was ebbing. After three days more here, when the bodies of their companions

The Price of Empire: The Donner Party

had restored their vitality a little, he got them into motion again, on December 30. In the literature of the Donner party, these people who made the venture over the divide are called "the Forlorn Hope," and this bivouack in the blizzard has the name they gave it, "the Camp of Death."

They knew they were off the trail now but the good weather that succeeded the storm held. Gradually they got down to where patches of bare ground showed through. "Gradually" is a word: the meaning is men and women who were all but dead falling forward step by step through a white desolation. Five or six miles a day, a mile or two when the flame burned weaker. The dried flesh of their companions was gone. Getting down to country where bare ground was common enough to justify it, they made another meal: they cooked and ate the rawhide of their snowshoes. After that there was nothing to eat. Everyone but Eddy wanted to kill the two Indians. Eddy would not; he told the Indians what was being considered and they silently disappeared.

Eddy determined to strike out ahead. He took the gun and made a trail for the preservation of them all. Mary Graves went with him, the two of them staggering a little faster than the others could and gradually getting out of sight. So Eddy killed a deer. His frontiersman's craft enabled him to identify a place where one had bedded for the night. He and Mary knelt and prayed, and pretty soon they saw it. He contrived the swinging snapshot which frontier gaffers used when their strength was gone. He wounded the deer, crawled toward it, and cut its throat. He and Mary cooked the guts and that night slept soundly within gunshot of the others.

Farthest of all from him, the Fosdicks heard the shots that Eddy fired to hearten them. Jay Fosdick correctly interpreted them. If he could get to Eddy and the meat, he said, he would live. But he died and Sarah wrapped his body in their remaining blanket and lay down beside him to die. She did not die but woke again in the morning and started out alone, only to meet some of the others who were coming back to find the Fosdick corpses—to get meat. Eddy called them in and they spent the day drying as much venison and human flesh as they had not eaten.

There were two men left now. When the new food was exhausted, William Foster began to plead with Eddy to kill one of the survivors. Eddy refused. If any member of this party had to die in order to keep the others alive, William Eddy said, he and Foster would fight it out.

The next day they saw bloody footprints in a patch of snow. A little later they found the two Indians stretched out on the ground, dying. Foster could not be denied now and Eddy protested with words only, for it was no longer rational to protest. Foster shot the Indians, they butchered the bodies, and that night they ate again. But Eddy ate only grass.

It was on January 12 that they came at dusk to the brush huts of a tiny Indian village. Lowly Diggers lived there but the squaws wept at sight of these living dead and the children wailed with them.[8]

The Diggers subsisted on acorns and pine nuts, and these they shared with the survivors. Half carrying them from village to village, they brought them down to the edge of a white settlement. Relief parties set out immediately up the mountain—an act of heroism, for January was not yet out and the winter's worst storms were still to come. The First Relief stumbled over the pass on February 18. At first they could not find the huts, so buried were they in the snow. But then, up out of a hole in the white blanket, came "wailing mummies," their cries a "lunatic talk" of winds and death, and a clawing competition for survival.[9] Eddy's wife and little girl were dead; so were eight of the twelve Donner children, George Donner, and many others. The Reed children, Mrs. Reed, and Eddy's small son had survived.

Safe in the base camp, down the terrible mountain's western slope, Patty Reed revealed a secret:

Before leaving the huts she had wrapped up her treasure in a little bundle. Doubtless it had been a solace through long days of dust along the trail last summer and she had cherished it when the wagons parked at night beneath twisted buttes or when she came footsore to bed in the Wasatch or when the grownups argued or despaired along the Humboldt. Leaving the lake she had hidden it under her dress, knowing that the men would make her throw away even so slight a weight as this. There was a tiny glass saltcellar, one of those jewels that are precious to children. There was a small wooden doll with black hair and black eyes. And there was a lock of gray hair, her grandmother's hair. She had wrapped them all in a shred of lawn dotted with blue flowers. Now she was safe in California and could bring out the treasure and settle down to play.[10]

And now life could go on. For some the "golden shore" had become a reality. The price of empire had been paid.

27

The Emancipation of Frederick Douglass

"Very well," thought I,
"knowledge unfits a child to become a slave."

In Eastern Maryland is a small district called Tuckahoe, thinly popu-
lated, with worn-out soil, dilapidated farms and fences, and indigent and
spiritless inhabitants. Here I was born and spent the first years of my
childhood.[1] The dwelling of my grandmother and grandfather had few
pretensions. It was a log hut of clay, wood, and straw. To my child's eye,
however, it was a noble structure. My grandmother enjoyed the high privilege of living thus, with no other burden than her own support and the care
of the little children. The children were not her own, but her grandchildren.

Living here, with my dear old grandparents, it was a long time before
I knew myself to be a *slave.* I knew many other things before I knew that.
Grandmother and grandfather were the greatest people in the world to me;
and being with them so snugly, knowing no higher authority over me than
that of a grandmamma, for a time there was nothing to disturb me. But, as
I grew older, I learned by degrees the sad fact that the "little hut" belonged
not to my dear grandparents, but to some person who lived a great distance off, and whom my grandmother called, with every mark of reverence,
"OLD MASTER." I further learned the sadder fact that not only the house
but grandmother herself (grandfather was free) and all the little children
around her belonged to this mysterious personage. And I was not long in
finding out another fact, still more grievous to my childish heart. "Old
master" only allowed the children to live with grandmother for a limited
time. As soon as they were big enough, they were promptly taken away.

Though I was quite too young to comprehend the full import of this and mostly spent my childhood in gleesome sports, a shade of disquiet rested upon me.

But it is not within the power even of slavery to write indelible sorrow, at a single dash, over the heart of a child. The slave-boy escapes many troubles which befall and vex his white brother. He seldom has to listen to lectures on propriety. He has no pretty little verses to learn, no nice little speeches to make for aunts or uncles to show how smart he is. He is never chided for handling his little knife and fork improperly—for he uses none. He is never reprimanded for soiling the tablecloth—for he takes his meals on the clay floor. He is never expected to act like a nice little gentleman —for he is only a rude little slave. Thus, freed from all restraint, the slave-boy can be a genuine boy.

When the time of my departure was decided upon, my grandmother, knowing my fears, kept me ignorant of the dreaded event. During the whole journey, which I remember as if it were yesterday, she kept the sad fact from me. As the day advanced, I found myself in the midst of children of many colors—black, brown, copper, and nearly white. I had not seen so many children before. Great houses loomed up in different directions, and a great many men and women were at work in the fields. I could not help feeling that our being there boded no good to me. Grandmamma looked sad. Affectionately patting me on the head, she told me to go play with the little children. "They are kin to you," said she; "go and play with them." She pointed out my brothers and sisters, who stood in the group. Though I had sometimes heard of them, I really did not understand what they were to me, or I to them. We had never nestled and played together. My poor mother, like many other slave-women, had many children but no family.

Entreated to do so, I went to the back of the house to play. Play, how-ever, I did not, but stood with my back against the wall, watching the others. At last one of the children who had been in the kitchen ran up to me in a sort of roguish glee, exclaiming, "Fed, Fed! Grandmammy gone!" I ran into the kitchen to see for myself and found it even so. My brothers and sisters came around me and said, "Don't cry," and gave me peaches and pears, but I flung them away. It was now late in the afternoon. The day had been a wearisome one, and I know not how or where, but I suppose I sobbed myself to sleep.

Now it was that I came to know my mother. My knowledge of her is very scanty, but distinct. She was tall and finely proportioned, of deep black, glossy complexion, and among the other slaves was remarkably sedate in her manner. How she acquired the knowledge, I know not, but she was the only one of all the colored people in Tuckahoe who knew how to read, though I only learned this after her death.

She was hired out to a Mr. Stewart, who lived about twelve miles from old master's, and, being a field hand, she seldom had leisure by day for the performance of the journey. She was obliged to walk, unless chance flung in her way an opportunity to ride one way. The iron rule of the plantation, always violently enforced in that area, makes flogging the penalty for failing to be in the field before sunrise. "I went to see my child," is no excuse to the overseer. It is deemed a foolish whim for a slave-mother to manifest concern for her children.

One of my mother's visits I remember very vividly. I had on that day offended old master's cook, "Aunt Katy" (called "Aunt" by way of respect). I do not now remember the nature of my offense on that particular occasion, but she had adopted that day her favorite mode of punishing me, namely making me go without food all day after breakfast. The first hour or two after dinnertime, I succeeded pretty well in keeping up my spirits. Sundown came, but no bread, and in its stead there came the threat that she "meant to starve the life out of me!" Brandishing her knife, she chopped off the heavy slices for the other children and put the loaf away, muttering all the while her savage designs upon myself. I sat by the fire and brooded over my hard lot, too hungry to sleep. While I sat in the corner, I caught sight of an ear of Indian corn on the kitchen shelf. Quickly I shelled off a few grains, which I put in some ashes and covered with embers—all at the risk of a brutal thumping. My corn was not long in roasting. I eagerly pulled them out and placed them on my stool in a clever little pile. Just as I began to eat, in came my mother. I shall never forget the indescribable expression on her countenance when I told her that I had had no food since morning and that Aunt Katy had threatened to starve me. She took the corn from me and gave me a large ginger cake, meanwhile reading Aunt Katy a lecture which she never forgot. My mother threatened to complain to old master. Though harsh and cruel himself at times, he did not sanction the meanness and oppressions of Aunt Katy. That night I learned that I was not only a child, but *somebody's* child. I was victorious and prouder on my mother's knee than a king on his throne. But my triumph was short. I dropped off to sleep and waked in the morning to find my mother gone.

I do not remember having seen my mother after this occurrence. Death soon ended the little communication that had existed between us. I was not allowed to visit her during any part of her long illness. The heartless form of slavery rises between mother and child, even at the bed of death.

Gradually I became aware of the ranks into which the great plantation was divided. My old master was himself subservient to a great lord, being the chief butler on Col. Lloyd's plantation. His duties were numerous, and in almost all important matters he answered in Col. Lloyd's stead. The overseers of all the farms received the law from his mouth. The colonel himself seldom addressed an overseer or allowed an overseer to address him. Old master carried the keys of all the store houses, measured out the allowances for the slaves, superintended the storing of all goods, dealt out the raw material to all the handicraftsmen, shipped all saleable produce

The Emancipation of Frederick Douglass

to market, and had the general oversight of the coopers', wheelwrights', blacksmiths', and shoemakers' shops.

Old master (or Capt. Anthony, as he was generally called) was not considered a rich slaveholder, but was pretty well off. He owned about thirty "head" of slaves, whereas Col. Lloyd possessed a thousand. At the time of which I am now writing, there were slaves on the plantation who had been brought directly from the coast of Africa. I could scarcely understand them when I first went among them, and I am persuaded I could not have been dropped anywhere on the globe where I could reap less in the way of knowledge from my immediate associates. Even "Mas' Daniel," the youngest son of Col. Lloyd, by his association with his father's slaves, had measurably adopted their dialect and ideas. At the same time, he could not give his black playmates his company without giving them his intelligence as well. Without knowing this, I spent much of my time with Mas' Daniel.

Perplexing questions now began to claim my thoughts. Why am I a slave? Why are some people slaves and others masters? Was there ever a time when this was not so? Asking, I was told "God up in the sky" made everybody; He made white people to be masters and black people to be slaves. This did not satisfy me. Once engaged in the inquiry, I was not long in finding out the true solution. It was not color but crime, not God but man that afforded the explanation. Nor was I long in finding out another important truth—what man can make, man can unmake. There were slaves here direct from Guinea. There were many who could say that their fathers and mothers were stolen from Africa—forced from their homes and compelled to serve as slaves. This knowledge filled me with a burning hatred of slavery. I could not have been more than seven or eight when I began to make this subject my study. It was with me in the woods and fields, along the shore of the river, and wherever my boyish wanderings led me. Though I was at that time quite ignorant of the existence of free states, I distinctly remember being, even then, most strongly impressed with the idea of being a freeman some day.

It is the boast of slaveholders that their slaves enjoy more of the physical comforts of life than the peasantry of any country in the world. My experience contradicts this. The men and women slaves on Col. Lloyd's farm received as their monthly allowance of food eight pounds of pickled pork (often tainted) or their equivalent in fish of the poorest quality. With this they got one bushel of Indian meal and one pint of salt. This was the entire monthly allowance for a full grown slave, working constantly in the open field from morning until night every day except Sunday.

The yearly allowance of clothing consisted of two tow-linen shirts (such linen as the coarsest crash towels are made of), two pair of trousers most sleazily put together, one pair of yarn stockings, and one pair of shoes of the coarsest description. Children who were unable to work in the field had neither shoes, stockings, jacket nor trousers. Their clothing consisted of two coarse tow-linen shirts per year. When these failed them, as they often did, they went naked until the next allowance day.

Beds were unknown to field hands, nothing but a coarse horse blanket was given them, and this only to adults. The children stuck themselves in holes about the quarters, often in the corner of the huge chimneys, with their feet in the ashes to keep them warm. Time to sleep was of far greater importance than the want of beds, however, for, when the day's work was done, most of the slaves had their washing, mending and cooking to do, and many of their sleeping hours were consumed in preparations for the coming day. The slaves were summoned by the driver's horn at the first gray streak of morning, and more were whipped for oversleeping than for any other fault.

On the other hand, in the sacred precincts of the great house, the home of the Lloyds, immense wealth and lavish expenditure furnished all that could please the eye or tempt the taste. Behind the tall-backed, elaborately wrought dining chairs stood fifteen servants, who constituted the black aristocracy of the plantation—men and maidens discriminately selected with a view to their industry, faithfulness, personal appearance, agility, and address. They resembled the field hands in nothing except color. The delicate colored maid rustled in the scarcely worn silk of her young mistress, while the servant men were equally well attired from the overflowing wardrobe of their young masters. Viewed from his own table, the colonel was a model of hospitality. For weeks during the summer months, his house was, literally, a hotel. Who could say that the servants of Col. Lloyd were not well clad and cared for after witnessing one of his magnificent entertainments? Who could say that these slaves did not seem to glory in being the chattels of such a master?

I was not ten years old when I left Col. Lloyd's plantation for Baltimore. I shall never forget the ecstasy with which I received the intelligence that my old master had determined to let me go to Baltimore to live with Mr. Hugh Auld, a brother to my old master's son-in-law, Thomas Auld. I received this information about three days before my departure. They were three of the happiest days of my childhood. I spent the largest part of them in the creek, washing off the dead skin from my feet and knees, for I had been told I would not get a pair of trousers unless I scrubbed off all the dirt and mange.

I arrived in Baltimore on a Sunday morning and was speedily conducted to my new home. Mr. and Mrs. Hugh Auld met me at the door with their little son, Thomas, whose care was to constitute my future occupation. In fact, it was to "little Tommy," rather than to his parents that old master made a present of me. He was affectionately told by his mother that "there was *his* Freddy," and I was told to "be kind to little Tommy." My new mistress happily proved to be all that she seemed. The crouching servility of a slave was not understood nor desired by her. So far from deeming it

The Emancipation of Frederick Douglass

impudent in a slave to look her straight in the face, she seemed ever to say, "Look up, child, don't be afraid." Mr. Auld was altogether a different character. He set out to get on by becoming a successful ship builder. This was his ambition, and it fully occupied him. While he was sour, he was never cruel to me, according to the notion of cruelty in Maryland. The first year or two I spent in his house he left me almost exclusively to the management of his wife.

Hearing my mistress read the bible soon awakened my curiosity in respect to this mystery and roused in me the desire to learn. I asked her to teach me to read and, without hesitation, the dear woman began the task. Very soon I was master of the alphabet and could spell words of three or four letters. My mistress, being proud of my progress and supposing that her husband would be as well pleased, made no secret of what she was doing for me. Master Hugh was amazed at the simplicity of his spouse and unfolded to her the peculiar rules necessarily observed by masters and mistresses in the management of their human chattels. He promptly forbade the continuance of her instruction, telling her that the thing was unlawful and unsafe and could only lead to mischief. To use his own words, "He should know nothing but the will of his master. If you teach that nigger how to read the bible, there will be no keeping him."

His words sunk deep into my heart and awakened within me a slumbering train of vital thought. It was a new revelation, dispelling a painful mystery against which my youthful understanding had struggled in vain, to wit: the white man's power to perpetuate the enslavement of the black man. "Very well," thought I, "knowledge unfits a child to be a slave." And from that moment I understood that knowledge was the direct pathway from slavery to freedom.

I lived in the family of Master Hugh for seven years, during which I learned to read and write. In attaining this knowledge, I was compelled to resort to indirection. I used my young white playmates in the street as teachers. Carrying a copy of Webster's spelling book in my pocket when sent on errands or when play time was allowed me, I would take a lesson in spelling with my young friends. Sometimes, seated on a curbstone or a cellar door, I would say to them, "You will be free as soon as you are twenty-one and can go where you like. Have I not as good a right to be free?" Over and over again they told me they believed I had as good a right to be free as they. Such conversations strengthened my love of liberty.

When I was about thirteen, I had enough money to buy the "Columbian Orator," a rich treasure of speeches, all redolent of the principles of liberty, which poured floods of light on the nature and character of slavery. As I read, behold! the very discontent so graphically predicted by Master Hugh came upon me, and light penetrated the moral dungeon where I dwelt.

Often I overheard Master Hugh or his company speaking with much warmth and excitement about "abolitionists." I very soon discovered that slavery was under consideration whenever they were alluded to. This made the term very interesting to me, and I set about finding out who and what the abolitionists were and why they were so obnoxious to the slave-holders. The dictionary afforded me very little help. It taught me that aboli-tion was the "act of abolishing," but it left me in ignorance as to the thing to be abolished. A city newspaper gave me the incendiary information I sought. Ever and anon, too, I could see some terrible denunciation of slavery in our papers—copied from abolition papers in the north, and always accompanied by comments on the injustice of such denunciations. A still deeper train of thought was stirred. I saw that there was*fear* as well as rage. When I met with a slave to whom I deemed it safe to talk on the subject, I would impart to him as much of the mystery as I had been able to penetrate. The insurrection of Nathaniel Turner had been quelled, but the alarm and terror had not subsided. Cholera was becoming a threat, and the thought was present that God's judgments were abroad in the land.

My mind was now seriously awakened to the subject of religion, and I seemed to live in a new world. I loved all mankind—slaveholders not ex-cepted, though I abhorred slavery more than ever. While seeking religious knowledge, I became acquainted with a good old colored man named Lawson. Uncle Lawson lived near Master Hugh's house, and I went often with him to prayer-meeting. The old man could only read a little. I could teach him "the letter," but he taught me "the spirit." High refreshing times we had together, singing, praying, and glorifying God. He was my spiritual father, and he fanned my already intense love of knowledge into a flame by assuring me that I was to be a useful man in the world. When I would say to him, "How can these things be—what can I do?" his simple reply was, "The Lord can make you free; only have faith in God."

I was too young to think of running away immediately. Besides, I wished to learn how to write before going, as I might have occasion to write my own pass. With playmates for teachers, fences and pavements for copy books, and chalk for pen and ink, I learned the art of writing. I then set about improving my hand by copying the italics in Webster's spelling book. I took old copy books of Master Tommy's and pen and ink, and between the lines I wrote other lines as nearly like his as possible. In addition, sleeping as I did in the kitchen loft seldom visited by the family, I got a flour barrel and a chair and, on the barrel head, copied from the bible, the Methodist hymn book and others late at night when all the family were asleep.

In 1833, when I was about 16, Master Hugh had a misunderstanding with his brother, Thomas. As a means of punishing his brother, Master Thomas [who had come into legal possession of me through the death of old master] ordered him to send me home to St. Michael's down the Chesa-peake Bay. In the house of Master Thomas I was made—for the first time in seven years—to feel the pinchings of hunger. I was allowed neither to

The Emancipation of Frederick Douglass

teach nor to be taught. With a single exception, the whole white community frowned on instructing either slaves or free colored persons. That exception was a pious young man named Wilson, who asked me to assist him in teaching a little Sabbath school. We commenced operations with some twenty scholars. Here, thought I, is something worth living for. Our first Sabbath passed delightfully. At our second meeting I learned that there was some objection to the Sabbath school, and, sure enough, we had scarcely got to work—good work, simply teaching a few colored children how to read the gospel of the Son of God—when in rushed a mob headed by Master Thomas and two others, who, armed with sticks and missiles, drove us off and commanded us never to meet for such a purpose again.

The many differences springing up between myself and Master Thomas, owing to the clear perception I had of his character and the boldness with which I defended myself against his capricious complaints, led him to declare that I was unsuited to his wants. City life had almost ruined me for every good purpose, he complained. I had now lived with him nearly nine months, and he had given me a number of severe whippings without any visible improvement in my character or conduct. He resolved to put me out "to be broken."

There was nearby a man named Edward Covey, who enjoyed the reputation of being a first rate hand at breaking young negroes. This Covey was a poor farm-renter, and his reputation was of immense advantage to him, enabling him to get his farm tilled with very little expense, compared with what it would have cost him without it. Some slaveholders thought it an advantage to let Mr. Covey have the government of their slaves a year or two, almost free of charge, for the sake of the excellent training such slaves got under his happy management! Like some horse breakers noted for their skill, who ride the best horses in the country without expense, Mr. Covey could have under him the most fiery bloods of the neighborhood for the simple reward of returning them to their owners *well broken.*

The morning of the first of January, 1834, with its chilling wind and pinching frost, quite in harmony with the winter in my mind, found me with my little bundle of clothing on the end of a stick, bending my way toward Covey's. I was now about to sound the profounder depths in slave life.

I had been at my new home but three days before Mr. Covey gave me a bitter foretaste of what was in reserve for me. I was to get a load of wood from a forest about two miles from the house. For this work Mr. Covey gave me a pair of *unbroken* oxen. I had no knowledge of the art of managing horned cattle, even trained ones. The mile from the house to the woods gate passed with very little difficulty. But on reaching the woods the animals took fright and started off ferociously, carrying the cart full tilt against trees, over stumps, and dashing from side to side. After running thus for several minutes, they were finally brought to a stand by a tree against which they dashed with great violence, upsetting and tearing the cart and entangling themselves among sundry young saplings. I managed to put the cart together and cut down the saplings in which they were caught, and, finding and chopping the wood and filling the cart, returned to the house. The waste of time, however, brought a brutal chastisement from Mr. Covey. Under his heavy blows blood flowed freely and wales were left on my back as large as my little finger.

I remained with Mr. Covey one year, and during the first six months that I was there I was whipped, either with sticks or cow-skins, every week. We were kept at hard work in the fields or the woods from dawn until darkness was complete and at certain seasons till eleven and twelve o'clock at night. Part of the time Covey, who had had his training as an overseer, watched us. It was, however, scarcely necessary for him to be actually present in the field for his work to go on industriously. By a series of adroitly managed surprises which he practiced, I was prepared to expect him at any moment. He carried this kind of trickery so far that he would sometimes mount his horse and make believe he was going to St. Michael's. And thirty minutes afterwards, you might find his horse tied in the woods and the snake-like Covey lying flat in the ditch with his head lifted above its edge, watching our every movement.

I shall never be able to narrate the mental experience through which it was my lot to pass during the first half of my stay at Covey's. I was made to drink the bitterest dregs of slavery. It was never too hot or too cold; it could never rain, blow, snow, or hail too hard for us to work in the field. Work, work, work was scarcely more the order of the day than of the night. The longest days were too short for him, and the shortest nights were too long for him. I was somewhat unmanageable when I first went there; but a few months of this discipline tamed me. Mr. Covey succeeded in breaking me. I was broken in body, soul and spirit. My natural elasticity was crushed; my intellect languished; the disposition to read departed; the cheerful spark that lingered about my eye died; the dark night of slavery closed in upon me, and behold a man transformed into a brute!

The transformation, however, was not complete. After six months an incident occurred that restored the slave's spirits and altered the attitude of the master. One sweltering August day, while working in the treading yard, Douglass collapsed from the heat. Covey, after kicking him and gashing his head with a large pointed slab of hickory, turned back to the other slaves. When Douglass revived, he escaped into the woods and, going to Thomas Auld, begged to be taken from Covey. Auld, however, refused to do so or even to feed him. The next morning, when Douglass returned to the farm, Covey leaped on him from behind a fence corner. Seeing the whip in his hand, the slave evaded his tormenter and again slipped into the woods. As he lay there that evening, a friend came by on his way to visit his free wife and took Douglass home with him. Refreshed by a hearty meal and a good night's sleep, the slave went back to the farm again the following morning. It was Sunday, and he met Covey driving his wife to church. Smiling pleasantly, Covey asked him if he would be so good as to drive the pigs out of the yard. Douglass did not run afoul of him all that day, but the next morning the white man's Sunday manners had vanished, and he stalked the slave in the barn and, seizing him by the leg, began to slip a rope over his feet. Douglass, however, invigorated by his long rest, turned on him savagely. "Are you going to resist, you scoundrel?" asked Covey, amazed. "Yes sir," replied Douglass. A struggled ensued, and, when it became evident that he could not subdue the slave unassisted, Covey called for help. His cousin responded, but Douglass felled him with one smashing blow and returned to his foe. Two different Negroes now came on the scene and, one after the other, refused to help the master. The fight continued for two full hours, during which time Douglass made no attempt to injure his antagonist but only fended off his blows. Finally Covey gave up the contest and gasped, "Now, you scoundrel, go to your work. I would not have whipped you half so much as I have if you had not resisted." "During the whole remaining six months I lived there," wrote Douglass with satisfaction, "Covey never again laid on me the weight of his finger in anger."

At the end of the year, Auld placed him with still another man, from whom he attempted unsuccessfully to escape. Thomas Auld's feud with his brother had by now been resolved, so he allowed the refractory slave to return to Master Hugh in Baltimore. There, hired out to a shipbuilder, he at once came into bitter conflict with the white laborers in the yard. These carpenters, furious at the competition with wageless workers and fearful that emancipation would "place the white working man on an equality with negroes," had in recent years turned against their black co-workers.

Until a very little while before I went there in 1836, white and black ship carpenters worked side by side. Some of the blacks were first rate workmen and were given jobs requiring the highest skill. All at once, however, the white carpenters swore they would no longer work on the same stage with free negroes.

The spirit which this movement awakened was one of malice and bitterness toward colored people generally, and I suffered with the rest. My fellow apprentices very soon began to feel it degrading to work with me. They began to put on high looks and to talk contemptuously of how "the niggers" wanted to take over the country. They did their utmost to make it impossible for me to stay. I could manage any of them singly. But finally I was beset by four of them at once. One came in front, armed with a brick; there was one at each side, and one behind, and they closed up around me.

While I was attending those in front, I received a blow on my head from behind, dealt with a heavy hand-spike. Stunned, I fell, and they rushed upon me and began to pound me with their fists. Finally one planted a blow with his boot in my left eye, which seemed to burst my eyeball. When they saw my eye completely closed, my face covered with blood, they left me. Not fewer than fifty white men had stood by and seen this brutal outrage committed, and not a man of them all interposed a single word of mercy. No one said, "That is enough." But some cried out, "Kill him—kill him—kill the d—d nigger!"

After making my escape from the ship yard, I related the story to Master Hugh, who took me to the magistrate with a view to procuring the arrest of those who had assaulted me. But the magistrate said, "I am sorry, Sir, but I cannot move in this matter except upon the oath of *white* witnesses." If I had been killed in the presence of a thousand blacks, their combined testimony would not have been sufficient to arrest a single murderer. Master Hugh took me to another yard, where I rapidly became expert in the use of calking tools, and in the course of a single year was able to command the highest wages paid to journeymen calkers in Baltimore.

Here then were better days. Many of the young colored calkers could read, write and cipher. Some of them had high notions about mental improvement; and the free ones organized what they called the "East Baltimore Mental Improvement Society." It was intended that only free persons should attach themselves to this society, but I was admitted, and was several times assigned a prominent part in its debates. I owe much to the society of these young men. I was living among freemen and was, in all respects, equal to them by nature and by attainments. Why should I be a slave?

I was now getting a dollar and fifty cents per day. I contracted for it, worked for it, earned it, and collected it. It was rightfully mine. And yet, upon every returning Saturday night, this money was demanded and taken from me by Master Hugh. I became more and more dissatisfied. To make a contented slave, you must make a thoughtless one. It must not depend upon mere force; the slave must know no Higher Law than his master's will. If there be one crevice through which a single drop can fall, it will certainly rust off the slave's chain.

In 1838 Frederick Douglass made good his escape from bondage. In his account he deliberately omitted the details of his flight in order not to prejudice the chances of others who might follow in his path. Douglass became one of the most ardent and articulate voices in the North for abolition. His story, published in 1855, when slavery was "at the bar of public opinion," is still deeply relevant.

The Emancipation of Frederick Douglass

Richmond Militiamen at the Time of the
Trial of John Brown at Harper's Ferry

Valentine Museum, Richmond,
Virginia. Cook Collection.

28

The Making of
Johnny Reb

Such men as these of the South
were bound to come often into conflict.

Occasionally a writer with a gift for synthesis undertakes to capture in words the spirit of some era or culture. A generalization of this sort is in part an artistic production and one in which the minorities, the exceptions, and the unique individuals are often ignored or at least treated superficially. Nevertheless, at its best, such a re-creation can throw invaluable light on the society it examines. One of the most stimulating studies of this type in American historical literature is *The Mind of the South,* by W. J. Cash, a native Southerner. The following reading is taken from the early portion of this work—the portion dealing with the development and nature of the "great South" in the years preceding the Civil War.

Cash begins by stressing the frontier nature of the antebellum South —how in the seventy years following the invention of the gin, the Cotton Kingdom burst from its confines along the Atlantic Seaboard and spread across the Piedmont, down to the Gulf, on to the Mississippi, and beyond.

Men who, as children, had heard the war-whoop of the Cherokee in the Carolina backwoods lived to hear the guns at Vicksburg. And thousands of other men who had looked upon Alabama when it was still a wilderness and upon Mississippi when it was still a stubborn jungle, lived to fight— and to fight well, too—in the ranks of the Confederate armies. The inference is plain. It is impossible to conceive the great South as being, on the whole, more than a few steps removed from the frontier stage at the beginning of the Civil War. Take a concrete case.

A stout young Irishman brought his bride into the Carolina upcountry about 1800. He cleared a bit of land, built a log cabin of two rooms, and sat down to the pioneer life. One winter, with several of his neighbors, he loaded a boat with whisky and the coarse woolen cloth woven by the women, and drifted down to Charleston to trade. There, remembering the fondness of his woman for a bit of beauty, he bought a handful of cotton seed, which she planted about the cabin with the wild rose and the honey- suckle—as a flower. Afterward she learned, under the tutelage of a new neighbor, to pick the seed from the fiber with her fingers and to spin it into yarn. Another winter the man drifted down the river, this time to find the half-way station of Columbia in a strange ferment. There was a new won- der in the world—the cotton gin—and the forest which had lined the banks of the stream for a thousand centuries was beginning to go down. Fires flared red and portentous in the night—to set off an answering fire in the breast of the Irishman.

Land in his neighborhood was to be had for fifty cents an acre. With twenty dollars, the savings of his lifetime, he bought forty acres and set himself to clear it. Rising long before day, he toiled deep into the night, with his wife holding a pine torch for him to see by. Aided by his neighbors, he piled the trunks of the trees into great heaps and burned them, grubbed up the stumps, hacked away the tangle of underbrush and vine, stamped out the poison ivy and the snakes. A wandering trader sold him a horse, bony and half-starved, for a knife, a dollar, and a gallon of whisky. Every day now—Sundays not excepted—when the heavens allowed, and every night that the moon came, he drove the plow into the earth, with uptorn roots bruising his shanks at every step. Behind him came his wife with a hoe. In a few years the land was beginning to yield cotton—richly, for the soil was fecund with the accumulated mold of centuries. Another trip down the river, and he brought home a mangy black slave—an old and lazy fellow reckoned of no account in the rice-lands, but with plenty of life in him still if you knew how to get it out. Next year the Irishman bought fifty acres more, and the year after another black. Five years more and he had two hundred acres and ten Negroes. Cotton prices swung up and down sharply, but always, whatever the return, it was almost pure velvet. For the fertility of the soil seemed inexhaustible.

Chapters from the American Experience

When he was forty-five, he quit work, abandoned the log house, which had grown to six rooms, and built himself a wide-spreading frame cottage. When he was fifty, he became a magistrate, acquired a carriage and built a cotton gin and a third house—a "big house" this time. It was not, to be truthful, a very grand house really. Built of lumber sawn on the place, it was a little crude and had not cost above a thousand dollars, even when the marble mantel was counted in. Essentially, it was just a box, with four rooms, bisected by a hallway, set on four more rooms bisected by another hallway, and a detached kitchen at the back. Windswept in winter, it was difficult to keep clean of vermin in summer. But it was huge, it had great columns in front, and it was eventually painted white, and so, in this land of wide fields and pinewoods it seemed very imposing.

Meantime the country around had been growing up. Other "big houses" had been built. There was a county seat now, a cluster of frame houses, stores, and "doggeries" [saloons] about a red brick courthouse. A Presbyterian parson had drifted in and started an academy, as Presbyterian parsons had a habit of doing everywhere in the South. The Irishman had a piano in his house, on which his daughters, taught by a vagabond German, played as well as young ladies could be expected to. One of the Irishman's sons went to the College of South Carolina, came back to grow into the chief lawyer in the county, got to be a judge, and would have been Governor if he had not died at the head of his regiment at Chancellorsville.

As a crown on his career, the old man went to the Legislature, where he was accepted by the Charleston gentlemen tolerantly and with genuine liking. He grew extremely mellow in age and liked to pass his time in company, arguing about predestination and infant damnation, proving conclusively that cotton was king and that the damyankee didn't dare do anything about it, and developing a notable taste in the local liquors. Tall and well-made, he grew whiskers after the Galway fashion—the well-kept whiteness of which contrasted very agreeably with the brick red of his complexion—donned the long-tailed coat, stove-pipe hat, and string tie of the statesmen of his period, waxed innocently pompous, and, in short, became a really striking figure of a man.

Once, going down to Columbia for the inauguration of a new Governor, he took his youngest daughter along. There she met a Charleston gentleman who was pestering her father for a loan. Her manner, formed by the Presbyterian parson, was plain but not bad, and she was very pretty. Moreover, the Charleston gentleman was decidedly in hard lines. So he married her.

When the old man finally died in 1854, he left two thousand acres, a hundred and fourteen slaves, and four cotton gins. The little newspaper

The Making of Johnny Reb

which had recently set up in the county seat spoke of him as "a gentleman
of the old school" and "a noble specimen of the chivalry at its best"; the
Charleston papers each gave him a column; and resolutions of respect
[were introduced] into the Legislature.[1]

Thus, rising from humble circumstances during this period, many
Southerners rapidly assumed the veneer and some the substance of
traditional Southern gentility. But Cash makes it clear that his Irishman
pursued his objectives with more integrity and less ruthlessness than
did many of the "nouveaux" planters. The old Virginia leadership was
"gradually overshadowed and swallowed up into the new master class
of cotton." And, while visitors like Frederick Olmstead denounced the
newcomers as "the vulgar rich" and seaboard aristocrats like Charleston
lawyer D. R. Hundley regarded them as "unprincipled boors" and "Cotton Snobs," planters of the new breed (like their Northern counterparts)
confidently took command of their section—engrossing all the best
lands and seizing political control of the South.[2]

This aristocracy of newly propertied backwoodsmen ruled over a
fluid society of yeomen farmers and "crackers." The yeomen tilled the
relatively rich lands left by the Cotton Kings, and some of them rose in
time to the ranks of the aristocracy. At the end of the spectrum, the
poorest of the yeomen merged imperceptibly into the third class of the
"great South," the shiftless "crackers," whom Cash describes with typical verve.

The whole pack of them exhibited, in varying measure, a distinctive
physical character—a striking lankness of frame and slackness of muscle
in association with a shambling gait, a misshapeliness of head and feature,
a peculiar sallow swartness, or alternatively a not less peculiar and a not
less sallow faded-out colorlessness of skin and hair. Their practice of
agriculture was generally confined to a little lackadaisical digging—
largely by the women and children—in forlorn corn patches. The men
might plow a little, hunt a little, fish a little, but mainly passed their time
on their backsides in the shade of a tree, communing with their hounds and
a jug of what, with a fine feeling for words, had been named "bust-head."

This life, in its essence, was simply a progressively impoverished version of the life of the old backwoods. The forest was presently in large part
destroyed by the plantation and the prevailing wastefulness. Hence the
hunter who had formerly foraged for the larder while his women hoed the
corn found himself with less and less to do. Lacking lands and markets
which would repay any extensive effort as a farmer, lacking any incentive

which would even serve to make him aid the women at tasks which habit had fixed as effeminate, it was the most natural thing in the world for him to sink deeper and deeper into idleness and shiftlessness. More, the pass- ing of the forest increasingly deprived his table of the old abundant variety which the teeming wild life had afforded. Increasingly his diet became a monotonous and revolting affair of cornpone and the flesh of razorback hogs. And so, increasingly, he was left open to the ravages of hookworm, malaria and nutritional diseases [which sometimes led him to eat dirt in a search for the elements lacking in his diet].[3]

These apathetic "crackers" were a far cry from the driving nouveaux plantation lords or the relatively industrious yeomen of the cotton South. Their natural economic and political interests were at odds with those of the leaders who swallowed up the choicest lands, worked them with wageless slave labor, and legislated consistently in their own be-half. Yet, when the time for decision came, these crackers closed ranks with their class enemies against the Northerners. Why? asks Cash. He finds the answer in their common background and environment, and in certain psychological overtones of slavery.

At the core about which most Southerners of whatever degree were likely to be built [lay] a backcountry pioneer farmer or the immediate descendant of such a farmer. A man, indeed, who, because of one, two, or more generations in the backcountry was an even more uncomplex sort than had been the original immigrants from Europe. In some respects, perhaps as simple a type as Western civilization has produced in modern times.

The Southerner was primarily a direct product of the soil. He galloped to hounds in pursuit of the fox precisely as the [English] squire did [but] for quite other reasons. It was not that hoary and sophisticated class tradition dictated it as the proper sort [of entertainment] for gentlemen. It was simply and primarily for the same reason that in his youth and often into late manhood, he ran spontaneous and unpremeditated foot-races, wrestled, drank Gargantuan quantities of raw whisky, let off wild yells, and hunted the possum:—because the thing was already in his mores when he emerged from the backwoods, because he was a hot, stout fellow, full of blood and reared to outdoor activity.

Inevitably, then, the dominant trait of this mind was an intense individ-ualism. The thin distribution of the population over vast reaches of country, the virtual absence of law and government save in their most rudimentary stages, the fact that at every turn a man was thrown back wholly upon his

The Making of Johnny Reb

own resources—all these combined to give his native individualism the widest scope and to spur it on to headlong growth.

And what the frontier had begun, the world of the plantation was admirably calculated to preserve. The plantation tended to find its center in itself: to be an independent social unit, a self-contained and largely self-sufficient little world of its own. Despite the striking gregariousness which had long been growing up in counterbalance, the Southerner, whoever and wherever he was, would be likely to be much alone. Or if not strictly alone, then companied only by his slaves and members of his own family, to all of whom his individual will would stand as imperial law.

And what is true of the planter is true also for the poorer whites under this plantation order. The farmers and the crackers were in their own way self-sufficient too—as fiercely careful of their prerogatives of ownership, as jealous of their sway over their puny domains, as the grandest lord.

The individualism of the plantation world, like that of the backcountry before it, [was] far too much concerned with bald, immediate, unsupported assertion of the ego, which placed too great stress on the inviolability of personal whim, and which was full of the chip-on-shoulder swagger and brag of a boy—one, in brief, of which the essence was the boast, voiced or not, on the part of every Southerner, that he would knock hell out of whoever dared to cross him.

However careful they might be to walk softly, such men as these of the South were bound to come often into conflict. And being what they were —and their world being what it was—conflict with them could only mean immediate physical clashing, could only mean fisticuffs, the gouging ring, and knife and gun play.

Nor was it only private violence that was thus perpetuated. In this world of ineffective social control, the tradition of vigilante action, which normally lives and dies with the frontier, not only survived but grew so steadily that already long before the Civil War and long before hatred for the black man had begun to play any direct part in the pattern (of more than three hundred persons said to have been hanged or burned by mobs between 1840 and 1860, less than ten per cent were Negroes) the South had become peculiarly the home of lynching.

To the end of his service [the Confederate soldier] could not be disciplined. He slouched. He would never learn to salute briskly. His "Cap'n" and his "Gin'ral" were likely to pass his lips with a grin—were charged always with easy, unstudied familiarity. And down to the final day at Appomattox his officers knew that the way to get him to execute an order without malingering was to flatter and to jest, never to command too brusquely and forthrightly. And yet by virtue of precisely these unsoldierly

Chapters from the American Experience

qualities, he was one of the world's very finest fighting men. Allow what you will for *esprit de corps,* for this or for that, the thing that sent him swinging up the slope at Gettysburg was nothing more or less than his conviction, the conviction of every farmer among what was essentially only a band of farmers, that nothing living could cross him and get away with it.

In that void of pointless leisure which was his, the poor white turned his energies almost wholly to elaborating the old backcountry pattern of amusement and distinction—became one of the most complete romantics and one of the most complete hedonists ever recorded.

To stand on his head in a bar, to toss down a pint of raw whisky at a gulp, to fiddle and dance all night, to bite off the nose or gouge out the eye of a favorite enemy, to fight harder and love harder than the next man, to be known eventually far and wide as a hell of a fellow—such would be his focus. To lie on his back for days and weeks, storing power as the air he breathed stores power under the sun of August, and then to explode, as that air explodes in a thunderstorm, in a violent outburst of emotion—in such fashion would he make life not only tolerable but infinitely sweet.

And what is true of the poor white was true in a fashion of the planter and yeoman farmer as well. In every rank men lolled much on their verandas or under their oaks, sat much on fences, dreaming. In every rank they exhibited a striking tendency to build up legends about themselves and to translate these legends into explosive action—to perform with a high, histrionic flourish, and to strive for celebrity as the dashing blade.

Closely allied to this romanticism and hedonism is the Southern fondness for rhetoric, which flourished here far beyond even its American average; it early became a passion—and not only a passion but a primary standard of judgment of leadership.

But to speak of the love of rhetoric is at once to suggest the love of politics. The politics of the South was a theater for the play of the purely personal. It was an area wherein one great champion confronted another or a dozen, and sought to outdo them in rhetoric and splendid gesturing. It swept back the loneliness of the land, it brought men together under torches, it filled them with the contagious power of the crowd, it unleashed emotion and set it to leaping and dancing, it caught the very meanest man up out of his own tiny legend into the gorgeous fabric of the legend of this or that great hero.[4]

Despite their tendency to create heroes, Southerners in general did not believe that the great planters possessed any qualities which, given a modicum of luck, they themselves might not attain.

The Making of Johnny Reb

The Southerner's primary approach to his world was not through the idea of class. He never really got around in his subconsciousness to thinking of himself as being, before all else, a member of a caste, with interests and purposes in conflict with the interests and purposes of other castes. The groundwork in this case was the tradition of the backcountry and the never entirely obliterated remembrance of the community of origins. If, being a poor white or a farmer, you knew that your planter neighbor was a kinsman, you were normally going to find it as difficult to hate him as to think of him as being made of fundamentally different stuff from yourself —a "shining one" begotten by God for the express purpose of ruling you. The Southern social order had [furthermore] not sealed up the exit entirely. Always it was possible for the strong, craving lads who still thrust up from the old sturdy root-stock to make their way out and on: to compete with the established planters for the lands of the Southwest, or even to carve out wealth and honor in the very oldest regions.

Similarly, if you were a planter, and recalled that as a youth you had hunted the possum with that slouching fellow passing there, or danced the reel with the girl who had grown unbelievably into the sun-faded woman yonder, why, the chances were that, for all your forgetfulness when your ambition was involved, for all your pride in your Negroes, and your doctrinaire contempt for incompetence, there was still at the bottom of you a considerable community of feeling with these people.

Fully three-quarters of the planters were accustomed to having their farmer neighbors and cousins at their boards now and then; nor was it any rare thing for a great man with political ambitions to seize on a dozen crackers at a camp-meeting or a party rally and bear them off to his home to sleep on his best beds and make merry with his best liquor—or anyhow his second-best liquor.

The famous Southern manner served wonderfully for a balance wheel in the Southern social world and so as a barrier against the development of bitterness. If the common white was scorned, yet that scorn was so softened in its passage down through the universal medium of this manner that it glanced off harmless. When he frequented public gatherings, what he encountered would seldom be naked hauteur. Rather, there would nearly always be a fine gentleman to lay a familiar hand on his shoulder, to inquire by name after the members of his family, maybe to buy him a drink, certainly to rally him on some boasted weakness or treasured misadventure, and to come around eventually to confiding in a hushed voice that that damned nigger-loving scoundrel Garrison, in Boston—in short, to patronize him in such fashion that to his simple eyes he seemed not to be patronized at all but actually deferred to, to send him home, not sullen and vindictive, but glowing with the sense of participation in the common brotherhood of white men.

For if the plantation had introduced distinctions of wealth and rank among the men of the old backcountry, it had also introduced that other vastly ego-warming and ego-expanding distinction between the white man and the black. This common white was himself made by extension a member of the dominant class—was lodged solidly on a tremendous superiority. Come what might, he would always be a white man. And before that vast and capacious distinction, all others were foreshortened, dwarfed, and all but obliterated.[5]

Over this volatile society, in the early 1830s, fell the shadow of conflict with the "damyankee," who, it was clear, would soon hold complete control over the national government and who now turned his wrathful tongue upon the South's "peculiar" and basic institution.*

In this inevitable conflict the South was steadily driven back upon the defensive. It was running counter to the moral notions of its time in embracing slavery at the hour when the rest of the West was decisively giving it up.

Worst of all the South itself definitely shared in these moral notions. Of the 130 abolition societies established before 1827 by Lundy, the forerunner of Garrison, more than a hundred were in the South. And in the days of their sway the old colonial gentry had been so disturbed by the institution that numbers of them had followed the lead of Thomas Jefferson in pronouncing it an insufferable crime.[6]

But the economic urgencies of the new order had changed all that. The South's political leaders were now insisting that slavery offered the labor system best adapted to a democratic society, and her religious

---

*It was against the Yankee that the Southerner came to concentrate all the romantic pride that had for decades been stimulated by the literature of his section. Edmund Wilson *(Patriotic Gore: Studies in the Literature of the American Civil War* [New York: Oxford University Press, 1962]) incisively discusses the role of romantic Southern letters in developing the section's vision of itself as the champion of the chivalric plantation world against the vulgar tradesmen of the North.

When the war was over, Mark Twain would speak of the "measureless harm" done to Southern civilization by Sir Walter Scott and the Romantic tradition in literature, with its emphasis on fantasy and "sham chivalry." And Sidney Lanier, one of the most talented Southern contributors to the tradition, would contend that the conflict arose when the "peasants" of the North learned that they could become "lords" by wealth, and "so Trade arose and overthrew Chivalry" *(Ibid.* , pp. 438, 444–45, 552).

The Making of Johnny Reb

leaders were announcing that, since God in His infinite wisdom had established each in his just place, man should not question the order of things. Nevertheless the Yankee's tirades against the institution upon which their way of life was founded stirred old doubts and prodded the sense of guilt that they could never bury as deeply as they wished.

The stark fact remains: the relationship rested on force. The black man occupied the position of a mere domestic animal, without will or right of his own. The lash lurked always in the background. Its open crackle could often be heard where field hands were quartered. Into the gentlest houses drifted now and then the sound of dragging chains and shackles, the bay of hounds, the report of pistols on the trail of a runaway. And, as the advertisements of the time incontestably prove, mutilation and the mark of the branding iron were pretty common.

But the South could not and must not admit it, of course. It must prettify the institution, must begin to boast of its own Great Heart. To have heard them talk, indeed, you would have thought that the sole reason some of these planters held to slavery was love and duty to the black man. He was a child whom somebody had to look after. Mrs. Stowe did not invent the figure of Uncle Tom, nor did Christy invent that of Jim Crow—the banjo-picking, heel-flinging, hi-yi-ing happy jack of the levees and the cotton fields. All they did was to modify them a little for their purposes. In essentials, both were creations of the South—defense-mechanisms, answers to the Yankee and its own doubts.

But there was another factor which was perhaps even more important for the growth of sentimentality than this: the influence of the presence of the Negro in increasing the value attaching to Southern woman. For, as perpetuator of white superiority in legitimate line, and as a creature absolutely inaccessible to the males of the inferior group, she inevitably became the focal center of the fundamental pattern of pride.

Nor, in this connection, must we overlook the specific role played by the Negro woman. Torn from her tribal restraints and taught an easy complaisance for commercial reasons, she was to be had for the taking. Boys on and about the plantation inevitably learned to use her, and having acquired the habit, often continued it into manhood and even after marriage. For she was natural, and could give herself up to passion in a way impossible to wives inhibited by Puritanical training. There were many men in the South who rigidly abstained from such liaisons, and scorned those who indulged. Nevertheless every Southern community abounds in stories which run to the tune of "the *image,* my dear, the living *image,* of old Colonel Bascombe himself!"

Chapters from the American Experience

But this set up conflict with domestic sentiment. And such sentiment, without regard to the influence of the Negro's presence, was even stronger in the Southerner than in the American generally. In the isolation of the plantation world the home was necessarily the center of everything; family ties acquired a strength and validity unknown in more closely settled communities; and, above all, there grew up an unusually intense affection and respect for the women of the family.

Yet if such a woman knew that the maid in her kitchen was in reality half-sister to her own daughter, if she suspected that her husband sometimes slipped away from her bed to the arms of a mulatto wench, or even if she only knew or suspected these things of her sons, why, of course she was being cruelly wounded in the sentiments she held most sacred. And even though she feigned blindness, as her convention demanded she should—even if she actually knew or suspected nothing—the guilty man, supposing he possessed any shadow of decency, must inexorably writhe in shame and an intolerable sense of impurity under her eyes.

Join to this the fact that the Yankee's hate (and maybe his envy) had not been slow to discover the opening in the Southern armor, that his favorite journals were filled with "screamers" depicting every Southerner as a Turk wallowing in lechery, and it is plain that here was a situation which was not to be tolerated.

And the only really satisfactory escape here, as in so many other instances, would be fiction. On the one hand, the convention must be set up that the thing simply did not exist, and on the other, the woman must be compensated by glorifying her; the Yankee must be answered by proclaiming from the housetops that Southern Virtue was superior to any on earth. She was the South's Palladium, this Southern woman—the shield-bearing Athena gleaming whitely in the clouds. There was hardly a sermon that did not begin and end with tributes in her honor, hardly a brave speech that did not open and close with the clashing of shields and the flourishing of swords for her glory. At the last, I verily believe, the ranks of the Confederacy went rolling into battle in the misty conviction that it was wholly for her that they fought.

This Old South, in short, was a society beset by the specters of defeat, of shame, of guilt—a society driven by the need to bolster its morale, to nerve its arm against waxing odds, to justify itself in its own eyes and in those of the world. Hence a large part of its history from the day that Garrison began to thunder in Boston is the history of its efforts to achieve that end, and characteristically by means of romantic fictions.

And of all these fictions, the most inevitable and obviously indicated was just that one which we know today as the legend of the Old South—

The Making of Johnny Reb

the legend of which the backbone is the assumption that every planter was in the most rigid sense of the word a gentleman.

Enabling the South to wrap itself in contemptuous superiority, to sneer down the Yankee as low-bred, crass, and money-grubbing, and even to beget in his bourgeois soul a kind of secret and envious awe, it was a nearly perfect defense-mechanism. And the stage was magnificently set for its acceptance. For the Yankee, accustomed by long habit to thinking of the South purely in terms of Virginia, had the association of plantation and aristocrat fixed in his mind with axiomatic force. And what was true of the Yankee was equally true of the world in general, which received the body of its impressions of the South directly from him.

Nor was this all. It was for the principal Western nations an age of nostalgia. An age in which, underneath all the solemn self-congratulation on Progress, there was an intensive revulsion against the ugliness of the new industrialism and the drab monotony of the new rule of money-bags miscalled democracy, and a yearning back toward the colorfulness and the more or less imaginary glory of the aristocratic and purely agricultural past. It was an age which was not only ready but eager to believe in the Southern legend as a sort of projection ground for its own dreams of a vanished golden time.

All the South would join in believing that Southern culture outran not merely the Yankee's but even that of mankind as a whole, [and] represented perhaps the highest level ever attained.

It was the conflict with the Yankee which really created the concept of the South as an object of patriotism, in the minds of the Southerners. In this loyalty the common white participated as fully as any other Southerner. If he had no worth-while interest at stake in slavery, if his real interest ran the other way about, he did nevertheless have that, to him, dear treasure of his superiority as a white man, which had been conferred on him by slavery; and so was as determined to keep the black man in chains as the angriest planter. Morever, this struggle against the Yankee and the surging emotion of patriotism it set off provided a perfect focus for his romantic instincts and for his love of self-assertion and battle—a chance to posture and charge and be the dashing fellow.

Add up [all this] and you arrive, with the precision of a formula in mathematics, at the solid South. You can understand how farmer and white-trash were welded into an extraordinary and positive unity of passion and purpose with the planter—how it was that, when [critics] began at last on the eve of the Civil War to point out the wrongs of the common white and to seek to arouse him to recognizing them, they could get no response; how, on the contrary, when the guns spoke at Sumter, the

Chapters from the American Experience

masses sprang to arms, with the famous hunting yell soaring in their throats; how, against ever mounting odds and in the face of terrible privations, the South could hold its ranks firm even in the long gloom of the closing years of the war, fight its magnificent fight, and yield only when its man power was definitely spent.[7]

South Street from Maiden Lane, 1828

Watercolor by William J. Bennett. The Edward W. C. Arnold Collection, lent by the Metropolitan Museum of Art. Photo courtesy Museum of The City of New York.

29

Two Faces
of the American
Industrial Revolution

If ever a permanent inequality of conditions and aristocracy
again penetrate the world,
it may be predicted that this is the gate
by which they will enter.
—Alexis de Tocqueville[1]

In the decades preceding the Civil War, while attention focused on Western empire and on the impending conflict, a gradual and profound revolution was under way in the economy of the nation—a revolution that would transform America from a relatively uncomplicated agricultural and commercial land to a towering competitor for world markets and industrial leadership. This transformation, which had already been at work in Europe and England, received its initial impetus here in the cities of the Northeastern seaboard. In the course of a single generation, small, half-rural communities were converted into dynamic industrial centers with many of the aspects and problems of the modern metropolis.

Allan Nevins has told the story of one of the economic innovators whose lives spanned this period—Peter Cooper, ironmaster, New Yorker of exceptional dimensions, a representative of the new breed of pioneer that contributed so substantially to the Industrial Revolution in America.

In our admiration for the venturesome wilderness hunter in fringed buckskin and the heroic frontier farmer in homespun, we are wont to forget the pioneer industrialist. . . . The change he wrought was as picturesque as anything in American life. . . . Our industrial age began, and a thousand shrewd, speculative, aggressive men pushed it forward with astonishing rapidity.

Among them all . . . none was more typical than Peter Cooper. He was not, of course, at all typical of industry in the form it took after the Civil War, still less of the industrialist of today. He was typical of the pioneering or experimental age in American industry; of the period when new devices, new processes, new combinations were being worked out by trial and error. . . .

. . . In youth a painstaking workman, he always remained essentially a master craftsman . . . and to him the ideal society was one of capable, independent farmers and craftsmen. . . . He became the head of great undertakings, a multi-millionaire, a national power; yet even in later years the tall, keen-eyed, long-jawed gentleman . . . immaculate in white chin-whiskers, black stock, and frock coat, gave the impression of being ready at any moment to drive a bolt, put a belt on a pulley, or correct a blueprint. Like Horace Greeley, he kept the tang of the rural atmosphere in which he had been reared. To be sure, he had been born in New York City. But that was when it had fewer than 35,000 people; and his youth was passed largely in the country above Peekskill. . . .

. . . [Peter's father] was storekeeper, hatter, shoemaker, brewer, and farmer, sometimes all at once; and to eke out the limited return from these callings he would scour the woods on off days for wild honey and fur, which he sold. . . . As the family grew, its means became pinched, and Peter, between early ill-health and hard work at home, got almost no education. . . .

. . . Peter early displayed great manual dexterity and an extraordinary aptitude for mechanics. One of his first occupations was helping to make hats by pulling the hair out of rabbit-skins, when his head was just above the table. Before long he knew how to make every part of a hat. He also assisted his mother at an early age with the family washing. They placed the soiled clothes in a half-barrel of soapsuds, and he pounded them with a long-handled wooden club. It was tiresome work, and he soon devised a crude washing-machine. "I constructed a wheel . . . ," he later wrote. "On each side of this wheel I attached a handle for a pounder. . . . I made a double lever . . . fastened by a wheel on each side of it. A post in the top of this wheel, connected with this double lever, enabled me to . . . work both pounders at once; and by means of a ratchet attachment I caused them to strike in a new place every time." . . .

. . . At seventeen . . . when Jefferson was ending his second term, and New York City had perhaps 80,000 people, he descended upon the little metropolis. After some search for a place, he apprenticed himself for four years to John Woodward, of Burtis & Woodward, the leading coach-builders.... He received his board and $25 a year, and lodged with his Grand- mother....

New York, of which Peter Cooper was soon to become so prominent a figure, was then what Washington Irving called a handy city. Everyone knew everybody else. The leafy, ill-paved highways, the swine that basked in Broadway and Wall Street, the single theatre on John Street, the reliance on pumps for water, the high piles of hickory cordwood in the back yards, the universal pride in Trinity Church, the leather-capped watchmen who nightly called the hours in the streets, the general use of the Battery as a summer promenade, the interest in the Boston, Albany, and Philadelphia stage-coaches which, with much horn-blowing, rolled once daily to and from the City Hotel, the curiosity whenever some rich merchant bought a new carriage, the concern over the number of country traders who came in every spring and fall—all this proclaimed the place but an overgrown town.... At night the town was practically dark, a few smoky oil lamps shedding faint circles of illumination; no public street-cleaners existed, every property-owner being responsible for the space in front of his premises to the middle of the street; and in most of the streets open gutters took the place of sewers.... Every few years a pestilence of yellow fever would revisit the city, people would flee by thousands, and till the autumn frosts New York would appear half dead. In short, it was a quaint, inconvenient, unsanitary, very crude, and very delightful little city....

... Like other apprentices ... [Peter Cooper] had to be up at daybreak ... [to do chores and go] on errands—to the Hudson waterfront for lumber, to the auction stores downtown ... for upholstery, to the Fly Market ... for food. His physical endurance was prodigious, and he could work sixteen hours without fatigue. He soon knew by sight the principal men in the town: politicians ... savants ... editors ... merchants.... He accompanied Woodward to talk with out-of-town customers at the City Hotel. ... Above all, he became expert at his craft....

... [He] learned much more than carriage-making, for he was the very type of Hogarth's Industrious Apprentice.... Instead of spending ... time with ... other apprentices ... [indulging] in "sports of all kinds" [in the little city's 3,500 licensed drinking places and its numerous "disorderly houses"], writes Peter Cooper, "I made it a practise to go to a little room furnished by my Grandmother ... in one of the buildings she had on Broadway at the time and there I employed myself in various things." In this garret, buying candle-butts for light, he practised ornamental wood-carving, and sold his pieces to Woodward and other coach-builders. Ashamed of his lack of education, he read and reread the Bible, Pope's *Essay on Man*, Burns, and a few other British authors.... [Here too] he gave rein to his genius for mechanics. His first device was a machine for mortis-

Two Faces of the American Industrial Revolution

ing the hubs of carriages, theretofore done by hand, which had so much merit that Woodward bought it from him. . . .

His apprenticeship ended, Peter Cooper shrewdly rejected John Woodward's offer to set him up in business. . . . [He had] doubts about the trade [which was not as lucrative as might be supposed]. . . . Instead, . . . he became acquainted with a man who was making machines for shearing the nap from cloth, and accepted employment as a mechanic at the then generous wage of $1.50 a day. . . . Before three years elapsed he had saved enough money to buy the rights for New York State of an improved cloth-shearing machine, . . . and he commenced its manufacture on his own account. . . .

For some years his business remained profitable. . . . Imports of foreign cloth were cut off by the war [of 1812], textile manufacturing boomed in New England and the Middle States, and . . . he found a ready sale for his machines—in which . . . he soon made numerous improvements. As money flowed in he saved it. [He married and] now had a new outlet for his inventiveness—the home:

. . . "We did not keep servants then . . . so that when I went home from my work nightly I often found my wife rocking the cradle. . . . I went to my shop and got up a pendulous cradle that not only kept going, but by an attachment, I gave it a musical instrument that would sing the child to sleep. It had a still further advantage, for by placing a cloth on the frame, its swinging motion would keep the flies off the little one. One day a Yankee pedlar came along, and seeing the invention, for which I had a patent, insisted on my selling him the right to make them in, and for the State of Connecticut. I asked him how much he would offer. "I'll give you my horse and wagon and all there is in it." On that we concluded the bargain. . . .

The peace of 1815 . . . overthrew Peter Cooper's little machinery business, for many textile factories were forced to the wall by British competition. . . . His first step was to turn his . . . machine factory into a furniture shop. His second, since the shop paid badly, was to sell it and his house for what he could get, . . . and despite total inexperience, set up as a grocer. This was with some member of his wife's family. . . . He remained there three years, becoming sole owner; and he then bought an unexpired lease for . . . the . . . six or eight lots . . . and two buildings. . . . His grocery was on the corner, and he erected four frame houses to be rented. He and his thrifty wife let no source of income escape. She baked what Peter called "the best bread in New York" for the grocery. . . . Money flowed in steadily, and Peter Cooper was ready for his great opportunity.

One day in 1827 . . . a hardware dealer . . . of whom Cooper had bought tools when an apprentice . . . asked him why he did not take over . . . [a] glue factory . . . [which] had been mismanaged, and Peter Cooper purchased it for only $2,000. Now thirty-six years of age . . . at last he found his field. There was need for a good American glue. All thus far manufactured was of poor quality; that imported from the British Isles and France was costly; and Cooper saw the possibility of a large market. "I determined to make the best glue that could be produced, and found out every method and ingredient to that end." He tried experiments, took out patents, and by 1830 had equalled the best imported glues. . . . [He was soon working with another product, isinglass.] The American market was largely supplied by Russia at $4 a pound, but Peter Cooper manufactured a fair quality at 75¢. Finally, some years later, he began making the first table gelatin to be sold in packages. Mrs. Cooper wrote the recipes printed on the packets, and housewives were soon buying it in large quantities.

. . . For many years in the twenties and thirties he gave . . . the humble glue factory . . . incessant labor. At first he had no manager, no agent, no salesman, no bookkeeper—nothing but a force of workmen. Soon after dawn he would be at the factory lighting fires and preparing for work. In the afternoon he drove to the city and made his sales; at home in the evening he wrote letters and held business conferences. His bookkeeping was rudimentary, and at the end of the year he used to drive about town settling balances in gold. . . .

. . . Hooves of bullocks when Peter Cooper began his business sold for a cent apiece. He drove up the price to 12¢, and took all the city could supply. Henry Astor, brother of John Jacob Astor, was for years the city's largest slaughterer, and every morning Peter Cooper's carts could be seen standing at his establishment. . . .

. . . Glue was increasingly needed for furniture-making, . . . for the inking-rolls used in printing, for book-binding, the leather-trade, and household uses. Isinglass was in demand for clarifying wines and spirits, making jelly, ice-cream, and candy, giving lustre to textiles, and manufacturing ink, courtplaster, and household cement. For every housewife who had made her own calvesfoot jelly, a hundred shortly learned to use Peter Cooper's gelatin. He was soon growing rich, but his family continued to live in . . . plain . . . style, with one maid, one stableman, and a one-horse chaise instead of a carriage. . . .

Thus, as Adams gave way to Jackson, and Jackson to Van Buren [as New York became a city of 300,000]; . . . as men became familiar with railroads, national conventions, illuminating gas, penny newspapers, and Abolitionists, Peter Cooper rose to be one of the important American capitalists. . . . [He] became more dignified . . . grew the throat-whiskers which set off his face like a ruff, wore his hair long with flaring bangs over the ears, donned gold-rimmed spectacles with four octagonal lenses, one beside each eye as well as in front of it, and dressed with careful neatness. . . . In some ways he was still ignorant, even illiterate. His correspondence was ungrammatical . . . his speech incorrect, his manner, though courteous, a bit uncouth; but he was manifestly growing. He was a prominent

Two Faces of the American Industrial Revolution

Unitarian, he was active in civic movements, and his warm human sympathy and practical benevolence were becoming widely known.[2]

In 1828 a Maryland land boom followed the beginning of work on the Baltimore & Ohio Railroad, and Peter Cooper bought a 3,000-acre tract in Baltimore. When the railroad floundered in its first attempts to push tracks westward, Cooper examined his property with a view to making other uses of it. He cut timber and mined iron ore from it and built charcoal kilns, a lumber mill, and a furnace for smelting his iron. The metal he produced was not of high quality, but he made and sold cast-iron rails for sidings. The Baltimore & Ohio succeeded now in moving its lines to the West, and Cooper became interested in building for that company an American engine that would compete with the English imports.

. . . In England the lines were remarkably straight, with slight grades and no curves except of wide radius; the rougher American landscape demanded curves with as short a radius as 200 feet.

Peter Cooper set to work . . . in the fall of 1829. Always self-confident, he was positive that when finished his locomotive would pull cars around a curve of only 150 feet in radius; positive also that he could show English manufacturers that the crank with which they applied power to the wheels could be replaced by a more efficient device. As he writes in . . . [a] scrap of autobiography:

"I came back to New York for a little bit of a brass engine of mine—about one-horse-power—it had a three and a half inch cylinder and fourteen inch stroke—and carried it back to Baltimore. I got some boiler iron and made a boiler about as high as an ordinary wash-boiler, and then how to connect the boiler to the engine I didn't know.

"I couldn't find any iron pipes. The fact is that there were none for sale in this country. So I took two muskets and broke off the wood part, and used the barrels for tubing to the boiler, using one on one side and the other on the other. I went into a coachmaker's shop and made this locomotive, which I called the *Tom Thumb* because it was so insignificant. I didn't intend it for actual service but only to show the directors what could be made." . . .

The boiler of the *Tom Thumb* was . . . placed upright on a small car; the lower part served as the firebox, and the upper part contained the vertical tubes . . . improvised from musket barrels. To force air through the wood-burning firebox, he devised a blower, driven by a drum fastened to one of the car-wheels, over which passed a cord attached by a pulley to the blower-shaft. . . .

. . . The leading stage proprietors of Baltimore . . . challenged . . . [Cooper's *Tom Thumb*] to a race; and, hitching a gallant gray of beauty and speed to another car on the second track, met the engine one day at the Relay House. . . . At this point the race began . . . away went horse and engine, the snort of one and the puff of the other keeping time and tune. At first, the gray led, for he started with an instant bound, while the locomotive did not get under speedy way till the rotation of the wheels gave the blower a strong draft. Writes . . . [railroad attorney] Latrobe:

"The horse was perhaps a quarter of a mile ahead when the safety valve of the engine lifted and the thin blue vapor issuing from it showed an excess of steam. The blower whistled, the steam blew off in vapory clouds, the pace increased, the passengers shouted, soon . . . the race was neck and neck, nose and nose—then the engine passed the horse, and a great hurrah hailed the victory. But it was not repeated; for just at this time, when the gray's master was about giving up, the band which drove the pulley which drove the blower slipped from the drum, the safety valve ceased to scream, and the engine for want of breath began to wheeze and pant. In vain Mr. Cooper, who was his own engineman and fireman, lacerated his hands in attempting to replace the band upon the wheel; in vain he tried to urge the fire with light wood; the horse gained on the machine, and passed it; and although the band was presently replaced, and steam again did its best, the horse was too far ahead to be overtaken and came in the winner of the race. But the real victor was Mr. Cooper notwithstanding."

Peter Cooper . . . made an improvement in the fan belt which rendered a repetition of the accident impossible. Next day the *Tom Thumb* was hauling passengers and freight again, but the horse was out of competition with the railroad forever.[3]

Cooper sold his Baltimore property for a handsome profit and returned to New York, where he built a foundry and entered the business that was to make him one of the great iron magnates of the country. He bought mining properties with ore of high quality, built rolling mills, and produced unexcelled rails and wire. During the 1850s he pioneered in the use of iron for structural beams.

Meanwhile, Cooper had given the active management of his iron business over to his son and to his son-in-law, Abram Hewitt, and was free to turn his wealth and his inventive abilities to a dream he had entertained for many years. As early as 1825 he had purchased the first lot of a tract in the center of New York that he planned to use for a free institute of higher learning for workingmen. Over the years he bought adjoining strips of this land until, by the early fifties, he owned an entire block and was ready to begin the erection of Cooper's Union. The institution, which opened in 1857, embodied ideas as new as Cooper's various innovations in industry. It was to "give regular free night courses in applied science, in social and political science (these always to have preeminence) and in other branches of knowledge," to "offer a free reading room, art galleries, and scientific collections," to give instruction to "respectable females in the arts of design," to include "a thorough polytechnic school," and in general to "improve and elevate the working classes of the city."[4]

Through the quarter century and more that remained to him, Cooper guided the course of this institution, serving as its shepherd in matters of policy and as its financial "angel." As he entered his patriarchal years, Cooper lent the weight of his prestige to many local and national causes, crusading for social, economic, and political reform—for the emancipation of the slaves, the destruction of bossism in New York, currency reform, and federal action to curb monopolies. Some of his financial proposals were overly simple, many had to wait until the twentieth century for implementation. But all were directed toward the amelioration of the workingman's lot. To wage these crusades more effectively, he began, in late middle age, a rigorous program of study in the art of self-expression.

At a time when most men think their education over, Peter Cooper really began his. Unable in 1850 to write a letter without ludicrous errors in grammar and spelling, woefully ignorant on many subjects, he trained himself in the next fifteen years to be a remarkably forcible and effective pamphleteer on public questions. . . . Amid the confusion, waste, and graft of the Gilded Age he stood erect to do battle for the Jeffersonian and Jacksonian principles that he had breathed in with the air of his young manhood. . . . [With a new-found clarity and an habitual compassion, he wrote] a few years after Appomattox: "I consider the persistent class legislation of Congress since the war, a worse despotism than that of Great Britain before the Revolution, because it reduces the laboring classes to periodic distress and starvation, that are worse than any despotism ever was; for monopolizing corporations, whether in the shape of banks or railroads, have no soul."[5]

Peter Cooper died in 1883, at the age of ninety-two. New York City paid him a final tribute of stirring sincerity, and E. L. Godkin, eulogizing him in the lead editorial of *Nation*, wrote: "There has been no such funeral in the city in our time. . . . Peter Cooper was honored because he was a man who . . . [united] the highest integrity with the highest success, and who . . . at every stage used his success . . . to make the world a happier and easier abode for such of his fellow-men as he could reach."[6]

In his inventiveness, his drive, his versatility, and his climb to success, Peter Cooper was typical of the rising industrialists of the pre–Civil War North. In his engrossing concern for the welfare of the worker and his deeply democratic orientation, he was less representative.

The Industrial Revolution brought changes that affected the working and living standards of men in all levels of urban society. In the primarily agricultural economy of earlier days, city workers had been less dependent on their jobs for subsistence, often having their own gardens and farm animals, which tided them over in times of unemployment. Many of them had had small shops of their own, where they handcrafted goods which now came under the crushing competition of machine products. Shoemakers, hatters, hand-loom weavers, and other craftsmen found themselves gradually forced out of business and into the factories whose machine processes had displaced their older methods. Under the new, more specialized economy, any period of depression brought disaster to large numbers of workers.

As industry expanded, owners became more remote from their workmen and often from active management, and workers were driven with increasing ruthlessness. The typical workingman labored (under unsanitary and unsafe conditions) from eleven to fourteen hours a day for six days a week. Studies initiated by two leading newspapers in the early 1850s determined that the average workingman's family required $11 per week for subsistence. But such a worker did not usually earn half that amount. And so his wife and his children, too, worked at the factory. In manufacturing areas few children over twelve were to be found in school, and as late as 1880 one Massachusetts child in eleven never attended school at all.[7]

Yet, in certain industries and in some areas the owners made a handsome profit from their operations. In New Hampshire, for instance, the thirteen leading textile mills (having a total capitalization of more than $11.5 million) earned, over a long period of time, an annual return on their investment of 7.85 percent.[8] And still, few industries more completely exploited their workers than the textile factories. There working hours extended in some cases to sixteen hours out of the twenty-four, and the wages—meager at best—were often not paid entirely in cash. A portion of the earnings of many mill operatives in New England was reserved for board and room in approved boardinghouses. The managers of such establishments in one mill town received from the factory 25¢ per day for a male boarder and 17.5¢ a day for a woman. For this sum they housed and fed the workers and reported to the factory management on the activities of their boarders. Infractions of the rules as to "moral" behavior, conversation, and church attendance (or in the case of "single females" a ten o'clock curfew) might result in dismissal.[9] In many industries it was common to pay part of the wages in merchandise from the lucrative company stores, and workers were in some cases encouraged to put their small savings in banks to which the businesses that employed them had ready access.[10]

Yet, if the worker chafed at such wretched conditions or compared his lot with that of the owner, there was little he could do to better his position, for his services were a glut on the market. The Eastern seaboard had, for most of its history, suffered a labor shortage, as the vast open spaces of the West provided a preferable alternative to industrial employment. However, during the 1840s the situation was reversed as the result of an abrupt influx of immigrants. In the first fifty years of our existence as a nation, about a million immigrants entered the country. But, in the single decade beginning in 1846, three times that number flooded in.[11] Furthermore, the newcomers tended to concentrate in the Eastern cities and factory towns. And they were eager for any kind of work, at almost any wage offered.

If the average worker of this time burned out his life in a perpetual struggle for existence, the conditions of the immigrant populations of the Northeastern cities were even more depressed. And nowhere was this more true than among the Irish newcomers who inundated the well-ordered, insular community of Boston during the decade and a half before the Civil War.

Although several large factory complexes had grown up around Boston, the city itself remained, in the mid-forties, "a town of small traders, of petty artisans and handicraftsmen, and of great merchant princes."[12] Into this exclusive little community, stingy of promise to newcomers, few immigrants had previously ventured, for most had come to America with sufficient funds to move on to the Midwestern farmlands. With the Irish it was different.

Irish peasants had lived in poverty for generations, growing grain and potatoes on their small rented plots, selling the grain to pay for the use of the land, and subsisting almost entirely on the potatoes. But, during the first half of the nineteenth century, a series of events, economic and political, disrupted their marginal existence and drove them from Ireland. By 1855, 50,000 of these impoverished peasants had descended upon Boston, which in 1850 had boasted a total population of only 137,000. They came without funds to move on, without even the means to survive, save for the charity of the city or of Irish friends who had come before. These unskilled farm workers flooded the labor market. Some found part-time employment on public works, in stables, as janitors, and in other menial labor. The largest number to find work at first were the servants who filled a long-standing shortage of domestic help. Irish waiters became common. Numbers of these immigrants were enticed by labor contractors into gangs for railroad construction, where they were often paid less than promised and commonly charged such unreasonable prices for their food that they returned to Boston as poor as they had left it. Then, as Boston began to industrialize in the face of such an abundant supply of cheap labor, the fortunate among the Irish found employment in industry: in textile, shoe, paper, and furniture factories; in sugar-refining plants and shipyards; and in copper, brass, and iron foundries. But even the immigrant who gained steady employment found that, although he worked seven days a week for fifteen hours a day under a discipline much harsher than any he had known, he seldom had sufficient money to feed and clothe his family. At night he returned home to ghettos that would have been unthinkable in the Boston of a few years before.[13] Historian Oscar Handlin describes the living conditions of these early Irish immigrants:

Within easy reach of . . . the commercial heart of Boston . . . its docks and markets, offices and counting houses, stores and work-shops . . . were two centers whose development made them the logical receiving points for the Irish. . . . Both the North End, which in its more prosperous days had contained many fine mansions, and less elegant but eminently respectable Fort Hill . . . had once been purely residential, but the encroachment of trade impaired their fashionableness, draining off many old dwellers. . . . [Other parts of the city, particularly] the West End . . . and . . . South Boston . . . experienced a similar transition. . . .

The . . . housing of the Irish required an extensive process of adaptation on the part of Boston real estate. The simplest form was conversion of old mansions and disused warehouses into tenements. In many cases, boardinghouse keepers, wishing to profit by the new demand, took over properties which, after a few alterations, emerged as multiple dwellings. In other cases, a sublease system developed, whereby a contractor . . . leased an old building at an annual rental, subdivided it into immigrant flats, and subrented it at weekly rates. . . . Solely interested in immediate income . . . sublandlords encouraged a host of evils. . . .

Despite its lack of conveniences or sanitation, and its general inflammability, the remodeled type was far superior to any other available to the Irish. . . .

New dwellings, completely free of restrictions, displayed every stratagem for economy at the expense of the most humble amenities. . . . [The] enterprising landowners utilized unremunerative yards, gardens, and courts to yield the maximum number of hovels that might pass as homes. The abundant grounds surrounding well-built early Boston residences, and the hitherto unusable sites created by the city's irregular streets, once guarantees of commodious living, now fostered the most vicious Boston slums. Every vacant spot, behind, beside, or within an old structure, yielded room for still another. . . .

The whole brood of evils typical of this development materialized in Half Moon Place. . . . This pest hole consisted of a very limited tract, originally vacant, between the rear of the Broad Street tenements and Fort Hill. . . . A rise in the value of land led to the excavation of additional portions of the hill, and the erection of tottering rookeries with their backs flush upon it. Not one of these melancholy warrens, moldering at their very conception, opened directly upon the street. The inhabitants . . . [could go] to the main thoroughfare through two gaps between the Broad Street buildings . . . [or up the hill by] a battered staircase, "Jacob's Ladder," which led to the comparative heaven of Humphrey Place above.

Remodeled or new, these dwellings promoted a steady succession of evils. . . . No standards of decency and comfort were too low. . . .

Immigrant rents were everywhere high beyond all reason because of the system whereby middlemen demanded dual and sometimes triple profits, and secured returns greater than on any other real estate in the city. . . .

. . . [These "homes"] were "not occupied by a single family or even by two or three families; but each room, from garret to cellar [was] . . . filled with a family . . . of several persons, and sometimes with two or more. . . ." Every nook was in demand. Attics, often no more than three feet high, were popular. And basements were even more coveted, particularly in the Fort Hill area; by 1850 the 586 inhabited in Boston contained from five to fifteen persons in each, with at least one holding thirty-nine every night.

Underground dwellings enjoyed refreshing coolness in the hot summer months and coal-saving warmth in the winter. . . . But . . . [built] entirely beneath the street level, they enjoyed no light or air save that which dribbled in through the door leading down, by rickety steps, from the sidewalk above. Innocent of the most rudimentary plumbing, some normally held two or three feet of water, and all were subject to periodic floods and frequent inundations by the backwater of drains at high tide. Above all, there was little space. Some windowless vaults no more than eighteen feet square and five feet high held fourteen humans. . . .

The most serious danger inherent in immigrant quarters was the complete neglect of sewerage equipment and sanitation of any kind. In many cases . . . the absolute lack of facilities obliged the occupants "to supply their necessities as best they" could. Where drainage systems existed, they were inefficient and insufficient. . . . Usually residents relied on yard hydrants and water-closets "exposed to the transient custom of tenants or outsiders" alike. Many houses had "but one sink, opening into a contracted and ill-constructed drain, or . . . into a passageway or street, and but one privy, usually a mass of pollution, for all the inhabitants, sometimes amounting to a hundred." No one was responsible for the care of these communal instruments, and as a result they were normally out of repair. Abominably foul and feculent, perpetually gushing over into the surrounding yards, they were mighty carriers of disease. . . .

Inadequate housing, debarment from the healing sun, and inescapable filth took their toll in sickness and lives. Boston had been a healthy city before the 1840s, a city in which the life-span was long and disease rare.

Smallpox, for instance, no longer existed by 1845. . . . But after [that year] . . . the pestilence flourished. . . . Nor was this the only scourge . . . to plague the city. Year after year endemic or contagious maladies returned to haunt the depressed areas. In 1849 the cholera spread from Philadelphia and New York to Boston. Despite feverish efforts to halt it, the epidemic swept through the congested courts in the hot summer months, reaping a full harvest of victims. . . . In all, more than 500 of the 700 fatalities were Irish. . . .

More vicious in the long run than the spectacular ills were those which, conceived in squalor, quietly ate away resistance before delivering their final blow. Most important was tuberculosis. This disease had declined in Boston until 1845, but thereafter revived in the hovels of the Irish . . . reaching the unprecedented peak of 4.57 deaths per thousand . . . in 1855. . . .

. . . So many died soon after arrival that it was said the Irish lived an average of only fourteen years after reaching Boston. . . . Far from lowering the mortality [rate of the city], as the injection of a young and medium-aged group should have, the immediate effect of immigration . . . in Boston . . . was to boost it . . . [until, for the five-year period ending 1850, it was] twice as high as for the rest of Massachusetts . . . and higher even than the English slums.[14]

If the conditions in the Irish ghettos of Boston were more grotesquely harsh than most, still, the other industrial centers also had their diseased areas, smaller but similarly blighted, and workers in factory cities everywhere lived and labored in a squalor and want that verged on the obscene.

So, the climb of Peter Cooper and the struggle of the Irish immigrants in Boston cut two different facets in the great industrial rock crystal of the transition period—a crystal in which may be seen the end of the old economic era and the rise and the challenge of the new.

Harper's Ferry, Virginia

Lithograph by E. Sachse & Co. after A. Weidentosh.

30

The Sword of Gideon

And the angel of the Lord appeared unto him, and said unto him,
The Lord is with thee, thou mighty man of valour.
—Judges 6:12.

In the village of Charlestown, on the beautiful Shenandoah River of
upland Virginia, John Brown was preparing for death. There was little
in his manner that betrayed him as the man whose band had killed in
cold blood in Kansas and assaulted the sleeping hamlet of Harpers
Ferry, Virginia—little to suggest that the poet-historian, Stephen Vincent Benét would one day call him

> A stone flung from a sling, against a wall . . .
> A cold prayer hardened to a musket ball.[1]

To the men who guarded him he seemed more like a kindly rural pastor
as he scanned his Bible, marking a few more Old Testament passages.
On the last day he gave this treasure to a confectioner who had been
kind to him, distributed his other books and his silver watch to the
guards who had come to respect him in spite of themselves, and spoke
words of comfort to those of his men who would soon follow him to the
scaffold. To his family he wrote a loving and pious farewell:

> My dear shattered & broken family be of good cheer & believe & trust
> in God, for "he doeth all things well." I am waiting the hour of my public
> murder with great composure of mind and cheerfulness, feeling the strong-

est assurance that in no other possible way could I be used to so much advance the cause of God and of humanity, & that nothing that either I or all my family have sacrificed or suffered will be lost.

I beseech you every one to make the bible your daily & nightly study. My dear younger children will you listen to the last poor admonition of one who can only love you? Oh be determined at once to give your whole hearts to God. Do not be vain and thoughtless, but sober minded. Live in habitual contentment with very moderate circumstances, and teach this to your children & children's children: "Owe no man anything but to love one another." Nothing can so tend to make life a blessing as the consciousness that you love & are beloved. Abhor with undying hatred that "sum of all villainies," slavery. Remember that "he that is slow to anger is better than the mighty, and he that ruleth his spirit than he that taketh a city."

And now dearly beloved, Farewell. To God & the word of his grace I commend you all.[2]

Not the message of a man assailed by conscience. Rather, the proud testament of one making the supreme sacrifice for a great truth—that slavery constituted an affront to God and must be destroyed. And also the defiant assertion that any means had been justified in the furtherance of that cause.

Brown had declared "eternal war" against slavery early in his life. As a very young child in Connecticut, he had heard his Abolitionist father decry its evils and, as a teen-ager in Ohio, had undergone an experience that crystallized his hatred. In a brief autobiographical note written years later, he described that episode and revealed at the same time other aspects of his youth: the frontier privations endured, the comfort found in the Puritan principles of his ancestors, the stress placed on responsibility and physical accomplishment, and the austere narrowness to which his intense mind was so early shaped.

I cannot tell you of anything in the first four years of John's life worth mentioning [he wrote, alluding to himself in the third person] save that at that early age he was tempted by three large brass pins belonging to a girl who lived in the family & stole them. In this he was detected by his Mother, &, after having a full day to think of the wrong, received a thorough whipping.

When John was in his sixth year a poor Indian boy gave him a yellow marble, the first he had ever seen. This he thought a great deal of & kept a good while, but at last he lost it beyond recovery. About five months after this he caught a young squirrel, tearing off his tail in doing it & getting severely bitten himself. He however got the little bob tail squirrel perfectly tamed & almost idolized his pet. This too he lost & for a year or two John was mourning and looking at all the squirrels he could see to try & discover Bobtail. You may laugh when you come to read about it, but these were sore trials to John, whose earthly treasures were very few & small. These were the beginning of a severe but much needed course of discipline which he passed through, & which, it is to be hoped, taught him that the Heavenly Father sees it best to take all the little things out of his hands which He has ever placed in them.

I must not neglect to tell you of a very bad & foolish habit to which John was somewhat addicted. I mean telling lies, generally to screen himself from blame or from punishment.

At eight years old, John was left a motherless boy, which loss was complete & permanent, for, notwithstanding his father again married to a sensible, intelligent, and on many counts very estimable woman, yet he never adopted her in feeling, but continued to pine after his own Mother for years.

He would always choose to stay at home & work hard rather than go to school. By the time he was twelve years old he was sent off more than a hundred miles through the wilderness alone with cattle, & he would have thought his character much injured had he been obliged to be helped in any such job.

During the War of 1812, his father furnished troops with beef cattle, & what John saw in this connection so disgusted him with military affairs that he would neither train or drill, but paid fines & got along like a Quaker until his age finally cleared him of military duty.

Also during the war, he saw a slave boy near his own age and of very active intelligence and kindly beaten with iron shovels or any other thing that came to hand. This brought John to reflect on the wretched, hopeless condition of slave children, and led him to swear eternal war with slavery.

He never attempted to dance in his life, nor did he ever learn to know one pack of cards from another. He learned nothing of grammar, but acquired some taste for reading, which formed the principal part of his early education. By reading the lives of great & good men, he grew to dislike vain & frivolous conversation & persons.

He became very strong & large for his age, & from fifteen to twenty he spent most of his time working at the tanning trade and serving as foreman in his father's establishment. The habit so early formed of being obeyed rendered him in after life too much disposed to speak in an imperious way.

At a little past twenty years, led by his own inclination & prompted also by his father, he married a remarkably plain but neat and industrious & economical girl, of earnest piety & good common sense.[3]

The Sword of Gideon

His wife bore him seven children before she died. Brown now imposed on his own household the rigid discipline that had marked his youth. Determined that his children should not fall into the "habit of lying," which had caused him so many hours of self-recrimination, he inflicted harsh punishments on them. There was no room in his austere world for childish flights of imagination. One son was "thrashed severely" at the age of three for confusing a dream with reality. But tears filled the father's eyes as he executed this punishment. One of his daughters, recalling that he frequently spent sleepless nights tending sick youngsters or neighbors, insisted that "no one outside his own family could ever know the strength and tenderness of his character."[4]

This benevolent despotism Brown extended to the apprentices and journeymen serving under him at the tannery, where all workmen were required to attend church each Sunday and family worship every morning. In the shop Brown showed an early preference for his own justice. When a journeyman stole a calf hide, he punished the recreant by forbidding all other workers to speak to him—a punishment which became so trying as the months went by that the journeyman gave up his job.

By this time (while still in his early twenties), Brown had become engrossed in the slavery question. One journeyman remembered that he considered it "as much his duty to help a Negro escape as it was to help catch a horse thief." Of each new settler, "his first inquiry was whether he was an observer of the Sabbath, opposed to slavery and a supporter of the gospel and common schools. If so, all was right with him; if not he was looked upon by Brown with suspicion."[5]

When he was twenty-five, Brown moved his family to Richmond, Pennsylvania, where he at once became a pillar of the community.

Between May and the first of October, Brown cleared twenty-five acres of timber lands, built a fine tannery, sank vats, and had leather tanning in them. He was of marked value to the new settlement by his devotion to religion and to civil order. He surveyed new roads, was instrumental in erecting school-houses, procuring preachers and "encouraging everything that would have a moral tendency."[6]

Here Brown remarried, and this marriage produced thirteen more children, of whom seven died in childhood and two at Harpers Ferry. Here also he built a hiding place for fugitive slaves—a "roughly boarded room" in his haymow, well ventilated and equipped and so skillfully concealed under the hay that "a man might stand on the trap-door and yet see no signs of the hiding-place."[7] He began now to think of other ways he might help the oppressed race. To his brother in Ohio he wrote:

I have been trying to devise some means whereby I might do something practical for my poor fellowmen who are in bondage, and we have agreed to get at least one Negro boy or youth and bring him up as we do our own, give him a good education, and above all, try to teach him the fear of God. If we could get a school a-going hero for blacks we might, under God, do more towards breaking their yoke than in any other way. If once the Christians in the free states began teaching the blacks, the slaveholding states would find themselves driven to set about the work of emancipation immediately.[8]

Brown was thirty-four when he entertained this peaceable hope that a school for black children, by encouraging a general program of Negro education in the North, might lead to the destruction of slavery. He did not entertain it for long. Within half a decade he turned from the idea of evolutionary techniques to the dream of revolution. One of his sons recorded how, one evening in the later 1830s, Brown told his family that henceforth he would use any means, including force, against slavery:

We were seated around the open fireplace in the kitchen of the old house when he first informed us of his determination to make war on slavery by force and arms. After spending considerable time setting forth in most impressive language the hopeless condition of the slave, he asked who of us were willing to make common cause with him in doing all in our power to "break the jaws of the wicked and pluck the spoil out of his teeth." He named each of us in succession, and, receiving an affirmative answer from each, he kneeled in prayer. He then administered to us an oath which bound us to secrecy and devotion to the purpose of fighting slavery by force and arms to the extent of our ability.[9]

But still Brown's resolve took no particular direction. After the Pennsylvania period his financial affairs flagged. He bought several farms on credit, suffered heavily in the Depression of 1837, and finally went into bankruptcy. He tried, in many ways and many places, to recoup his fortunes—worked at surveying, raised sheep, organized wool producers, became a wool merchant—all with marked lack of success and by means sufficiently dubious to involve him in numerous litigations. Despite his business worries, Brown's interest in slavery continued.

The Sword of Gideon

In Springfield, Massachusetts, where he moved his family in the late 1840s (and where his living room remained unfurnished so that the savings might be used for fugitive slaves), he became deeply involved with the militant Boston Abolitionists. In that volatile atmosphere he attended countless meetings, read in Greeley's *Tribune* that slavery should be opposed with "Sharp's rifles," and shared plans with such Negro Abolitionists as Frederick Douglass. In 1851, in reaction to the Fugitive Slave Law, he took his first definite step toward forcible rebellion. Against the "slave catchers" attempting to return fugitive slaves to the South, he organized a group of blacks for guerrilla warfare and advised them:

Should one of your number be arrested, you must collect together as quickly as possible so as to outnumber your adversaries. Let no able-bodied man appear on the ground unequipped, or with his weapons exposed to view. Your plans must be known only to yourself, and with the understanding that all traitors must die, wherever caught and proven to be guilty. "Whosoever is fearful or afraid, let him return and depart early from Mount Gilead." Do not delay one moment after you are ready; you will lose all your resolution if you do. Let the first blow be the signal for all to engage; and do not do your work by halves, but make clean work with your enemies.[10]

So, his mind filled with the Old Testament parallel, speaking easily of treason in the name of right, Brown began his career of inciting to riot and to murder.

He began also to formulate plans for the campaign that would be his last great contribution to the cause. Reading of the mountain guerrilla warfare of Spanish revolutionaries, he conceived of a well-organized thrust down the Alleghenies into the Deep South. He and a loyal force would move down the backbone of the range, descending to raid the plantations at either side and returning to the mountains with hordes of liberated slave recruits.

While Brown dreamed of evoking a massive slave uprising in the heart of the South, his sons, who had settled in Kansas, wrote urging him to join them there in the struggle to save that state from slavery. Brown replied, at first, that his attention was engaged elsewhere, but, as word came of the depredations of the proslavery "Border Ruffians" against the "Free Soil" settlers along the Missouri border, he decided to go to Kansas and there test the guerrilla tactics he had been studying. He joined his sons and their families near the village of Osawatomie, Kansas, in the fall of 1855 and immediately became active in the leadership of the Free Soilers. When the Free Soil town of Lawrence was ravaged by raiders in May, 1856, the Browns at once sought vengeance on the proslavery settlement along the Pottawatomie River. The self-justification with which they approached their mission of murder was reflected years later in the words of one of Brown's sons: "Some radical retaliatory measure—some killing—was necessary. We started for the Pottawatomie country, which was the headquarters for the pro-slavery men, to pick off men prominent in enforcing Border Ruffian laws."[11] Late on the night of May 24, they descended upon the scattered settlement, and, before they were done, they had "picked off" five unarmed men. The wife of one of the victims later told how the Browns had worked:

It was about eleven o'clock when we heard a knock. My husband got up and went to the door. Those outside inquired for Mr. Wilkinson and where he lived. My husband told them that he would show them and opened the door. Several men came into the house, armed with pistols and large knives, and saying they were from the army. They told my husband that he and the boys must surrender. They first took my husband out of the house, then they took two of my sons—the oldest ones—and went away. My son John was spared, because I asked them in tears to spare him. Shortly afterward I heard the report of pistols.

My husband and two boys, my sons, did not come back any more. I went out next morning in search of them, and found my husband and William, my son, lying dead in the road near together, about two hundred yards from the house. My other son I did not see.[12]

Her youngest son completed the testimony: "I saw my other brother lying dead on the grass near a ravine. His fingers and arms were cut off, his head cut open; there was a hole in his breast. William's head was cut open, a knife hole was in his jaw and another in his side. My father was shot in the forehead and stabbed in the breast."[13]

Proslavery newspapers broke into a frenzy of war hysteria. "Let Slip the Dogs of War," they cried; civil war "reigns" in Kansas, and the South must rally with men and money.[14]

Even the Free Soilers reacted to this bloodletting with repugnance, refusing to shelter the outlaws. They were accustomed to vigilante justice, but such frontier justice usually followed a code of its own. The victims of the Pottawatomie raid had died without the opportunity to present their case in the crudest court or even to compose themselves for death.

The Sword of Gideon

Brown and his men took refuge in the forest. There life became a prolonged camp meeting, with the "exalted character" of the "Captain" dominating the scene. Strong and sinewy, with an inflexible mouth, a prominent Roman nose, and penetrating, slightly hooded blue eyes, Brown reminded his men of an eagle, and they sat at his feet like disciples while he spread the word of the gospel and the doctrine of anarchy.[15]

In this camp no manner of profane language was permitted, nor any man of immoral character. His toes protruding from his boots, Old Brown made prayers in which all the company united every morning and evening. The old man would say that the Lord had directed him in visions what to do, that, for himself, he did not love warfare, but peace, acting only in obedience to the will of the Lord, fighting God's battles for His children's sake.

He exhibited at all times the most affectionate care for each of us. He attended to the cooking. We had two meals daily, of bread baked in skillets, washed down with creek water mixed with ginger and molasses. Nevertheless, we kept in excellent spirits; we considered ourselves as one family, determined that victory or death might find us together. We were united as brothers by love towards the man who, with tender words and wise counsel, in the depth of the wilderness, prepared a handful of young men for the work of laying the foundation of a free commonwealth. His words have ever remained firmly engraved on my mind. He admonished us not to care whether a majority, no matter how large, opposed our principles and opinions. We should never allow ourselves to be tempted by any consideration to acknowledge laws and institutions to exist as of right, if our conscience and reason condemned them.[16]

Now the Free Soilers along the Missouri border suffered a rash of atrocities in retaliation for Brown's raids. A peace emissary was ambushed and killed with corrosive acid, and another innocent man, riding in his buggy, suffered a barbaric death as a result of a six-dollar bet that the perpetrator could "scalp an Abolitionist" within two hours. In the rush of anger against the proslavery men, Free Soiler feeling toward Brown subsided. By July he was able boldly to enter Lawrence and call on a newsman there. Soon he was outfitted with a "spick and span four-mule team," a wagon loaded with provisions, and fine mounts for his men, and was leading forays in the warfare that raged up and down the border.[17]

By the fall of the year the new governor of the Kansas Territory had effected a measure of peace, and Brown decided to move on. He made his way across the North, collecting funds and building sympathy. In Boston especially, his praises were sung from the pulpit, in public forums, in newspapers, and in private meetings. Amos Lawrence, the industrial giant of the Lowell Mills, hailed him as a "true Puritanic warrior"; journalist Artemus Ward praised his "pluck"; and Emerson admired his "simple, artless goodness."[18] A small but powerful committee formed to collect funds for Brown and to promote "whatever attacks he might make on slavery." The committee tempered its enthusiasm when one of Brown's men betrayed his plans for an assault against the Southern heartland to a United States Senator, who promptly warned that, if the money and arms collected should be used for other purposes than the defense of Kansas, "it might be of disadvantage to the men who were induced to contribute." Brown was given $500 and the arms thus far collected, with the understanding that he use them in Kansas. When he returned to Boston, he would be given at least $2,000 more to use in any way he saw fit, so long as the committee was not made privy to his plans.[19]

Consequently, in the fall of 1858, Brown returned to Kansas, where he led a raid into Missouri that culminated in the killing of one slaveholder, the theft of numerous horses, and the liberation of eleven slaves. Again, the cries of vengeance and talk of war across the South. And again, the mixed reaction among Northerners, with many who had helped slaves cross to Canada questioning the right to raid a slave state and bring them out by violence. But others obviously approved, for, despite a large reward on his head and despite his insistence on taking traveled roads, Brown was not captured. By wagon, by train, and by boat, he took his eleven Negroes slowly across the country, north to Canada.

Meanwhile the Boston Abolitionists continued their money-raising activities. By early July, 1859, they had given Brown the promised funds, and he was ready to launch his great campaign. He had settled on the little community of Harpers Ferry in northern Virginia as the initial point of attack. This picturesque village at the confluence of the Shenandoah and the Potomac had attracted his attention for several reasons. It offered easy access to the mountain range down which he intended to move as he swept into the South. Its quick capitulation might woo the great state of Virginia from the slavery cause. And, it was the site of a federal armory for the manufacture of weapons and a federal arsenal where lay a cache of arms he could use to equip the slave population.

The Sword of Gideon

Here Brown arrived, under the name of I. Smith, on July 4. After reconnoitering briefly, he rented a piece of property, known as the Kennedy Farm, on the Maryland side of the Potomac. He sent for his daughter, Annie, and his daughter-in-law, Martha (both still in their teens), to come and cook for the men and serve as sentries.

The summer wore away while they waited for arms and for reinforcements from Kansas and the North. During this interval Brown told his men, for the first time, of the exact nature of his plan. The news that it was not to be a simple raid followed by quick retreat evoked bitter criticism and threats of desertion. But Brown rallied them all. The Negroes were straining at their bonds, he told his men. Many white settlers in the area abhorred slavery. "When I strike the bees will begin to swarm," he promised. "If God be for us, who can be against us?"[20] They were not completely convinced by his reasoning, but his earnestness moved them. The plan proceeded. They waited out the long dog days of August and September in fairly good spirits. Annie Brown later described the care with which they hid the men and the constant threat posed by an inquisitive neighbor.

The middle room in the second story was used for dining and general living, as the stairway from the men's quarters above came down into that room. Sometimes Mrs. Huffmaster, who was a worse plague than the flees, would be seen coming with her brood of little ones while the men were at the table eating. They would then gather up all the things, table-cloth and all, and go so quietly upstairs that no one would believe they existed, finish their meal up there and come back down bringing the things, when the visitor had gone.

The men did nearly all the washing. We spread the clothes on the fence and on the ground to dry. Martha and I would bring them in as fast as they dried, but Mrs. Huffmaster would have some excuse to come to the garden, and then she would tell us, "Your men folks has a right smart lot of shirts." No one can ever imagine the pestering torment that little barefooted woman and her children were to us. Martha called them the little hen and chickens.

We were in constant fear that people would become suspicious. The rifles were in boxes called "furniture" and were used to sit on in the dining room. I had to tell people that "my mother was coming soon and that she was very particular and had requested us not to unpack her furniture until she arrived."

Father encouraged debating on all subjects among the men, although he did not always agree with them on religion. It is claimed they were a wild, ignorant, fanatical or adventurous lot of rough men. This is not so. They were sons of good families well trained by orthodox religious parents, too young to have settled views on many subjects. Judging by the rules laid down by Christ, I think they were uncommonly good Christians if the term Christian means follower of Christ's example, and too great lovers of freedom to endure to be trammeled by church or creed. The mission was an effort to help those who were oppressed and could not help themselves—a practical application of the Golden Rule. I heard them ask father one day if the money to pay the expenses was furnished by orthodox church members or liberal Christians. He said he must confess it came from the liberal ones.

To while away the time the men read magazines, sang, told stories, played cards and checkers, studied military tactics, and drilled. When there was a thunderstorm they would jump about and play, making all kinds of noise to rest themselves.[21]

Funds ran low, but the men remained determined. Watson Brown, whose wife had borne him a son just before he left, wrote her:

I do want to see you and the little fellow very much but must wait. There was a slave near where we live whose wife was sold to go South the other day and he was found hanging in the orchard, dead, the next morning. I cannot come home as long as such things are done here. I sometimes think perhaps we shall not meet again. [And later,] we are all eager for the work and confident of success. There was another slave murdered near our place the other day, making in all five slaves murdered and one committed suicide near our place since we lived here. I can but commend you to our friends if I should never see you again.[22]

In October sufficient money arrived to enable them to make final preparations. On the evening of the 16th, leaving three of his small force to guard the guns and the pikes he had had made for Negro insurgents, Brown and eighteen men swung in double file down the Potomac River road toward Harpers Ferry.

Capturing the Potomac bridge guard, they entered the unsuspecting town and took possession of the arsenal. Without any particular strategy, they split up, some taking over the Shenandoah bridge, others the armory, and a group of six moving up the heights above the village and thence south into the country. There they took as hostages Colonel Lewis Washington (a great-grandnephew of the first President) and one of his neighbors. "Freeing" the slaves of these two gentlemen farmers, they returned with their entourage to Harpers Ferry and delivered their prisoners to Brown at the enginehouse of the armory.

Shortly after midnight the eastbound Baltimore & Ohio train was stopped by the insurgents, and the first casualty occurred. Ironically, the victim was a free Negro, the baggagemaster, who was shot while searching for a missing watchman. As the night wore on, word of the attack spread through the village, but no antislavery townsmen swelled Brown's forces. On the contrary, the citizens began to arm themselves against him.

From an outpost at the rifle works, Brown's lieutenant sent messages urging retreat. Still Brown waited for the whites and the slave population to join him. No bees swarmed.

During the early morning Brown released the captive train, which crossed the Potomac bridge and quickly telegraphed an alarm to Maryland and the capital. At the same time a latter-day Paul Revere pounded south into nearby Charlestown with the news, and by ten o'clock a body of state militia from Charlestown had formed hastily and set out for Harpers Ferry. They arrived about noon and cut off escape to the North by capturing both bridges. Firing had now become general and fatalities numerous; the killing of the town's mayor roused the entire citizenry. In midafternoon Brown's outpost in the rifle works fell. Young Watson Brown, dispatched by his father under a flag of truce to discuss terms, was wounded and dragged himself back to the enginehouse to die. At dusk three companies of militiamen arrived from Maryland, and before midnight a U.S. Cavalry officer named Robert E. Lee rode in from Washington and drew a ring of marines tightly around the armory.

As the night passed and no assistance came, it grew evident to the men penned in the enginehouse that defeat was imminent. Blinded by the justice of his cause to expect help where it was not forthcoming, Brown had misjudged the situation badly. He had overestimated the strength of antislavery sentiment among the well-paid federal mechanics of Harpers Ferry. He had ignored the fact that the slave population of the community consisted primarily of house servants, relatively well treated and disinterested in revolution. And he had failed to take into consideration the speed and strength with which the state militias and federal forces would rally against him.

At dawn a small squad of marines assaulted the enginehouse door, beating it in with a ladder. As they entered, Colonel Washington, standing among the prisoners, pointed to Brown and said, "This is Osawatomie." Brown was "the coolest and firmest man I ever saw in defying danger and death," Washington recorded. "With one son dead by his side and another shot through, he felt the pulse of his dying son with one hand and held his rifle with the other, and commanded his men with the utmost composure, encouraging them to be firm and to sell their lives as dearly as they could."[23]

Marine Commander Green sprang at Brown, lunging at him with his light sword and bringing him to his knees. The sword bent double in striking Brown's belt or a bone; taking the bent weapon in both hands, Green showered blows upon Brown's head, which laid him flat, brought the blood, and seemed as if they must reach the skull, but the weapon was too light to inflict a mortal wound. By failing to buckle on his regulation sabre, Green had unintentionally done a profound service to the cause that John Brown had at heart, and that Green, later a Confederate officer, hated.[24]

Brown was taken to Charlestown, tried, found guilty, and sentenced to death. Throughout the trial he capitalized to the fullest on the tremendous propaganda value of the situation. He had come to Virginia, he said, to carry out a measure that was "perfectly justifiable, to aid those suffering great wrong." "You may dispose of me very easily; I am nearly disposed of now; but," he warned, "the settlement of this Negro question must come up sooner than you are prepared for it." Enjoined by Governor Wise of Virginia to "think upon eternity," Brown replied, "Governor, I have, from all appearances, not more than fifteen or twenty years the start of you in that journey, and whatever my tenure here I am prepared to go. There is an eternity behind and an eternity before, and the little speck in the center, however long, is but comparatively a minute. It behooves you slaveholders to prepare more than it does me."[25] "Jesus of Nazareth was doomed in like manner," he told a reporter. "Why should not I be?" Asked by a friend whether a rescue should be attempted, he replied, "I am worth now infinitely more to die than to live."[26]

On December 2, in accordance with his sentence, he left his cell and climbed into a wagon for the journey to the scaffold. No slaves were present to hail his passing, as he had asked that they might be, for the streets were filled with soldiers. To a bystander he handed the message that would stir Northern hearts: "I, John Brown, am now quite certain that the crimes of this guilty land will never be purged away but with blood."[27]

"This is a beautiful country," he commented as, seated on his coffin, he drew up to the place of execution.[28]

The Sword of Gideon

There were fifteen hundred soldiers present to see that this one old man was hanged. But, watch him as they might, they could detect no sign of flinching. With alacrity the despised Abolitionist climbed down from the wagon and ascended the scaffold. Cheerfully he shook the hands of those near him and bade others adieu. Not when the cap was drawn over his head, his arms pinioned at the elbows, the noose slipped around his neck, was there a single waver. Even in all the unpicturesqueness of his ill-fitting suit and trousers and loose carpet-slippers, John Brown was a wonderfully dignified and impressive figure because of the serenity of his spirit. While the three companies that had been his escort deployed slowly into place, he stood erect as a soldier of the Lord. As if to test his courage to the end, they were a long twelve minutes filing into place, while John Brown showed Virginia how a brave man could die.

"The sheriff asked him," writes Colonel J. T. L. Preston, who stood hard by, "if he should give him a private signal, before the fatal moment. He replied in a voice that sounded to me unnaturally natural—so composed was its tone and so distinct its articulation—that it did not matter to him, if only they would not keep him too long waiting." But the little-drilled troops took forever in moving into place. However, come the word did at last. A single blow of the hatchet in the sheriff's hand and "the would-be Cataline of the South" was hanging between heaven and earth.[29]

"So perish all such enemies of Virginia! All such enemies of the Union! All such foes of the human race!" intoned the officer in charge. And in Albany, New York, a 100-gun salute hailed the birth of a martyr.[30]

Brown's work was done. As the South had been driven to the rim of the maelstrom by his acts of violence, now his moving words and courageous death sent waves of emotionalism across the North. The eloquent voice of New England Abolitionism enshrined him. "Weep for Captain Brown!" cried Thoreau. "Marvellous old man! He has abolished slavery in Virginia," exclaimed Wendell Phillips, and William Lloyd Garrison thundered of his "resurrection."[31] More quickly now the nation moved toward polarization. North and South, moderates who had hoped for a peaceable, permanent solution of the great quandary were swept into one extreme or the other, or saw their influence diminish.

In the name of a great and just cause, a narrowly intense, autocratic old man, ignorant of many things, driven by a vision of himself as an Old Testament instrument of justice, had flaunted the rule of law and brought the country closer to civil conflict. And, in Boston, in Kansas, across the North, citizens who might have stopped him at the first illegal words or at the commission of the earliest crimes had, by default, done the same—had shared in the denial of the constitutional process.

The Puritan warrior who had chosen to be a law unto himself could 379face death with composure—even with complacency. The sword of Gideon had done its duty. His truth was marching on.

Hospital scene in the Union camp at Gettysburg showing a physician about to amputate
a soldier's leg, 1863.

31

That the Nation
Might Live

The grand old ensign—which these people coming
would rob of half its stars—
stood up, and the west wind kissed it
as the sergeants sloped its lance towards the enemy

The fissure of fear and hatred that severed the nation in 1861 moved across the land. On the wooded bluffs of Shiloh and Fredericksburg, in the swamps along the James, over the creeks of Bull Run and Antietam, and in the forests of Chancellorsville, it took visible form in the battle lines of civil conflict. Now, on July 3, 1863, a few miles south of the town of Gettysburg, Pennsylvania, it had assumed the shape of an old stone wall, hurriedly reinforced with fence rails and mud, zigzagging along the crest of a sprawling rise. It shimmered back the glare and heat of the noonday sun, until the men behind it struggled to remain alert, and those across the valley below shielded their eyes to keep it in focus.

Two days of fighting had left undecided the issue of whether Meade's Army of the Potomac, entrenched now on the crest of Cemetery Ridge, could repel Lee's invasion of the North. The day before, the Confederates had come close to carrying the strategic heights commanding the Union left and had effected a lodgement up the slope on the Union right. But they had been repulsed from "Little Round Top" on the left, and in the course of this morning their advanced position on the right had been thrust back by a Union counterassault. The sounds of that engagement had now died away, and for more than an hour a torpid silence had lain over the countryside, dulling awareness that one of the most decisive and important battles of the war was about to begin.

General Gibbon, commander of the Union Second Corps, examined the disposition of his men along the thousand feet of the line's center where the wall dipped below the crest, jutting forward around a clump of trees. Satisfied, he returned with his staff officers to the ambulance that served as their headquarters. There, in the shade of a peach orchard, they ate lunch and lay down to rest. The general's aide, Lieutenant Frank Haskell, later described the scene to his brother:

We dozed in the heat and lolled upon the ground, with half open eyes. Our horses were hitched to the trees munching oats. A great lull rested upon all the field. For want of something better to do, I looked at my watch. It was five minutes before one o'clock. I stretched myself upon the ground, and suddenly there came the distinct sharp sound of one of the enemy's guns, square over to the front, and we saw directly above the crest the smoke of the bursting shell. In an instant, before a word was spoken, the report of gun after gun in rapid succession smote our ears and their shells plunged down and exploded all around us. We sprang to our feet and started for the front.

The men of the infantry have seized their arms, and behind their works, behind every rock in every ditch wherever there is any shelter, they hug the ground, silent, quiet, little harmed. The enemy's line is some two miles long, concave on the side toward us, and their range is from one thousand to eighteen hundred yards. One hundred and twenty-five rebel guns, we estimate, are now active, firing ten- to twenty-four–pound projectiles of many shapes. From the cemetery on our right to Round Top hill on our left, with over a hundred guns, our batteries reply. We thought, at the second Bull Run, at Antietam, and at Fredericksburg, that we had heard heavy cannonading; they were but holiday salutes compared to this. The projectiles shriek long and sharp. They hiss, they scream, they growl, they sputter. The shells swoop down among the battery horses. A half dozen of them stumble, their legs stiffen, their vitals and blood smear the ground. Men hobble back from the crest, or, pale and weak, lie on the ground with the mangled stump of an arm or leg, dripping their life-blood away. We saw them but a moment since there among the flame, with brawny arms and muscles of iron wielding the rammer and pushing home the cannon's plethoric load.

Half past two o'clock, an hour and a half since the commencement, and still the cannonade did not in the least abate. Our infantry was still unshaken, had suffered very little. The enemy, probably supposing our infantry was massed behind the crest and the batteries, fired too high, cut his fuses to the shells too long.

Chapters from the American Experience

Our batteries had been hurt much more severely. A great number of horses had been killed, in some batteries more than half of all. Guns had been dismounted. Many caissons, limbers and carriages had been de- stroyed, and usually from ten to twenty-five men to each battery had been struck, at least along our part of the crest. Our ammunition was exhausted, our guns fouled, our batteries unfit for further immediate use.

At three o'clock almost precisely the last shot hummed, and bounded and fell, and the cannonade was over. Men began to breathe more freely, and to ask, What next? Some batteries from the artillery reserve were moving up to take the places of the disabled ones; the smoke was clearing from the crests. There was a pause between acts, with the curtain soon to rise upon the final catastrophe of Gettysburg.[1]

During the closing minutes of the artillery attack, across the fields behind the Confederate line, an officer was hurriedly scribbling a note to his sweetheart. General George Pickett wrote of the attack his infantry division was about to make on the enemy and of the doubts that assailed his immediate superior, General Peter Longstreet, at the prospect of flinging his men across the rolling, open terrain up the slope against a defended position.

A summons came from Old Peter, and I immediately rode where he and Marse Robert [E. Lee] were making a reconnaissance of Meade's position.

"Great God!" said Old Peter as I came up. "Look, General Lee, at the insurmountable difficulties between our line and that of the Yankees—the steep hills, the tiers of artillery, the fences, the heavy skirmish line—and we'll have to fight our infantry against their batteries."

"The enemy is there, General Longstreet, and I am going to strike him," said Marse Robert in his firm, quiet, determined voice.

I rode with them along our line of prostrate infantry. The men had been forbidden to cheer, but they arose and lifted in reverential adoration their caps to our beloved commander. Oh, the responsibility for the lives of such men as these! Well, my darling, their fate and that of our beloved Southland will be settled ere your glorious brown eyes rest on these scraps of penciled paper.

Our line of battle faces Cemetery Ridge. The men are lying in the rear, and the hot July sun pours its scorching rays almost vertically down on them. The suffering is almost unbearable. I have never seen Old Peter so grave and troubled. For several minutes after I had saluted him he looked at me without speaking. Then in an agonized voice, the reserve all gone, he said, "Pickett, I am being crucified. I have instructed Alexander to give you your orders, I can't."

While he was yet speaking, a note was brought to me from Alexander.

That the Nation Might Live

After reading it I handed it to Pete, asking if I should obey and go forward. He looked at me for a moment, then held out his hand. Presently, clasping his other hand over mine without speaking, he bowed his head on his breast. I shall never forget the look on his face nor the clasp of his hand, and I saw tears glistening on his cheeks and beard. The stern old war horse, God bless him, was weeping for his men and, I know, praying too that this cup might pass from them. It is almost three o'clock.
YOUR SOLDIER[2]

"I would gladly have given up my position rather than share in the responsibilities of that day," Lieutenant General Longstreet wrote later.

It was thus I felt when Pickett and his brave men marched over the crest of our knoll and began his descent of the slope. As he passed me he rode gracefully, with his jaunty cap raked well over on his right ear and his long auburn locks, nicely dressed, hanging almost to his shoulders. He seemed rather a holiday soldier than a general at the head of a column which was about to make one of the grandest, most desperate assaults recorded in the annals of wars. Armistead and Garnett, two of his brigadiers, were veterans of nearly a quarter of a century's service. Their minds seemed absorbed in the men behind, and in the bloody work before them. Kemper, the other brigadier, was younger but had experienced many severe battles. He was leading my old brigade that I had drilled on Manassas plains before the first battle on that field. The troops advanced in well-closed ranks and with elastic step, their faces lighted with hope. Before them lay several fences, a field of corn, a little swale running through it and then a rise from that point to the Federal stronghold.[3]

Beyond the stone wall that marked the limit of the "Federal stronghold," Union General Gibbon and his aide, Lieutenant Haskell, had moved below the crest and out of sight of the enemy. Suddenly they noted that their chief of artillery was galloping about, giving rapid orders as to the guns that had been brought up from the reserve. A moment later someone shouted that the Confederate infantry was advancing across the fields, and Haskell and his general hurried to the crest.

None on that crest now needed to be told that the enemy was advancing. Every eye could see his legions sweeping upon us. Regiment after regiment and brigade after brigade moved from the woods and rapidly took their places in the lines forming the assault. Pickett's proud division, with some additional troops, held their right; Pettigrew's their left. The first line at short interval was followed by a second, and that succeeded by a third, the columns between supporting the lines. More than half a mile their front extended, dull gray masses, man touching man, rank pressing rank, and line supporting line. The red flags waved; their horsemen galloped up and down; the arms of eighteen thousand men gleamed in the sun. Right on they moved, as with one soul, in perfect order, through orchard and meadow, and cornfield, magnificent, grim, irresistible.

All was orderly and still upon our crest. The men had little need of commands. The survivors of a dozen battles, they knew well enough what this array in front portended and would be prepared to act when the time should come. The click of the locks as each man raised the hammer to feel that the cap was on the nipple, the sharp jar as a musket touched a stone upon the wall, the clicking of iron axles as guns were rolled by hand a little further to the front—were quite all the sounds that could be heard.

General Gibbon rode down the lines. "Don't hurry men. Let them come up close before you fire, and then aim low and steadily." Along the lines in front, the grand old ensign that first waved in battle at Saratoga in 1777—and which these people coming would rob of half its stars—stood up, and the west wind kissed it as the sergeant sloped its lance towards the enemy. I believe that not one of us but blessed his God that he was loyal to it, the emblem of the Republic waving there before those flaunting rags of treason advancing across the fields.

Five minutes had elapsed since first the enemy emerged from the woods—no great space of time surely, but long enough for us to note that upon our ability to hold the crest and repel the assault depended the honor of the Army of the Potomac and defeat or victory at Gettysburg. And it was long enough for the Rebel storm to drift across more than half the space that had at first separated it from us.

Our skirmishers opened a spattering fire along the front, and, fighting, retired upon the main line. Then the thunder of our guns shook and reverberated again through the air, and their sounding shells struck the enemy. The General said I had better go and tell General Meade of this advance. To gallop to General Meade's headquarters and be again upon the crest was but the work of a minute. All our available guns were now active, and from the fire of shells, as the range grew shorter and shorter, they changed to shrapnel, and from shrapnel to canister.

But in spite of shells, and shrapnel, and canister—without wavering or halting—the hardy lines of the enemy continue toward us. Their right flank sweeps near Stannard's bushy crest, and his concealed Vermonters rake it with a well-delivered fire of musketry. The gray lines do not halt or reply, but, withdrawing a little from that extreme, still move on. And so across all that broad open ground they have come, nearer and nearer, with our guns bellowing in their faces, until now a hundred yards, no more, divide our ready left from their advancing right.

The eager men there are impatient to begin. Let them. The breastworks flame. As if our bullets were the fire coals that touched off their muskets, the enemy in front pauses and his countless level barrels blaze back at us. The rattling storm soon spreads to the right. All along each hostile front the volleys blaze and roll, as thick the sound as when a summer hailstorm pelts the city roofs.

Now our batteries become silent, for they have been the targets of the concentrated Rebel bullets and some of them have spent all their canister. But they are not silent before Rhorty has been killed, Woodruff has fallen mortally wounded, and Cushing, firing almost his last canister, has dropped dead among his guns, shot through the head. The conflict is left to the infantry alone.

Save myself, there is now not a mounted officer near the engaged lines. The conflict is tremendous, but I have seen no wavering in all our line. Then —my God, it is true—the larger portion of Webb's brigade, there by the group of trees at the angle of the wall, is breaking from the cover of their works, and, without orders or reason, with no hand lifted to check them, is falling back.

A great magnificent passion comes on me at the instant. My sword, that has always hung idle by my side, the sign of rank only in every battle, I draw, bright and gleaming—the symbol of command. As I meet the tide of these rabbits, the damned red flags of the rebellion begin to thicken and flaunt along the wall they have just deserted, and one is already waving over the guns of the dead Cushing. I order these men to "halt," and "face about" and "fire," and they obey. General Webb comes to my assistance. He is on foot, but does all he can to repair the breach and avert calamity. The men soon regain confidence. This portion of the wall has been lost to us. But Webb's men, with their bodies partially protected by the abruptness of the crest, now send back in the enemies' faces as fierce a storm.

Red flags accumulate at the wall before us. Webb's men are falling fast, and it becomes apparent that, however well they may do, they will soon be overpowered. I gallop to the left to see if Hall and Harrow can not send some of their commands to reinforce Webb. As I attain the rear of Hall's line it is easy to see the reason and the manner of this gathering of Rebel flags in front of Webb. The enemy is concentrating all his right against the point in our line near the trees at the angle of the wall. There is the stress of his assault; there would he drive his fiery wedge to split our line. In front of Harrow's and Hall's brigades he has been able to advance no nearer than when he first halted to deliver fire; these commands have not yielded an inch.

Not a moment must be lost. I find Colonel Hall just in rear of his line.

Chapters from the American Experience

"Webb is hotly pressed and must have support, or he will be overpowered." In briefest time five friendly colors are hurrying to the point of attack, and Hall's men are fighting gallantly beside Webb's. General Harrow I do not see, but his fighting men will answer as well; all the men that I can find I take over to the right at the double quick.

As we move near, I can see that the enemy's right, under Hall's fire, is beginning to stagger and break. The men see too, and, as they sweep to their places and open fire, they roar, and this says more plainly than words—for the deaf could see it in their faces, and the blind could hear it in their voices—*the crest is safe.*

As our position has changed, so has the enemy's. Before this Second Division he is massed, the main bulk of his force covered by the ground that slopes to his rear, with his front at the stone wall. Between his front and us extends the very apex of the crest. Twelve of our regiments in three brigades are below or behind the crest, in such a position that by the exposure of the head and upper part of the body above the crest they can deliver their fire in the enemy's faces along the top of the wall. Formation of companies and regiments in regular ranks is lost. Commands, companies, regiments, and brigades are blended and intermixed, an irregular extended mass—men enough, if in order, to form a line of four or five ranks along the whole front of the division. The twelve flags of the regiments wave defiantly at intervals along the front. At the stone wall stream nearly double this number of enemy battle flags.

Though no abatement in the general din has been noticeable during these changes in position, now it is as though a new battle, deadlier, stormier than before, has sprung from the body of the old. The jostling, swaying lines on either side boil, and roar, and dash their flamy spray —two hostile billows of a fiery ocean. Thick flashes stream from the wall, thick volleys answer from the crest. No threats or expostulation now, only example and encouragement. All depths of passion are stirred, all combative fires—down to their deep foundations. Individuality is drowned in a sea of clamor, and timid men, breathing the breath of the multitude, are brave.

The dead and wounded lie where they stagger and fall—there is no humanity for them now. None can be spared to care for them. The men do not cheer or shout; they growl. And over that uneasy sea, heard with the roar of musketry, sweeps the muttered thunder of a storm of growls. Now the loyal wave rolls up as if it would overleap its barrier, the crest. "Forward to the wall" is answered by the Rebel counter-command, "Steady, men!" and the wave swings back.

Again it surges, and again it sinks. These men of Pennsylvania, on the soil of their own homesteads—the first to flee the wall—must be the first to storm it. "Major, lead your men over the crest, they will follow." "By

That the Nation Might Live

the tactics I understand, my place is in the rear of the men." "Your pardon, sir; I see your place is behind your men. I thought you were fit to lead."

"Captain, come on with your men." "Let me first stop this fire in the rear, or we shall be hit by our own men." "Never mind the fire in the rear, let us take care of this in front first."

"Sergeant, forward with your color. Let the Rebels see it close to their eyes once before they die." The color sergeant of the 72nd Pennsylvania, grasping the stump of the severed lance in both his hands, waves the flag above his head and rushes towards the wall. "Will you see your color storm the wall alone?" One man only starts to follow. Almost half way to the wall, down go color bearer and color to the ground—the gallant sergeant is dead.

The line springs—the crest of the solid ground, with a great roar, heaves forward its maddened load—men, arms, smoke, fire—a fighting mass. It rolls to the wall. Flash meets flash. The wall is crossed.

A moment ensues of thrusts, yells, blows, shots, and undistinguishable conflict, followed by a shout universal. The last and bloodiest fight of the great battle of Gettysburg is ended and won.

When the vortex of battle passion had subsided, and we were calm enough to look about us, we saw that, as with us, the fighting elsewhere was ended. In that moment the judgment almost refused to credit the senses. Were these abject wretches about us, whom our men were driving together in flocks, the jaunty men of Pickett's Division, whose steady lines and flashing arms but a few moments since had come sweeping up the slope to destroy us? Were these red cloths that our men tossed about the "fiery Southern crosses," the battle flags of the rebellion that had waved defiance at the wall?[4]

Across the fields, from his advanced position with supporting guns, Confederate artillery chief, Colonel Alexander—to whom General Longstreet had delegated the responsibility of initiating the charge—watched the retreat sadly as it moved toward and past him.

Human life was being poured out like water. Of Pickett's three brigadiers, Garnett and Armistead were killed and Kemper dangerously wounded. We ceased fire in order to save ammunition in case the enemy should advance, but held our ground as boldly as possible, though we were entirely without support, and very low on ammunition.

About that time General Lee, entirely alone, rode up and remained with me for a long time. He then probably first appreciated the full extent of the disaster as the disorganized stragglers made their way back past us. He urged the retreating stragglers to rally as soon as they got back to cover, saying that the failure was his fault, not theirs.

Little by little we got some guns to the rear to replenish and refit, and get in condition to fight again, and some we held boldly in advanced positions all along the line. Sharp-shooters came out and worried some of the men, and single guns would fire on these, sometimes very rapidly, and manage to keep them back; some parts of the line had not even a picket in front. But the enemy's artillery generally let us alone, and I certainly saw no reason to disturb the *entente cordiale*. Night came very slowly, but came at last.[5]

General Pickett, who, despite his daring, was one of the "fortunates" to return to the Confederate lines, sought release for his anguish by penning another brief note to his fiancée:

My brave boys were so full of hope and confident of victory as I led them forth! Over on Cemetery Ridge the Federals beheld a scene which has never previously been enacted—an army forming in line of battle in full view, under their very eyes—charging across a space nearly a mile in length, pride and glory soon to be crushed by an overwhelming heartbreak.

Well, it is all over now. . . .

I can still hear them cheering as I gave the order, "Forward!" the thrill of their joyous voices as they called out, "We'll follow you, Marse George, we'll follow you! Oh, how faithfully they followed me on—on—to their death, and I led them on—on—on—Oh, God!

I can't write you a love letter today, my Sally. But for you, my darling, I would rather, a million times rather, sleep in an unknown grave. Your sorrowing SOLDIER[6]

The Confederates retreated to the Potomac and beyond. The jubilant Union men rejoiced, resting on their laurels. President Lincoln came to Cemetery Ridge and said his immortal words. And the hill, with its graves and its stone wall, was left to sleep in the summer heat. The fissure of war had moved on.

Abraham Lincoln

Alexander Gardner, April 10, 1865.
Courtesy Library of Congress.

32

O Captain, My Captain

With malice toward none; with charity for all.

When Abraham Lincoln died, the nation mourned him as one of its greatest leaders. Yet, four years before, he had come to the Presidency under a cloud of derision and doubt. In part Lincoln's rapid emergence as a national demigod rose out of the events through which he piloted the country and out of the circumstances of his death. But, in large measure, it was wrought by the man himself, for, as he wrestled, day by day, with the burden that had been laid upon him, his subtle skills, deep understanding, and inspirational strength of character became increasingly evident to the nation. Threading his way through those dark years of civil conflict, Lincoln recorded some of his thoughts in speeches and in letters, and his friends and enemies entered their impressions of the President and his words in their diaries and memoirs. From these it is possible to put together a sketch of Lincoln as he rose to unparalleled challenges and of the Americans as they came to recognize his strength and to revere him.*

Among the Southern elite, on the eve of the inauguration, one heard

*For a judgment of Lincoln as a conscious contriver of his own legend, who "created himself as a poetic figure" and sold the North and posterity on his views as to the "meaning of the Civil War," see Edmund Wilson, *Patriotic Gore: Studies in the Literature of the American Civil War* (New York: Oxford University Press, 1962), pp. 99–130.

"from all quarters" that the "vulgarity" of Lincoln and his wife were "beyond credence," says Mary Chestnut's *Diary from Dixie*. The President-elect was the kind always to be found "at the corner stores, sitting on boxes, whittling sticks, and telling stories as funny as they are vulgar."[1]

The stereotype circulated freely through the North too. "Abraham Lincoln looks very awkward," wrote a woman correspondent for a Massachusetts paper. "Mrs. Lincoln is very dumpy and very good-natured and very gorgeous; she stuns me with her low-necked dresses and the flower-beds which she carries on the top of her head."[2] Even in his own party, Radicals criticized his "cringing and whining" attitude toward the South, and some Moderates, appalled at the chirruping optimism of his pre-inauguration speeches, wondered whether they had not elected a "simple Susan."[3]

Emerson—or at least the Abolitionist in Emerson—commented biliously on Lincoln's "bad manners."

You cannot refine Mr. Lincoln's taste, extend his horizon, or clear his judgment; he will not walk dignifiedly through the traditional part of the President of America, but will pop out his head at each railroad station and make a little speech, and get into an argument with Squire A and Judge B. But this we must be ready for, and let the clown appear, and hug ourselves that we are well off, if we have got good nature, honest meaning, and fidelity to public interest instead of an elegant roué.[4]

Newspaper cartoons pictured Lincoln as a gangling, straggle-haired oaf, squeezed into ill-fitting clothes and speaking in exaggerated frontier vernacular. Gleefully they made capital of the fact that, warned of a mass assassination plot in Baltimore, he had yielded to the urgings of friends and slipped secretly into Washington under heavy guard. "Lanky Lincoln came to town, In night and wind and rain, sir, Wrapped in a military cloak, Upon a special train, sir," quipped the *Louisville Courier*. Cartoonists drew him enveloped in a cloak-and-dagger greatcoat or dancing outlandishly into the capital in a skirt of Highland plaids.[5]

The scion of the illustrious Adams family was in Washington that winter—young Henry Adams, who was serving as his father's private secretary and who would one day write an autobiography in which he described morosely and with great artistry his unavailing lifelong search for an education. Henry had voted for Lincoln and had observed with distaste the inescapable air of conspiracy that permeated the capital.[6]

He found particularly obnoxious the "hundreds of Southern gentlemen" —leaders of Washington society—who were "engaged in the plainest breach of faith and the blackest secret conspiracy" and who had noth- ing to contribute to anyone's education except "bad temper, bad manners, poker, and treason."* But, typically, though Adams found the opposition comtemptible, he cherished few hopes for the incoming administration. Attending the "melancholy function" called the Inaugural Ball, he "looked anxiously" to the new President for some "sign of character," but found none.[7] Years later he would write:

> He saw a long, awkward figure; a plain, ploughed face; a mind, absent in part, and in part evidently worried by white kid gloves; features that expressed neither self-satisfaction nor any other familiar Americanism, but rather the same painful sense of becoming educated and of needing education that tormented a private secretary; above all a lack of apparent force. Any private secretary in the least fit for his business would have thought, as Adams did, that no man living needed so much education as the new President but that all the education he could get would not be enough.[8]

Thus, with influential Americans from every part of the country conceding his honesty but despairing of his judgment and his educability and lampooning him as a vulgar clown, the new President assumed his heavy responsibilities.

On the evening of his arrival in Washington, he met with delegates from the seven states that had seceded. One of the Southerners asserted that the responsibility lay with Lincoln whether there would be war and the grass "grow in the streets of our commercial cities." Lincoln replied that, if it depended on him, the grass would "not grow anywhere except in the fields."

"Then you will yield to the just demands of the South?" pressed his interrogator. At this Lincoln responded soberly that he did not know just what his actions and opinions might be in the future but that he was sure of one thing. In taking the oath of office, he would swear to preserve, protect, and defend the Constitution—not just as he would like to have it, but as it was—and this he intended to do. The Constitution must be respected and obeyed in "every part of every one of the United States," he warned, "let the grass grow where it may."[9]

*Secession badges were sold openly and Confederate ladies wore short striped skirts and blue blouses ornamented with seven stars (symbolic of the seven states already in rebellion).

O Captain, My Captain

In his inaugural message on March 4, Lincoln sounded this same note. After first assuring the South that he had no intention of interfering with slavery in the states where it existed and promising to uphold the Fugitive Slave Law, he warned that the Union was "perpetual" and the "acts of violence . . . against the authority of the United States" were "insurrectionary or revolutionary." The Union, he pledged, would "defend and maintain itself."

A rebellious minority must not be permitted to thwart the will of the majority, he insisted; for the will of the majority must prevail in a free land. Unanimity is impossible among all citizens of a great country. Therefore control must be vested in either the majority or a minority. If any minority rules permanently, the people are not free. It follows then, that "the only true sovereign of a free people" is the will of the majority. This will must be restrained by Constitutional checks and kept responsive to changes in public opinion, but it is the only possible instrument of freedom. Rejecting "the majority principle" leads only to "anarchy or despotism in some form."

Lincoln begged the South to "think calmly" on their action—to wait for justice to work its way out through the democratic process:

Why should there not be a patient confidence in the ultimate justice of the people? Is there any better or equal hope in the world? . . . If the Almighty Ruler of Nations, with his eternal truth and justice, be on your side of the North, or on yours of the South, that truth and that justice will surely prevail by the judgment of this great tribunal of the American people. . . .

. . . Intelligence, patriotism, Christianity, and a firm reliance on Him who has never yet forsaken this favored land are still competent to adjust, in the best way, all our present difficulty.

He put the onus for any possible war directly on the South:

In *your* hands, my dissatisfied fellow-countrymen, and not in *mine,* is the momentous issue of civil war. The Government will not assail *you.* You can have no conflict without being yourselves the aggressors. *You* have no oath registered in Heaven to destroy the Government, while I shall have the most solemn one to "preserve, protect, and defend it."

Lincoln concluded on a conciliatory note:

I am loath to close. We are not enemies, but friends. We must not be enemies. Though passion may have strained, it must not break our bonds of affection. The mystic chords of memory, stretching from every battle-field and patriot grave to every living heart and hearthstone all over this broad land, will yet swell the chorus of the Union, when again touched, as surely they will be, by the better angels of our nature.[10]

Describing the inaugural ceremony, one young major wrote to his father in Massachusetts:

When the address closed and the cheering subsided, Taney rose, and, almost as tall as Lincoln, he administered the oath, Lincoln repeating it; and as the words, "preserve, protect and defend the Constitution" came ringing out, he bent and kissed the book; and for one, I breathed freer and gladder than for months. The man looked a man, and acted a man and a President.[11]

On April 12, with the firing on Fort Sumter, the "bonds of affection" broke. The nation was at war. Lincoln recognized the crucial impor-tance of placing the blame for aggression firmly on the South. With Virginia and three other states now joining the Confederacy, the border states of Kentucky and Missouri had come to hold the balance of power between the sections, and the need to keep them in the Union became imperative. Nor could the North afford to appear the aggressor in the eyes of England and France, whose possible alliance with the South presented a constant threat.

In a message to Congress, which he called into special session in July, Lincoln made it clear that the assault on the federal garrison at Fort Sumter could not be justified on the grounds of self-defense. Southern-ers had opened the bombardment "without a gun in sight, save only a few in the fort sent to that harbor years before for their own protec-tion." By this attack, "the assailants of the government began the con-flict of arms." Deep issues were at stake, he said; the war was a testing —a testing by fire—of all free government.

This issue embraces more than the fate of these United States. It pre-sents to the whole family of man the question whether a constitutional republic or democracy—a government of the people by the same people —can or cannot maintain its territorial integrity against its own domestic foes. It presents the question whether discontented individuals, too few in numbers to control administration according to organic law in any case, can always, upon the pretenses made in this case, or on any other pre-

O Captain, My Captain

tenses, break up their government, and thus practically put an end to free government upon the earth. It forces us to ask: "Is there, in all republics, this inherent and fatal weakness?" "Must a government, of necessity, be too strong for the liberties of its own people, or too weak to maintain its own existence?"[12]

"Union" was to be the theme of Lincoln's administration. All else was secondary. "My policy is to have no policy," he told his secretary, and this flexibility would apply to all *means* employed.[13] But not to the ultimate objective. To the preservation of the Union—as the democratic hope of the world—he dedicated himself and his administration with undeviating purpose.

Lincoln's first practical task was to create an army. At the outbreak of hostilities the Union Army had only a few thousand soldiers, and these were, for the most part, scattered along the frontier. Lincoln issued a call for men at once, and enthusiastic Northerners rushed to the colors while their wives and mothers sewed them uniforms (of considerable variety in fabric and styling), their fathers polished up the family pistols to supplement their scanty arms, and German drill sergeants shouted "Eyes vront! Toes oud! Leetle finger mit de seam de banteloons!"[14] On July 21, with fine spirit and confidence, the first units of this army went into battle at Bull Run. By nightfall they were in pell-mell retreat, their morale shattered.

Two days later Lincoln appeared unexpectedly at their camp. He wanted, he told General William T. Sherman (then a colonel), to talk to "the boys." Sherman asked him to "discourage all cheering, noise, or any sort of confusion." They had had enough of that before Bull Run; what they needed was "cool, thoughtful, hard-fighting soldiers—no more hurrahing, no more humbug." "He took my remarks in the most perfect good-nature," recorded Sherman in his *Memoirs.* [15] They came to the first camp, and Lincoln stood up in his carriage to address the men.

[He] made one of the neatest, best, and most feeling addresses I ever listened to [Sherman wrote], referring to our late disaster at Bull Run, the high duties that still devolved on us, and the brighter days yet to come. At one or two points the soldiers began to cheer, but he promptly checked them, saying: "Don't cheer, boys. I confess I rather like it myself, but Colonel Sherman here says it is not military; and I guess we had better defer to his opinion." In winding up, he explained that, as President, he was commander-in-chief; that he was resolved that the soldiers should have

every thing that the law allowed; and he called on one and all to appeal to him personally in case they were wronged. The effect of this speech was excellent.
We passed along in the same manner to all the camps of my brigade; and Mr. Lincoln complimented me highly for the order, cleanliness, and discipline that he observed. Indeed, he assured me that it was the first bright moment [he] had experienced since the battle.[16]

In the crowd at the last camp, Sherman noticed an officer with whom he had had a confrontation at reveille that morning. The officer, a lawyer, had complained at not being paid and said he was going home, whereupon Sherman had warned that, if he tried to leave without permission, he would "shoot him like a dog." Hearing Lincoln's promise to listen to complaints, the malcontent came forward and said:

"Mr. President, I have a cause of grievance. This morning I went to speak to Colonel Sherman, and he threatened to shoot me," [Sherman's account continues]. Mr. Lincoln, who was still standing, said, "Threatened to shoot you?" "Yes sir, he threatened to shoot me." Mr. Lincoln looked at him, then at me, and—stooping his tall spare form toward the officer—said to him in a loud stage-whisper, easily heard for some yards around: "Well, if I were you, and he threatened to shoot, I would not trust him, for I believe he would do it." The officer turned about and disappeared, and the men laughed. Soon the carriage drove on, and I explained the facts to the President, who answered, "I thought you knew your own business best." I thanked him for his confidence, and assured him that what he had done would go far to enable me to maintain good discipline, and it did.[17]

While the Union Army gradually took shape, the navy underwent a similar transition. Less than a week after the firing on Fort Sumter, Lincoln proclaimed a blockade of the entire Confederate seaboard. On paper such a blockade looked good, for the South, with its highly specialized economy, depended heavily on imports. But many Northerners doubted the practicality of proposing to isolate 3,500 miles of Rebel coastline (rich in long, navigable inland passages) with a navy that was virtually nonexistent. Foreign powers tended to greet the announcement with amused contempt. A navy paymaster analyzed the problems Lincoln faced in enforcing his ban.

When Mr. Lincoln issued this proclamation we had only forty-two ships in commission in our navy. Most of them were absent on foreign stations, and only one efficient war-ship . . . was available for immediate service. . . .

There were twenty-eight old ships of war lying dismantled at the various navy-yards. Those that were worth repairing were fitted for sea as rapidly as possible. All the available merchant vessels that could be made to carry a battery, including tugs and old New York ferry-boats, were purchased and converted into fighting ships as hastily as the limited facilities of the Northern ports would permit. . . .

The total number of seamen at all the Northern naval stations available for immediate detail amounted to only two hundred and seven; and it must be remembered that it was as important that they should be trained to handle heavy guns at sea as that they should be good seamen. . . . Officers and men from the merchant service freely offered themselves. Gunnery schools were established at the naval stations for their instruction. As fast as the volunteers could be given an elementary training in the handling of heavy guns, they were sent to sea. This was continued for three years, by which time we had six hundred and fifty vessels and over fifty thousand men afloat. . . .

. . . At the beginning of the war . . . blockade-running was carried on from Chesapeake Bay to the mouth of the Rio Grande, by vessels of all sorts, sizes and nationalities. . . .

. . . The British . . . felt confident that they could monopolize the Southern cotton and the markets of the Confederacy; but when it was found . . . that the perils to their beautiful vessels and precious cargoes increased as fast as their efforts to surmount them [and even faster] . . . they finally gave up the business, admitting that the blockade was a success.[18]

Long before events had justified Lincoln's course in proclaiming this blockade, an incident rose out of it which threatened to end the war with a Southern victory. In the fall of 1861 the Union sloop of war *San Jacinto*, under the freewheeling Captain Charles Wilkes, stopped the British packet *Trent* and forcibly carried off two Confederate diplomats, James Mason and John Slidell. Across the North the news of this escapade was greeted with joy. But the British leaders, furious, demanded that the Americans set the two men free or expect war with Britain. Members of the Cabinet and Senator Charles Sumner (Chairman of the Committee on Foreign Relations) met constantly with the President, seeking a solution to this grave crisis. Perhaps no other decision of the war would be more crucial. With time running out, they convened on Christmas Day to hear Secretary of State William H. Seward present the draft of a letter he proposed to send to England. It would, he felt, enable them to salve American patriotic sentiment and, at the same time, accede to British demands. He suggested they assume the position that, since the two diplomats were "contraband," Captain Wilkes should have seized ship and all—and delivered it to a prize court. In taking the two men from the British vessel, he had followed a tactic in which the British had often indulged—a tactic that violated American principles. Therefore they were returning the Confederate envoys. The reaction of Lincoln and his Cabinet to this proposal was mixed.

Adroit as Seward had shown himself to be in finding a way out of this deadlock, his colleagues were slow to be convinced. To give way to detested Albion, even when a pistol was pointed at Uncle Sam's head, came hard. . . . Though the cabinet discussed the matter from ten o'clock in the morning till two in the afternoon, no conclusion had been reached. It was therefore decided to adjourn and meet the following morning. After all the others had left the cabinet room, Lincoln and Seward found themselves alone. "You will go on, of course," Lincoln said to Seward, "preparing your answer, which, as I understand it, will state the reasons why they ought to be given up. Now I have a mind to try my hand at stating the reasons why they ought*not* to be given up. We will compare the points on each side." Lincoln did formulate such an argument and it is now preserved among his papers. . . . When the cabinet reconvened the next morning, however, Lincoln did not present his thesis. All seven men now accepted Seward's answer. After the cabinet broke up, Lincoln and Seward again held a private session. Seward referred to their talk of the day before. "You thought you might frame an argument for the other side?" Lincoln smiled and shook his head. "I found that I could not make an argument that would satisfy my own mind," he said. "That proved to me that your ground was the right one."[19]

"It was a pretty bitter pill to swallow," Lincoln later admitted.[20] But victory was the objective; their pride was expendable.

Victory was not coming easily. Following the disaster at Bull Run, Lincoln had turned to General George B. McClellan for military leadership, making him first Commander of the Army of the Potomac and the General-in-Chief of the Army. Young McClellan, who possessed real ability as an organizer, quickly trained and disciplined the troops and began planning his strategy. The fall season went by, and McClellan continued to drill and plan. As it became evident that he would not get an offensive under way before the winter rains, criticism of him grew widespread and bitter.

O Captain, My Captain

Lincoln and Seward called on the general one evening to discuss the situation. An hour passed while they waited for him to return from a wedding he was attending. When he came in, McClellan went directly upstairs to bed without speaking to his illustrious visitors. Horrified, Lincoln's personal secretary described the breach and added: "I merely record this unparalleled insolence of epaulettes without comment. . . . Coming home, I spoke to the President about the matter but he seemed not to have noticed it especially, saying it was better at this time not to be making points of etiquette and personal dignity."[21]

Committees of eminent men called on the President to protest the general's inaction—to raise a question as to his courage and even his loyalty. Still Lincoln waited, refusing to act against McClellan or to criticize him further than to admit that the general had "the slows," and that, if McClellan did not "want to use" the army, he would like to "borrow" it.[22]

February came, and with it the sudden illness and death of Lincoln's son, Willie, and the beginning of a long and morbid mourning and withdrawal on the part of Mrs. Lincoln. Pressing military problems impinged on Lincoln's grief. McClellan, whom he had sent to Harpers Ferry to reopen the Baltimore & Ohio Railroad and destroy enemy batteries on the river, discovered belatedly that the pontoon boats with which he had planned to make a bridge across the Potomac were too wide to pass through the river locks. Lincoln called in the general's father-in-law, General Marcy. His secretary noted his harassed words of rebuke:

Why in the nation . . . couldn't the General have known whether a boat would go through that lock before spending a million dollars getting them there? I am no engineer, but it seems to me that if I wished to know whether a boat would go through a hole or a lock, common-sense would teach me to go and measure it. I am almost despairing at these results. Everything seems to fail.[23]

McClellan was reduced from his position as general-in-chief and left only with the command of the Army of Potomac. There followed an unenthusiastic, unsuccessful campaign against Richmond. "The fact is," said Lincoln wearily, "the people have not yet made up their minds that we are at war with the South."

[They] have got the idea into their heads that we are going to get out of this fix somehow by strategy! That's the word—*strategy!* General

McClellan thinks he is going to whip the Rebels by strategy; and the army has got the same notion. They have no idea that the War is to be carried on and put through by hard, tough fighting, that it will hurt somebody; and no headway is going to be made while this delusion lasts.[24]

Believing that the North could only win the war by taking the offensive, Lincoln was deeply discouraged by such lukewarm campaigning. He began for the first time to consider, as a military expedient, the emancipation of the slaves in Rebel territory. He had long hated slavery and had fought against its extension, but, recognizing the overwhelming difficulties that immediate emancipation would raise, he had favored a gradual freeing of the slaves. However, the military disappointments, the threat of foreign intervention, and the pressure from powerful elements in the Republican Party brought him, in July, 1862, to the point where he was seriously considering the move. Later he explained how pragmatically his decision had developed:

It had got to be midsummer, 1862. Things had gone on from bad to worse, until I felt that we had reached the end of our rope on the plan of operations we had been pursuing; that we had about played our last card, and must change our tactics, or lose the game! I now determined upon the adoption of the emancipation policy; and, without consultation with, or the knowledge of the Cabinet, I prepared the original draft of the proclamation, and, after much anxious thought, called a Cabinet meeting upon the subject.[25]

The Cabinet did not endorse Lincoln's idea, and (at Seward's suggestion) he decided to defer further discussion of it until the long string of military setbacks had been interrupted by some sort of victory. That way, he said, he would not appear to be issuing a proclamation which, like the "Pope's bull against the comet," could not possibly be enforced.[26]

Then, in September, came the measured victory at Antietam, and Lincoln decided to act. Secretary of the Treasury Chase described the Cabinet meeting which Lincoln called on September 22. After some pleasantries, Lincoln "took a graver tone" and said:

Gentlemen: I have, as you are aware, thought a great deal about the relation of this war to Slavery. I think the time has come now [for acting on the matter]. I wish it were a better time. I have got you together to hear what I have written down. I do not wish your advice about the main matter

O Captain, My Captain

—for that I have determined for myself. This I say without intending anything but respect for any one of you. But I already know the views of each on this question. I have considered them as thoroughly and carefully as I can. If there is anything in the expressions I use, or in any other minor matter, which any one of you thinks had best be changed, I shall be glad to receive the suggestions. I know very well that many others might, in this matter, as in others, do better than I can. But I am here. I must do the best I can, and bear the responsibility of taking the course which I feel I ought to take.[27]

The next morning the press announced that, on January 1, 1863, the President would declare free all slaves in areas then in rebellion. From the workers of the mill town of Manchester, England, dependent for their livelihood on cotton, came the following decisive response:

Heartily do we congratulate you and your country on this humane and righteous course.... One thing alone has, in the past, lessened our sympathy with your country ... —Negro slavery....

... [The] vast progress you have made ... fills us with hope that every stain on your freedom will shortly be removed.... And if you have any ill-wishers here, be assured they are chiefly those who oppose liberty at home, and that they will be powerless to stir up quarrels between us, from the very day in which your country becomes, undeniably and without exception, the home of the free.[28]

Delighted at this evidence that his proclamation would indeed deter foreign intervention, Lincoln replied that the heroic words of the Manchester workers, at the very time when the crisis was causing them such suffering, offered an assurance of "the ultimate and universal triumph of justice, humanity, and freedom" and that this "interchange of sentiment" gave promise that the "peace and friendship" existing between the two nations would be "perpetual."[29]

Predictably, American reaction to Lincoln's proclamation ran the gamut from unrestrained joy to hysterical rejection. Within his own party it heightened ideological differences between the warring factions. To the Moderates, including Lincoln and most of his Cabinet, the step presented great difficulties. Fearing that abrupt emancipation would disrupt the nation's economic and social fabric, they had played for time to work out some plan of gradual emancipation, under which the slaveholders would be compensated for their loss and the slaves would be trained for self-support or colonized to the Caribbean or to

Africa. Some of the Moderates agreed with Lincoln that the proclamation had become necessary; many did not. The Radicals, on the other hand, found in emancipation the realization of one of their major objectives in the war. Led by Senator Sumner of Massachusetts and Congressman Thaddeus Stevens of Pennsylvania, the Radicals had, from the beginning of Lincoln's administration, spearheaded the opposition organization within the Republican Party. Long resentful of Southern political power, they favored a ruthless prosecution of the war and, as part of their general program, the emancipation of the slaves.

Throughout his administration much of Lincoln's energy was diverted to the task of stemming the tide of Radicalism, which grew constantly stronger as, under the pressure of war, extremism mounted in the North. He did everything possible, short of capitulating to their harshest measures, to keep the cooperation of the Radicals. Sumner he wooed assiduously, letting it be known that he had given his secretary instructions to admit the Senator to him anytime he called, night or day. Even when their persistent investigations of the army and their pressure for the appointment of Radical generals became obstructive, Lincoln continued to conciliate them, holding their talents within his government. On his Cabinet, Secretary of the Treasury Salmon P. Chase was one of the Radicals' ablest representatives.

When, late in 1862, the national elections went against the Republicans and the Union Army suffered another painful defeat at Fredericksburg, the Radicals launched a campaign to drive the Moderates from the Cabinet. Lincoln's dismissal of McClellan did not sufficiently appease them, and they turned their sights first on Secretary of State Seward, who had supported the general and had disapproved of the Emancipation Proclamation. A caucus of Republican Senators bitterly accused Lincoln and Seward, charging the Secretary of wielding undue influence over the President. In the face of this criticism Seward submitted his resignation. J. G. Randall describes how Lincoln worked his way through this emergency.

Lincoln was face to face with a challenge to his position and leadership, a crisis which involved the success of the government and the fate of the nation. If senators could push him around, his effectiveness would be seriously weakened, with the possibility of further disaster to the Union cause. The men who were using the caucus of Republican senators as their instrument were the President's "bitterest enemies"; they were "doing all in their power to break him down."

Lincoln's technique rose to the occasion. It was arranged that a commit-

O Captain, My Captain

tee of the senators should call on the President on the evening of Thursday, December 18, and state their demands. Patiently the nation's Executive listened while senators presented the case against Seward—his lukewarmness and responsibility for failure. "To use the Pres[iden]t's quaint language, while they believed in the Pres[iden]t's honesty, they seemed to think that when he had in him any good purposes, Mr. S[eward] contrived *to suck them out of him unperceived.*"

404

Lincoln arranged that the senatorial committee should meet him again on the [next] evening. That morning he had a long and earnest session of his cabinet. Enjoining secrecy, he reported the resignation of Seward and the conference with the senators. The President stated how "shocked and grieved" he was to hear the senators' objections to Seward, knowing as he did how there had never been any disagreements in the cabinet "though there had been differences," and how their confidence and zeal had "sustained and consoled" him.

Having given the cue for the cabinet's attitude—cooperation with the President and among themselves—Lincoln made an adroit move. He contrived it so that when the senatorial committee of nine came again they found themselves confronted by the whole cabinet except Seward. One effect of this was that Chase, who had talked with some of the senators in the anti-Seward sense, found himself in a situation in which he could not do otherwise than confirm the President's statement of essential harmony in the cabinet. The mere confronting of the legislators with the cabinet, in a meeting of which Lincoln was moderator, gave the President a notable advantage. It was one thing for senators to use strong language in a caucus; it was quite another to do it face to face with President and cabinet. When questioned directly by the President, only four of the solons stuck to their guns in insisting upon Seward's removal.

As with the senators, so with the secretaries. For any cabinet member to associate himself with a senatorial drive against a colleague would put him clearly in the wrong. "This Cabinet," said Stanton, "is like yonder window. Suppose you allow it to be understood that passers-by might knock out one pane of glass—just one at a time—how long do you think any panes would be left in it?" At length the meeting of President, cabinet, and senators broke up "in a milder spirit" than when it met. The senators had shot their bolt, yet no explosion had occurred.

Thus ended Friday. Next day Washington buzzed with rumors that the whole cabinet had resigned and the President was in receipt of a number of new slates. Holding another cabinet meeting, Lincoln found himself in possession of another resignation. What happened is best told in the language of Gideon Welles: "Chase said he had been painfully affected by the meeting of last evening and informed the President he had prepared his resignation 'Where is it?' said the President quickly, his eye lighting up in a moment. 'I brought it with me,' said Chase. 'Let me have it,' said the President, reaching his long arm and fingers toward C[hase], who held on, reluctant to part with the letter. Something further he wished to say, but the President did not perceive it, but took and hastily opened the letter. 'This,' said he, 'cuts the Gordian knot.' "[30]

To a friend who found him beaming soon after the Cabinet heads had left, Lincoln said (referring to a farm custom of keeping a balanced load on each side of a horse), "Yes, Judge, I can ride on now, I've got a pumpkin in each end of my bag." Then Lincoln wrote to both Seward and Chase, saying that their services were indispensable and urging them to continue their duties. Now the Secretary of the Senate called on Lincoln to say he hoped that "the President would not let Mr. Chase resign," adding as an afterthought, "nor Mr. Seward." Through him Lincoln served notice on the Radicals. *"If one goes, the other must,"* he said; *"they must hunt in couples."* The two men returned to the Cabinet, and the crisis was over.[31]

Lincoln's cordiality to many of the Radical leaders was not entirely a matter of opportunism. Though they represented, in their attitude toward the South, the antithesis of his own philosophy, he genuinely liked some of them personally. Sumner, so different from Lincoln in many ways, was a warm personal friend and a frequent guest at the President's leisure evenings in his office. On such informal occasions the President's "ample feet" usually adorned his desk.

The fastidious Sumner with his elegantly tailored brown coat, maroon vest and lavendar pantaloons made a strange companion for the easygoing President, whose garb on these informal evenings was likely to be a faded, long-skirted dressing-gown, belted around the waist, and an old, worn pair of carpet slippers. Lincoln's and Sumner's sharp disagreement over reconstruction policies never dampened their personal friendship. Mrs. Lincoln was also fond of Sumner and often invited him to drive with her and the President and to attend their theater parties. But whenever Lincoln, at ease in his office, heard Sumner's goldheaded cane thumping down the White House corridor, he deferred to the Senator's pompous dignity by dropping his feet to the floor.[32]

The President's warm, gregarious nature, his simple friendliness

O Captain, My Captain

with all kinds of people, comes through clearly in his secretary's description of life at the White House:

It would be hard to imagine a state of things less conducive to serious and effective work, yet in one way or another the work was done. In the midst of a crowd of visitors who began to arrive early in the morning and who were put out, grumbling, by the servants who closed the doors at midnight, the President pursued those labors which will carry his name to distant ages. There was little order or system about it; those around him strove from beginning to end to erect barriers to defend him against constant interruption, but the President himself was always the first to break them down. He disliked anything that kept people from him who wanted to see him, and although the continual contact with importunity which he could not satisfy, and with distress which he could not always relieve, wore terribly upon him and made him an old man before his time, he would never take the necessary measures to defend himself. He continued to the end receiving these swarms of visitors, every one of whom, even the most welcome, took something from him in the way of wasted nervous force.

Of course it was not all pure waste; Mr. Lincoln gained much of information, something of cheer and encouragement, from these visits. He particularly enjoyed conversing with officers of the army and navy, newly arrived from [duty].

The inventors were more a source of amusement than annoyance. They were usually men of some originality of character, not infrequently carried to eccentricity. Lincoln had a quick comprehension of mechanical principles. He would sometimes go out into the waste fields that then lay south of the Executive Mansion to test an experimental gun or torpedo. He used to quote with much merriment the solemn dictum of one rural inventor that "a gun ought not to rekyle; if it rekyled at all, it ought to rekyle a little forrid." He was particularly interested in the first rude attempts at the afterwards famous mitrailleuses [embryonic machine guns]; on one occasion he worked one with his own hands at the Arsenal, and sent forth peals of Homeric laughter as the balls, which had not power to penetrate the target set up at a little distance, came bounding back among the shins of the bystanders.[33]

The train of petitioners was endless:

Time and again, after listening to someone's woes, the President would send him to Stanton, Welles, Seward or some other person in authority with a brief but precious missive: . . . "Can this man be accommodated?" . . . Will the Secretary of War please have the matter corrected "or explain

to me wherein the hitch is?" ... The doors of military prisons opened for untold numbers of repentant Confederates at the behest of Lincoln's terse endorsement: "Let this man take the oath and be discharged."
... It would be difficult to estimate how many tired, scared, or homesick boys in the Union army who fell asleep on picket duty, ran away in battle, or slipped off without leave to visit wives or parents were spared ... by a terse telegram from Lincoln: ... "Let him fight instead of being shot."
Lincoln's orders to [Secretary of War] Stanton often display sly humor. The crabbed Secretary must have snorted with disgust when he read Lincoln's order: "Please have the adjutant general ascertain whether ———— is entitled to promotion. His wife thinks he is." ... Stanton had learned that he could oppose the President up to a point; but to go beyond that point might bring him a rebuff such as: "I personally wish ———— ... to be appointed a Colonel of a colored regiment—and this regardless of whether he can tell the exact shade of Julius Caesar's hair."[34]

Lincoln was quite aware of the mockery with which tales about his social awkwardness (particularly his discomfort in white gloves) were told.* He once said that, throughout his life, he had "endured a great deal of ridicule" and had "received a great deal of kindness, not quite free from ridicule."[35] He grew especially sensitive to the carping criticism of his "frontier humor" and "backwoods tales." One night in 1863, when military worries weighed heavily on him, Lincoln was awakened by three army officers (one of them a tipsy major) bearing an urgent message. One of the two colonels later recalled the interview:

After the servant returned and announced that the President would receive us, we sat for some time in painful silence. At length we heard slow, shuffling steps come down the carpeted stairs, and the President entered the room as we respectfully rose from our seats. That pathetic figure has ever remained indelible in my memory. His tall form was bowed, his hair disheveled; he wore no necktie or collar, and his large feet were partly incased in very loose, heelless slippers . . . that made . . . flip-flap sounds. . . .

*One of the most popular of these anecdotes recounted how, in the process of welcoming an Illinois friend to a formal reception, Lincoln burst his white kid glove with a loud pop. Raising "his brawny hand up before him, looking at it with an indescribable expression, he said—while the whole procession was checked, witnessing this scene—'Well, my old friend, this is a general bustification. You and I were never intended to wear these things.' " See Ward Hill Lamon, *Recollections of Abraham Lincoln, 1847-1865* (Chicago: A. C. McClurg & Co., 1895), p. 96.

O Captain, My Captain

It was the face that, in every line, told the story of anxiety and weariness. The drooping eyelids, looking almost swollen; the dark bags beneath the eyes; the deep marks about the large and expressive mouth; the flaccid muscles of the jaws were all so majestically pitiful that I could almost have fallen on my knees and begged pardon for my part in the cruel presumption that had thus invaded his repose. . . .

The merely formal talk being over, [a] little pause in the conversation ensued. The gaunt figure of the President had gradually slid lower on the slippery sofa, and his long legs were stretched out in front, the loose slippers half-fallen from his feet, while the drowsy eyelids had almost closed over his eyes, and his jaded features had taken on the suggestion of relaxation in sleep.

Deeply moved by the President's evident fatigue, and by his cordial treatment of us in spite of our presumptuous call, Colonel Van Buren and I were about rising to make our adieux when, to our dismay, the Major slapped the President on his knee and said: "Mr. President, tell us one of your good stories."

If the floor had opened and dropped me out of sight, I would have been happy.

The President drew himself up, and turning his back as far as possible upon the Major, with great dignity addressed the rest of us, saying: "I believe I have the popular reputation of being a story-teller, but I do not deserve the name in its general sense; for it is not the story itself, but its purpose, or effect, that interests me. I often avoid a long and useless discussion by others or a laborious explanation on my own part by a short story that illustrates my point of view. So, too, the sharpness of a refusal or the edge of a rebuke may be blunted by an appropriate story, so as to save wounded feeling, and yet serve the purpose. No, I am not simply a story-teller, but story-telling as an emollient saves me much friction and distress."[36]

Sadly, Hay recorded the transition this tremendous strain wrought on Lincoln:

As time wore on and the war held its terrible course, upon no one of all those who lived through it was its effect more apparent than upon the President. He bore the sorrows of the Nation in his own heart. The cry of the widow and the orphan was always in his ears; the awful responsibility resting upon him as the protector of an imperiled republic kept him true to his duty, but could not make him unmindful of the intimate details of the vast sum of human misery involved in a civil war.

Chapters from the American Experience

Under this frightful ordeal his demeanor and disposition changed—so gradually that it would be impossible to say when the change began; but he was in mind, body, and nerves a very different man at the second inauguration from the one who had taken the oath in 1861. He continued always the same kindly, genial, and cordial spirit he had been at first; but the boisterous laughter became less frequent year by year; the eye grew veiled by constant meditation on momentous subjects; the air of reserve and detachment from his surroundings increased.[37]

Finally, in July, 1863, came the long-awaited military triumph. It came in double measure—the sweeping victory at Gettysburg and the conquest of Vicksburg. Asked to deliver an address at the ceremony commemorating the Battle of Gettysburg, Lincoln spoke a few lines which he said, the world would "little note, nor long remember." In words that have been remembered by millions who have forgotten the details of the battle, he articulated and purified the motives for which Northerners fought:

Fourscore and seven years ago our fathers brought forth on this continent a new nation, conceived in liberty, and dedicated to the proposition that all men are created equal.

Now we are engaged in a great civil war, testing whether that nation, or any nation so conceived and so dedicated, can long endure. We are met on a great battlefield of that war. We have come to dedicate a portion of that field as a final resting-place for those who here gave their lives that the nation might live. It is altogether fitting and proper that we should do this. But, in a larger sense, we cannot dedicate—we cannot consecrate—we cannot hallow—this ground. The brave men, living and dead, who struggled here have consecrated it, far above our poor power to add or detract. . . . It is for us the living, rather, to be dedicated here to the unfinished work which they who fought here have thus far so nobly advanced. It is rather for us to be here dedicated to the great task remaining before us—that from these honored dead we take increased devotion to that cause for which they gave the last full measure of devotion—that we here highly resolve that these dead shall not have died in vain—that this nation, under God, shall have a new birth of freedom and that government of the people, by the people, for the people, shall not perish from the earth.[38]

But Lincoln's joy over Gettysburg was tempered by the fact that the Southern rout had not been consummated, that Lee had escaped south-

O Captain, My Captain

ward across the Potomac with his army. The search for military leadership continued. Not until the next spring, 1864, did Lincoln at last find a general-in-chief who satisfied him. He came from the Western front, from the victories of Vicksburg and Chattanooga. Early in the war Lincoln had found respite from the Eastern defeats in the exploits of Brigadier General Ulysses S. Grant at Forts Henry and Donelson. Remembering those successes, Lincoln had stood by him when, in the spring of 1862, his losses at Shiloh brought a campaign for his dismissal. "I can't spare this man," he said, after he had heard Grant's detractors out; "he fights."[39] Vicksburg and Chattanooga had vindicated Lincoln's judgment and his loyalty.

Now Grant energetically assumed the task of finishing the war. Reserving for himself the leadership of the Army of the Potomac, he divided his old command of the Army of Mississippi between General ("Rock of Chickamagua") Thomas (who would hold back the Confederates in Tennessee) and General Sherman (who would bring his troops eastward to Atlanta and to the sea). Lee's army was soon closely invested between Richmond and Petersburg.

By the time Lincoln delivered his second inaugural address, victory was almost assured. Laying aside the bitterness of four years of war, he returned to the theme of Union. To vindictive Northerners, he pleaded compassion. He pointed out the tearing tragedy of civil strife—where antagonists share so much, where "Both read the same Bible, and pray to the same God; and each invokes His aid against the other." Eloquently he called upon the people of both the North and the South to put away their burden of hatred:

Fondly do we hope—fervently do we pray—that this mighty scourge of war may speedily pass away. Yet, if God wills that it continue until all the wealth piled by the bondman's two hundred and fifty years of unrequited toil shall be sunk, and until every drop of blood drawn with the lash shall be paid by another drawn with the sword, as was said three thousand years ago, so still it must be said: "The judgments of the Lord are true and righteous altogether."

With malice toward none; with charity for all; with firmness in the right, as God gives us to see the right, let us strive on to finish the work we are in; to bind up the nation's wounds; to care for him who shall have borne the battle, and for his widow, and his orphan—to do all which may achieve a just and lasting peace among ourselves, and with all nations.[40]

"To bind up the nation's wounds" had been Lincoln's primary goal from the hour of his becoming President. For four years he had devoted all his energies to holding the South in the Union (first by persuasion and then by force), to keeping the factious North united in the common endeavor, and to preventing England and France from throwing their decisive power against the Union. As victory drew near, he turned his superb talents to the task of effecting a genuine reconciliation, on which might be based a "just and lasting peace." As Grant said later, had Lincoln lived, he "would have proven the best friend the South could have had."[41]

That there were those in the South who recognized this compassion was made clear when, early in 1865, Lincoln and three peace commissioners from the Confederacy made a premature attempt to bring about a reconciliation.

On February 3 Lincoln and Seward sat down with the three Confederates in the cabin of the *River Queen* under the guns of Fortress Monroe. Frail Alexander H. Stephens [Vice President of the Confederacy], for whom Lincoln had entertained a genuine fondness and admiration since their days in Congress, arrived bundled in a tremendous overcoat with numerous scarves and vestments. The President watched him good-humoredly as he unwrapped his puny body, and remarked later to Grant that it was the smallest nubbin for so much shucking that he had ever seen.

For four hours there was a swift interplay of acute minds across the council table. Lincoln would make no bargain with an enemy in arms. When Hunter [of Virginia] retorted that Charles I had negotiated with persons in arms against his government, the President replied that he was not posted on history; all that he distinctly remembered about the matter was that Charles had lost his head. Hunter said he understood that Lincoln looked upon the leaders of the Confederacy as traitors. Lincoln granted that was "about the size of it." There was a moment's silence. Then Hunter smiled. "Well, Mr. Lincoln," he observed, "we have about concluded that we shall not be hanged as long as you are President—if we behave ourselves."[42]

Toward the end of March Lincoln was again on the *River Queen* — this time planning, with Generals Grant and Sherman and Admiral Porter, the final encirclement of Lee's army. Sherman recorded in his *Memoirs* that, while the North was chanting "Hang Jeff Davis to a sour apple tree," Lincoln encouraged his generals to let the hated Rebel leader slip through their fingers.

O Captain, My Captain

During this interview I inquired of the President if he was all ready for the end of the war. What was to be done with the rebel armies when defeated? And what would be done with the political leaders, such as Jeff Davis. . . . He said he was all ready; all he wanted of us was to defeat the opposing armies, and to get the men composing the Confederate armies back to their homes, at work on their farms and in their shops. As to Jeff Davis, he was hardly at liberty to speak his mind fully, but intimated that he ought to clear out, "escape the country," only it would not do for him to say so openly.[43]

On Palm Sunday, April 9, Lee surrendered at Appomattox, and the war came to an end. Five days later on the evening of Good Friday, Lincoln was shot by an assassin and mortally wounded.

During the early morning hours, while they waited, and through the days of mourning, Americans recalled the words, acts, and gestures of the man who had been their President. For a small interval of time, all caviling ceased. And men remembered that, confronted with the almost insuperable task of bringing the South back into the Union in the face of a divided North and hostile foreign powers, Lincoln had somehow succeeded. Ambling about with such seeming aimlessness—deferring, acceding, shifting—by some inscrutable magic, he had brought the nation to victory. Impelled by the tragedy of the hour, they probed how this could have been.

Some few of the more philosophical may have wondered whether the magic had been so inscrutable after all—whether the war effort, the victory had not been simply the response of the American experience to its greatest challenge. After all, Lincoln's open-mindedness, his willingness to compromise if need be, his frontiersman's caution (as moving through bear traps)—were these not part of the American heritage? His humor, his intellect with its earthy practicality, his inflexible pursuit of the basic objective—had not many other Americans shared these gifts? The skill he showed with words was not unique in that day of the American Renaissance. Surely Lincoln's philosophy—the democracy of the open society (which his life embodied)—was the American credo. And that other dimension (more rare, admittedly)—the magnanimity to his enemies, the compassion, the understanding—was it not a keystone of the faith which had helped build America?

Having deduced that all had been strands from the American fabric, no single quality unique, they would have gone on to conclude that it was in the putting together that the uniqueness had emerged. That such a mind, and such a heart, and such a gift for eloquence should have come together at that point in time and space—there the magic became inscrutable.

Feeling some of these things, acutely aware that he had suffered for them, had labored and died for them, the Americans grieved as they buried him. They exalted him as a sacrifice for their frailties and as the symbol of their perfectibility. They wrote great stirring odes in his memory. And they made of him a legend.

O Captain, My Captain

References

1. Iliad of the New World

[1]Salvador de Madariaga, *Hernan Cortes: Conqueror of Mexico* (London: A. P. Watt & Son, 1942, and Coral Gables, Fla.: University of Miami Press, 1967), p. 15.

[2]Francisco López de Gómara, *Cortés: The Life of the Conqueror by His Secretary*, ed. and trans. by Lesley Byrd (Berkeley and Los Angeles: University of California Press, 1964), pp. 24-25. Reprinted by permission of The Regents of the University of California.

[3]Madariaga, *op. cit.*, p. 16.

[4]*Ibid.*, p. 11.

[5]*Ibid.*

[6]William H. Prescott, *History of the Conquest of Mexico*, Vol. 1 (New York: Thomas Y. Crowell & Co., 1843), pp. 226–27. Material from this source has been condensed and modernized.

[7]*Ibid.*, p. 228.

[8]Séjourné presents an interesting thesis that the Tlascalan rulers had capitulated to the Aztecs and that a secret treaty had been consummated whereby "military fairs" or battles would be arranged when the Aztecs wished it so that they might have a ready supply of captives to serve as sacrifices for their religious rites. Laurette Séjourné, *Burning Water: Thought and Religion in Ancient Mexico* (New York: The Vanguard Press, Inc., 1956), pp. 31-34.

This book also analyzes the Aztec character in terms of a dichotomy between the barbarism of their own culture and the moral code and conscientiousness instilled in them as a result of their conquest of the more civilized Toltecs. It draws a parallel between the life and teachings of the Toltec leader and demigod Quetzalcoatl and those of Jesus of Nazareth.

[9]Prescott, *op. cit.*, p. 380.

[10]*Ibid.*, p. 399.

[11]*Ibid.*, p. 407.

[12]*Ibid.*, p. 454.

[13]*Ibid.*, p. 484.

[14]*Ibid.*, p. 487.

[15]*Ibid.*, pp. 492-93.

[16]*Ibid.*, p. 493.

[17]*Ibid.*, II, pp. 55-56.

[18]*Ibid.*, pp. 72-73.

¹⁹*Ibid.*, pp. 85-90, 92, 95-98.
²⁰*Ibid.*, pp. 103, 107-14.
²¹*Ibid.*, pp. 291-92, 301-2.
²²*Ibid.*, p. 316.

2. The Challenge

¹Richard Hofstadter, William Miller, Daniel Aaron, *The United States: The History of a Republic* (Englewood Cliffs, N.J.: Prentice-Hall, Inc., 1957), p.19.
²Julian S. Corbett, *Drake and the Tudor Navy*, Vol. 1 (London and New York: Longmans, Green, & Co., 1899), pp. 265-66. Material from this source has been condensed and revised.
³*Ibid.*, pp. 263-65.
⁴*Ibid.*, pp. 269-76.
⁵Samuel de Champlain, *The Voyages and Explorations of Samuel de Champlain, 1604-1616*, Vol. I, eds. and trans. Edward Gaylord Bourne and Annie Nettleton Bourne (New York: Allerton Book Co., 1922, copyright 1904 by Williams-Barker Co.), pp. 202-16. Condensed and modernized.
⁶Morris Bishop, *Champlain: The Life of Fortitude* (New York: Alfred A. Knopf, Inc., 1948), pp. 223-25.
⁷Champlain, *op. cit.*, p. 84.
⁸Bishop, *op. cit.*, pp. 223n-24n.

3. The Starving Time

¹George F. Willison, *Behold Virginia! The Fifth Crown* (New York: Harcourt, Brace & Company, 1951), p. 4. Material from this source has been condensed.
²*Ibid.*, p. 28.
³*Ibid.*, p. 23.
⁴Philip L. Barbour, *The Three Worlds of Captain John Smith* (Boston: Houghton Mifflin Company, 1964), p. 144.
⁵ Willison, *op. cit.*, pp. 108-17.
⁶*Ibid.*, p. 119.

4. The Genesis of a Patriarch, Puritan Style

¹Robert C. Winthrop, *Life and Letters of John Winthrop*, Vol. II (Boston: Little, Brown and Company, 1869, 1895), p. 18. Material from this source has been condensed and partially modernized.
²Edmund S. Morgan, *The Puritan Dilemma: The Story of John Winthrop* (Boston: Little, Brown and Company, 1958), p. 7.
³Samuel Eliot Morison, *Builders of the Bay Colony* (Boston: Houghton Mifflin Company, 1930), p. 54.
⁴Winthrop, *op. cit.*, I, 56-57.
⁵*Ibid.*, pp. 60-61, 64.
⁶*Ibid.*, pp. 68, 72.
⁷*Ibid.*, p. 65.
⁸*Ibid.*, p. 80.

[9]*Ibid.*, pp. 69-70.
[10]*Ibid.*, p. 72.
[11]*Ibid.*, p. 94.
[12]*Ibid.*, p. 72.
[13]*Ibid.*, p. 76.
[14]*Ibid.*, p. 77.
[15]*Ibid.*, p. 261.
[16]*Ibid.*, pp. 135, 138.
[17]*Ibid.*, p. 290.
[18]*Ibid.*, p. 397.
[19]*Ibid.*, p. 235.
[20]*Ibid.*, p. 234.
[21]*Ibid.*, p. 261.
[22]See Morgan, *op. cit.*, p. 19.
[23]Winthrop, *op. cit.*, I, 295-96.
[24]*Ibid.*, p. 342.
[25]*Ibid.*, p. 296.
[26]*Ibid.*, pp. 309-10, 312-13. For an excellent discussion of the nonreligious motives for the migration, see Thomas J. Wertenbaker, *The Puritan Oligarchy: The Founding of American Civilization* (New York: Charles Scribner's Sons, 1947), pp. 35-39.
[27]Winthrop, *op. cit.*, I, 307.
[28]*Ibid.*, p. 340.
[29]*Ibid.*, p. 370.
[30]*Ibid.*, pp. 388-89.
[31]*Ibid.*, 18-19.
[32]*Ibid.*, p. 22.
[33]John Winthrop, *Winthrop's Journal: History of New England*, Vol. I, ed. James Kendall Hosmer (New York: Charles Scribner's Sons, 1908), pp. 70-71.
[34]*Ibid.*, pp. 238-39.
[35]R. Winthrop, *op. cit.*, II, 430.
[36]*Ibid.*, p. 19.

5. The Rise of a Rebel, Puritan Style

[1]Samuel Hugh Brockunier, *The Irrepressible Democrat, Roger Williams* (New York: The Ronald Press Company, 1940), p. 80. Contemporary quotations have been slightly modernized.
[2]*Ibid.*, p. 39.
[3]*Ibid.*, p. 41.
[4]Cotton Mather, "Little Foxes; or The Spirit of Rigid Separatism in One Remarkable Zealot," in *Magnalia Christi Americana*, Vol. II (New York: Russell & Russell, Publishers, 1967, reproduced from the 1852 edition), p. 495. Quotations from this source have been partially modernized.
[5]Brockunier, *op. cit.*, pp. 41, 42.
[6]Mather, *op. cit.*, p. 496.
[7]Brockunier, *op. cit.*, pp. 54-55.
[8]Roger Williams, *The Bloudy Tenent of Persecution for Cause of Conscience*, in *The Complete Writings of Roger Williams*, Vol. III (New York: Russell & Russell, Publishers, 1963, first printed in 1644 and reproduced from the 1866 edition), pp. 249-50. Quotations from this source have been partially modernized.

[9]*Ibid.*, pp. 3-4.

[10]Robert C. Winthrop, *Life and Letters of John Winthrop*, Vol. II (Boston: Little, Brown and Company, 1869, 1895), p. 430.

[11]Brockunier, *op. cit.*, p. 42

[12]*Ibid.*

[13]*Ibid.*, p. 45.

[14]Mather, *op. cit.*, II, 496.

[15]Brockunier, *op. cit.*, p. 46.

[16]*Ibid.*, p. 47.

[17]*Ibid.*

[18]*Ibid.*, p. 48.

[19]*Ibid.*, p. 49. See also Cyclone Covey, *The Gentle Radical: A Biography of Roger Williams* (New York: The MacMillan Company, Publishers, 1966), p. 94.

[20]Brockunier, *op. cit.*, p. 56.

[21]*Ibid.*, p. 57.

[22]*Ibid.*

[23]*Ibid.*, p. 58.

[24]*Ibid.*, p. 59.

[25]*Ibid.*, p. 60.

[26]*Ibid.*, p. 61.

[27]*Ibid.*

[28]*Ibid.*, p. 62.

[29]*Ibid.*

[30]*Ibid.*, p. 63.

[31]*Ibid.*, pp. 64-65.

[32]*Ibid.*, p. 68.

[33]*Ibid.*, pp. 84-85.

[34]*Ibid.*, p. 87.

[35]*Ibid.*, p. 89.

[36]*Ibid.*, p. 90.

[37]Ola Elizabeth Winslow, *Master Roger Williams: A Biography* (New York: The Mac-Millan Company, Publishers, 1957), p. 153.

[38]*Ibid.*, p. 156.

[39]*Ibid.*, pp. 155-56.

[40]*Ibid.*, p. 157.

[41]Mather, *op. cit.*, II, 495, 499.

[42]James Bryce, in Irving Berdine Richman, *Rhode Island: Its Making and Its Meaning* (New York: G. P. Putnam's Sons, 1908), pp. vi-viii. Condensed.

6. The Emergence of a Yankee, Puritan Style

[1]Samuel Sewall, *Diary of Samuel Sewall, 1674-1729*, Vol. I, in *Collections of the Massachusetts Historical Society*, Vols. V, VI, VII (Boston, 1878), p. 328. Material from the source has been condensed and partially modernized. The reader who wishes to explore Sewall's diary further is referred to the American Bookshelf's one-volume edition: Mark Van Doren, ed., *Samuel Sewall's Diary* (New York: Russell & Russell, Publishers, 1963).

[2]Sewall, *op. cit.*, III, 84-85.

[3]*Ibid.*, p. 194.

[4]*Ibid.*, p. 424.

[5]*Ibid.*, pp. 476 and 417.

[6]*Ibid.*, pp. 15-16, 103-4, 420, 432-33; II, 36-37.
[7]*Ibid.*, I, 225, 369, 419-20, 422-23.
[8]*Ibid.*, p. 281.
[9]*Ibid.*, III, 91; I, 184.
[10]*Ibid.*, pp. 308-9
[11]*Ibid.*, pp. 332, 383, xviii, 384.
[12]*Ibid.*, p. 113.
[13]*Ibid.*, p. 468.
[14]*Ibid.*, III, 71.
[15]*Ibid.*, I, 43.
[16]*Ibid.*, II, 231-32.
[17]*Ibid.*, I, 44 5.
[18]*Ibid.*, III, 87.
[19]*Ibid.*, I, 38, 301.
[20]*Ibid.*, II, 71.
[21]*Ibid.*, p. 44; I, 435.
[22]*Ibid.*, II, 258.
[23]*Ibid.*, III, 144.
[24]*Ibid.*, pp. 262-67, 269-75.

7. Blood on the Quarterdeck

[1]George Francis Dow, ed., *Slave Ships and Slaving* (Salem, Mass.: Marine Research Society, 1927), p. xvii.
[2]For a good account of the African slave trade, see Daniel P. Mannix, in collaboration with Malcolm Cowley, *Black Cargoes: A History of the Atlantic Slave Trade, 1518-1865* (New York: The Viking Press, 1962).
[3]Dow, *op. cit.*, p. 78. This book is a skillful and interesting condensation of the multivolume eighteenth-century collections of voyages mentioned in the text. Material from this source has been condensed.
[4]*Ibid.*, pp. 78-79.
[5]*Ibid.*, pp. 61-62.
[6]*Ibid.*, p. 59.
[7]*Ibid.*, pp. 62-63.
[8]*Ibid.*, pp. 82-85.
[9]*Ibid.*, pp. 67-70.
[10]Captain Charles Johnson, *A General History of the Robberies and Murders of the Most Notorious Pyrates*, Vol. I (4th ed.) (London: T. Woodward, 1726). (An updated version was published in 1926 by Routledge & Kegan Paul, Ltd., London.) Material from this source has been condensed and modernized.
[11]*Ibid.*, pp. 74-76, 86-88.
[12]Shirley Carter Hughson, *The Carolina Pirates and Colonial Commerce, 1670-1740,* in *Johns Hopkins University Studies in Historical and Political Science*, ed. Herbert B. Adams, Twelfth series, V, VI, VII (Baltimore: The Johns Hopkins Press, 1894), pp. 70-72, 74-76. Condensed and revised.
[13]Johnson, *op. cit.*, pp. 80-85, *passim.*

8. Travelers to the Middle Colonies

[1]J. Hector St. John de Crevecoeur, *Letters from an American Farmer* (New York: Fox, Duffield & Company, 1904), pp. 54-55. Condensed and slightly revised.

[2]For the thesis that the melting-pot concept of America should be replaced by a salad-bowl metaphor, see Carl N. Degler, *Out of Our Past: The Forces that Shaped Modern America* (New York: Harper & Row, Publishers, 1959), pp. 295-96.

[3]Sarah Kemble Knight, *The Private Journal of a Journey from Boston to New York in the Year 1704* (Albany: Frank H. Little, 1865), pp. 25-28. Material from this source has been condensed and substantially modernized.

[4]*Ibid.*, p. 53.

[5]*Ibid.*, p. 66.

[6]*Ibid.*, pp. 66-69.

[7]Alexander Hamilton, *Gentleman's Progress, The Itinerarium of Dr. Alexander Hamilton, 1744*, Carl Bridenbaugh, ed. (Chapel Hill: University of North Carolina Press, Institute of Early American History and Culture, Williamsburg, 1948), p. 74. Spelling modernized.

[8]*Ibid.*, p. 73.

[9]*Ibid.*, pp. 71-72.

[10]*Ibid.*, p. 89.

[11]*Ibid.*, pp. 42-43, 88.

[12]Peter Kalm, *Travels into North America*, 2d ed., in John Pinkerton, *A General Collection of the Best and Most Interesting Voyages and Travels*, Vol. XIII (London, 1812), pp. 398, 422, 407, 569, 513. Material from this source has been condensed and modernized.

[13]*Ibid.*, p. 458.

[14]*Ibid.*, p. 455.

[15]*Ibid.*, pp. 386-87.

[16]*Ibid.*, p. 390.

[17]*Ibid.*, p. 387.

[18]*Ibid.*, p. 386.

[19]*Ibid.*, pp. 391-92.

[20]*Ibid.*, p. 395.

[21]*Ibid.*, p. 396.

[22]*Ibid.*, p. 409.

[23]*Ibid.*, p. 406.

[24]*Ibid.*, p. 564.

[25]*Ibid.*, pp. 499-503.

[26]*Ibid.*, pp. 460-61, 587.

9. The Tidewater Gentleman

[1]See Thomas J. Wertenbaker, *Patrician and Plebian in Virginia* (Charlottesville, Va.: Michie Co., 1910).

[2]Daniel J. Boorstin, *The Americans: The Colonial Experience* (New York: Random House, Inc., 1958), pp. 102-3. The generalized discussions of the Virginia gentleman in the following reading are derived primarily from this incisive source, which has been condensed.

[3]*Ibid.*, p. 103.

[4]James Thomas Flexner, *George Washington: The Forge of Experience (1732-1775)* (Boston: Little, Brown and Company, 1965), p. 21.

[5]*Ibid.*, p. 238.

[6]*Ibid.*, p. 237.

[7]*Ibid.*, p. 244.

[8]*Ibid.*, pp. 244-45.

[9]*Ibid.*, p. 266. Asked later to write his memoirs of the Revolution, he demurred on the grounds that he was too conscious of his "defective education." (*Ibid.*, p. 24)

[10]Boorstin, *op. cit.*, pp. 105-6, 108.

[11]See Paul Leland Haworth, *George Washington: Farmer* (Indianapolis: The Bobbs-Merrill Co., Inc., 1915), pp. 60-70 for Washington's land problems.

[12]See Edward Townsend Booth, *Country Life in America* (New York: Alfred A. Knopf, Inc., 1947), pp. 67-68.

[13]See photographs in Haworth, *op. cit.*

[14]Bernard Fäy, *George Washington, Republican Aristocrat* (Boston: Houghton Mifflin Company, The Riverside Press, 1931), p. 150.

[15]Boorstin, *op. cit.*, pp. 111, 114-16.

[16]*Ibid.*, pp. 117-19, 122-23.

[17]*Ibid.*, p. 121.

10. Encounter at Quebec

[1]Francis Parkman, *Montcalm and Wolfe* (New York: Crowell-Collier & MacMillan, Inc., 1962 [set from the 1884 edition]), p. 316. This account is a condensation of Parkman's work.

[2]*Ibid.*, pp. 472-73.

[3]*Ibid.*, p. 475.

[4]*Ibid.*, pp. 485-90.

[5]*Ibid.*, pp. 499-500.

[6]*Ibid.*, pp. 525-26.

[7]*Ibid.*, pp. 536-47.

[8]*Ibid.*, p. 560.

11. Benjamin Franklin: Universal American

[1]Herman Melville, *Israel Potter* (Boston: L. C. Page & Company, 1925), p. 82.

[2]Benjamin Franklin, *The Autobiography of Benjamin Franklin*, eds. Leonard W. Labaree, Ralph L. Ketcham, Helen C. Boatfield, and Helene H. Fineman (New Haven: Yale University Press, 1964), pp. 75-76. Used by permission of the University of California Press. Spelling slightly modernized.

[3]*Ibid.*, pp. 53-54.

[4]*Ibid.*, p. 62.

[5]Carl Van Doren, *Benjamin Franklin* (New York: The Viking Press, 1938), p. 28. Condensed. Much of this reading is a compilation of excerpts from different parts of this penetrating study, to which the reader is enthusiastically referred.

[6]Franklin, *op. cit.*, p. 70.

[7]*Ibid.*, pp. 125-26.

[8]*Ibid.*, pp. 149-50.

[9]*Ibid.*, pp. 151-52.

[10]*Ibid.*, pp. 158-59.

[11]Van Doren, *op. cit.*, pp. 73, 90.

[12]*Ibid.*, p. 260.

[13]*Ibid.*, pp. 295-96.
[14]*Ibid.*, pp. 416-17.
[15]*Ibid.*, pp. 619-20, 622-23.
[16]*Ibid.*, pp. 744-45, 753-54.
[17]*Ibid.*, pp. 776, 772, 777-78.
[18]*Ibid.*, p. 782.

12. John Adams, Reluctant Revolutionary

[1]John Adams, *The Works of John Adams*, 10 volumes (Boston: Little, Brown and Company, 1851–1856), IX, 339. Material from this source has been condensed and slightly modernized.

[2]For a colorful account of the delegates' departure from Boston, see Catherine Drinker Bowen, *John Adams and the American Revolution* (Boston: Little, Brown and Company, 1950), pp. 449-53.

[3]Adams, *op. cit.*, II, 342.

[4]*Ibid.*, pp. 342-45.

[5]*Ibid.*, pp. 346-51.

[6]*Ibid.*, pp. 350-51.

[7]*Ibid.*

[8]*Ibid.*, p. 353.

[9]*Ibid.*, p. 338; IX, 339.

[10]*Ibid.*, II, 523-25.

[11]*Ibid.*, pp. 124-25.

[12]*Ibid.*, pp. 86-87.

[13]*Ibid.*, pp. 90, 92.

[14]*Ibid.*, p. 85.

[15]*Ibid.*, p. 107.

[16]*Ibid.*, p. 144.

[17]*Ibid.*, p. 154.

[18]*Ibid.*, p. 153.

[19]*Ibid.*, III, 448-64.

[20]*Ibid.*, II, 150-51.

[21]*Ibid.*, III, 465-68.

[22]*Ibid.*, II, 212.

[23]*Ibid.*, p. 208.

[24]*Ibid.*, p. 214.

[25]*Ibid.*

[26]*Ibid.*, p. 229.

[27]*Ibid.*, p. 230.

[28]*Ibid.*, p. 231.

[29]*Ibid.*, p. 232.

[30]*Ibid.*, pp. 232-33.

[31]*Ibid.*, pp. 255-57.

[32]*Ibid.*, p. 308.

[33]*Ibid.*

[34]*Ibid.*, pp. 308-9.

[35]*Ibid.*, p. 314.

[36]*Ibid.*, p. 316.

[37]*Ibid.*, III, 516-74.

³⁸Carl Becker, *The Eve of the Revolution* (New Haven: Yale University Press, 1921), p. 183.

³⁹Adams, *op. cit.*, II, 315, 313.

⁴⁰*Ibid.*, p. 312.

⁴¹*Ibid.*

⁴²*Ibid.*, p. 313.

⁴³Gilbert Chinard, *Honest John Adams* (Boston: Little, Brown and Company, 1933), p. 66.

⁴⁴Adams, *op. cit.*, II, 336.

⁴⁵Cited in Bowen, *op. cit.*, p. 434.

⁴⁶Adams, *op. cit.*, IX, 333.

⁴⁷*Ibid.*, II, 323-24.

⁴⁸Cited in Bowen, *op. cit.*, p. 442.

⁴⁹John C. Miller, *Sam Adams, Pioneer in Propaganda* (Stanford: Stanford University Press, 1936), p. 308.

⁵⁰Adams, *op. cit.*, II, 338.

⁵¹*Ibid.*, p. 357.

⁵²*Ibid.*, p. 395; IX, 348.

⁵³*Ibid.*, p. 346.

⁵⁴George F. Willison, *Patrick Henry and His World* (Garden City, N.Y.: Doubleday & Company, Inc., 1969), p. 245.

⁵⁵Adams, *op. cit.*, II, 360.

⁵⁶*Ibid.*, p. 362.

⁵⁷*Ibid.*, p. 401.

⁵⁸Chinard, *op. cit.*, p. 80.

⁵⁹Adams, *op. cit.*, II, 407.

⁶⁰*Ibid.*, pp. 401, 395.

13. Mosaic of Freedom

¹Henry Steele Commager and Richard B. Morris, eds., *The Spirit of 'Seventy-Six: The Story of the American Revolution as Told by Participants* (Indianapolis: The Bobbs-Merrill Co., Inc., 1958), p. 901. The reader will enjoy browsing further among the rich resources of this fine collection.

²*Ibid.*, p. 352.

³*Ibid.*, p. 804.

⁴*Ibid.*, p. 809.

⁵*Ibid.*, p. 813.

⁶Reprinted by permission of G. P. Putnam's Sons from *The American Revolution*, by Hugh F. Rankin, p. 346. Copyright © 1964 by Hugh F. Rankin. Material from this source has been condensed.

⁷See Walter Millis, *Arms and Men: A Study in American Military History* (New York: G. P. Putnam's Sons, 1956), pp. 33-37, for an elaboration of the importance of the mass levies of armed patriots.

⁸Commager and Morris, *op. cit.*, p. 476.

⁹*Ibid.*, p. 714.

¹⁰Rankin, *op. cit.*, p. 166.

¹¹*Ibid.*, pp. 176-77.

¹²*Ibid.*, pp. 177-78.

¹³*Ibid.*, p. 205.

[14]Commager and Morris, *op. cit.*, pp. 519-20.
[15]*Ibid.*, pp. 1211-12.
[16]*Ibid.*, pp. 1214-15.
[17]*Ibid.*, p. 1217.
[18]*Ibid.*, pp. 1217-18.
[19]*Ibid.*, p. 1218.
[20]*Ibid.*, p. 1289.

14. E Pluribus Unum

[1]Catherine Drinker Bowen, *Miracle at Philadelphia: The Story of the Constitutional Convention May to September 1787* (Boston: Little, Brown and Company, 1966), pp. 294-305. Material from this source has been condensed.
[2]John C. Miller, *Alexander Hamilton, Portrait in Paradox* (New York: Harper & Row, Publishers, 1959), p. 212.
[3]Linda Grant De Pauw, *The Eleventh Pillar: New York State and the Federal Constitution* (Ithaca, N.Y.: American Historical Association, Cornell University Press, 1966), p. 206.
[4]*Ibid.*, p. 187.
[5]*Ibid.*, p. 186.
[6]*Ibid.*, p. 199.
[7]Clinton Rossiter, *Alexander Hamilton and the Constitution* (New York: Harcourt, Brace & World, Inc., 1964), p. 61.
[8]De Pauw, *op. cit.*, p. 189.
[9]*Ibtd.*, p. 186.
[10]*Ibid.*, p. 193.
[11]*Ibid.*, pp. 200-202.
[12]*Ibid.*, p. 202.
[13]*Ibid.*, pp. 206-7.
[14]*Ibid.*, pp. 209-10.
[15]*Ibid.*, p. 209.
[16]*Ibid.*, p. 222.
[17]*Ibid.*, p. 244.
[18]*Ibid.*, pp. 229-30.
[19]*Ibid.*, p. 233.
[20]*Ibid.*, p. 237.
[21]Bowen, *op. cit.*, p. 305.
[22]*Ibid.*, pp. 306-7, 309-10.

15. A Pendulum Is Set in Motion: Hamilton and Jefferson

[1]Gilbert Chinard, *Thomas Jefferson, the Apostle of Americanism* (Ann Arbor, Mich.: The University of Michigan Press, 1957), p. 356.
[2]Thomas Jefferson, *The Writings of Thomas Jefferson*, Vol. XV, Monticello edition, Andrew A. Lipscomb, ed. (Washington, D.C.: The Jefferson Memorial Association, 1904), p. 43.
[3]*Ibid.*, III, 320.
[4]Dumas Malone, *Jefferson and the Rights of Man*, Vol. II of *Jefferson and His Time* (Boston: Little, Brown and Company, 1951), pp. 259-60.

⁵*Ibid.*, pp. 258-63.

⁶Claude G. Bowers, *Jefferson and Hamilton: The Struggle for Democracy in America* (Boston: Houghton Mifflin Company, The Riverside Press, 1925), pp. 92-93. Material from this source has been condensed.

⁷*Ibid.*, p. 94.

⁸*Ibid.*, pp. 22-23.

⁹*Ibid.*, p. 24.

¹⁰Dumas Malone, "Jefferson, Hamilton, and the Constitution," in *Thomas Jefferson, A Profile*, ed. by Merrill D. Peterson (New York: Hill and Wang, 1967), p. 169.

¹¹Louis M. Hacker, *Alexander Hamilton in the American Tradition* (New York: McGraw-Hill Book Company, 1957), p. 7.

¹²Malone, *Jefferson and the Rights of Man*, p. 270.

¹³Bowers, *op. cit.*, p. 69.

¹⁴Thomas Jefferson, *The Writings of Thomas Jefferson*, Vol. VI, collected and edited by Paul Leicester Ford (New York: G. P. Putnam's Sons, 1896), p. 154.

¹⁵Alexander Hamilton, *The Works of Alexander Hamilton*, Vol. X, ed. by Henry Cabot Lodge (New York: G. P. Putnam's Sons, The Knickerbocker Press, 1904), pp. 45-46.

¹⁶Malone, *Jefferson and the Rights of Man*, p. 357.

¹⁷*Ibid.*, p. 358.

¹⁸Bowers, *op. cit.*, pp. 87, 89.

¹⁹Hamilton, *op. cit.*, VII, 304-6.

²⁰Jefferson, *op. cit.*, VI, Ford edition, 102.

²¹*Ibid.*

²²*Ibid.*, p. 104.

²³*Ibid.*, p. 105.

²⁴*Ibid.*, p. 109.

²⁵Bowers, *op. cit.*, pp. 107-8.

²⁶Jefferson, *op. cit.*, VII, Ford edition, 327.

²⁷*Ibid.*, p. 329.

²⁸*Ibid.*, VI, 518.

²⁹*Ibid.*, VII, 96.

³⁰*Ibid.*, p. 99.

³¹See Malone, "Jefferson, Hamilton, and the Constitution," pp. 173-74. See also Dumas Malone, *Jefferson and the Ordeal of Liberty*, Vol. III of *Jefferson and His Time* (Boston: Little, Brown and Company, 1962), pp. 400-403.

³²Hamilton, *op. cit.*, X, 143.

³³*Ibid.*, p. 151.

³⁴*Ibid.*, pp. 200-201.

³⁵*Ibid.*, p. 181.

³⁶*Ibid.*, p. 280.

³⁷*Ibid.*, p. 241.

³⁸*Ibid.*, p. 288.

³⁹John C. Miller, *Alexander Hamilton: Portrait in Paradox* (New York: Harper & Row, Publishers, 1959), p. 458.

⁴⁰Hamilton, *op. cit.*, X, 295. Condensed.

⁴¹*Ibid.*, pp. 296, 299-300.

⁴²Nathan Schachner, *Aaron Burr, A Biography* (New York: Frederick A. Stokes Company, 1937), pp. 171, 174-75.

⁴³Bowers, *op. cit.*, p. 454.

⁴⁴*Ibid.*, p. 479; Hamilton, *op. cit.*, VII, 316, 348.

⁴⁵Bowers, *op. cit.*, p. 480.

[46]Hamilton, *op. cit.,* X, 22, 20.
[47]*Ibid.,* p. 387, 395-96.
[48]*Ibid.,* pp. 396-97.
[49]*Ibid.,* p. 401.
[50]*Ibid.,* pp. 412-13.
[51]*Ibid.,* pp. 413-14, 417-18. Condensed.
[52]Bowers, *op. cit.,* pp. 486-87.
[53]*Ibid.,* p. 488.
[54]*Ibid.,* p. 490.
[55]Malone, *Jefferson and the Ordeal of Liberty,* pp. 504-5.
[56]Bowers, *op. cit.,* pp. 507-9.
[57]Jefferson, *op. cit.,* III, Monticello edition, 319.
[58]Bowers, *op. cit.,* p. 510.

16. Star of Empire

[1]Bernard De Voto, ed., *The Journals of Lewis and Clark* (Boston: Houghton Mifflin Company, 1953), p. 482. This skillfully edited work combines in a single volume entries from the journals of Lewis, Clark, and others in their company, collated chronologically and carefully annotated in such a way as to present an unusually clear and vivid account of the expedition. This reading is condensed from the De Voto edition. Entries from the journals are slightly modernized.

[2]Alexander Mackenzie, leading fur-trade promoter (1801), quoted *ibid.,* pp. xxxi-xxxii.
[3]*Ibid.,* pp. 35-36.
[4]*Ibid.,* p. 39.
[5]*Ibid.,* p. 38, 41.
[6]*Ibid.,* pp. 43-44.
[7]*Ibid.,* p. 90.
[8]*Ibid.,* p. 111.
[9]*Ibid.,* p. 113.
[10]*Ibid.,* p. 117.
[11]*Ibid.,* p. 130.
[12]*Ibid.,* p. 136.
[13]*Ibid.,* p. 167.
[14]*Ibid.,* p. 168.
[15]*Ibid.,* p. 169.
[16]*Ibid.,* p. 175.
[17]*Ibid.,* pp. 181-82.
[18]*Ibid.,* p. 183.
[19]*Ibid.,* p. 189.
[20]*Ibid.,* pp. 185-86.
[21]*Ibid.,* pp. 188-89.
[22]*Ibid.,* pp. 190-91.
[23]*Ibid.,* pp. 196-97.
[24]*Ibid.,* p. 198.
[25]*Ibid.,* pp. 199-201.
[26]*Ibid.,* p. 202.
[27]*Ibid.*
[28]*Ibid.,* pp. 202-3.

17. The Defenders of New Orleans

[1]James Parton, *Life of Andrew Jackson*, Vol. I (Boston: Houghton Mifflin Company, The Riverside Press, 1859), p. 584. The material for this reading is condensed from Parton and from Alexander Walker, *The Life of Andrew Jackson* (New York: Derby & Jackson, 1858). Both these colorful old sources, which have been slightly revised here, make use of many vivid first-hand accounts of the battle.

[2]Parton, *op. cit.*, I, 581-82.

[3]*Ibid.*, p. 587.

[4]Walker, *op. cit.* p. 53.

[5]*Ibid.*, p. 69.

[6]*Ibid.*, p. 72.

[7]*Ibid.*, p. 15.

[8]*Ibid.*, p. 18.

[9]*Ibid.*, p. 73.

[10]Parton, *op. cit.*, II, 13-14.

[11]Harry L. Coles, *The War of 1812* (Chicago: University of Chicago Press, 1965), p. 212.

[12]Parton, *op. cit.*, II, 34-37.

[13]*Ibid.*, p. 55; Walker, *op. cit.*, p. 139.

[14]Parton, *op. cit.*, II, 56.

[15]*Ibid.*, p. 62.

[16]Walker, *op. cit.*, pp. 154-55; Parton, *op. cit.*, II, 74.

[17]*Ibid.*, pp. 63-64.

[18]Walker, *op. cit.*, p. 126.

[19]Parton, *op. cit.*, II, 72-73.

[20]*Ibid.*, p. 85.

[21]Walker, *op. cit.*, pp. 167-68.

[22]*Ibid.*, p. 174.

[23]Parton, *op. cit.*, II, 141.

[24]*Ibid.*, p. 140.

[25]Walker, *op. cit.*, pp. 242-43.

[26]Marquis James, *The Life of Andrew Jackson* (Indianapolis: The Bobbs-Merrill Co., Inc., 1938), p. 240.

[27]Parton, *op. cit.*, II, 179.

[28]Walker, *op. cit.*, p. 319.

[29]Parton, *op. cit.*, II, 173-74; Walker, *op. cit.*, p. 312.

[30]*Ibid.*, pp. 327, 338.

[31]*Ibid.*, pp. 327-33.

18. The Man Behind the Robes

[1]Joseph Story, *Miscellaneous Writings*, Vol. IV (Boston: James Munroe and Company, 1835), p. 199.

[2]For an account of sectionalism and nationalism in the crisis of 1819, see Leonard W. Levy and Merrill D. Peterson, eds., *Major Crises in American History*, Vol. I (New York: Harcourt, Brace & World, Inc., 1962), pp. 269-77.

[3]Albert J. Beveridge, *The Life of John Marshall*, Vol. IV (Boston: Houghton Mifflin Company, The Riverside Press, 1929), pp. 61-62. The material presented here on Marshall's personal life is condensed from this classic biography.

[4]*Ibid.*, p. 64.
[5]*Ibid.*, pp. 76-77.
[6]*Ibid.*, p. 67.
[7]*Ibid.*, pp. 81-82.
[8]*Ibid.*, p. 83.
[9]*Ibid.*, p. 81.
[10]*Ibid.*, pp. 86-89.
[11]John Stokes Adams, ed., *An Autobiographical Sketch by John Marshall* (Ann Arbor: University of Michigan Press, 1937), pp. 9-10.
[12]Henry P. Johnston, ed., *The Correspondence and Public Papers of John Jay*, Vol. IV (New York: G. P. Putnam's Sons, 1893), p. 285.
[13]Felix Frankfurter, *Of Law and Men* (New York: Harcourt, Brace & World, Inc., 1956), p. 4.
[14]John P. Roche, ed., *John Marshall: Major Opinions and Other Writings* (Indianapolis: The Bobbs-Merrill Co., Inc., 1967), pp. 173-74.
[15]*Ibid.*, pp. 179-81.
[16]*Ibid.*, p. 187.

19. Pioneers of the Old Northwest: The Lincoln Family

[1]John G. Nicolay and John Hay, *Abraham Lincoln, A History*, Vol. I (New York: The Century Co., 1890). Material from this source has been condensed and slightly revised.
[2]*Ibid.*, pp. 28-46.

20. Before the Mast

[1]Richard Henry Dana, *Two Years Before the Mast*, Vol. XXIII of *The Harvard Classics* (New York: P. F. Collier & Son, 1909), p. 373. This reading is a condensation of parts of Dana's classic account.
[2]See Raymond A. Rydell, *Cape Horn to the Pacific* (Berkeley: University of California Press, 1952).
[3]Dana, *op. cit.*, p. 373.
[4]*Ibid.*, pp. 7-12.
[5]*Ibid.*, pp. 77-109, *passim.*
[6]*Ibid.*, p. 288.

21. Enter the Self-made Man and the Machine

[1]Arthur M. Schlesinger, Jr., *The Age of Jackson* (Boston: Little, Brown and Company, 1946), pp. 38-39.
[2]Richard Hofstadter, *The American Political Tradition and the Men Who Made It* (New York: Alfred A. Knopf, Inc., 1948), pp. 45-46, 49, 54.
[3]*Ibid.*, p. 48.
[4]For a discussion of property qualifications and the popularizing of the vote in Presidential elections, see Richard P. McCormick, "New Perspectives on Jacksonian Politics," in *American Historical Review*, Vol. LXV, No. 2, January, 1960, pp. 288-301.
[5]Hofstadter, *op. cit.*, p. 52.
[6]Robert V. Remini, *The Election of Andrew Jackson* (Philadelphia: J. B. Lippincott Co.,

1963), p. 25. Material on the election techniques of the Jacksonians is from this valuable source, which has been condensed.

[7]George Dangerfield, *The Era of Good Feelings* (New York: Harcourt, Brace & World, Inc., 1952), pp. 352-53.

[8]Remini, *op. cit.*, pp. 59, 65.

[9]*Ibid.*, p. 72.

[10]*Ibid.*, p. 89.

[11]*Ibid.*, p. 170.

[12]*Ibid.*, pp. 84-85, 101-2, 108-11, 116.

[13]*Ibid.*, pp. 181, 183. See also p. 187.

[14]*Ibid.*, p. 101.

[15]*Ibid.*, pp. 67, 102-3.

[16]*Ibid.*, pp. 104-7.

[17]*Ibid.*, pp. 117-18.

[18]*Ibid.*, pp. 112-15.

[19]*Ibid.*, pp. 69, 97, 100, 73-76, 68.

[20]See Dangerfield, *op. cit.*, pp. 9-10.

[21]Remini, *op. cit.*, p. 125.

[22]Hofstadter, *op. cit.*, p. 67.

22. Storm Warning in South Carolina

[1]Charles M. Wiltse, *John C. Calhoun, Nullifier, 1829-1839* (Indianapolis: The Bobbs-Merrill Co., Inc., 1949), p. 147.

[2]*Ibid.*, pp. 150-51.

[3]David Franklin Houston, *A Critical Study of Nullification in South Carolina* (New York: Longmans, Green & Co., 1896), p. 13.

[4]William W. Freehling, *Prelude to Civil War: The Nullification Controversy in South Carolina, 1816-1836* (New York: Harper & Row, Publishers, 1965), pp. 10-11.

[5]*Ibid.*, p. 11.

[6]*Ibid.*, pp. 13-15.

[7]*Ibid.*, pp. 21-23.

[8]University of Chicago, *The People Shall Judge*, Vol. I (Chicago: University of Chicago Press, 1949), p. 672; Freehling, *op. cit.*, p. 251.

[9]Thomas Hart Benton, *Thirty Years' View, or, A History of the Working of the American Government for Thirty Years, from 1820 to 1850*, Vol. I (New York: D. Appleton and Company, 1854), p. 311.

[10]Frances Anne Kemble, *Journal of a Residence on a Georgian Plantation in 1838-1839*, John A. Scott, ed. (New York: Alfred A. Knopf, Inc., 1961), pp. 38-39.

[11]Freehling, *op. cit.*, p. 250.

[12]Marquis James, *Andrew Jackson: Portrait of a President* (Indianapolis: The Bobbs-Merrill Co., Inc., 1937), p. 311. Material from this source has been condensed. James is Jacksonian in his interpretations. For positions in defense of Calhoun, see Wiltse, *op. cit.*; and Margaret L. Coit, *John C. Calhoun, American Portrait* (Boston: Houghton Mifflin Company, 1950).

[13]James, *op. cit.*, p. 306.

[14]*Ibid.*, pp. 312-24.

23. Emerson: A Voice for America

[1]Ralph Waldo Emerson, "The Poet," *The Harvard Classics*, Vol. V, Charles W. Eliot, ed. (New York: P. F. Collier & Son, 1909), p. 186.

[2]Hildegarde Hawthorne, *Youth's Captain: The Story of Ralph Waldo Emerson* (New York: Longmans, Green & Co., 1935), p. 1. Used by permission of David McKay Company, Inc.

[3]*Ibid.*, p. 7.

[4]*Ibid.*, pp. 26, 28.

[5]Ralph Waldo Emerson, *Journals,* Vols. I–IX (Boston: Houghton Mifflin Company, The Riverside Press, 1909–1913), IX, 265. The *Journals* and *Essays* of Emerson have been condensed in this reading.

[6]*Ibid.*, p. 538.

[7]Phillips Russell, *Emerson, The Wisest American* (New York: Brentano's Publishers, 1929), p. 32.

[8]Hawthorne, *op. cit.*, p. 38.

[9]Russell, *op. cit.*, p. 7.

[10]Emerson, *Journals,* I, 70.

[11]*Ibid.*, IX, 532.

[12]*Ibid.*, I, 139, 141-42.

[13]Russell, *op. cit.*, p. 79.

[14]Emerson, *Journals,* II, 409.

[15]*Ibid.*, p. 395.

[16]Russell, *op. cit.*, p. 76.

[17]*Ibid.*, pp. 68-69.

[18]*Ibid.*, p. 85.

[19]Ralph L. Rusk, *The Life of Ralph Waldo Emerson* (New York: Charles Scribner's Sons, 1949), p. 167.

[20]Russell, *op. cit.*, p. 91.

[21]Saul K. Padover, *The Genius of America: Men Whose Ideas Shaped Our Civilization* (New York: McGraw-Hill Book Company, 1960), p. 183.

[22]Emerson, "Address to Divinity Students," *The Harvard Classics,* V, 26-28.

[23]Emerson, "Nature," *The Harvard Classics,* V, 239-40, 247-48.

[24]Emerson, "Address to Divinity Students," pp. 30-32, 39, 38.

[25]Emerson, "Self-Reliance," *The Harvard Classics,* V, 63-88, *passim.*

[26]*Ibid.*, pp. 76-77, 87-88.

[27]Emerson, *Journals,* IX, 370, 371, 541.

[28]Emerson, "Address to Divinity Students," p. 38; "An American Scholar," *The Harvard Classics,* V, 23.

[29]Emerson, "New England Reformers," *The Harvard Classics,* V, 268.

[30]Emerson, *Journals,* IX, 305.

[31]*Ibid.*, p. 456.

[32]*Ibid.*, pp. 463-64.

[33]*Ibid.*, p. 552.

[34]Emerson, "An American Scholar," p. 16.

[35]*Ibid.*, p. 23.

[36]*Ibid.*, pp. 23-24.

[37]Emerson, "The Poet," p. 186.

24. Pitchforks and Panaceas

[1]Nathaniel Hawthorne, *The Blithedale Romance* (Boston: Houghton Mifflin Company, The Riverside Press, 1894), p. 76.

[2]Henry W. Sams, ed., *Autobiography of Brook Farm* (Englewood Cliffs, N.J.: Prentice-

Hall, Inc., © 1958), pp. 6-7. Material from this source has been condensed.

³*Ibid.*, p. 8.

⁴*Ibid.*, pp. 9-10, 12.

⁵*Ibid.*, p. 216.

⁶John Thomas Codman, *Brook Farm: Historic and Personal Memoirs* (Boston: Arena Publishing Co., 1894), pp. 4-5.

⁷Charles Crowe, *George Ripley, Transcendentalist and Utopian Socialist* (Athens, Ga: University of Georgia Press, 1967), p. 144.

⁸Codman, *op. cit.*, p. 6.

⁹Nathaniel Hawthorne, *Passage from the American Note-Books*, Vol. IX of *Complete Works* (Boston: Houghton Mifflin Company, The Riverside Press, 1868), pp. 217-18.

¹⁰*Ibid.*, pp. 226-35, *passim*.

¹¹Sams, *op. cit.*, pp. 22-23.

¹²Hawthorne, *Note-Books*, pp. 235-44.

¹³Edith Roelker Curtis, *A Season in Utopia: The Story of Brook Farm* [1961] (New York: Russell & Russell, 1970), p. 115.

¹⁴Hawthorne, *Blithedale Romance*, p. 164.

¹⁵Curtis, *op. cit.*, p. 87.

¹⁶Vernon L. Parrington, *Main Currents in American Thought*, Vol. II (New York: Harcourt, Brace & Company, 1927), p. 443.

¹⁷See Curtis, *op. cit.*, pp. 67, 74.

¹⁸Ralph Waldo Emerson, "Historic Notes of Life and Letters in New England," in *Lectures and Biographical Sketches* (Boston: Houghton Mifflin Company, 1883), p. 345.

¹⁹Sams, *op. cit.*, p. 87.

²⁰See Curtis, *op. cit.*, pp. 105-6.

²¹Emerson, *op. cit.*, p. 331.

²²Sams, *op. cit.*, pp. 95-97.

²³Codman, *op. cit.*, p. 44.

²⁴*Ibid.*, p. 57.

²⁵Curtis, *op. cit.*, p. 174.

²⁶Codman, *op. cit.*, pp. 44-45.

²⁷*Ibid.*, p. 76-77.

²⁸Sams, *op. cit.*, pp. 171-74.

²⁹*Ibid.*, p. 193.

³⁰Emerson, *op. cit.*, p. 343.

³¹Hawthorne, *Blithedale Romance*, p. 18.

25. A Lone Star

¹Sam Houston, *The Autobiography of Sam Houston*, Donald Day and Harry Herbert Ullom, eds. (Norman, Okla.: University of Oklahoma Press, 1954), p. 4.

²Marquis James, *The Raven: A Biography of Sam Houston* (Indianapolis: The Bobbs-Merrill Co., Inc., 1929), pp. 15-17, 19. Material from this source has been condensed.

³*Ibid.*, pp. 20-23.

⁴*Ibid.*, p. 27.

⁵*Ibid.*, p. 29.

⁶Houston, *op. cit.*, p. 46.

⁷James, *op. cit.*, p. 157.

[8]Marion Karl Wisehart, *Sam Houston, American Giant* (Washington: Robert B. Luce, Inc., 1962), p. 62.

[9]*Ibid.*

[10]Jacques Barzun, *Romanticism and the Modern Ego* (Boston: Little, Brown and Company, 1943), p. 24.

[11]Wisehart, *op. cit.*, p. 124.

[12]Houston, *op. cit.*, p. 98; Wisehart, *op. cit.*, p. 167.

[13]Houston, *op. cit.*, pp. 100, 101.

[14]*Ibid.*, p. 101.

[15]*Ibid.*, p. 102.

[16]*Ibid.*, p. 111.

[17]Wisehart, *op. cit.*, p. 211.

[18]*Ibid.*, p. 219.

[19]James, *op. cit.*, p. 244.

[20]*Ibid.*, pp. 248-55.

[21]Wisehart, *op. cit.*, p. 260.

[22]*Ibid.*, pp. 567, 570.

[23]*Ibid.*, p. 576.

[24]James, *op. cit.*, p. 412.

[25]Wisehart, *op. cit.*, p. 650.

26. The Price of Empire: The Donner Party

[1]George Berkeley, *Works* (Oxford: Clarendon Press, 1871), III, 232.

[2]Bernard De Voto, *The Year of Decision: 1846* (Boston: Houghton Mifflin Company, The Riverside Press, 1942), pp. 151-52, 158-60. The following account of the Donner disaster is condensed from this brilliant study, which the reader will enjoy in its entirety. It contains many other fascinating tales, all blended together with great skill into the biography of one crucial year in American history.

[3]*Ibid.*, pp. 153, 159.

[4]*Ibid.*, pp. 342-43.

[5]*Ibid.*, pp. 344-46.

[6]*Ibid.*, pp. 348-49.

[7]*Ibid.*, pp. 353-54.

[8]*Ibid.*, pp. 357–58, 398-401, 421-23.

[9]*Ibid.*, pp. 428–29.

[10]*Ibid.*, p. 439.

27. The Emancipation of Frederick Douglass

[1]Frederick Douglass, *My Bondage and My Freedom* (New York: Miller, Orton & Mulligan, 1855), Part I, *My Life as a Slave.* This reading is a condensation of Douglass' stirring account, which has been slightly revised.

28. The Making of Johnny Reb

[1]W. J. Cash, *The Mind of the South* (New York: Alfred A. Knopf, Inc., 1941), pp. 10, 14-17. The material from this source has been condensed.

Chapters from the American Experience

²*Ibid.*, p. 20.
³*Ibid.*, pp. 24-25.
⁴*Ibid.*, pp. 29-33, 42-44, 50-53.
⁵*Ibid.*, pp. 35-41, *passim.* To Cash's provocative interpretation should be added recent **433** psychological insights into the elements of racial prejudice. See, for example, Milton R. Barron, *American Minorities* (New York: Alfred A. Knopf, Inc., 1957) and Gordon W. Allport, *The Nature of Prejudice* (Garden City, N. Y.: Doubleday & Company, Inc., 1958).
⁶*Ibid.*, pp. 60-61.
⁷*Ibid.*, pp. 61-62, 65-67, 82-86.

29. Two Faces of the American Industrial Revolution

¹Alexis de Tocqueville, *Democracy in America*, II (Boston: John Allyn, Publishers, 1882), p. 197.
²Allan Nevins, *Abram S. Hewitt; With Some Account of Peter Cooper* (New York: Harper & Row, Publishers, 1935), pp. 45-62.
³*Ibid.*, pp. 67-70.
⁴*Ibid.*, p. 176.
⁵*Ibid.*, pp. 268-69.
⁶*Ibid.*, p. 445.
⁷Foster Rhea Dulles, *Labor in America* (New York: Thomas Y. Crowell Co., 1960), p. 78; Allan Nevins, *Ordeal of the Union*, Vol. II (New York: Charles Scribner's Sons, 1947), p. 291. See also Norman Ware, *The Industrial Worker, 1840-1860* (Boston: Houghton Mifflin Company, The Riverside Press, 1924), p. 58.
⁸*Ibid.*, p. 299.
⁹*Ibid.*
¹⁰*Ibid.*
¹¹Dulles, *op. cit.*, p. 78.
¹²Oscar Handlin, *Boston's Immigrants: A Study in Aculturation* (Cambridge, Mass.: The Belknap Press of Harvard University Press, 1959), p.11.
¹³See *ibid.*, pp. 25-53, for a discussion of Irish backgrounds.
¹⁴*Ibid.*, pp. 91-98, 101-16, *passim.*

30. The Sword of Gideon

¹Stephen Vincent Benét, *John Brown's Body* (Garden City, N.Y.: Doubleday, Doran and Company, Inc., 1929), p. 375.
²Oswald Garrison Villard, *John Brown, 1800-1859: A Biography Fifty Years After* (Boston: Houghton Mifflin Company, The Riverside Press, 1910), pp. 551-53. Almost all of this reading is condensed from Villard's classic biography, which has been slightly revised.

Brown is still a controversial figure. For a different interpretation of his personality, see Allan Nevins, *The Emergence of Lincoln*, Vol. II: *Prologue to Civil War, 1859-1861* (New York: Charles Scribner's Sons, 1950).
³Villard, *op. cit.*, pp. 1-7.
⁴*Ibid.*, pp. 19, 20.
⁵*Ibid.*, p. 22.
⁶*Ibid.*, p. 23.
⁷*Ibid.*, p. 26.

[8]*Ibid.*, pp. 43-44.
[9]*Ibid.*, pp. 45-46.
[10]*Ibid.*, p. 51.
[11]*Ibid.*, p. 152.
[12]*Ibid.*, pp. 158-60.
[13]*Ibid.*, p. 160.
[14]*Ibid.*, p. 189.
[15]*Ibid.*, pp. 57-58.
[16]*Ibid.*, pp. 198-200.
[17]*Ibid.*, pp. 220, 235.
[18]*Ibid.*, pp. 273, 282; Nevins, *op. cit.*, p. 26.
[19]Villard, *op. cit.*, p. 339.
[20]*Ibid.*, pp. 413, 321.
[21]*Ibid.*, pp. 416-20.
[22]*Ibid.*, p. 416.
[23]*Ibid.*, p. 453.
[24]*Ibid.*
[25]*Ibid.*, pp. 461, 463.
[26]*Ibid.*, pp. 545-46.
[27]*Ibid.*, p. 554.
[28]*Ibid.*, p. 555.
[29]*Ibid.*, pp. 556-57.
[30]*Ibid.*, p. 557.
[31]Henry David Thoreau, "A Plea for Captain John Brown," in *A Yankee in Canada, with Anti-Slavery and Reform Papers* (Boston: Ticknor and Fields, 1866), p. 181; Villard, *op. cit.*, pp. 562, 560.

31. That the Nation Might Live

[1]Frank Aretas Haskell, "The Battle of Gettysburg," in *American Historical Documents, 1800-1904*, Vol. XLIII, *The Harvard Classics* (New York: P. F. Collier & Son, 1910), pp. 394-97, 401-2. Lieutenant Haskell is described by the *Harvard Classics* as "one of the most distinguished soldiers of the Army of the Potomac." He died in June, 1864, leading a charge at the Battle of Cold Harbor.
[2]Otto Eisenschiml and Ralph Newman, *Eyewitness: The Civil War As We Lived It* (New York: Grosset & Dunlap, The Universal Library, 1956), p. 492.
[3]*Battles and Leaders of the Civil War*, Vol. III (New York: The Century Co., 1884), III, 345-46.
[4]Haskell, *op. cit.*, pp. 403-12.
[5]*Battles*, III, 366-67.
[6]Eisenschiml and Newman, *op. cit.*, p. 500.

32. O Captain, My Captain

[1]Mary B. Chestnut, *A Diary from Dixie* (New York: D. Appleton and Company, 1905), pp. 12, 19.
[2]Robert S. Harper, *Lincoln and the Press* (New York: McGraw-Hill Book Company, 1951), p. 94.
[3]T. Harry Williams, *Lincoln and the Radicals* (Madison and Milwaukee: The Univer-

sity of Wisconsin Press, 1965), pp. 22, 21.

[4]Ralph Waldo Emerson, *Journals*, Vol. IX (Boston: Houghton Mifflin Company, The Riverside Press, 1913), p. 557.

[5]Carl Sandburg, *Abraham Lincoln: The War Years*, Vol. I (New York: Harcourt, Brace & World, 1939), p. 84. See also I, 78, 80, 82.

[6]See Margaret Leech, *Reveille in Washington, 1860-1865* (New York: Harper & Row, Publishers, 1941), p. 49.

[7]Henry Adams, *The Education of Henry Adams: An Autobiography* (Boston: Houghton Mifflin Company, The Riverside Press, 1918), pp. 100, 107–8.

[8]*Ibid.*, p. 107.

[9]L. E. Chittenden, *Recollections of President Lincoln and His Administration* (New York: Harper & Row, Publishers, 1891), p. 75.

[10]Abraham Lincoln, *Complete Works*, Vol. II, John G. Nicolay and John Hay, eds. (New York: The Century Co., 1894), pp. 1-7.

[11]Henry Steele Commager, ed., *The Blue and the Gray*, Vol. I (Indianapolis: The Bobbs-Merrill Co., Inc., 1950), p. 14.

[12]Lincoln, *op. cit.*, II, 57-58.

[13]Carl Sandburg, "Lincoln, Man of Steel and Velvet," Address to a Joint Session of Congress, February 12, 1959, in *The National Geographic*, February, 1960, p. 239.

[14]Charles M. Segal, ed., *Conversations with Lincoln* (New York: G. P. Putnam's Sons, 1961), p. 119. The reader will find a wealth of Lincoln material in this source and also in: Paul M. Angle, ed., *The Lincoln Reader* (New Brunswick, N. J.: Rutgers University Press, 1947); and Courtland Canby, ed., *Lincoln and the Civil War: A Profile and a History* (New York: George Braziller, Inc., 1960).

[15]William T. Sherman, *Memoirs of General William T. Sherman*, Vol. I (2nd ed.) (New York: D. Appleton and Company, 1887), p. 217.

[16]*Ibid.*, p. 218.

[17]*Ibid.*, pp. 217-19.

[18]Commager, *op. cit.*, II, 848-53.

[19]Burton J. Hendrick, *Lincoln's War Cabinet* (Boston: Little, Brown and Company, 1946), pp. 207-8.

[20]Horace Porter, *Campaigning with Grant* (New York: The Century Co., 1897), p. 408.

[21]John Hay, *Lincoln and the Civil War in the Diaries and Letters of John Hay*, Tyler Dennett, ed. (New York: Dodd, Mead & Company, Inc., 1939), p. 35.

[22]Segal, *op. cit.*, p. 151.

[23]*Ibid.*, p. 160.

[24]Sandburg, *War Years*, I, 553.

[25]Francis B. Carpenter, *Six Months at the White House with Abraham Lincoln* (New York: Hurd and Houghton, 1866), pp. 20-21.

[26]Segal, *op. cit.*, p. 199.

[27]Salmon P. Chase, *The Diary and Correspondence of Salmon P. Chase*, Annual Report of the American Historical Association, Vol. II (Washington: Government Printing Office, 1903), pp. 87-88.

[28]Commager, *op. cit.*, I, 549-51.

[29]*Ibid.*, p. 552.

[30]J. G. Randall, *Lincoln the President*, Vol. II (New York: Dodd, Mead & Company, Inc., 1945), 244-48. Condensed.

[31]Sandburg, *War Years*, I, 648-49.

[32]Benjamin P. Thomas, *Abraham Lincoln, A Biography* (New York: Alfred A. Knopf, Inc., 1952), p. 476.

³³John Hay, "Life in the White House in the Time of Lincoln," in *The Century Illustrated Monthly Magazine*, XLI, Nov. 1890–Apr. 1891, 33-34.

³⁴Thomas, *op. cit.*, pp. 462-63.

³⁵Hay, "Life in the White House," p. 33.

³⁶Condensed from Rufus Rockwell Wilson, ed., *Lincoln Among His Friends: A Sheaf of Intimate Memories* (Caldwell, Idaho: The Caxton Printers, Ltd., 1942), pp. 331-33.

³⁷Hay, "Life in the White House," pp. 36-37.

³⁸Lincoln, *op. cit.*, II, 439.

³⁹Sandburg, *War Years*, I, 478.

⁴⁰Lincoln, *op. cit.*, II, 657.

⁴¹Ulysses S. Grant, *Personal Memoirs of U. S. Grant*, Vol. II (New York: Charles L. Webster & Company, 1886), p. 523.

⁴²Thomas, *op. cit.*, p. 502.

⁴³Sherman, *op. cit.*, II, 326.

Index

439

2819